International Law-making

This book explores law-making in international affairs and is compiled to celebrate the fiftieth birthday of Professor Jan Klabbers, a leading international law and international relations scholar, who has made significant contributions to the understanding of the sources of international legal obligations and the idea of constitutionalism in international law. Inspired by Professor Klabbers' wide-ranging interests in international law and his interdisciplinary approach, the book examines law-making through a variety of perspectives and seeks to break new ground in exploring what it means to think and write about law and its creation.

While examining the substance of international law, these contributors raise more general concerns, such as the relationship between law-making and the application of law, the role and conflict between various institutions and the characteristics of the formal sources of international law. The book will be of great interest to students and academics of legal theory, international relations and international law.

Rain Liivoja is a Senior Research Fellow at the Asia Pacific Centre for Military Law, Melbourne Law School, and an Affiliated Research Fellow of the Erik Castrén Institute of International Law and Human Rights, University of Helsinki.

Jarna Petman is Deputy Director of the Erik Castrén Institute of International Law and Human Rights and Senior Lecturer (professor *ad interim*) of International Law, University of Helsinki.

Routledge Research in International Law

Available:

International Law and the Third World
Reshaping Justice
Richard Falk, Balakrishnan Rajagopal and Jacqueline Stevens (eds)

International Legal Theory
Essays and Engagements, 1966–2006
Nicholas Onuf

The Problem of Enforcement in International Law
Countermeasures, the Non-Injured State and the Idea of International Community
Elena Katselli Proukaki

International Economic Actors and Human Rights
Adam McBeth

The Law of Consular Access
A Documentary Guide
John Quigley, William J. Aceves and Adele Shank

State Accountability under International Law
Holding States Accountable for a Breach of *Jus Cogens* Norms
Lisa Yarwood

International Organisations and the Idea of Autonomy
Institutional Independence in the International Legal Order
Richard Collins and Nigel D. White (eds)

Self-Determination in the Post-9/11 Era
Elizabeth Chadwick

Participants in the International Legal System
Multiple Perspectives on Non-State Actors in International Law
Jean d'Aspremont (ed.)

Sovereignty and Jurisdiction in the Airspace and Outer Space
Legal Criteria for Spatial Delimitation
Gbenga Oduntan

International Law in a Multipolar World
Matthew Happold (ed.)

The Law on the Use of Force
A Feminist Analysis
Gina Heathcote

The ICJ and the Development of International Law
The Lasting Impact of the Corfu Channel Case
Karine Bannelier, Théodore Christakis and Sarah Heathcote (eds)

UNHCR and International Refugee Law
From Treaties to Innovation
Corinne Lewis

Asian Approaches to International Law and the Legacy of Colonialism
The Law of the Sea, Territorial Disputes and International Dispute Settlement
Jin-Hyun Paik, Seok-Woo Lee and Kevin Y L Tan (eds)

The Right to Self-determination Under International Law
"Selfistans," Secession, and the Rule of the Great Powers
Milena Sterio

Reforming the UN Security Council Membership
The Illusion of Representativeness
Sabine Hassler

Threats of Force
International Law and Strategy
Francis Grimal

The Changing Role of Nationality in International Law
Alessandra Annoni and Serena Forlati

Criminal Responsibility for the Crime of Aggression
Patrycja Grzebyk

Regional Maintenance of Peace and Security under International Law
The Distorted Mirrors
Dace Winther

International Law-making
Essays in Honour of Jan Klabbers
Rain Liivoja and Jarna Petman (eds)

Forthcoming titles in this series include:

International Law, Regulation and Resistance
Critical Spaces
Zoe Pearson

The Cuban Embargo under International Law
El Bloqueo
Nigel D. White

The Changing Nature of Customary International Law
Methods of Interpreting the Concept of Custom in International Criminal Tribunals
Noora Arajärvi

Technology and the Law on the Use of Force
New Security Challenges in the Twenty-first Century
Jackson Maogoto

Criminal Diversity in International Law
The Effectiveness of the UNESCO Convention on the Protection and Promotion of the Diversity of Cultural Expressions
Lilian Hanania

The United Nations and Collective Security
Gary Wilson

International Law-making
Essays in Honour of Jan Klabbers

Edited by
Rain Liivoja and Jarna Petman

LONDON AND NEW YORK

First published 2014
by Routledge
2 Park Square, Milton Park, Abingdon, Oxfordshire OX14 4RN

and by Routledge
711 Third Avenue, New York, NY 10017

First issued in paperback 2015

Routledge is an imprint of the Taylor & Francis Group, an informa business

© 2014 selection and editorial matter, Rain Liivoja and Jarna Petman; individual chapters, the contributors

The right of Rain Liivoja and Jarna Petman to be identified as editors of this work has been asserted by them in accordance with sections 77 and 78 of the Copyright, Designs and Patents Act 1988.

All rights reserved. No part of this book may be reprinted or reproduced or utilised in any form or by any electronic, mechanical, or other means, now known or hereafter invented, including photocopying and recording, or in any information storage or retrieval system, without permission in writing from the publishers.

Trademark notice: Product or corporate names may be trademarks or registered trademarks, and are used only for identification and explanation without intent to infringe.

British Library Cataloguing in Publication Data
A catalogue record for this book is available from the British Library

Library of Congress Cataloging-in-Publication Data
International law-making : essays in honour of Jan Klabbers / [edited by] Rain Liivoja, Jarna Petman.
pages cm. – (Routledge research in international law)
Includes index.
1. International law. I. Liivoja, Rain, editor of compilation. II. Petman, Jarna, editor of compilation. III. Klabbers, Jan, honouree.
KZ3410.I582 2013
341–dc23
2013020820

ISBN 13: 978-1-138-93761-1 (pbk)
ISBN 13: 978-0-415-65956-7 (hbk)

Typeset in New Baskerville by
FiSH Books Ltd, Enfield.

Contents

Biographical notes	x
Table of cases	xvii
Table of treaties	xxiv
Table of other relevant instruments	xxxi
Preface RAIN LIIVOJA AND JARNA PETMAN	xl

PART I
Legislation and globalisation   1

1 Legislating for humanity: May states compel foreigners
   to promote global welfare?   3
   EYAL BENVENISTI

2 Declaratory legislation: Towards a genealogy of
   neoliberal legalism   17
   MARTTI KOSKENNIEMI

3 Legalism and the 'dark' side of global governance   39
   FRIEDRICH KRATOCHWIL

4 Global legislation and its discontents   57
   GIANLUIGI PALOMBELLA

5 Informal international law as presumptive law:
   Exploring new modes of law-making   75
   JOOST PAUWELYN, RAMSES A. WESSEL AND JAN WOUTERS

6   Mankind's territory and the limits of international
    law-making   103
    WOUTER G. WERNER

PART II
Domestic and international   119

7   (International) Law!   121
    INGER ÖSTERDAHL

8   Perspectivism in law   136
    KAARLO TUORI

9   Law-making through comparative international law?
    Rethinking the role of domestic law in the international
    legal system   149
    RENÉ URUEÑA

PART III
Institutions and participants   169

10 International responsibility and problematic law-making   171
    KATJA CREUTZ

11 Law-making and international environmental law: The
    legal character of decisions of conferences of the parties   190
    MALGOSIA FITZMAURICE

12 In search of a voice: EU law constraints on Member
    States in international law-making   211
    PANOS KOUTRAKOS

13 'In principle the full review': What justice for Mr Kadi?   225
    PÄIVI LEINO

14 Law-making by human rights treaty bodies   249
    GEIR ULFSTEIN

PART IV
Uncertainties and gaps 259

15 Peremptory law-making 261
ENZO CANNIZZARO

16 Law-making and the law of the sea: The BP *Deepwater Horizon* oil spill in the Gulf of Mexico 271
JAMES E. HICKEY, JR.

17 Slowly but surely? The challenge of the responsibility to protect 283
MARJA LEHTO

18 Treaties, custom and universal jurisdiction 298
RAIN LIIVOJA

19 Making the right choice: Constructing rules for anti-terrorist operations 313
JARNA PETMAN

Index 330

Biographical notes

Eyal Benvenisti, LLB (Jerusalem) 1984, LLM (Yale) 1988, JSD (Yale) 1990, is Anny and Paul Yanowicz Professor of Human Rights at Tel Aviv University Faculty of Law. He is Global Visiting Professor at New York University School of Law (since 2003) and Associate Member of the Institut de Droit International (2011). He is the recipient, most recently, of the European Research Council Advanced Grant for research on 'Sovereigns as Trustees of Humanity: The Obligations of Nations in an Era of Global Interdependence' (GlobalTrust) (2013–2018).

Enzo Cannizzaro is Professor of International and European Union Law at the University of Roma 'La Sapienza'. He has also taught as a Visiting Professor at the Law School of the University of Michigan, in Ann Arbor, and at the University Pantheon Assas, Paris 2. He has researched and lectured in a number of prestigious international institutes. He has written extensively on both international law and European Union Law. His publications in English include the edited volumes *Customary International Law on the Use of Force: A Methodological Approach* (Martinus Nijhoff, 2005), *International Law as Law of the European Union* (Brill, 2011) and *The Law of Treaties beyond the Vienna Convention* (Oxford University Press, 2011).

Katja Creutz is a doctoral candidate in international law at the Erik Castrén Institute of International Law and Human Rights, University of Helsinki. She holds a Master of Political Sciences from Åbo Akademi University (2000), and an LLM from the University of Helsinki (2004). In her doctoral dissertation she focuses on international responsibility by exploring state responsibility and international criminal law from a critical standpoint. Katja has pursued her doctoral studies as a member of the Centre of Excellence in Global Governance Research (2006–2011) and as a member of the Finnish and Nordic Graduate School in Human Rights Research. Besides her current post-graduate studies, she has authored studies on international post-conflict governance and privatisation of security commissioned by the Finnish Ministry for Foreign Affairs.

Malgosia Fitzmaurice holds a chair of public international law at the Department of Law, Queen Mary, University of London. She specialises in international environmental law, the law of treaties, indigenous rights and polar law, with a particular interest in Arctic matters, such as its biodiversity. She has lectured widely in the UK and abroad at various universities and participated in many international conferences. In 2001, she was invited to deliver keynote lectures on 'International Protection of the Environment' at The Hague Academy of International Law. She is the Editor in Chief of *International Community Law*. Her previous teaching positions include Readership in international law at the Department of Law, University of Amsterdam. She also worked at the Iran–United States Claims Tribunal in The Hague. She is also a part-time Nippon Professor of Marine Environmental Law at the International Maritime Law Institute at Malta.

James E. Hickey, Jr. is Professor of Law and former Director of International and Comparative Law Programs at Maurice A. Deane School of Law at Hofstra University, where he teaches energy and international law courses. He has twice been a Visiting Fellow at the Lauterpacht Centre for International Law at Cambridge University. He has practiced energy and international law with two Washington DC law firms. He is past Chair of the American Bar Association (ABA) Special Committee on Electric Industry Restructuring. He has been a Consultant to the Energy Charter Secretariat in Brussels and a Special Assistant to the National Petroleum Council. He sits on the Book Publications Board of the ABA Section of Environment, Energy and Resources and is a Fellow of the American Bar Foundation. He has authored and co-authored four books and over 60 publications. He received his undergraduate degree from the University of Florida, his JD degree from the University of Georgia and his PhD in International Law from the University of Cambridge (Jesus College). He has visited and taught at numerous universities around the world.

Jan Klabbers holds the Academy of Finland Martti Ahtisaari Chair, on leave from his regular position as Professor of International Law at the University of Helsinki. He studied international law and political science at the University of Amsterdam, where he also obtained his doctorate (1996, with distinction). He taught international law and European Union law at the University of Amsterdam (1990–1996) and has been Professor of International Law (as well as occasionally Professor of International Organisations Law) at the University of Helsinki since 1996, where he has received three different teaching awards. He was director of the Academy of Finland Centre of Excellence in Global Governance Research 2006–2011. He has held visiting professorships at, amongst others, the Graduate Institute in Geneva (2008) and the University of Paris Panthéon–Assas (2011), and was one of the inaugural fellows at the Straus Institute for the Advanced Study of Law and Justice at New York University (2009–10). His main publications include *The Concept of Treaty* in *International Law* (1996), *An Introduction to International Institutional Law* (2002, 2nd edn. 2009), *Treaty Conflict and the European Union* (2008), *International Law* (2013) and, as co-author, *The Constitutionalization of International Law* (2009).

Martti Koskenniemi is Academy Professor of International Law at the University of Helsinki and Director of the Erik Castrén Institute of International Law. He is also Hauser Visiting Global Professor of Law at New York University. He was the Arthur Goodhart Visiting Professor of Legal Science at Cambridge (2008–2009), a member of the UN International Law Commission (2002–2006) and Counsellor at the Ministry for Foreign Affairs of Finland (1978–1994). His publications include *From Apology to Utopia: The Structure of International Legal Argument* (2nd edn, Cambridge University Press, 2005) and *The Gentle Civilizer of Nations: The Rise and Fall of International Law 1870–1960* (Cambridge University Press, 2001).

Panos Koutrakos is Professor of European Union Law at City University London. He is the joint editor of *European Law Review*. He is the author of *The EU Common Security and Defence Policy* (Oxford University Press, 2013), *EU International Relations Law* (Hart, 2006) and *Trade, Foreign Policy and Defence in EU Constitutional Law* (Hart, 2001), the editor of *European Foreign Policy: Legal and Political Perspectives* (Edward Elgar, 2011) and the co-editor (with Malcolm Evans) of *Beyond the Established Legal Orders: Policy Interconnections Between the EU and the Rest of the World* (Hart, 2011) and (with Christophe Hillion) of *Mixed Agreements Revisited: The EU and Its Member States in the World* (Hart, 2010). In addition to EU external relations, Panos writes on the law of the single market. In 2007, he was awarded a Jean Monnet Chair in European Law by the European Commission. He has held visiting posts at the Universities of Antwerp, Melbourne, Sydney, New South Wales, Iowa and Michigan.

Friedrich Kratochwil studied philosophy and classics at the Ludwig Maximilian University of Munich (LMU Munich) and received an MA from Georgetown University and PhD in political science from Princeton University. He has published widely on international relations, social theory and international law and organisation. He taught at the universities of Maryland, Columbia, Denver and Penn before returning to Europe in 1995 and becoming chair of international relations at LMU Munich and at the European University Institute in Florence (2003–2011). He is Visiting Professor at the Central European University in Budapest and International Scholar at Kyng Hee University in Seoul. His latest book, *The Puzzles of Politics*, was published by Routledge in 2011 and *The Status of Law in World Society: Meditations on the Role and Rule of Law* will appear in the Cambridge series on International Relations in 2014.

Marja Lehto is Finland's ambassador to Luxembourg since 2009. She has served as the head of the public international law unit of the Finnish Ministry for Foreign Affairs (MFA) and as the legal adviser of the Finnish UN Mission in New York. She has led intergovernmental negotiations at the UN and at the European level and held the chairmanship of the Council of Europe expert committee on terrorism (CODEXTER) in 2006 to 2007. Ambassador Lehto holds a PhD in international law (University of Lapland) and a Master's degree in political science (University of Helsinki). She has published academic articles on a number of international law matters ranging from the law of the sea to state succession, peace and security, terrorism and international humanitarian law. Her book entitled *Indirect Responsibility for Terrorist Acts* was published by Martinus Nijhoff in 2009.

Päivi Leino is an Adjunct Professor of European Union Law at the University of Helsinki. She holds a Doctor of Laws degree from the University of Helsinki (2005), a Master of Laws (with distinction, 2001) and a Diploma from the General Course (1998) from the London School of Economics and a Master's degree in international law from the Åbo Akademi University (2000). Her doctoral thesis *Universality as Particularity: The Politics of Human Rights in the European Union* discussed the effects of the politicisation of human rights language in the EU. She has worked as Legal Counsellor at the Ministry of Justice and Ministerial Counsellor at the Prime Minister's Office, Finland, being responsible for the negotiations of various legislative files, including the Treaty of Lisbon and the EU Fundamental Rights Agency. She has also worked as an Assistant Professor in international law and EU law at the University of Helsinki and as a research fellow at the Erik Castrén Institute of International Law and Human Rights.

Rain Liivoja is a Senior Research Fellow and Project Director for the Law of Armed Conflict at the Asia Pacific Centre for Military Law, Melbourne Law School. He is also an Affiliated Research Fellow of the Erik Castrén Institute of International Law and Human Rights, University of Helsinki. Rain's research interests include the law of armed conflict, the law of treaties, state jurisdiction and comparative military justice. He is a member of the Board of Directors of the International Society for Military Law and the Law of War and book review editor of the *Finnish Yearbook of International Law*. Rain holds a doctorate in international law from the University of Helsinki.

Inger Österdahl is Professor in Public International Law at Uppsala University in Sweden. She is a member of the International Law Association's Committee on the Use of Force and a member of the editorial board of the *Nordic Journal of International Law* (*NJIL*). Her research has mainly concerned the international use of force, humanitarian law, human rights, international organisations, constitutional EU law and national constitutional law. Among her recent publications are 'The Neutral Ally: The European Security and Defence Policy and the Swedish Constitution' (*NJIL*, 2009); 'The Use of Force: Sweden, the *Jus ad Bellum* and the European Security and Defence Policy' (*NJIL*, 2010); 'Challenge or Confirmation? The Role of the Swedish Parliament in the Decision-making on the Use of Force' (*NJIL*, 2011); and 'Just war, just peace and the *jus post bellum*' (*NJIL*, 2012).

Gianluigi Palombella is Professor of Legal Philosophy at the University of Parma, Italy, and Robert Schuman/GGP Fellow at the European University Institute (EUI) in Florence. He has previously been Braudel Senior Fellow at the EUI, Inaugural Fellow of the Straus Institute at New York University and MacCormick Fellow at the Edinburgh Law School. He has written extensively in various languages about fundamental rights, constitutionalism and the rule of law, authored several books, the most recent *E' possibile una legalità globale?* (*Is a Global Legality Possible?*) (il Mulino, 2012), and has edited *Relocating the Rule of Law* (with Neil Walker) (Hart, 2009) and *Rule of Law and Democracy* (with Leonardo Morlino) (Brill, 2010).

Joost Pauwelyn is Professor of International Law at the Graduate Institute of International and Development Studies (IHEID) in Geneva, Switzerland, and Co-Director of the Institute's Centre for Trade and Economic Integration (CTEI). He is also Senior Advisor with the law firm of King & Spalding LLC and General Editor of the *Journal of International Dispute Settlement*. His area of expertise is international economic law, in particular, the law of international trade and investment. Before joining the Graduate Institute in 2007, he was a tenured Professor at Duke Law School, Durham, USA. He also served as Legal Officer at the World Trade Organization from 1996 to 2002 and practiced law at a major Brussels law firm. Joost has been a Visiting Professor at Georgetown, Stanford and Harvard law schools.

Jarna Petman, LLD habil., is Deputy Director of the Erik Castren Institute of International Law and Human Rights, and Senior Lecturer (professor *ad interim*) of international law, University of Helsinki. She is also, *inter alia*, a Member of the European Committee of Social Rights of the Council of Europe and a Commissioner of the International Commission of Jurists. Recipient of a number of teaching awards, she has been teaching mainly within the different areas of public international law and legal theory in Finland and abroad, and has published primarily within the fields of human rights, the law governing the use of force and legal theory. She has served on various domestic and international boards of academic associations in international law, international studies, and law and literature. She is the Editor-in-Chief of the *Finnish Yearbook of International Law*.

Biographical notes xv

Kaarlo Tuori is Academy Professor and Professor of Jurisprudence at the University of Helsinki. He is also the Director of the Centre of Excellence Foundations of European Law and Polity, financed by the Academy of Finland. His main research fields are legal and constitutional theory, as well as the foundations of European Law. His recent publications include *Ratio and Voluntas: The Tension between Reason and Will in Law* (Ashgate, 2011) and *The Many Constitutions of Europe* (edited with Suvi Sankari, Ashgate, 2010). He is the Finnish member and the Vice-President of the Venice Commission of the Council of Europe.

Geir Ulfstein is Professor of International Law, University of Oslo. He has published in different areas of international law, including the law of the sea, international environmental law, international human rights and international institutional law. Ulfstein is co-editor of the book series Studies on Human Rights Conventions (Cambridge University Press) and member of the Executive Board of the European Society of International Law. He has been Director of the Norwegian Centre for Human Rights at the University of Oslo.

René Urueña is Professor and Director of the International Law Program, Universidad de Los Andes (Bogotá, Colombia). He was a Research Fellow at the University of Helsinki, where he lectured on international law. He was also a fellow at the Institute for International Law and Justice, at the New York University School of Law. He holds a PhD (*eximia cum laude*) and an LLM (*laudatur*) in international law, both from the University of Helsinki. He graduated with a law degree from the Universidad de Los Andes (Colombia), and holds a post-graduate degree in economics from the same university. His most recent book is *No Citizens Here: Global Subjects and Participation in International Law* (Martinus Nijhoff, 2012).

Ramses A. Wessel is Professor of the Law of the European Union and other International Organizations, and Co-Director of the Centre for European Studies at the University of Twente. He is Member of the standing Netherlands' Governmental Advisory Committee on Issues of Public International Law; Member of the Governing Board of the Centre for the Law of EU External Relations (CLEER) in The Hague; Editor-in-Chief and founder of the *International Organizations Law Review*, Editor of *Nijhoff Studies in European Union Law* and member of the Editorial Board of the *Netherlands Yearbook of International Law*. Ramses studied international law and international relations at the Universities of Groningen and Utrecht. His general research interests lie in the field of international and European institutional law, with a focus on the law of international organisations, matters of global governance, the relationship between international and EU law, European foreign, security and defence policy and EU external relations in general.

Wouter G. Werner is Professor of Public International Law at VU University Amsterdam, chair of European Cooperation in Science and Technology (COST) Action on the fragmentation and constitutionalisation of international law and co-founder of the Center on the Politics of Transnational Law. His main fields of interest are international legal theory, the interplay between international law and international politics and the international legal regime on the use of force. Recent publications concern the concept of humanity across international law and bio-law, the politics of legal cosmopolitanism, critical analyses of Carl Schmitt's international legal theory and the political implications of the International Criminal Court.

Jan Wouters is full Professor of International Law and International Organizations, Jean Monnet Chair *ad personam* EU and Global Governance and Director of the Leuven Centre for Global Governance Studies and Institute for International Law at the University of Leuven. As Visiting Professor at Sciences Po (Paris) and the College of Europe (Bruges) he teaches EU external relations law. He is President of the Flemish Foreign Affairs Council and practices law as Of Counsel at Linklaters, Brussels. He is Member of the Royal Flemish Academy of Belgium for Sciences and Arts. He is Editor of the *International Encyclopedia of Intergovernmental Organizations*, Deputy Director of the *Revue belge de droit international* and editorial board member in ten international journals. He has published widely on international law and various sub-fields thereof, EU law and corporate and financial law.

Table of cases

International

International Court of Justice and Permanent Court of International Justice

Ahmadou Sadio Diallo (Republic of Guinea v. Democratic Republic of the Congo), ICJ Reports (2010-II) 692 253–4
Applicability of the Obligation to Arbitrate under Section 21 of the United Nations Headquarters Agreement of 26 June 1947 (Advisory Opinion), ICJ Reports (1988) 12 151
Application of the Convention on the Prevention and Punishment of the Crime of Genocide (Bosnia and Herzegovina v. Yugoslavia) (Preliminary Objections), ICJ Reports (1996) 595 ....185, 187
Application of the Convention on the Prevention and Punishment of the Crime of Genocide (Bosnia and Herzegovina v. Serbia and Montenegro), ICJ Reports (2007) 43 180
Armed Activities on the Territory of the Congo (Democratic Republic of the Congo v. Uganda), ICJ Reports (2005) 168 ....269, 320, 321
Armed Activities on the Territory of the Congo (New Application: 2002) (Democratic Republic of the Congo v. Rwanda) (Jurisdiction and Admissibility), ICJ Reports (2006) 6 325
Arrest Warrant of 11 April 2000 (Democratic Republic of the Congo v. Belgium), ICJ Reports (2002) 3 ....269, 298, 301, 311
Avena and Other Mexican Nationals (Mexico v. US), ICJ Reports (2004) 12 151
Barcelona Traction, Light and Power Company Limited (Belgium v. Spain), ICJ Reports (1970) 3.......................................52, 266–7
Certain Criminal Proceedings in France (Republic of the Congo v. France) (Order), ICJ Reports (2010) 635 312
Certain German Interests in Polish Upper Silesia (Germany v. Poland), PCIJ Reports (1925) Ser. A, No. 7 151
Certain Questions of Mutual Assistance in Criminal Matters (Djibouti v. France), ICJ Reports (2008) 177..312
Corfu Channel (UK v. Albania), ICJ Reports (1949) 4 ....11, 113, 264–5

xviii   Table of cases

*Dispute Regarding Navigational and Related Rights
(Costa Rica v. Nicaragua)*, ICJ Reports (2009) 213..............................11–12
Fisheries (UK v. Norway), ICJ Reports (1951) 116..151
Frontier Dispute (Benin/Niger), ICJ Reports (2005) 90...................................151
Jurisdictional Immunities of the State (Germany v. Italy: Greece Intervening),
General List No. 143, ICJ, Judgment of 3 February 2006...............269–70
LaGrand (Germany v. US), ICJ Reports (2001) 466..151
*Legal Consequences of the Construction of a Wall in the Occupied
Palestinian Territory (Advisory Opinion)*, ICJ Reports (2004) 136...268, 321
Legality of the Use of Force (Serbia and Montenegro v. Belgium),
CR 1999/15, Oral Proceedings of 10 May 1999.....................................288
Legality or Threat of Use of Nuclear Weapons (Advisory Opinion),
ICJ Reports (1996) 226..268, 321
The SS "Lotus" (France/Turkey), PCIJ Publications Ser. A, No. 10
(1927) 5, 11, 301
*Military and Paramilitary Activities in and against Nicaragua
(Nicaragua v. US)*, ICJ Reports (1986) 14....................157, 267–8, 318, 320
Nottebohm (Liechtenstein v. Guatemala) (Second Phase),
ICJ Reports (1955) 4..151
*Questions Relating to the Obligation to Prosecute or Extradite (Belgium v.
Senegal)*, General List No. 144, ICJ, Judgment of 20 July 2012.............269
*Reparation for Injuries Suffered in the Service of the United Nations
(Advisory Opinion)*, ICJ Reports (1949) 174...252
*Reservations to the Convention on the Prevention and Punishment of the
Crime of Genocide (Advisory Opinion)*, ICJ Reports (1951) 15..............265–6
Right of Passage over Indian Territory (Portugal v. India), ICJ Reports
(1960) 6 11
United States Diplomatic and Consular Staff in Teheran (US v. Iran),
ICJ Reports (1980) 3..267

Arbitral Panels

The 'Alabama' Claims (US v. Great Britain) (1871) 29 UNRIAA 125............151
Azurix Corp. v Argentina, ICSID Case No. ARB/01/12,
Award of 14 July 2006..151
British Claims in the Spanish Zone of Morocco (Great Britain v. Spain)
(1925) 2 UNRIAA 615 10
Iron Rhine ('Ijzeren Rijn') Railway (Belgium v. The Netherlands) (2005)
27 UNRIAA 35..11
Island of Palmas (Netherlands v. US) (1928) 2 UNRIAA 829......................9, 10
Mondev International Ltd. v. US, ICSID Case No. ARB(AF)/99/2,
Award of 11 October 2002..165
Nykomb Synergetics Technology Holding AB v. Latvia, SCC Case No. 118/
2001, Award of 16 December 2003, 11 ICSID Reports 158..................151

Table of cases xix

International Criminal Tribunals

Prosecutor v. Tadić, Case no. IT-94-1, ICTY Appeals Chamber, Decision on the Defence Motion for Interlocutory Appeal on Jurisdiction, 2 October 1995 ....8, 113
Prosecutor v. Tadić, Case No. IT-94-I-A, ICTY Appeals Chamber, Judgment, 15 July 1999 318
Prosecutor v. Bemba Gombo, ICC Pre-Trial Chamber II, *Amicus Curiae* Observations on Superior Responsibility Submitted by Amnesty International, 20 April 2009 306

Human Rights Treaty Bodies

Al-Jedda v. UK, Application no. 27021/08, ECtHR Grand Chamber, Judgment of 7 July 2011 ....133–4, 241, 326
Al-Saadoon and Mufdhi v. UK, Application no. 61498/08, ECtHR Fourth Section, Decision of 3 July 2009................................323
Al-Skeini and Others v. UK, Application no. 55721/07, ECtHR Grand Chamber, Judgment of 7 July 2011 326
Andreou v. Turkey, Application 45653/99, ECtHR Fourth Section, Decision of 3 June 2008 323
Banković and Others v. Belgium and 16 Other Contracting States, Application no. 52207/99, ECtHR Grand Chamber, Decision of 12 December 2001 ....322–4, 326
Chahal v. UK, Application no. 22414/93, ECtHR Grand Chamber, Judgment of 15 November 1996..240–1
Cyprus v. Turkey, Application no. 25781/94, ECtHR Grand Chamber, Judgment of 10 May 2001..323
Djavit An v. Turkey, Application no. 20652/92, ECtHR Chamber, Judgment of 20 February 2003 323
Ilascu and Others v. Moldova and Russia, Application no. 48787/99, ECtHR Grand Chamber, Judgment of 8 July 2004 323
Isaak and Others v. Turkey, Application no. 44587/98, ECtHR Third Section, Decision of 28 September 2006 323
Issa v. Turkey, Application no. 31821/96, ECtHR Second Section, Decision of 16 November 2004 323–4
Loizidou v. Turkey (Preliminary Objections), Application no. 15318/89, Decision of 23 March 1995..323
Medvedyev and Others v. France, Application no. 3394/03, ECtHR Grand Chamber, Judgment of 29 March 2010........................323
Nada v. Switzerland, Application no. 10593/08, ECtHR Grand Chamber, Judgment of 12 September 2012 ....134, 247
Pad and Others v. Turkey, Application no. 60167/00, ECtHR Third Section, Decision of 28 June 2007..323
Sayadi and Vinck v. Belgium, Communication no. 1472/2006, HRC, Views of 22 October 2008, UN Doc. CCPR/C/94/D/1472/2006...241–2

xx   *Table of cases*

Solomou and Others v. Turkey, Application no. 36832/97, ECtHR Fourth
    Section, Decision of 24 June 2008..323

World Trade Organization

*India – Patent Protection for Pharmaceutical and Agricultural Chemical
    Products*, WT/DS50/AB/R, 19 December 1997 151
*United States – Import Prohibition of Certain Shrimp and Shrimp
    Products*, WT/DS58/AB/R, 12 October 1998................................3, 13, 64
*United States – Measures Concerning the Importation, Marketing and Sale
    of Tuna and Tuna Products*, WT/DS381/AB/R, 16 May 2012 ....3, 13
United States – Sections 301–310 of the Trade Act of 1974,
    WT/DS152/R, 22 December 1999 151

Courts of the European Communities/Union

*Air Transport Association of America v. Secretary of State for Energy
    and Climate Change*, Case C-366/10, Judgment of
    21 December 2011 (not yet reported)......................................3, 13–14, 16
*Air Transport Association of America v. Secretary of State for Energy and
    Climate Change*, Case C-366/10, Opinion of Advocate General
    Kokott of 6 October 2011 14
Bosphorus Hava Yollari Turizm ve Ticaret AS, Case C-84/95, [1996]
    ECR I-3953..228
Commission v. Austria, Case C-205/06, [2009] ECR I-1301 ....221, 222
Commission v. Belgium, Case C-170/98, [1999] ECR I-5493 221
Commission v. Council, Case C-25/94, [1996] ECR I-1469.........................217
Commission v. Finland, Case C-118/07, [2009] ECR I-10889 ....221, 222
Commission v. Germany, Case C-433/03, [2005] ECR I-6985..............213, 214
Commission v. Greece, Case C-45/07, [2009] ECR I-701 ....214, 215, 216
Commission v. Ireland, Case C-459/03, [2006] ECR I-4635 ....217, 222
Commission v. Kadi, Joined Cases C-584/10 P, C-593/
    10 P, and C-595/10 P, Judgment of 18 July 2013
    (not yet reported) 133, 226, 236, 246–8
Commission v. Luxembourg, Case C-266/03, [2005]
    ECR I-4805...213, 214, 222
Commission v. Portugal, Case C-62/98, [2000] ECR I-5171 221
Commission v. Sweden, Case C-249/06, [2009] ECR I-1335 ....221, 222
Commission v. Sweden, Case C-246/07, [2010] ECR I-3317 ..213, 218–20, 222
Commission v. UK, Case C-32/79, [1980] ECR 2403..................................214
Commission v. UK, Case C-804/79, [1981] ECR 1045................................214
Commission v. UK, Case C-416/85, [1988] ECR 3127................................215
Convention No 170 ILO on Safety in the Use of Chemicals at Work,
    Opinion 2/91, [1993] ECR I-1061 215–16

Draft Convention of International Atomic Energy Agency, Opinion 1/78,
  [1978] ECR 2151 219
France v. Commission, Case C-327/91, [1994] ECR I-3641 99
France v. Commission, Case C-233/02, [2004] ECR I-2759 99
Fulmen and Fereydoun Mahmoudian v. Council, Joined Cases T-439/10
  and T-440/10, Judgment of 21 March 2012 (not yet reported) 237
Hassan v. Council and Commission, and Ayadi v. Council, Cases
  C-399/06 P and C-403/06, [2009] ECR I-11393 226
Kadi v. Council and Commission, Case T-315/01,
  [2005] ECR II-3649 .... 226–33, 245
*Kadi and Al Barakaat International Foundation v. Council
  and Commission*, Joined Cases C-402/05 P and
  C-415/05 P, [2008] ECR I-6351 .... 126, 132, 136, 226–37, 244–5
*Kadi and Al Barakaat International Foundation v. Council and
  Commission*, Joined Cases C-402/05 P and C-415/05 P, [2008]
  ECR I-6351, Opinion of Advocate General
  Poiares Maduro of 16 January 2008 .... 228, 230, 232–3, 244–5
Kadi v. Commission, Case T-85/09, [2010]
  ECR II-5177 .... 226, 229, 234–7, 244
Kramer, Joined Cases 3, 4 and 6/76, [1976] ECR 1279 213
Lesoochranárske zoskupenie VLK, Case C-240/09, [2011] ECR I-1255 224
Manufacturing Support & Procurement Kala Naft v. Council, Case
  T-509/10, Judgment of 25 April 2012 (not yet reported) 237
Merck Genéricos v. Merck, Case C-431/05, [2007] ECR I-7001 224
Meroni v. High Authority, Cases 9/56 and 10/56, [1957–1958]
  ECR 133 and 157 99
Organisation des Modjahedines du peuple d'Iran v. Council, Case
  T-228/02, [2006] ECR II-4665 235
Othman v. Council and Commission, Case T-318/01, [2009]
  ECR II-1627 .... 226, 237
Parliament v. Council, Case C-130/10, Judgment of 19 July 2012
  (not yet reported) 234
People's Mojahedin Organization of Iran v. Council, Case T-256/07,
  [2008] ECR II-3019 235
People's Mojahedin Organization of Iran v. Council, Case T-284/08,
  [2008] ECR II-3487 235
A. Racke GmbH & Co. v. Hauptzollamt Mainz, Case C-162/96, 228
  [1998] ECR I-3655 228
Sison v. Council, Case C-266/05 P, [2007] ECR I-1233 232
Tay Za v. Council, Case C-376/10 P, Judgment of 13 March 2012
  (not yet reported) 227, 229
*Yusuf and Al Barakaat International Foundation v. Council and
  Commission*, Case T-306/01, [2005] ECR II-3533 228

xxii Table of cases

Domestic

Australia

Polyukhovich v. Commonwealth [1991] HCA 32, (1991) 172 CLR 501
 (High Court) 298

Brazil

*Instituto Brasileiro de Executivos de Financas v. Comissão de Valores
 Mobiliários*, Medida Cautelar n. 17.350 – RJ (2010/0168534-8),
 7 October 2010 (Superior Tribunal de Justiça) 100

Canada

A. v. Ontario Securities Commission [2006] CanLII 14414
 (Ontario Supreme Court) 100

Finland

Prosecutor v. Bazaramba, District Court of Itä-Uusimaa, 11 June 2010...305–6
Prosecutor v. Bazaramba, Court of Appeal of Helsinki, 30 March 2012......306

Israel

Attorney General v. Eichmann (1961) 36 ILR 5 (District Court
 of Jerusalem) 305
Attorney General v. Eichmann (1962) 16(3) PD 2033, 36 ILR 277
 (Supreme Court) 305
HCJ 769/02 *Public Committee against Torture in Israel et al.
 v. Government of Israel et al.* (2006) 53(4) PD 817,
 46 ILM 375 (Supreme Court) 319–21

The Netherlands

City Crash v. Het college van burgemeester en wethouders van 's-Hertogenbosch,
 LJN BP2750, 2 February 2011 (Raad van State) 99
*De Staat der Nederlanden v. Knooble B.V.; Knooble B.V. v. De Stichting
 Nederlands Normalisatie Instituut*, LJN BO4175, 16 November 2010
 (Gerechtshof's-Gravenhage) 99

United Kingdom

Al-Skeini and Others v. Secretary of State for Defence [2007] UKHL 26,
 [2008] 1 AC 153 (House of Lords) 322–6

R. v. Bow Street Metropolitan Stipendiary Magistrate, ex parte
  Pinochet Ugarte (No.3) [1999] UKHL 17, [2000] 1 AC 147
  (House of Lords) 159, 308
RB (Algeria) v. Secretary of State for the Home Department [2009] UKHL 10....226

United States

Banco Nacional de Cuba v. Sabbatino, 193 F Supp. 375
  (US District Court, Southern District of New York, 1961) ...154, 155, 161
Banco Nacional de Cuba v. Sabbatino, 307 F 2d 845
  (US Court of Appeals, 2nd Circuit, 1962)..............................154, 155, 161
Banco Nacional de Cuba v. Sabbatino, 376 US 398
  (US Supreme Court, 1964) 154, 155, 161
Environmental Defense Fund v. Massey, 986 F 2d 528
  (US Court of Appeals, DC Circuit, 1993) 3
Free Enterprise Fund v. Public Company Accounting Oversight Board,
  561 US 1 (US Supreme Court, 2010) 100
Hamdan v. Rumsfeld, 415 F 3d 33 (US Circuit Court,
  DC Circuit, 2005) 317
Hamdan v. Rumsfeld, 548 US 557 (US Supreme Court, 2006) 317–18
Medellín v. Texas, 552 US 491 (US Supreme Court, 2008) 164
Parker v. Brown, 317 US 341 (US Supreme Court, 1943) 99
The Paquete Habana, 175 US 677 (US Supreme Court, 1900) 307–8
US v. Yousef, 327 F3d 56 (US Court of Appeals, 2nd Circuit, 2003) 302

Table of treaties

Charter of the United Nations, 26 June 1945, in force 24 October 1945
................47, 115, 126, 133, 228, 230, 242, 265, 284–5, 289, 292, 294, 296
    Article 2..267, 268
    Article 39...181
    Article 48...228
    Article 102...81
    Chapter VII..132, 181, 283, 290, 292
Statute of the International Court of Justice, 26 June 1945,
    in force 24 October 1945
    Article 38..76, 79, 86
General Agreement on Tariffs and Trade (GATT 1947),
    30 October 1947, in force 1 January 1948, 55 UNTS 194 56
Convention on the Prevention and Punishment of the Crime of
    Genocide, GA Res. 260 A (III), 9 December 1948, in force
    12 January 1951, 78 UNTS 277 265
    Preamble 308
    Article 6 308
Geneva Conventions, 12 August 1949, in force
    21 October 1950, 75 UNTS 31, 85, 135 and 287...........269, 308, 316, 318
    Common Article 2...317–18, 320
    Common Article 3...316, 317–19
Geneva Convention (III) Relative to the Treatment of Prisoners
    of War, 12 August 1949, in force 21 October 1950, 75 UNTS 135
    Article 4...316
European Convention for the Protection of Human Rights and
    Fundamental Freedoms, 4 November 1950, in force 3 September
    1953, 213 UNTS 222 ....66, 132, 324–6
    Article 1...322, 324
    Article 2...322
    Article 3...322
    Article 13...240
Treaty on the Functioning of the European Union (Treaty of Rome;
    TFEU), 25 March 1957, in force 1 January 1958, OJ 2010 C 83/47
    Article 64...221

Article 66	221
Article 75	221, 234
Article 215	234
Article 258	215
Article 263	231
Article 275	234
Article 347	228
Article 351	220–1, 228
ex-Article 10	215
ex-Article 60	227
ex-Article 301	227

Convention on the High Seas, 29 April 1958, in force
30 September 1962, 450 UNTS 11 276
    Article 24 281

Convention on the Continental Shelf, 29 April 1958, in force
10 June 1964, 499 UNTS 311 .... 276, 279
    Article 2 278
    Article 5 .... 277–8, 281

Convention on the Territorial Sea and the Contiguous Zone,
29 April 1958, in force 10 September 1964, 516 UNTS 205 276
    Article 2 278

Convention on Fishing Conservation of the Living Resources of the
High Seas, 29 April 1958, in force 20 March 1966, 559 UNTS 285 276

North-East Atlantic Fisheries Convention, 24 January 1959, in force
27 June 1963, 486 UNTS 157 213

Antarctic Treaty, 1 December 1959, in force 23 June 1961,
402 UNTS 71
    Preamble 111

Vienna Convention on Consular Relations, 24 April 1963, in force
19 March 1967, 596 UNTS 261
    Article 36 164

International Covenant on Civil and Political Rights (ICCPR),
GA Res. 2200A (XXI), 16 December 1966, in force
23 March 1976, 999 UNTS 171 .... 250, 269
    Article 1 .... 6, 11
    Article 23 163–4
    Article 40 .... 250, 252
    Article 47 6

Optional Protocol to the International Covenant on Civil and
Political Rights, GA Res. 2200A (XXI), 16 December 1966,
in force 23 March 1976, 999 UNTS 171 252
    Article 5 252

Treaty on Principles governing the Activities of States in the
Exploration and Use of Outer Space, including the Moon and
Other Celestial Bodies (Outer Space Treaty), 27 January 1967,
in force 10 October 1967, 610 UNTS 205 .... 112, 115

Article 1..111
Article 5..111
Article 6..117
Article 7..117
Vienna Convention on the Law of Treaties, 23 May 1969,
   in force 27 January 1980, 1155 UNTS 331 ....203, 264, 267
Article 7..83
Article 11..210
Article 26..301
Article 30..203
Article 31..201, 203, 205
Article 34..302
Article 39..205
Article 41..205
Article 53..263–4, 268, 270
Article 60..206
Article 65..206
Article 66..206
Convention on Special Missions, GA Res. 2530 (XXIV),
   8 December 1969, in force 21 June 1985, 1400 UNTS 231 311
Convention for the Suppression of Unlawful Seizure of Aircraft,
   16 December 1970, in force 14 October 1971, 860 UNTS 105............300
Convention on Wetlands of International Importance, especially as
   Waterfowl Habitat (Ramsar Convention), 2 February 1971, in force
   21 December 1975, 996 UNTS 243..192–3
Article 6..192
Montreal Convention for the Suppression of Unlawful Acts against
   the Safety of Civil Aviation, 23 September 1971, in force
   26 January 1973, 974 UNTS 177 302
Convention on International Liability for Damage Caused by Space
   Objects, GA Res. 2777 (XXVI), 29 November 1971, in force
   1 September 1972, 961 UNTS 187...117
Act Concerning the Conditions of Accession and the Adjustments
   to the Treaties (Act of Accession), 22 January 1972, in force
   1 January 1973, OJ 1972 L 73/14
Article 102..213
Convention Concerning the Protection of the World Cultural and
   Natural Heritage, 16 November 1972, in force 17 December 1975,
   1037 UNTS 151
Preamble..112
Convention on the Prevention of Marine Pollution from Dumping
   (London Convention), 29 December 1972, in force 30
   August 1975, 1046 UNTS 120..192–3, 204–5
Article XIV..193

Table of treaties xxvii

Convention on International Trade in Endangered Species of
  Wild Fauna and Flora (CITES), 3 March 1973, in force
  1 July 1975, 993 UNTS 243 ....197, 199–200, 204–5
  Article VII 199
  Article XI 192
  Article XXIII 199
International Convention on the Protection from Pollution from
  Ships (MARPOL), 2 November 1973, in force 2 October 1983,
  1340 UNTS 184 194
  Article 16 194–5
International Convention for the Safety of Life at Sea
  (SOLAS Convention), 1 November 1974, in force
  25 May 1980, 1184 UNTS 3 214–15
Protocol (I) Additional to the Geneva Conventions of 12 August 1949,
  and Relating to the Protection of Victims of International Armed
  Conflicts, 8 June 1977, in force 7 December 1978, 1125 UNTS 3 316
  Article 51 320
Protocol (II) Additional to the Geneva Conventions of 12 August
  1949, and relating to the Protection of Victims of Non-International
  Armed Conflicts, Geneva, 8 June 1977, in force 7 December 1978,
  1125 UNTS 609 316
Protocol relating to the International Convention for the
  Prevention of Pollution from Ships, 17 February 1978, in force
  2 October 1983, 1340 UNTS 61 194
Convention on Long-range Transboundary Air Pollution,
  13 November 1979, in force 16 March 1983, 1302 UNTS 217
  Article 10 193
Agreement Governing the Activities of States on the Moon and Other
  Celestial Bodies (Moon Treaty), GA Res. 34/68, 5 December 1979,
  in force 11 July 1984, 1363 UNTS 3 112
  Article 4 111
Convention on the Elimination of All Forms of Discrimination against
  Women (CEDAW), GA Res. 34/180, 18 December 1979, in force
  3 September 1981, 1249 UNTS 13
  Article 5 255
  Article 8 249
Convention on the Conservation of Migratory Species of Wild
  Animals (Bonn Convention), 26 June 1979, in force
  1 November 1983, 1651 UNTS 333 ....193, 200
  Article II 200
Protocol to Amend the Convention on Wetlands of International
  Importance especially as Waterfowl Habitat (Paris Protocol),
  3 December 1982, in force 1 October 1986, 22 ILM 698 192
United Nations Convention on the Law of the Sea (UNCLOS),
  10 December 1982, in force 16 November 1994,
  1833 UNTS 3 ....59, 66, 112, 115, 217–18, 276, 279, 282

xxviii *Table of treaties*

Article 2..278
Article 56..278
Article 57..278
Article 58..116
Article 60..278
Article 77..278
Article 80..278
Article 82..279
Article 105..116
Article 136..111
Article 137..111
Article 145..281
Article 208..281
Article 282..217
Convention against Torture and Other Cruel, Inhuman or
  Degrading Treatment or Punishment, GA Res. 39/46,
  10 December 1984, in force 26 June 1987, 1465 UNTS 85..................300
Article 4..300
Article 5..300, 301
Article 7..300
Article 20..249
Vienna Convention on the Protection of Ozone Layer, 22 March
  1985, in force 22 September 1988, 1513 UNTS 323............................194
Article 2..194
Protocol to the 1979 Convention on Long-Range Transboundary
  Air Pollution on the Reduction of Sulphur Emissions or their
  Transboundary Fluxes by at least 30 per cent, 8 July 1985, in force
  2 September 1987, 1480 UNTS 215
Article 1..200
Montreal Protocol on Substances that Deplete the Ozone
  Layer, 16 September 1987, in force 1 January 1989,
  1522 UNTS 3..194, 198, 202, 206
Article 2..194
Article 8..196, 197
Additional Protocol to the American Convention on Human Rights
  in the Area of Economic, Social and Cultural Rights, Organization
  of American States, 17 November 1988, in force 16 November 1999,
  OAS Treaty Series No. 69
Article 7..51
Convention on Environmental Impact Assessment in a Transboundary
  Context (Espoo Convention), 25 February 1991, in force
  10 September 1997, 1989 UNTS 309...205
Basel Convention on the Control of Transboundary Movements of
  Hazardous Wastes and Their Disposal, 22 March 1989, in force
  5 May 1992, 1673 UNTS 126..203, 205, 210

Treaty on European Union (Maastricht Treaty; TEU),
7 February 1992, in force 1 November 1993, OJ 2012 326/13
- Article 4 212
- Article 6 144
- Article 24 234
- Protocol No. 6, Article 60 236

Convention on Biological Diversity, 5 June 1992, in force
29 December 1993, 1760 UNTS 79 ....191, 194
- Article 23 191
- Article 25 191
- Article 26 191
- Article 28 191
- Article 29 191
- Article 30 191

United Nations Framework Convention on Climate Change
(UNFCCC), 9 May 1992, in force 21 March 1994, 1771 UNTS 107 130
- Article 7 ....191, 193

General Agreement on Tariffs and Trade (GATT 1994), Annex 1A
of the Marrakesh Agreement Establishing the World Trade
Organization, 15 April 1994, in force 1 January 1995, 1867
UNTS 187 56

Agreement on Trade-Related Aspects of Intellectual Property Rights
(TRIPS Agreement), Annex 1C of the Marrakesh Agreement
Establishing the World Trade Organization, 15 April 1994, in
force 1 January 1995, 1869 UNTS 299 ....44, 98

United Nations Convention to Combat Desertification in Those
Countries Experiencing Drought and/or Desertification, in
particular in Africa, 17 June 1994, in force 26 December 1996,
1954 UNTS 3 194

Agreement for the Implementation of the United Nations Convention
of the Law of the Sea of 10 December 1982 Relating to the
Conservation and Management of Straddling Stocks and Highly
Migratory Fish Stocks, 4 August 1995, in force 11 December 2001,
2167 UNTS 3 282

Protocol to the 1972 Convention on the Prevention of Marine
Pollution by Dumping of Wastes and Other Matter, 11 July 1996,
in force 24 March 2006, 36 ILM 1 192

Convention on the Prohibition of the Use, Stockpiling, Production
and Transfer of Anti-Personnel Mines and on their Destruction
(Ottawa Convention), 18 September 1997, in force 1 March 1999,
2056 UNTS 211 284

Kyoto Protocol to the United Nations Framework Convention on
Climate Change, 11 December 1997, in force 16 February 2005,
2303 UNTS 148 ....196, 197, 198, 199, 205–6, 206–7, 208
- Article 6 196

Article 12 196
Article 17 ....196, 202
Article 18 ....197, 198, 202
Convention on Access to Information, Public Participation in
  Decision-making and Access to Justice in Environmental Matters
  (Aarhus Convention), 25 June 1998, in force 30 October 2001,
  2161 UNTS 447 205–6
Article 15 ....197, 198
Rome Statute of the International Criminal Court,
  17 July 1998, in force 1 July 2000,
  2187 UNTS 3 ....175–9, 182, 184, 284, 294, 304, 312
Article 7 ....184, 308
Article 8 184
Article 13 181
Article 16 181
Article 25 ....175, 177
Optional Protocol to the Convention on the Elimination of All Forms
  of Discrimination against Women, GA Res. 54/4, 6 October 1999,
  in force 22 December 2000, 2131 UNTS 83 254–5
Article 5 254–5
Article 7 256
Cartagena Protocol on Biosafety to the Convention on Biological
  Diversity, 29 January 2000, in force 11 September 2003, 2226
  UNTS 208 196
Article 7 196
Article 18 196
Constitutive Act of the African Union, 11 July 2000, in force
  26 May 2001, 2158 UNTS 3 284
Article 4 310
Stockholm Convention on Persistent Organic Pollutants
  (POPs Convention), 22 May 2001, in force 17 May 2004,
  2256 UNTS 119 218–20
Article 13 218
Article 22 219
Article 25 219
Treaty Establishing a Constitution for Europe, 29 October 2004,
  not in force, OJ 2004 C 310/1 ....136, 211
Treaty of Lisbon amending the Treaty on European Union
  and the Treaty establishing the European Community,
  13 December 2007, OJ 2007 C 306/1 ....211–12, 237
Convention on Cluster Munitions, 30 May 2008, in force
  1 August 2010, 48 ILM 357 284

Table of other relevant instruments

United Nations

General Assembly

GA Res. 96 (I), 11 December 1946	266
GA Res. 174 (II), 21 November 1947	173
GA Res. 217A (III), 10 December 1948	8, 269
GA Res. 3452 (XXX), 9 December 1975	269
GA Res. 43/131, 8 December 1988	287
GA Res. 45/100, 14 December 1990	287
GA Res. 49/53, 9 December 1994	175
GA Res. 53/152, 9 December 1998	112
GA Res. 56/82, 12 December 2001	173
GA Res. 56/83, 12 December 2001	172
GA Res. 60/1, 24 October 2005	283, 284, 291–5
GA Res. 60/288, 20 September 2006	238, 239
GA Res. 64/117, 16 December 2009	299
GA Res. 64/168, 18 December 2009	240
GA Res. 65/33, 6 December 2010	299
GA Res. 66/100, 9 December 2011	173
GA Res. 66/103, 9 December 2011	299
GA Res. 67/98, 14 December 2012	299
Declaration and treaty concerning the reservation exclusively for peaceful purposes of the seabed and the ocean floor underlying the seas beyond the limits of present national jurisdiction, and the use of the resources in the interest of mankind, UN Doc. A/6695, 18 August 1967	111
Report of the *Ad Hoc* Committee on the Establishment of an International Criminal Court, UN Doc. A/50/22, 6 September 1995	175
Report of the Special Committee on the Charter of the United Nations and on the Strengthening of the Role of the Organization, UN Doc. A/54/33 and Corr.1, 12 May 1999	288

Security Council

SC Res. 687, 8 April 1991	182
SC Res. 1368, 12 September 2001	320
SC Res. 1373, 28 September 2001	235, 237
SC Res. 1564, 18 September 2004	182
SC Res. 1593, 31 March 2005	182
SC Res. 1730, 19 December 2006	239
SC Res. 1904, 17 December 2009	239–40
SC Res. 1970, 26 February 2011	290, 294
SC Res. 1973, 17 March 2011	290, 294
SC Res. 1989, 17 June 2011	240
Press Release: Security Council Al-Qaida Sanctions Committee Deletes Entry of Yasin Abdullah Ezzedine Qadi from Its List, UN Doc. SC/10785, 5 October 2012	236
Statute of the International Tribunal for the Prosecution of Persons Responsible for Serious Violations of International Humanitarian Law Committed in the Territory of the Former Yugoslavia since 1991, approved by SC Res. 827, 25 May 1993, with later amendments	176
Statute of the International Criminal Tribunal for Rwanda, annexed to SC Res. 955, 8 November 1994, with later amendments	176

Secretary-General

'Implementing the Responsibility to Protect', Report of the Secretary-General, UN Doc. A/63/677, 12 January 2009	285, 290, 291
'In Larger Freedom: Towards Development', Security and Human Rights for All, Report of the Secretary-General, UN Doc. A/59/2005, 21 March 2005	285, 290, 296
'We the Peoples: The Role of the United Nations in the 21st Century', Report of the Secretary-General, UN Doc. A/54/2000, 27 March 2000	287, 295
'Early Warning, Assessment and the Responsibility to Protect', Report of the Secretary-General, UN Doc. A/64/864, 14 July 2010	290
'The Role of Regional and Sub-regional Arrangements in Implementing the Responsibility to Protect', Report of the Secretary-General, UN Doc. A/65/877–S/2011/393, 28 June 2011	290
'Responsibility to Protect: Timely and Decisive Response', Report of the Secretary-General, UN Doc. A/66/874, 25 July 2012	290

Commission on Human Rights/Human Rights Council

CHR Res. 2000/47, 25 April 2000	52
CHR Res. 2002/46, 23 April 2002	52
HRC Res. 13/26, 26 March 2010	240

Human Rights Committee

General Comment No. 33: The Obligations of States Parties under the Optional Protocol to the International Covenant on Civil and Political Rights, UN Doc. CCPR/C/GC/33, 5 November 2008.....253, 255

International Law Commission

Draft Articles on the Responsibility of International Organizations, in Report of the International Law Commission on the Work of its Sixty-third session (2011), UN Doc. A/66/10, ch. V 172, 174–5, 183
Draft Articles on the Responsibility of States for Internationally Wrongful Acts, in Report of the International Law Commission on the Work of its Fifty-third session (2001), UN Doc. A/56/10, ch. IV...172, 174–5, 178, 184
Draft Code of Crimes against the Peace and Security of Mankind, in Report of the International Law Commission on the Work of its Forty-eighth Session (1996), UN Doc. A/51/10, ch. II 172
Draft Statute for an International Criminal Court, in Report of the International Law Commission on the Work of its Forty-sixth Session (1994), UN Doc. A/49/10, ch. II................172, 175–7
Fragmentation of International Law: Difficulties arising from the Diversification and Expansion of International Law (finalized by Martti Koskenniemi), UN Doc. A/CN.4/L.682, 13 April 2006 165
Roberto Ago, 'Fifth Report on State Responsibility' UN Doc. A/CN.4/291, 22 March 1976 265
James Crawford, 'Third Report on State Responsibility: Addendum', UN Doc. A/CN.4/507/Add.4, 4 August 2000...........................184–5, 187
Report of the International Law Commission on the Work of its Fiftieth Session (1998), UN Doc. A/53/10 173
Report of the International Law Commission on the Work of its Fifty-third session (2001), UN Doc. A/56/10 266
State Responsibility: Draft Articles Provisionally Adopted by the Drafting Committee on Second Reading, UN Doc. A/CN.4/L.600, 21 August 2000 175

Programmes and Specialised Agencies

Universal Declaration on the Human Genome and Human Rights, UNESCO Doc. 29 C/Res.16, 11 November 1997
    Article 1...112
Code for the Construction and Equipment of Mobile Offshore Drilling Units, IMO Res. A.1023(26), 2 December 2009......................277

xxxiv *Table of other relevant instruments*

'Multilateral Environmental Agreements: Summary', Background Paper Presented by the Secretariat, UN Doc. UNEP/IGM/1/INF/1, 30 March 2001 190

Guidelines for Enhancing Compliance with Multilateral Environmental Agreements, UNEP Governing Council Decision SSVII/4, 15 February 2002, in in UN Doc. UNEP/GCSS.VII/6, Appendix I 197

Conference/Preparatory Commission on the Establishment of the International Criminal Court

Preparatory Committee on Establishment of International Criminal Court, 'Preparatory Committee on International Criminal Court Concludes First Session', Doc. L/2787, 12 April 1996 176

Preparatory Committee on the Establishment of an International Criminal Court, 'Summary of the Proceedings of the Preparatory Committee During the Period 25 March–12 April 1996', UN Doc. A/AC.249/1, 7 May 1996 176

Preparatory Committee on the Establishment of an International Criminal Court, UN Doc. A/AC.249/1997/WG.2/CRP.2, 13 February 1997 176

Preparatory Committee on the Establishment of an International Criminal Court, UN Doc. A/AC.249/1997/L.5, 12 March 1997 176

Report of the Committee of the Whole, Doc. A/CONF.183/8, 17 July 1998 177

Report of the Preparatory Committee on the Establishment of an International Criminal Court, UN Doc. A/CONF.183/2/Add.1, 14 April 1998 176

Working Group on General Principles of Criminal Law, 'Working Paper on article 23, paragraphs 5 and 6', UN Doc. A/CONF.183/C.1/WGGP/L.5/REV.2, 3 July 1998 176–7

Reports Submitted to United Nations Organs

'A More Secure World: Our Shared Responsibility', Report of the High-Level Panel on Threats, Challenges and Change, UN Doc. A/59/565, 2 December 2004 .... 283, 290, 292, 294

First Annual Report of the International Criminal Tribunal for the Former Yugoslavia, UN Doc. A/49/342-S/1994/1007, 29 August 1994 186

Report of the International Commission of Inquiry on Darfur to the United Nations Secretary-General, 25 January 2005 182

Report of the Special Rapporteur on the Promotion and Protection of Human Rights and Fundamental Freedoms while Countering Terrorism, UN Doc. A/65/258, 6 August 2010 240

Seventh Report of the Prosecutor of the International Criminal
   Court to the UN Security Council, 5 June 2008 182

Regional Organisations

African Union

African Union (Draft) Model National Law on Universal
   Jurisdiction over International Crimes, Meeting of
   Government Experts and Ministers of Justice/Attorneys
   General on Legal Matters (2012) 310–11
Decision on the Report of the Commission on the Abuse of
   the Principle of Universal Jurisdiction, Assembly/AU/
   Dec.199(XI) (1 July 2008) 309, 310
Decision on the Abuse of the Principle of Universal Jurisdiction,
   Assembly/AU/Dec.243(XIII) Rev.1 (3 July 2009) 311
Decision on the Abuse of the Principle of Universal Jurisdiction,
   Assembly/AU/Dec.271(XIV) (2 February 2010) 311
Decision on the Implementation of the Decisions of the
   International Criminal Court (ICC), Assembly/AU/
   Dec.419(XIX) (16 July 2012) 310, 312
Decision on the Abuse of the Principle of Universal Jurisdiction,
   Assembly/AU/Dec.420(XIX) (16 July 2012) 309

European Union

A Secure Europe in a Better World: European Security Strategy,
   European Council, 12 December 2003 211
Commission Implementing Regulation (EU) No 933/2012 of
   11 October 2012, OJ 2012 L 278/11 236
Commission Regulation (EC) No 2062/2001 of 19 October 2001,
   OJ 2001 L 277/25 225
Council Regulation (EC) No 2580/2001 of 27 December 2001,
   OJ 2001 L 344/70 235
Council Regulation (EC) No 881/2002 of 27 May 2002, OJ 2002
   L 139/9 225
Directive 2008/101/EC of the European Parliament and of the
   Council of 19 November 2008, OJ 2009 L 8/3 14
European Union Counter-Terrorism Strategy, EU Doc. 14469/4/05
   REV 4, 30 November 2005 239
Laeken Declaration: The Future of the European Union,
   European Council, SN 273/01, 15 December 2001 211
Presidency Conclusions: Tampere European Council,
   15–16 October 1999 238
Regulation (EC) No 1726/2003 of the European Parliament
   and of the Council of 22 July 2003, OJ 2003 L 249/1 3

xxxvi   *Table of other relevant instruments*

Regulation (EC) No 725/2004 of the European Parliament
and of the Council of 31 March 2004, OJ 2004 L 129/6 215
Report of the AU-EU Technical *Ad hoc* Expert Group on the
Principle of Universal Jurisdiction, EU Doc. 8672/1/09 REV
1 (April 2009) 298, 300
White Paper on European Governance, Commission of the
European Communities, COM (2001) 428 final, 25 July 2001,
OJ 2001 C 287/1 53

Meetings and Conferences of Parties to Treaties

Aarhus Convention

Decision I/7, 2002, UN Doc. ECE/MP.PP/2/Add.8 205
Decision II/5, 2005, UN Doc. ECE/MP.PP/2005/2/Add.6 205

Basel Convention

Decision VI/12, 2002, in UN Doc. UNEP/CWH.6/40,
Annex 197, 198, 205

Bonn Convention

Resolution 5.3, 16 April 1997, UNEP/CMS/ScCAP/Inf.4 200–1

CITES

Resolution Conf. 4.25 199
Resolution Conf. 5.11 204
Resolution Conf. 9.24 199
Resolution Conf. 9.6 199
Resolution Conf. 10.16 199–200
Resolution Conf. 11.11 199–200
Resolution Conf. 11.16 199
Resolution Conf. 13.6 199
Resolution Conf. 13.7 199
Resolution Conf. 14.3 205
Amendments to Appendices I and II of the Convention, adopted
by the Conference of the Parties at its seventh meeting in
Lausanne, Switzerland, from 9 to 20 October 1989 204

Espoo Convention

Decision II/4, 2001, in UN Doc. ECE/MP.EIA/4, Annex IV 205
Decision III/2, 2004, in UN Doc. ECE/MP.EIA/6, Annex II 205

London Convention

Res. LDC.21(9), 1985 204
Res. LDC.41(13), 1990 204–5
Res. LC.51(16), 1993 204

LRTAP

Report of the Seventh Session of the Executive Body, 1989,
  UN Doc. ECE/EB.AIR/20 200

Montreal Protocol

Decision II/8, 1990, in UN Doc. UNEP/OzL.Pro.2/3 204
Decision IV/18, 1992, in UN Doc. UNEP/OzL.Pro.4/15 198
Decision IV/5, 1992, in UN Doc. UNEP/OzL.Pro.4/15 205

SOLAS

International Ship and Port Facility Security Code, 12 December
  2002, UN Doc. SOLAS/CONF.5/34, Annex 1 214–5

UNFCCC/Kyoto Protocol

Decision 1/CP.17, 2007, in UN Doc. FCCC/CP/2011/9/Add.1 130
Decision 27/CMP.1, 2005, in UN Doc. FCCC/KP/CMP/2005/8/
  Add.3 205–6

Domestic Law

Austria

Strafgesetzbuch [Penal Code], 15 May 1974 303

Colombia

Constitución [Constitution], 4 July 1991 162–4
Código Penal [Penal Code], 24 July 2000 303

Cook Islands

Geneva Conventions and Additional Protocols Act 2002 308

Estonia

Karistusseadustik [Penal Code], 6 June 2001 303

xxxviii *Table of other relevant instruments*

Finland

Rikoslaki [Penal Code], 19 December 1889 .... 303, 305, 308
Asetus rikoslain 1 luvun 7 §:n soveltamisesta [Decree on the
 Application of Section 7 of Chapter 1 of the Penal Code],
 16 August 1996 306

France

La Constitution [Constitution], 28 September 1958
 Article 52 83
Code pénal [Penal Code], 22 July 1992 303
Circulaire relative à l'élaboration et à la conclusion des accords
 internationaux [Circular on the Preparation and Conclusion
 of International Agreements], 30 May 1997 83

Germany

Gemeinsame Geschäftsordnung der Bundesministerien
 [Common Ministerial Rules of Procedure], 5 October 2011 80
Strafgesetzbuch [Penal Code], 15 May 1871 303

Israel

Basic Law: Judicature, 28 February 1984 319

Switzerland

Schweizerisches Strafgesetzbuch [Penal Code], 21 December 1937 303

United Kingdom

Human Rights Act 1998 322
Prevention of Terrorism (Temporary Provisions) Act 1989 226

United States

1 USC § 112a 83
1 USC § 112b [Case-Zablocki Act] 83
22 CFR § 181.2, 5(b) 83
Oil Pollution Act of 1990 272
Clean Water Act of 1972 272
Constitution 80
Military Order, Detention, Treatment, and Trial of Certain
 Non-Citizens in the War against Terrorism, 13 November 2001 317
Military Commissions Act of 2006 318

Military Commissions Act of 2009 318

Miscellaneous Instruments

American National Standards Institute, 'ANSI Essential Requirements: Due Process Requirements for American National Standards', January 2013 98
Basel Committee on Banking Supervision, 'International Convergence of Capital Measurement and Capital Standards: A Revised Framework' ('Basel II'), 26 June 2004 81
British Standards Institute, 'BS 0:2011 – A Standard for Standards: Principles of Standardization', August 2011 98
Deutsches Institut für Normung, 'DIN 820', 2009 98
European Committee for Standardization and European Committee for Electrotechnical Standardization, 'CEN/CENELEC Internal Regulations – Part 2: Common Rules for Standardization Work', July 2012 98
Global Harmonization Task Force, 'Essential Principles of Safety and Performance of Medical Devices', Doc. GHTF/SG1/N41R9:2005, 20 May 2005 93
Institute of International Law, 'The Protection of Human Rights and the Principle of Non-intervention in Internal Affairs of States', Resolution of 13 September 1989 8
Institute of International Law, 'Universal criminal jurisdiction with regard to the crime of genocide, crimes against humanity and war crimes', Resolution of 26 August 2005 298
International Law Association, Committee on Formation of Customary (General) International Law, 'Final Report of the Committee, Statement of Principles Applicable to the Formation of General Customary International Law', 2000 307
ISEAL Alliance, 'Code of Good Practice for Setting Social and Environmental Standards', Version 5.0, January 2010 97

Preface

This is a book on international law-making, and more: this is also a compilation of papers celebrating the fiftieth birthday of our dear friend Jan Klabbers. Now one may think that a fiftieth birthday is a bit premature for such a gesture. As it so happens, however, it is a long tradition in the Finnish legal academia that prominent scholars, even if Dutch by origin, will be celebrated with a *liber amicorum* when turning fifty – with the presumption, of course, that further volumes will follow at regular intervals.

When we started pondering about the make-up of this particular volume, one of the first difficulties was to find a theme for the book, not least by virtue of the fact that Jan has in his prolific writings, in his inimitable style, touched upon every conceivable area of international law. As both of us have had the privilege of being a student of Jan's at some point in time, we finally ended up taking our cue from what we have learned from him. The thing is, in his teaching – as well as writing, for that matter – Jan tends to emphasise structural concerns rather than the minutiae of substantive, black-letter law. One such issue, on which he has indeed made a most significant contribution to legal scholarship, is the source of legal obligations. And so law-making soon seemed for us an appropriate theme for the book; a theme that would also allow Jan's friends of different intellectual persuasions to make a contribution.

When addressing the theme of law-making, we again took our cue from Jan, who often takes unconventional – some might say quirky – approaches to legal scholarship. And so the book was decidedly to be about 'international law-making' rather than the 'making of international law'. That is to say, it was to offer theoretical explorations into the very notion of law-making, whether in the global or regional, international or transnational realm, and into the limits and possibilities of competing global normative orders; it was to probe into the question of what qualifies as (international) law and how to distinguish it from non-law (and whether this is a meaningful distinction to begin with) – while at the same time offering discussions of a more technical kind about particular sources of international law and their inter-relationship, about the role of particular actors (international organisations, say) in developing those sources and about the differences and similarities in international law-making between different fields of human endeavour, for example.

And, sure enough, the contributors have delivered. The book begins with an exploration of the limits and possibilities of law-making in the global order. Accordingly, Eyal Benvenisti looks into the use of national regulation to unilaterally address global concerns. Martti Koskenniemi in his turn traces the intellectual trajectory of pursuits to grasp the intrinsic laws of modern sociability that leads from theology through law to political economy, while Friedrich Kratochwil examines critically the traditional liberal–cosmopolitan account of governance and the resulting transfer of the techniques of modern governmentality to the global level. Gianluigi Palombella analyses the idea of global legislation within a system that is fundamentally characterised by the lack of a central authority, stressing the potential of legality's non-instrumental side. Joost Pauwelyn, Ramses Wessel and Jan Wouters use Klabbersian notions – such as the broad concept of international agreement and the idea of 'presumptive law' – to shed more light on informal international law-making. Wouter Werner studies the invocation of the concept of 'mankind' in the work of Vitoria, Grotius and Vattel, and some modern treaties regulating non-sovereign territories.

The second part of the book examines the interplay and the distinction between domestic and international law. It is the argument of Inger Österdahl that the very distinction between international and non-international law begins to erode as law becomes more internationalised. Kaarlo Tuori adds a further layer to the discussion, namely European Union (EU) law, exploring the way in which legal actors are prisoners of their institutional and professional interests that dictate how to approach and define legal matters and what positions to take. René Urueña explores the interplay between international and domestic law by offering an alternative to the dominant dual approach that considers domestic courts, on the one hand, as enforcers of the international rule of law and, on the other, as organs of their respective state.

The third part concentrates on the varied roles that institutions and participants play in international law-making. Katja Creutz opens this part by exploring how the fragmented attempts at law-making by the International Law Commission can be seen to have contributed to problems in international responsibility rather than creating a functioning tool-box of remedies. Malgosia Fitzmaurice in her turn examines how Conferences of the Parties to multilateral environmental agreements shape, modify and, in some cases, broaden obligations of the parties to these treaties. Panos Koutrakos discusses the profound impact of EU law in constraining the ability of the member states to relate to third parties as sovereign subject of international law and explores the role of Europe's judges in the incremental development of this area of law. Päivi Leino, also addressing EU law, discusses the procedural deficiencies of the United Nations sanctions regime through the jurisprudence of EU courts in relation to one particular terrorism suspect.

Geir Ulfstein examines the legal basis for the different law-making functions of human rights treaty bodies and discusses the extent to which the treaty bodies should act as legal or policy organs.

The fourth and the final part highlights some of the uncertainties and gaps that emerge in law-making. Enzo Cannizzaro explores the processes of peremptory law-making by analysing the ways in which the contested concept of *jus cogens* has been applied in the jurisprudence of the International Court of Justice. James Hickey seeks to identify the legal uncertainties and gaps that have arisen in the law of the sea in light of the relatively new phenomenon of deepwater and ultra-deepwater oil and gas exploration, while Marja Lehto studies the uncertainties and gaps that potentially accompany the notion of 'responsibility to protect': should it be seen as an emerging norm of international law or as a failed project of international law-making? Rain Liivoja looks into the field of international criminal law, arguing that universal jurisdiction over crimes under international law can only be created through the development of customary law and not by means of incorporating procedural provisions into multilateral treaties. Jarna Petman uses the specific example of the 'war on terror' to critically explore the way in which international legal norms, human rights included, are made in the application.

We thank all the contributors – friends of Jan – in coming together to provide him with a lasting gift. We owe special gratitude to Routledge, especially Mark Sapwell and Katie Carpenter, for taking this book on board and for putting up with the tardiness of the editors. We also wish to thank the Larren Art Trust for their kind permission to use an artwork by Ron Waddams as the cover image. The painting, called 'Interdependence', is part of the Peace Quintet series, and well reflects Waddams' lifelong concern with humanitarian concerns – many of his works ponder on living without conflict and refer to the aims of the United Nations Charter. A fitting cover for a work celebrating the birthday of a true scholar in international law, would you not agree?

RL & JP
13 August 2013

Part I
Legislation and globalisation

1 Legislating for humanity

May states compel foreigners to promote global welfare?

Eyal Benvenisti

1 Introduction: What is 'legislation for humanity'?

Consider the following unilateral acts of legislation: the imposition by the US of sanctions on all actors, public and private, including foreign ones, who do not comply with the US's rules on illegal trafficking in humans;[1] the imposition by the US of trade restrictions on the global harvest of shrimp or tuna without US-approved techniques to protect sea turtles or dolphins;[2] or the imposition by the European Union (EU) of an obligation on any oil tanker visiting a port with the EU area, irrespective of their flag, to have a double-hull design,[3] or, most recently, the demand that non-EU air carriers landing in EU territory take part in the EU carbon emissions scheme that would apply also to those segments flown outside the EU area.[4] What is common to these and other unilateral regulatory efforts of this type is their aim: the unilateral attempt to prevent or remedy global public 'bads'. A major characteristic of this type of 'legislation for humanity' is the net burdens that it imposes on foreign producers and consumers in addition to the equivalent burdens it imposes on domestic actors.[5] Unlike the unilateral

---

1 See Janie A. Chuang, 'The United States as Global Sheriff: Using Unilateral Sanctions to Combat Human Trafficking', 27 *Michigan Journal of International Law* (2006) 437–94.
2 WTO Appellate Body, *United States – Import Prohibition of Certain Shrimp and Shrimp Products*, WT/DS58/AB/R, 12 October 1998 (*Shrimp/Turtle*); *United States – Measures Concerning the Importation, Marketing and Sale of Tuna and Tuna Products*, WT/DS381/AB/R, 16 May 2012 (*Tuna/Dolphin II*).
3 Regulation (EC) No 1726/2003 of the European Parliament and of the Council of 22 July 2003 amending Regulation (EC) No 417/2002 on the accelerated phasing-in of double-hull or equivalent design requirements for single-hull oil tankers, OJ 2003 L 249/1.
4 In Case C 366/10 *Air Transport Association of America v. Secretary of State for Energy and Climate Change*, Judgment of 21 December 2011 (not yet reported). For analysis and criticism see Andrea Gattini, 'Between Splendid Isolation and Tentative Imperialism: The EU's Extension of its Emission Trading Scheme to International Aviation and the ECJ's Judgment in the ATA Case', 61 *International & Comparative Law Quarterly* (2012) 977–91, at 982.
5 There is also the rarer possibility that the unilateral measure burdens only one's own nationals and state agencies. See, for example, *Environmental Defense Fund v. Massey*, 986 F 2d 528 (United States Court of Appeals for the District of Columbia Circuit, 1993) (environmental impact assessment required under US Law applied to a scientific station of a US Federal Agency in Antarctica, which the court regards as a 'global common'), but this type of legislation does not raise the problems discussed here.

extension of the continental shelf or exclusive economic zone that may not only be motivated by global welfare concerns but also carry benefits to the regulating state, the above examples do not offer exclusive benefits for the regulating state. Instead, they level the playing field by demanding competitors to abide by the same or equivalent constraints.[6]

Obviously, states that regulate public goods unilaterally do so not out of purely altruistic motives. They have strong self-interest in preventing human trafficking into their borders or in reducing global warming, and they are willing to bear the associated economic and other burdens. But at the same time they wish to ensure two related goals: to ensure that the measures imposed are effective, and to limit the associated economic burdens. To achieve both ends, they aim to regulate also the activities of foreign actors *worldwide*: the more stakeholders follow suit the more successful will the regulation be; similarly, if foreign competitors also comply with the regulation, the economic burden will be shared rather than shouldered only by the regulating state.

Accordingly, only economies that can sustain such heavy burdens and are confident that they can elicit compliance from at least some foreigners venture to unilaterally 'legislate for humanity' and enforce such laws on foreigners. Due to the limited number of such states and their relative strength, the unilateral measures that they adopt immediately raise concerns about 'imperialism' and 'hegemony', and are critiqued for flouting customary international law.[7] Beyond these rather simplistic worries, this type of unilateral legislation and enforcement raises various legitimacy questions. One set of questions relates to the appropriate scope of state sovereignty: Does international law on state sovereignty entail limits on the territorial scope of regulation that unilateral 'legislation for humanity' oversteps? Does such regulation impinge the sovereignty of other states? Another set of questions relates to the right to democratic participation or the lack of it in such instances: Does unilateral regulation infringe the rights of foreign stakeholders to take part in decision-making affecting their opportunities and interests? Can this democratic deficit be remedied by procedural or normative obligations that the legislating state must follow to ensure that the concerns and constraints of all affected stakeholders are taken into account?

This contribution seeks to outline answers to these questions by offering a theoretical framework that grounds the authority of states to legislate for humanity, and outlines the limits of such legislation, in political and moral

---

6   For a typology of unilateral measures in the environmental sphere see Richard Bilder, 'The Role of Unilateral State Action in Preventing International Environmental Injury', 14 *Vanderbilt Journal of Transnational Law* (1981) 51–95. On this general problem see also Daniel Bodansky, 'What's So Bad about Unilateral Action to Protect the Environment?', 11 *European Journal of International Law* (2000) 339–48, and Laurence Boisson de Chazournes, 'Unilateralism and Environmental Protection: Issues of Perception and Reality of Issues', 11 *European Journal of International Law* (2000) 315–38.

7   See references to such terms in sources cited in *supra* notes 4 and 5.

theory. The contribution is informed by the understanding that such a theoretical framework can clarify a fundamental distinction that inheres in contemporary international law on state sovereignty between two competing visions of sovereignty: between a solipsistic, *Lotus*-based, vision, and an alternative that sees sovereignty as embedded in global legal order from which states derive their authority. The first, widely shared concept of sovereignty regards the state as the source of legislative power for those under its jurisdiction and only for them. Under that view, global collective action problems should be resolved only through collective bargaining leading to international agreements. Such a concept of sovereignty is at odds with unilateral state action that affects rights and obligations of individuals outside its borders. The alternative vision that this contribution outlines challenges this approach. According to the alternative view, because sovereign states are, and should be, regarded as embedded in a global order of which they are parts and to which they owe certain obligations as 'trustees of humanity'. As such they are entitled to – indeed, in some instances they must – act unilaterally for the common good, as long as they meet rigorous conditions that ensure that the interest and opportunities of all affected stakeholders are seriously taken into account.

2 Why legislation for humanity is legitimate: The concept of sovereigns as trustees of humanity

This Part argues that states are authorized to take global interests and the interests of foreigners seriously into account when making policy choices, and may legislate unilaterally to promote such interests – indeed, they may even be bound to do so.[8] The argument rejects the solipsist vision of sovereignty as having exclusive law-making authority within its boundaries as incompatible with the very ideas that initially granted absolute authority to sovereigns. The idea of sovereignty as exclusive authority was congruent with democratic notions as long as there was a perfect or almost perfect fit between the sovereign and the citizens – those affected by the sovereign's policies.[9] Such a vision made eminent sense when sovereigns ruled discrete economies, separated from each other by rivers, deserts and other natural barriers, making cross-border externalities, such as pollution, a relatively rare event, to be resolved on the inter-sovereign level, negotiated by emissaries, ambassadors and, later, within international organisations. The solipsistic vision of sovereignty was enhanced by the notion of national self-determination that erected barriers to the demands of non-citizens to weigh

---

8   This part is based on Eyal Benvenisti, 'Sovereigns as Trustees of Humanity: On the Accountability of States to Foreign Stakeholders', 107 *American Journal of International Law* (2013) 295–333.

9   For such a functional justification of sovereignty, see Henry Sidgwick, *The Elements of Politics* (4th edn, Macmillan and Co., 1919) at 252 ('the main justification for the appropriation of territory to governments is that the prevention of mutual mischief among the human beings using it cannot otherwise be adequately secured').

in on domestic policymaking processes and shielded the domestic body politic from the obligation to internalize the rights and interests of non-citizens in their policymaking. Sovereignty has become an ostensibly neutral format that explained the exclusion of 'the other'.

But today's reality is significantly different. Sovereigns are hardly the owners of isolated mansions. They are more analogous to owners of small apartments in one densely packed high-rise in which about two hundred families live. In our global condominium, the 'technology' of global governance that operates through discrete sovereign entities no longer fits. What had previously been the solution to global collective action problems has now become part of the problem of global governance. Sovereigns routinely regulate resources that are linked in many ways with resources that belong to others. By their daily decisions on economic development, on conservation, or on health regulation, some states regularly shape the life opportunities of foreigners in faraway countries who are unable to participate meaningfully in shaping these measures either directly or by relying on their own governments to effectively protect them. The glaring misfit between the scope of the sovereign's authority and the sphere of the affected stakeholders leads to negative externalities as well as the loss of potential positive externalities imposed on the un- or under-represented stakeholders, namely outcomes that are often inefficient, undemocratic and unjust.

Instead, sovereignty should be regarded as embedded in a more encompassing global order, which is a source not only of powers and rights, but also of obligations that essentially require sovereigns to exercise their authority in ways that promote global goods while taking the interests of all affected individuals into account. Here I outline three distinct normative grounds for the authority cum obligation of sovereigns to weigh such other-regarding considerations: the first emphasizes sovereignty as the vehicle for the exercise of self-determination, the second focuses on the justification of government authority as an agent of human society and the third discusses the justification of exclusive ownership over portions of the earth.

2.1 The argument from self-determination

Externally, sovereignty epitomizes the freedom of the group to pursue its interests, to further its political status and to 'freely dispose of [its] natural wealth and resources'.[10] In fact, since its modern genesis, the claim to

---

10 International Covenant on Civil and Political Rights, GA Res. 2200A (XXI), 16 December 1966, in force 23 March 1976, 999 UNTS 171, Article 1. See also *ibid.*, Article 47: 'Nothing in the present Covenant shall be interpreted as impairing the inherent right of all peoples to enjoy and utilise fully and freely their natural wealth and resources.' See also Nico Schrijver, *Sovereignty over Natural Resources: Balancing Rights and Duties* (Cambridge University Press, 1997) (emphasising not only the rights of the sovereign people but also its duties as recognised by international law).

sovereignty has been inherently tied to the notion of freedom: from the Church, from empires, from colonial powers.[11] There was always a strong link between the collective and the personal claims. Mill noted that justice requires that all citizens have 'a voice in the exercise of that ultimate sovereignty [and] an actual part in the government'.[12] Otherwise '[e]veryone is degraded, whether aware of it or not, when other people, without consulting him, take upon themselves unlimited power to regulate his destiny'.[13] As Martti Koskenniemi put it, '[s]overeignty articulates the hope of experiencing the thrill of having one's life in one's own hands'.[14] Group self-determination stems from the right to *individual* self-determination, or what Joseph Raz calls individual 'self-authorship'.[15]

It is this internal aspect of sovereignty that is currently being challenged under contemporary global conditions. As the examples mentioned above indicate, domestic democratic processes are vulnerable to systemic failures that hamper individuals' ability to have a voice and take an actual part in government: if states legislate for humanity, the preferences of the foreign stakeholders might not count; on the other hand, if states are barred from unilaterally addressing global bads, the hold-out states that prevent a collective agreement obstruct the efforts of citizens who wish to promote human rights, reduce global warming or protect endangered species.

These examples and many others suggest that in today's world, the insular exercise of self-determination by national communities can prove to be oppressive to many – either in or outside the regulating state – and can undermine peoples' ability to have their lives in their own hands. True respect for the self-determination of the individual, and of that of many collectivities, and a real effort to ensure that individuals have their lives in their own hands must be translated into a concept of sovereignty that can minimize the systemic democratic failures that inhere in the sovereign-based system and that provides opportunities for individuals and communities to

---

11   However, as new states quickly realised already in the 19th century, sovereignty conferred much less autonomy and equality than they had anticipated: Arnulf Becker Lorca, 'Sovereignty beyond the West: The End of Classical International Law', 13 *Journal of the History of International Law* (2011) 7–73.

12   John Stuart Mill, *Considerations on Representative Government* (Barker, Son, and Bourn, 1861) at 57.

13   *Ibid.*, Chapter 8. See also John Stuart Mill, 'On Liberty', in J. S. Mill, *On Liberty and Other Writings 59* (Stefan Collini ed., Cambridge University Press, 1989 [1859]) at 59 ('He who lets the world, or his own portion of it, choose his plan of life for him, has no need of any other faculty than the ape-like one of imitation. He who chooses his plan for himself, employs all his faculties.')

14   Martti Koskenniemi, 'What Use for Sovereignty Today?', 1 *Asian Journal of International Law* (2011) 61–70, at 70.

15   Joseph Raz, *The Morality of Freedom* (Clarendon, 1986) at 204 ('An autonomous person is part author of his own life. ... A person is autonomous only if he had a variety of acceptable options to choose from, and his life became as it is through his choice of some of these options.')

exert effective influence on policymaking that affects them, even if the decision-maker is a foreign government.

2.2 The argument from equal moral worth

The Universal Declaration of Human Rights envisions all of human society – 'everyone' – as rights holders, entitled to 'universal respect'.[16] The Declaration does not allocate responsibilities among the different state parties who are the duty bearers, i.e., those who share collectively the duty to regard these obligations as 'a common standard of achievement'.[17] This implies that the entire system of state sovereignty is subject to the duty to respect human rights.[18] In subsequent human rights treaties, the states in turn allocated these shared responsibilities among themselves, assigning to each the prime (if not the sole) responsibility over the area under its jurisdiction. This, however, is a secondary allocation – an allocation that *itself* must be accounted for and justified and, if found wanting, corrected, because all the trustees are collectively required to protect everyone's human rights.[19] This inclusive vision can be best interpreted as a collective assignment of authority to sovereigns, on behalf of all human beings. To

---

16   Universal Declaration of Human Rights, GA Res. 217A (III), 10 December 1948, Preamble.
17   *Ibid.*
18   Joseph Raz, 'Human Rights in the Emerging World Order', 1 *Transnational Legal Theory* (2010) 31–47, at 42 ('human rights, as they function in the world order, set limits to sovereignty'); Institute of International Law, 'Protection of Human Rights and the Principle of Non-intervention in Internal Affairs of States', Resolution adopted at the Session of Santiago de Compostela, 13 September 1989, Article 1:

> Human rights are a direct expression of the dignity of the human person. The obligation of States to ensure their observance derives from the recognition of this dignity as proclaimed in the Charter of the United Nations and in the Universal Declaration of Human Rights. This international obligation, as expressed by the International Court of Justice, is *erga omnes*; it is incumbent upon every State in relation to the international community as a whole, and every State has a legal interest in the protection of human rights. The obligation further implies a duty of solidarity among all States to ensure as rapidly as possible the effective protection of human rights throughout the world.

Prosecutor v. Tadić, Case No. IT-94-1-I, ICTY Appeals Chamber, Decision on Defence Motion for Interlocutory Appeal on Jurisdiction, 2 October 1995, para. 97:

> [T]he impetuous development and propagation in the international community of human rights doctrines, particularly after the adoption of the Universal Declaration of Human Rights in 1948, has brought about significant changes in international law ... A State-sovereignty-oriented approach has been gradually supplanted by a human-being-oriented approach. Gradually the maxim of Roman law *hominum causa omne jus constitutum est* (all law is created for the benefit of human beings) has gained a firm foothold in the international community as well.

19   Charles Beitz, *The Idea of Human Rights* (Oxford University Press, 2009) at 137 (human rights are defined as interests sufficiently important to be protected by the state, and when states fail the failure is a suitable object of international concern).

paraphrase Madison, then, 'state governments are in fact but different agents and trustees of all human beings because the ultimate, residual, authority resides in humanity'.[20] It is humanity at large that assigns certain groups of citizens with the power to form national governments.

This vision is reflected also in the writings of Vattel, who maintained that sovereigns have an obligation to accommodate the absolutely necessary interests of every man, and should therefore consider such interests in good faith. Therefore, 'no nation can, without good reasons, refuse even a perpetual residence to a man driven from his country'.[21] A long tradition of scholarship has viewed 'the State as a unit at the service of the human beings for whom it is responsible',[22] or a social function of the global community of peoples,[23] and thus 'merely a part, a branch of humanity [which as such] must recognize in the legal community of states as the political unity of humanity a higher power than itself'.[24]

Accordingly, it may be possible to re-conceptualize Max Huber's famous vision of a global legal order that 'divides between nations the space upon which human activities are employed',[25] and allocates to each the responsibility towards other nations for activities transpiring in its jurisdiction that violate international law, as a relationship of trusteeship governed by international law. To paraphrase Huber's viewpoint: given the precedence of human rights, sovereigns can and should be viewed as organs of a global system that allocates competences and responsibilities for promoting the rights of all human beings and their interest in sustainable utilisation of global resources.

---

[20] As Madison noted in The Federalist Papers, '[t]he federal and State governments are in fact but different agents and trustees of the people [because] the ultimate authority ... resides in the people alone.' James Madison, 'The Influence of the State and Federal Governments Compared', Federalist No. 46 (29 January 1788).

[21] Emerich de Vattel, *The Law of Nations* (Joseph Chitty, trans., T. & J. W. Johnson & Co. 1883 [1758]) at paras 229, 231 ('[N]ature, or rather ... its Author, ... has destined the earth for the habitation of mankind; and the introduction of property cannot have impaired the right which every man has to the use of such things as are absolutely necessary – a right which he brings with him into the world at the moment of his birth.')

[22] Christian Tomuschat, 'International Law: Ensuring the Survival of Mankind on the Eve of a New Century – General Course on Public International Law', 281 *Recueil des Cours* (1999) 9–438, at 95. See also Christian Tomuschat, 'Obligations Arising for States Without or Against their Will', 241 *Recueil des Cours* (1993) 195–374; Bruno Simma, 'From Bilateralism to Community Interest in International Law', 250 *Recueil des Cours* (1994) 217–384.

[23] René-Jean Dupuy, *La Communaute internationale entre le mythe et l'histoire* (Economica/UNESCO, 1986) at 169–70.

[24] Carl Kaltenborn von Stachau, *Kritik des Völkerrechts* (G. Mayer, 1847) at 260–1, cited in Jochen von Bernstorff, *The Public International Law Theory of Hans Kelsen* (Cambridge University Press, 2010) at 19. This is the monist view, carefully explored by Kelsen: see Hans Kelsen, *Pure Theory of Law* (Max Knight trans., University of California Press, 1967) at 214–15, 333–47. See also Hans Kelsen, *General Theory of Law and State* (Anders Wedberg trans., Harvard University Press, 1949) at 383–8; Id., *Principles of International Law* (Rinehart & Co., 1952) at 440–7. On this matter see also von Bernstorff, *ibid.*

[25] *Island of Palmas (Netherlands v. US)* (1928) 2 UNRIAA 829, at 839.

As trustees of this global system – to paraphrase another statement of Huber's[26] – the competency of contemporary sovereigns to manage public affairs within their respective jurisdictions brings with it a corollary duty to take account of external interests and even to balance internal against external interests.

This vision of trusteeship does not downgrade state governments; to the contrary: it assigns them immensely important tasks. Among these is the task to legislate for humanity while taking the interests of foreigners into account, and the corresponding obligation of others to respect such legislation.

2.3 The argument from the exclusive power over portions of the Earth

Those states that legislate for humanity use their economic power or their unique geographic position as leverage for others to comply. Only countries that have a large consumer society like the US can unilaterally demand foreigners to comply with their consumer safety standards. Only centrally placed entities such as the EU can impose demands on foreign air carriers that need to land for refuelling en route. The decision to leverage that unique capability requires normative justification. For no state may regard its exclusive control over a portion of global resources as given.

A long tradition in international law that dates to Grotius, Wolff and Vattel suggests that sovereignty in the sense of exclusive ownership of parts of global resources originates from a collective regulatory decision at the global level, rather than being an entitlement that inheres in sovereigns.[27] Sovereign states therefore have an obligation to humankind to use the resources under their control with an eye toward global concerns.[28]

---

26 Huber's statement in the award re *British Claims in the Spanish Zone of Morocco (Great Britain v. Spain)* (1925) 2 UNRIAA 615, at 641: 'Responsibility is the necessary corollary of rights. All international rights entail international responsibility'. See Daniel-Erasmus Khan, 'Max Huber as Arbitrator: The *Palmas (Miangas)* Case and Other Arbitrations', 18 *European Journal of International Law* (2007) 145–70, at 156.

27 Martti Koskenniemi, 'Empire and International Law: The Real Spanish Contribution', 61 *University of Toronto Law Journal* (2011) 1–36, at 14–16 (emphasising Vitoria's conceptualisation of the prince's dominium over his commonwealth as deriving from the collective decision to delegate such authority to him).

28 Vattel, *The Law of Nations, supra* note 21, at para. 81:

> The cultivation of the soil deserves the attention of the government, not only on account of the invaluable advantages that flow from it, but from its being an obligation imposed by nature on mankind. The whole earth is destined to feed its inhabitants; but this it would be incapable of doing if it were uncultivated. Every nation is then obliged by the law of nature to cultivate the land that has fallen to its share.

See also Immanuel Kant, *Perpetual Peace: A Philosophical Essay* (M. Campbell Smith trans., Allen & Unwin, 1917 [1795]) (referring to the 'common right to the face of the earth, which belongs to human beings generally'); Georg Cavallar, *The Rights of Strangers the Global Community and Political Justice since Vitoria* (Ashgate, 2002).

Although the *Lotus*-based vision of sovereignty is more explicit in contemporary international law, the law is open to the trusteeship concept. Even the most formidable ground for justifying the 'sovereignty as independence' model, the right of peoples to self-determination that is an 'inherent' right, to be 'freely' exercised,[29] does not withstand the trusteeship concept. The right to self-determination does not free sovereign peoples from the obligation to conform to the duties international law imposes on all states. The principles of national self-determination and of national ownership of natural resources never meant supreme and unfettered authority to each people. While peoples cannot be subjected *to other peoples*, they remain subject to the constraints that apply to all.[30] The concept of trustee sovereignty respects and, in fact, enhances all individuals' and peoples' right to self-determination and the resulting right to maintain their culture and promote primarily the interests of their individual members.

Moreover, as I argue elsewhere,[31] the trusteeship concept of sovereignty runs through several doctrines of international law, as well as judicial and other decisions. Even if such doctrines and judgements do not explicitly embrace the trusteeship concept, this concept offers the best explanation for them. For example, the International Court of Justice (ICJ) was quick to find customary law obligations to allow maritime passage through straits subject to the sovereignty of the coastal state[32] and recognized the right of transit over foreign territory, subject to the territorial sovereign's limited authority to regulate such passage,[33] thereby adding at least some strength to the general claim of land-locked states to a right of transit through neighbouring states.[34] Similarly, an arbitral award sought to ensure that The Netherlands, which had granted Belgium the right of passage through its territory, confined its regulatory functions to measures required by environmental concerns.[35] In another dispute, the ICJ forced an interpretation of an 1858 treaty that had assigned to Costa Rica sovereignty over a river as ensuring that Nicaraguans inhabiting the Costa Rican bank of the river 'the right to use the river to the extent necessary to meet their essential

---

29 The tension between this freedom and the obligations towards others is already present in ICCPR, *supra* note 10, Article 1, as the freedom is 'without prejudice to any obligations arising out of international economic co-operation, based upon the principle of mutual benefit, and international law'.
30 See Alfred Verdross, 'Le fondement du droit international', 16 *Recueil des cours* (1927) 247–323, at 314 ('sa souveraineté ne désigne que le fait [que l'État souverain] est subordonné àucune *autre* puissance qu'au droit de gens' [emphasis in the original]).
31 Eyal Benvenisti, 'Sovereigns as Trustees of Humanity', *supra* note 8.
32 *Corfu Channel (UK/Albania)*, ICJ Reports (1949) 4, at 22.
33 *Right of Passage over Indian Territory (Portugal v. India)*, ICJ Reports (1960) 6, at 45.
34 Elihu Lauterpacht, 'Freedom of Transit in International Law', 44 *Transactions of the Grotius Society* (1958) 313–56.
35 *Iron Rhine ('Ijzeren Rijn') Railway (Belgium v. The Netherlands)* (2005) 27 UNRIAA 35.

requirements.'[36] This attitude fits well with the ICJ's general tendency to align international law with policies that promote global welfare.[37]

3 Implications of the trusteeship concept on law-making for humanity

That sovereignty is but a tool for promoting individual and collective welfare and self-authorship has mainly two implications for unilateral efforts to address global bads. The first implication concerns the authority of states to unilaterally legislate for humanity. The second implication is the concomitant obligation to take foreign interests into account.

3.1 The authority to legislate for humanity

The trusteeship concept offers a clear endorsement to democracies that wish to unilaterally promote global welfare. All three normative grounds for the trusteeship concept support this conclusion. As trustees of humanity, national decision-makers must regard themselves as partaking in a collective effort to promote global welfare. By exercising their individual sovereignty, they promote global welfare for all to benefit from, and they ensure that the global resources under their control are utilised in ways that promote global welfare. In fact, the sovereign-as-trustee concept even obliges states to pursue such policies. The fact that some states fail to cooperate should not hinder those who wish to act in pursuit of improving global standards, provided that they take into account the interests of others when devising policies (or reviewing them, in the case of national courts). For the same reason, those foreigners – including foreign states – affected by such unilateral policies must consider complying with them due to their own duty to take others' interests into account and to promote global welfare.

3.2 Constraints on unilateral law-making

The second implication the trusteeship concept works in the opposite direction: states that legislate for humanity must take the interests of others and humanity at large seriously into account. This has an institutional aspect: the legislative process must provide opportunity for foreign stakeholders to intervene in the process and shape its outcomes. And there is also a substantive aspect: the adopted policy must accommodate the legitimate interests of others, especially the interests of developing countries whose

---

36 *Dispute Regarding Navigational and Related Rights (Costa Rica v. Nicaragua)*, ICJ Reports (2009) 213.
37 Eyal Benvenisti, 'Customary International Law as a Judicial Tool for Promoting Efficiency', in Eyal Benvenisti and Moshe Hirsch (eds), *The Impact of International Law on International Cooperation* (Cambridge University Press, 2004) 85–116.

economies and capacities could incur excessive costs when modifying their priorities.

In general, the obligation to weigh the interests of foreign stakeholders does not *necessarily* imply an obligation to succumb to those interests, and does not even require full legal responsibility for ultimately preferring domestic interests in balancing the opposing claims. What it does imply as a minimum, however, is that sovereigns must give due respect to foreign stakeholders both procedurally and substantively. This is *a fortiori* the case when states justify their unilateral law-making as aimed at producing global public goods.

Among the considerations that unilateral lawmakers must weigh is the proper deference they should give to collective efforts to achieve similar goals through collective action. Unilateralists should not pre-empt or otherwise unfairly determine such collective outcomes. Collective efforts tend to be regarded as more legitimate in the eyes of relevant stakeholders and hence are likely to be more effective. They may also reflect the greater wisdom of the larger group that participates in the decision-making and also be more equitable to the different affected groups. Therefore, unilateral legislation must not be pursued unless good faith efforts to conclude an agreement between the representatives of the relevant states have failed. For the same reasons, unilateral law-making must remain open to the resumption of such discussions.

3.3 Recent practice

Although not articulated in this way, the World Trade Organization (WTO) Appellate Body may have been motivated by this approach. It has ruled twice on what I term 'legislation for humanity'. In the famous *Shrimp/Turtle* case,[38] the Appellate Body recognized the importing state's right to regulate foreign conduct that is likely to harm endangered species. But it rejected the regulations that were actually chosen both for procedural and substantive reasons: the legislating state must provide effective opportunities to foreign individuals who may be adversely affected by such policies to voice their concerns, and the rules must be flexible enough to accommodate the interests of those foreign stakeholders. The latter consideration was also emphasized by the Appellate Body in the *Tuna/Dolphin II* case.[39]

The judgement of the European Court of Justice in its 2012 *Air Transport Association* case may reflect a similar legitimate motivation, although this could be read only between the lines and with great effort. The explicit reasoning of the judgement is not convincing. The court refers to a rather

---

38 *Shrimp/Turtle, supra* note 2.
39 *Tuna/Dolphin II, supra* note 2 (finding that the US measure 'modifies the competitive conditions in the US market to the detriment of Mexican tuna products.')

simplistic notion of state sovereignty, emphasizing that 'European Union legislation may be applied to an aircraft operator when its aircraft is in the territory of one of the Member States and, more specifically, on an aerodrome situated in such territory, since, in such a case, that aircraft is subject to the unlimited jurisdiction of that Member State and the European Union.'[40] This unqualified statement, which does not recognize any limits to the prescriptive jurisdiction of the European states, is incompatible with basic principles of international law on state jurisdiction.[41]

However, and this is crucial from the perspective of 'legislating for humanity', the court did go to a great length to emphasize that the European directives imposing the emission trading obligations on foreign air carriers remained open to multilateral agreements and to adaptation to third countries' 'equivalent measures' so as 'to provide for optimal interaction between the Community scheme and that country's measures, after consulting with that country'.[42] With these references the court acknowledges the burdens imposed on third parties and indirectly outlines the parameters of unilateral acts that legitimately seek to promote global welfare.

---

40 *Air Transport Association of America*, *supra* note 4, para. 124; see also para. 125.
41 Gattini refers to this part of the judgement as 'ubuesque'. See Gattini, 'Between Splendid Isolation and Tentative Imperialism', *supra* note 4, at 980. Advocate General Kokott implies that the jurisdiction could be based on the 'effects doctrine': 'It is well known that air pollution knows no boundaries and that greenhouse gases contribute towards climate change worldwide irrespective of where they are emitted; they can have effects on the environment and climate in every State and association of States, including the European Union.' Case C-366/10 *Air Transport Association of America v. Secretary of State for Energy and Climate Change*, Opinion of Advocate General Kokott of 6 October 2011, para. 154. For a similar argument see Jonathan Remy Nash, 'The Curious Legal Landscape of the Extraterritoriality of U.S. Environmental Laws', 50 *Virginia Journal of International Law* (2010) 997–1020, at 999 ('for global air pollutants, it seems possible to claim that every nation might potentially have jurisdiction over all worldwide emissions.')
42 *Air Transport Association of America*, *supra* note 4, para. 33, citing Directive 2008/101/EC of the European Parliament and of the Council of 19 November 2008 amending Directive 2003/87/EC so as to include aviation activities in the scheme for greenhouse gas emission allowance trading within the Community, OJ 2009 L 8/3, Recitals 8 to 11, 14, 17 and 21 in the Preamble, which provide *inter alia* that

> [t]he Community and its Member States should continue to seek an agreement on global measures to reduce greenhouse gas emissions from aviation. The Community scheme may serve as a model for the use of emissions trading worldwide. The Community and its Member States should continue to be in contact with third parties during the implementation of this Directive and to encourage third countries to take equivalent measures. If a third country adopts measures, which have an environmental effect at least equivalent to that of this Directive, to reduce the climate impact of flights to the Community, the Commission should consider the options available in order to provide for optimal interaction between the Community scheme and that country's measures, after consulting with that country.

See also *Air Transport Association of America*, *supra* note 4, para. 38.

3.4 Reviewing sovereigns' discretion

The above discussion suggests that there is a fundamental difference between a situation where a state sets policies with respect to its own internal affairs – for example whether or not to allow the consumption within its territory of genetically modified food or how to distribute beef to domestic consumers – to a situation where the policy at stake is aimed at protecting global interests.[43] The fundamental difference between these types of regulation is the weight that should be assigned to the regulating state's discretion. While at least some deference to the discretion of the regulating state is due when that state focuses on its internal affairs and realizes the preferences of its citizens,[44] such deference is not called for when a state

---

43   On the general problem of 'standard of review' and the legitimate measure of deference to national measures in the context of trade and investment law see recently Caroline Henckels, 'Balancing Investment Protection and the Public Interest: The Role of the Standard of Review and the Importance of Deference in Investor-State Arbitration', 4 *Journal of International Dispute Settlement* (2013) 197–215; Stephan W. Schill, 'Deference in Investment Treaty Arbitration: Reconceptualizing the Standard of Review through Comparative Public Law', Society of International Economic Law (SIEL), 3rd Biennial Global Conference (2012) <ssrn.com/abstract=2095334>; Andreas von Staden, 'The Democratic Legitimacy of Judicial Review Beyond the State: Normative Subsidiarity and Judicial Standards of Review', 10 *International Journal of Constitutional Law* (2012) 1023–1049; Barnali Choudhury, 'Exception Provisions as a Gateway to Incorporating Human Rights Issues into International Investment Agreements', 49 *Columbia Journal of Transnational Law* (2011) 670–716. See also Alan O. Sykes, 'Domestic Regulation, Sovereignty, and Scientific Evidence Requirements: A Pessimistic View', 3 *Chicago Journal of International Law* (2002) 353–368, at 368. See also John H. Jackson, *World Trade and the Law of GATT* (Bobbs-Merrill, 1969) at 788; Robert Howse, 'Adjudicative Legitimacy and Treaty Interpretation in International Trade Law', in Joseph H. H. Weiler (ed.), *The EU, The WTO and The NAFTA: Towards a Common Law of International Trade?* (Oxford University Press, 2000) 35–70; Steven P. Croley and John H. Jackson, 'WTO Dispute Procedures, Standard of Review and Deference to National Governments', 90 *American Journal of International Law* (1996) 193–213.

44   This adds to the complexity of the factors that determine the appropriate standard of review. In the context of trade law, for example, the Appellate Body has over the years made it clear that it would be more deferential to trade restrictions prompted by human health considerations as opposed to other motives: Petros C. Mavroidis, *Trade in Goods: An Analysis of International Trade Agreements* (2nd edn, Oxford University Press, 2012) 331–335. See also Michael Ming Du, 'Autonomy in Setting Appropriate Level of Protection under the WTO Law: Rhetoric or Reality?', 13 *Journal of International Economic Law* (2010) 1077–1102, at 1100 ('the regulatory value protected by the disputed measure weighs heavily in the AB's judgment. If the value at stake is high, e.g. human health and safety or protection of the environment, the AB tends to respect the Member's judgment and to consider necessary very strict enforcement aimed at zero risk, even if that means a very heavy burden on imports.'); Robert Howse and Elisabeth Türk, 'The WTO Impact on Internal Regulations: A Case Study of the Canada–EC Asbestos Dispute', in Gráinne de Búrca and Joanne Scott (eds), *The EU and the WTO: Legal and Constitutional Issues* (Hart, 2001) 283–328, at 315 ('How far a member should be expected to go in exhausting all the regulatory alternatives to find the least trade-restrictive alternative is logically related to the kind of risk it is dealing with. Where what is at stake is a well-established risk to human life itself ... a member may be expected to act rapidly ...').

legislates for humanity. In this latter type of cases, the regulating state has no priority in setting global standards and hence is not entitled to a margin appreciation or any other deferential space. On the contrary, the state has obligations to third states and foreign citizens who are burdened by those standards. Therefore, when courts review unilateral acts of legislation for humanity for compatibility with the state's international obligations, they should critically examine whether such legislation is indeed 'necessary' to achieve a 'legitimate' *collective* goal.

4 Conclusion

In its recent *Air Transport Association* judgement,[45] the European Court of Justice failed to articulate a convincing legal basis for imposing the EU carbon emissions scheme on foreign air carriers flying outside the EU area.[46] As Andrea Gattini points out, the only possible basis for requiring all air carriers to comply with the EU scheme was for the EU to

> posit [itself] on a universal plane, in a supposed *civitas mundi*, but then the question inevitably pops up of why should the EU assume the role of legislator, fee collector, and lastly exclusive beneficiary of the revenues, for the sake of the entire world. ... [W]ithout that strong political underpinning, the legal arguments of the Court look scant and shaky.[47]

This contribution attempted to provide such a political underpinning. According to this theory, the unilateral law-making for humanity should not be deprecated as imperialist and hegemonic. Rather, international law should be positively open to initiatives of relatively strong actors to promote global public goods unilaterally, if they have the capacity, willingness and skills to do so, and if the procedures they follow while designing and enforcing the policies they adopt take all affected interests into account.[48] A new vision of sovereignty as trusteeship of humanity may encourage more such unilateral law-making, approved and implemented in an accountable manner that takes all affected interests into account.

---

45 *Supra* note 4.
46 Gattini, 'Between Splendid Isolation and Tentative Imperialism', *supra* note 4, at 980–3.
47 *Ibid.*
48 Compare Eyal Benvenisti, 'The US and the Use of Force: Double-Edged Hegemony and the Management of Global Emergencies', 15 *European Journal of International Law* (2004) 677–700 (discussing the extent the role of the US in providing global public goods by engaging with global terrorism and the legal implications that this role may entail).

2 Declaratory legislation
Towards a genealogy of neoliberal legalism

*Martti Koskenniemi**

In a famous speech at the House of Commons in 1947, Winston Churchill is reputed to have said, 'Democracy is the worst form of government, except for all those other forms that have been tried from time to time.' In this way, he found a memorable formulation for the widespread view of liberal legislation as a theory about the melancholy second best. Societies ought to be governed by laws that reflect the 'will of the people'. But human will is weak and manipulable. It is lead by passions that are altogether fickle and 'subjective'. As amateur psychologists, liberal philosophers and professional jurists, we have learned to juxtapose our 'will' with the firm objectivity of 'knowledge' – one matter of cunning desire; the other of reason and truth. Social life, we assume, including law is *both* about reason (knowledge) and will, about 'ratio and voluntas', knowledge and politics.[1] Churchill's formulation, however, points to awareness that the forms of knowledge so far available to assist in the government of society had either not operated well or had ended up in tragedy. Therefore, because of the absence of true social knowledge with directive power, we have had to reconcile ourselves with being ruled by 'will' (preferably by parliamentary will). 'Knowledge' and its accompanying 'reason' would still have a secondary role as its technical instruments. But they cannot sit on the driver's seat. Because we cannot be ruled by scientists we must accept being ruled by politicians. Instead of being based on scientific theorems, our laws emerge as the mundane outcomes of the legislative will.

All of this is so familiar that it is almost embarrassing to write it down. And all of this has been critiqued in legal and political theory many times over.[2] But it is useful to write it down because there have often been moments in history in which we of the secular West have also ceased to believe this, in

---

* All the translations in the text are by the author.

1 The classical articulation (and critique) of this view remains, Roberto Mangabeira Unger, *Knowledge and Politics* (Free Press, 1975). For a liberal re-statement, Kaarlo Tuori, *Ratio and Voluntas: The Tension between Reason and Will in Law* (Ashgate, 2011).

2 For a classical critique, the 'will theory', see Karl Olivecrona, *Rättsordiningen: Ideer och fakta* (Gleerups, 1966).

which we have become tired of the mistakes brought about by our reliance on *voluntas*. It has begun to appear an altogether contingent expression of uneducated desires, perhaps a surface for populist calls for instant gratification by politicians only concerned over re-election. Why should we honour such laws? A child stands in front of a shelf of sweets in a grocery shop and cries out 'I want!' As concerned parents we know that the child's merely 'wanting' it is not a sufficient reason for us to buy that bar of chocolate. We must decide on behalf of the child. And because we *know better* we pull the child from the shop by the hand no matter the ensuing noise. The same 'parental' intuition has also frequently entered the world of politics. Conservatives have used it to oppose legislative changes proposed without respect for the wisdom of the past. Radicals have used it to advance revolutionary transformation to grasp history's inner direction. Right-wing paternalisms and left-wing paternalisms have had a more or less stable presence in European polities in the twentieth and twenty-first centuries. They have rarely occupied the reins of power for long without venturing on the slippery slope towards fascism or communism. This is what Churchill, too, had in mind. For a society of imperfect humans, the principle of *voluntas* is safer than its alternative, the hubris of perfect knowledge.

But perfectionism is alive and well in the debates about international governance. Proposals for international legislation are still a more or less stable part of ideas of international government.[3] They build on the domestic analogy that views the international society as being in certain respects similar to the domestic one: ultimately, there ought to be an international parliament. This view was never unchallenged. Various 'realist' streams of thought held it ridiculously utopian, neglecting the nature of the international as a sphere on irreducible antagonism. But it was always a respected part of diplomacy, especially (and unsurprisingly) of the ethos of public international institutions. After the Cold War it may even have become the ruling ideology. International institutions were often seen as expressive of the *voluntas* of the members of an international (legal) community.

That moment is largely over. In the West we now live in a 'crisis' of governance. The EU decided to impose a government of technocrats on Greece and Italy. The point was not to give effect to some law-creating popular '*voluntas*' but to envisage technical responses to developments produced by (European, Greek) society itself. At a global scale, proposals for international legislation have been replaced by blueprints for regulation and governance by economic and technical expert groups and committees, operating at

---

[3] After the somewhat old-fashioned debates on 'international legislation' during the League of Nations and the early post-war era, the preferred English-language expression now is that of 'law-making' where treaty-law and custom still stand, however, as functional equivalents to domestic 'legislation'. Out of a huge amount of materials, see e.g. Alan Boyle and Christine Chinkin, *The Making of International Law* (Oxford University Press, 2007).

national, regional and global levels, in public and private institutions, seeking to tap on to the mechanisms of operation of a globalised world. The most important 'laws' in Europe or the world are not those enacted in parliaments but those managed by economic or technical experts so as to avoid collapse but ultimately so as to produce optimal outcomes. In this optimistic understanding, laws are not about what we 'want' but what we 'know' about the world: they declare truths that scientists, economists and technical experts have uncovered or will do so in the nearest future. Their 'validity' lies in the truth of those knowledges and they operate much the way concerned parents deal with disobedient children. 'I know better what is good for you.' There is, as I have elsewhere put it, a new naturalism on the rise.[4] Like the old one it, too, is paternalistic and it may be well to remember how that old naturalism operated and what presuppositions about human life and society accompanied it. In this essay I propose to do just that. I shall examine another moment – that of enlightenment France – where an old regime was felt to be in 'crisis' and new technologies were called upon to clear up the mess. The arbitrary will of the ruler was to be replaced by the objective vision of a (social) scientific knowledge that finally took the name of 'political economy'. Then, as now, this knowledge sought to liberate the spontaneous forces of a civil society. Then, as now, it was based on naturalist assumptions about the role of providence in human society.

I

In classic naturalism, human law was supposed to emerge from a complex set of derivations from an anterior and immutable natural law. According to Thomas Aquinas, natural law was the expression of divine law in human society. But although its first principles, given at creation, remained unchanging, its secondary principles could be modified by addition or subtraction. This could take place, for example, through *jus gentium* (law of nations) that arose either as 'conclusions' from natural law or as universally valid determinations of just ('artificial') relationship (as in just price or slavery).[5] By contrast, civil law arose from 'specific applications' of natural law for a political community.[6] In each case, 'legislation' coincided with the judgement by the ruler of what natural law demanded in view of the good of the community. The precise nature of this kind of legislative prudence – a notion Aquinas received from Aristotle – has been the object of much commentary. But there is no disagreement that it belongs to the capacity of

---

4   Martti Koskenniemi, 'Miserable Comforters: International Relations as a New Natural Law', 15 *European Journal of International Relations* (2009) 395–422.
5   Thomas Aquinas, 'Summa theologiae' Ia–IIae, Q 95 A 4 (in *Aquinas: Political Writings* [edited by Robert W. Dyson, Cambridge University Press, 2002] at 135–6) and IIa IIae Q 57 A 3 (163–4).
6   *Ibid.*, at Ia–IIae Q 95 A 4 (135).

human reasoning (and not will) the point of which was to relate a behavioural standard to the pursuit of supernatural happiness.[7]

The view of legislation as judicial determination extended from medieval kingship to the early modern legal theory propounded by Catholic intellectuals such as the members of the Salamanca school. Its 'founder', the Dominican cleric Francisco de Vitoria discussed Spanish imperial activities as well as the expansion of commerce in Europe and beyond by a law of nations derived from Aquinas' *Summa theologiae*. In his famous public lecture on the Indies of 1539, Vitoria quoted the *Institutes* of Gaius in support of the view that the law of nations 'is or derives from natural law'.[8] In his lecture course to his students, however, Vitoria put forward a somewhat more complex view. He recognised that under natural law, all things were common and humans were free and equal. But he lived in a time where kings were beginning to claim absolute rule and expanding commercial relations drew on exchanges of private property. If natural law was unchanging, then these matters could only have emerged though human legislation. In his *Commentaries* Vitoria suggested that these activities were governed by the law of nations. This lacked the intrinsic goodness of natural law; yet it was what was good in the novel world of empire and commerce.[9] Vitoria was seeking to fit a traditional legal-moral vocabulary to new political and economic events. To do so, he sought a middle-way between Thomistic theories of objective law and the nominalist doctrine of subjective rights. This led him to allow increasingly expansive scope for secular legislation. But while he stressed the importance of legislative power as part of civil sovereignty, he did *not* envision it in a voluntarist fashion: 'for human laws to be just and binding, the will of the legislator is not sufficient, since the law must also be moderate, and useful to the commonwealth'.[10] The Salamancans viewed legislation as a task of sovereign prudence, not essentially different from the act of judgement, an operation guided by virtue and the search for the common good.[11]

---

7   'For Aquinas, law is fundamentally and primarily connected with reason, *ratio*'. See Annabel Brett, *Liberty, Right and Nature: Individual Rights in Later Scholastic Thought* (Cambridge University Press, 1997) at 95 and generally 89–97. See further Joseph Canning, *A History of Medieval Political Thought 300–1450* (Routledge, 1996) at 131.
8   Francisco de Vitoria, 'On the American Indians', in *Vitoria: Political Writings*, edited by Anthony Padgen and Jeremy Lawrance (Cambridge University Press, 1991) at 278.
9   For the long discussion of the relations of natural law and the law of nations, see Francisco de Vitoria, *Comentarios a la Secunda secundae de Santo Tomás* (edited by Vicente Beltrán de Heredia, 6 vols, Salamanca, 1934–1952), vol. III, *De justitia*, Q 62 A 3 (12–17).
10 Vitoria, 'On Civil Power' in *Political Writings*, *supra* note 8, Q 3 A 1 (34).
11 For a discussion and further references, see Martti Koskenniemi, 'Empire and International Law: The Real Spanish Contribution', 61 *University of Toronto Law Journal* (2011) 12–16.

Scholasticism produced a view of legislation as an activity of monarchic prudence, operating within a theological view of human life as orientated towards supranatural beatitude. It also highlighted the authority of the Catholic church in assessing the legality of civil power and Spanish actions in the Indies.[12] This view was put to question with the rise of Protestantism. The violent schism between Christian confessions brought forward an increasingly absolutist view of monarchic powers. Looking for the right religious authority behind secular laws would only undermine the fragile social peace. As the Bordeaux lawyer Michel de Montaigne wrote in the course of the French religious wars: 'the laws maintain their credit, not because they are just but because they are laws'. To seek a deeper justification would only continue the interminable conflict. It was best to accept laws simply because they had been duly enacted. 'This is the mystical basis of their authority; they have no other'.[13] But such a tendentiously absolutist position could hardly stand without more. That 'more' was provided by that other French jurist, Jean Bodin who theorised legislative power as the 'first mark of sovereignty'. In his 1576 work *Six livres de la république*, Bodin moved the weight in sovereign power from judgement to legislation, but not so as to liberate the monarch to command whatever he might have desired. The ruler was bound by divine and natural law as well as the fundamental laws of the realm. The point of legislating – as is clear from the much too little read sixth book of the *Six livres* – was to provide for a well-governed, orderly society. What would be needed for what Bodin called a 'science of governing a state', he had suggested in an earlier study, was an in-depth view of the situation of one's country: 'In history, the best part of universal law is hidden'.[14] This would consist of organised knowledge of laws and legislation as instruments for the stability and growth of territorial regimes. This proposal was not that far from what his arch-enemies, counter-reformation intellectuals and raison d'état theorists working for the Pope had suggested. Against the '*politique*' faction, the latter were developing a 'Christian science of politics' to assist the (Catholic) Prince to governing his state in view of its history and resources so as to strengthen his relative position towards his neighbours.[15]

---

12 Vitoria, 'On Civil Power', in *Political Writings, supra* note 8, Prologue (3), and 'On the American Indians', *ibid.*, Introduction (235–8).
13 Michel de Montaigne, *Essays* (first published in 1580) (Penguin, 1993) at 353.
14 Jean Bodin, *Les six livres de la république* (abregé du texte de 1583 par Gérard Mairet, Libraire Générale française, 1993) at 99–100 and 276 *et seq.*, especially 326–32 (for the doctrine of 'harmonious government'). For the quote from that earlier work, see *Method for the Easy Comprehension of History* (translated by Beatrice Reynolds, Norton, 1945) at 8.
15 See especially Giovanni Botero, *The Reason of State* (edited and translated by P. J. and D. P. Waley, Routledge 1956) and commentary in Romain Descendre, *L'État du monde: Giovanni Botero entre raison d'État et géopolitique* (Droz, 2009).

The view of legislation as an instrument for translating the deep truths of a country's history and its human and material resources into massive governmental projects was used as the basis for his absolutist legal theory by Cardin Le Bret, Cardinal Richelieu's principal legal advisor. In his *De la souveraineté du Roi* (1632), Le Bret defined sovereignty both in terms of supreme authority *and* its directness to functional objectives. Its point was 'de procurer par toutes sortes de moyens le bien de ses subjects'.[16] It was not for public lawyers to speculate what these objectives might be, however. The king's authority in this respect was unlimited: 'sa première marque est de ne dépendre que de Dieu seul'.[17] This undermined the development or even the maintenance of a strong public law. Legislative measures in France tended to be seen as emanating from little else than royal pleasure. Therefore, as Louis XIV embarked on rationalising his administration, he invited the *avocat du roi*, Jean Domat from Clermont to Paris to reorder French private and public law by providing a much-needed theory of legislation to support them. As the only important naturalist of seventeenth century France, Domat supported absolutism but did not view the king as the embodiment of divine law. He had a sceptical view of the human capacity to goodness without strong guidance on the part of public power. His naturalism was wholly orientated towards directing self-interest to useful purposes. This meant dispensing God's justice in secular conditions – 'making God Himself rule' as Domat put this.[18]

It was an intrinsic quality of sovereignty that it was to be both absolute and extensive – not so as to give free reign to the sovereign's desires but to enable him to take the place of God in ruling for the community.[19] Writing on the 'duties of sovereigns' Domat insisted that monarchs study carefully divine law and avoid committing the sins of pride and vanity; they should make good choice of ministers and counsel and supervise their activity, keep good contacts with their neighbours and be prudent in raising new taxes. Domat regarded Roman law as 'written reason' that he weighed in view of Christian moral principles. The power to enact 'arbitrary laws' was to be exercised wholly in accordance with natural law and the king ought, whenever possible, himself to obey them.[20]

---

16 Cardin Le Bret, *De la souveraineté du Roy* in *Les Œuvres de Messire C Le Bret* (Du Bray, 1643) I.II (5).
17 *Ibid.*, I.I (1).
18 Jean Domat, *Quatre livres du droit public 1697* (Université de Caen – Bibliothèque de Philosophie politique et juridique, Texts et Documents, 1989) at I II (21). See further Marie-France Renoux-Zagamé, *Du droit de Dieu au droit de l'homme* (Presses Universitaires de France, 2003) at 129–143.
19 Domat, *Quatre livres, supra* note 18, I II (19–20, 21), I III (39–40).
20 *Ibid.*, I II II (45)

II

Domat's contribution to the theory of legislation was to view it as the unfolding of rational principles whose basis lay in Christian love and ethics.[21] Love of one's self was to be channelled with the help of laws to love of one's neighbour in ways that would ultimately benefit everyone.[22] Legislation under absolutism would become the rational pursuit of the common good. But Domat's religiously inclined naturalism did not prevent critics such as Abbé de Saint-Pierre from attacking the policies of the *ancien regime* precisely for their whimsical character – including the pursuit of *la gloire* in foreign policy. In his famous 'Plan for Perpetual Peace in Europe', written at the time of the Peace of Utrecht 1713, Saint-Pierre wanted to convince Europe's ruling houses that it was best for them to leave the search of immediate gratification by war and conquest. Promises, truces, commercial treaties, guarantees and alliances were all fragile and easily overridden. They, like the balance of power, were dependent on the whims of princes and changes of national fortune:

> Il est impossible que le Système de l'Équilibre rende la paix durable en Europe; qu'ainsi les malheurs de la Guerre se renouvelleront incessamant & dureront tant qu'il n'y aura pas entre les Souverainetez Chrétiennes une Société permanente qui leur donne sûreté suffisante de l'exécution des promesses faites dans les Traitez.[23]

Saint-Pierre thus proposed the establishment of a permanent institution, a *Union européenne* with 18 or 24 sovereign members (the number varied in different parts of the plan) all of which would be Christian, European States.[24] There were 12 'fundamental' and eight 'important' articles of the draft treaty on the Union.[25] Under it, members would agree to preserve European territorial and dynastic status quo. The Union was not to intervene in the affairs of its members for any other reason than for implementing the

---

21 William F. Church, 'The Decline of the French Jurists as Political Theorists 1660–1789', 5 *French Historical Studies* (1967) 1–16 at 16.
22 For the relative separateness with which Domat treats natural and arbitrary laws, see *ibid.*, at 18–19.
23 Charles Castel de Saint-Pierre, *Mémoire du projet pour render la paix perpetuelle* (pour le ministre M. de Torcy, 1 septembre 1712) Deuxième discours (73).
24 In making his proposal, Saint-Pierre wrote that he was following the examples of the constitution of the German–Roman Empire and the famous plan of the foreign minister of Henry IV, the Duke of Sully. Both claims were dubious. Saint-Pierre believed – wrongly – that the German estates had entered the empire as sovereigns and that Sully's specific plan had not really been to direct the plan against Austria. In fact, the German estates had never been sovereign and the hegemonic purposes of Sully's design were well known. See Patrick Riley, 'The Abbé de St. Pierre and Voltaire on Perpetual Peace in Europe', 137 *World Affairs* (1974) 186–94 at 187–9.
25 Abbé (Charles-Irénée Castel) de Saint-Pierre, *Mémoire*, Quatrième discours (271–366).

guarantees, including the suppression of any domestic dissent.[26] A permanent Senate was to be set up in which each sovereign would have one vote.[27] The Senate would organise European commerce on the basis of the most-favoured nation treatment and with the help of Chambers of Commerce. The Senate would also arbitrate between sovereigns, and a member refusing to execute a judgement would be declared the enemy of all.[28] Costs of joint operations (including against the Turks) would be borne by members in accordance with their relative wealth.

Saint-Pierre's plan was based on a Hobbesian view of human nature and European politics. It relied on utilitarian, self-interested calculations of the sovereigns themselves. We are slaves of our passions, he held, and when carried away by them, the only thing that can restrain us is the threat of an evil of greater intensity that any good that we can expect to attain.[29] As a young man, Saint-Pierre had had a great interest in the natural sciences. From them he received the idea of successful government as a kind of machine that ran with the energy of self-interest and passion. He understood political regimes and the international world as 'systems' that ought to be operated by laws that would maintain or redress the equilibrium between the parts so as to channel passionate energies for useful objectives. Legislation became a technique of good government.

Many eighteenth century jurists agreed. Europe was a 'system' and European politics was to be understood as an effort to manage it. But what kind of 'system' was it? In his work on the demise of 'universal empire' Montesquieu put forward a vivid contrast between the ancient and the modern worlds, the one extolling a spirit of conquest; the other governed by a spirit of commerce. It was pointless to admire Rome's military virtues. Its breathless search for glory and expansion had undone Rome in ancient times just as it had led Spain more recently to bankruptcy.[30] After the Romans, many European nations had sought to expand their hegemony over Europe. None had succeeded. The wider their grasp, the more vulnerable they had become.[31] This was a result of technological progress, raising standards of living, the dependency of the military on economic conditions dictated by commercial competition and the rapid expansion of scientific knowledge. As soon as a nation developed the means for conquest,

---

26 *Ibid.*, at 273. Article 2 provided that the union could take action to see to it that the monarchic or republican form is maintained but also that the internal electoral laws and capitulations are honoured (276–7) and article 3 that during periods of regency or otherwise weakness in ruling house, nothing threatens its security (279–81).
27 Article 1 in *ibid.*, at 271.
28 *Ibid.*
29 Abbé de Saint-Pierre, as cited in Merle L. Perkins, 'Civil Theology in the Writings of the Abbé de Saint-Pierre', 18 *Journal of the History of Ideas* (1957) 245.
30 Montesquieu, *Réflexions sur la Monarchie universelle en Europe* (introduction et notes par M. Porres, Droz, 2000) XVI (97).
31 *Ibid.*, X (85).

its neighbours would possess the means to counter it. Hegemony would be the source of decline of a nation and the laurels of its war remained 'sterile'. Today, he wrote, European nations had become so dependent on each other that war between them had become senseless. 'Europe is no longer but one nation that is composed of many'.[32]

Montesquieu's mature work, *L'Esprit des lois* (1748) then offered a holistic, even totalising image of the political, legal, cultural and economic conditions that characterised the three forms of modern government – republican, monarchic and despotic. Each had a single operating principle: honour, virtue or fear. He then produced a sociological and a historical view of the 'general spirit' of the laws that would serve best to govern each. Like in the earlier work, Montesquieu also observed a general development in Europe from conquest to commerce and the largest part of the book – almost one-fifth – described the history that had led to the latter, began with the maxim 'peace is the natural effect of trade'.[33] Montesquieu also associated commerce with liberty and celebrated the many virtues that accompanied the commercial spirit, namely 'frugality, economy, moderation, labor, prudence, tranquillity, order and rule'.[34] Indeed, Montesquieu understood that commerce would operate best without excessive interference from the State.[35]

Against this background, *The Spirit of the Laws* aimed to provide a modern theory of legislation. The 'spirit of the legislator', he wrote, 'ought to be that of moderation'.[36] Good laws were to correspond to the 'general spirit' of a nation. Finding out that spirit required painstaking scientific and historical studies of the 'manners of a People',[37] including close studies of what was needed by the adequate operation of the economic system. There was a natural law, of course, but its contents could not be separated from the national contexts where it operated.[38] In modern monarchies and republics, legislation was to be geared so that it allowed commerce to produce its goods within the constraints of the defining virtue of each. As is well known, Jean-Jacques Rousseau became a vocal critic of precisely this kind of commercial society. The culture of 'luxury' that he abhorred had been part of court life and inextricable from the problems of the old regime. Rousseau's critique was also an attack on the very ideas of sovereignty and legislation that had underpinned the natural law tradition.

---

32 *Ibid.*, XVIII (105).
33 Montesquieu, *The Spirit of the Laws* (translated by Thomas Nugent, Hafner, 1949) book XX.2 (vol. I, 316).
34 *Ibid.*, book V.6 (vol. I, 46). See further Eric MacGilvray, *The Invention of Market Freedom* (Cambridge University Press, 2011) at 99–100, 104–5.
35 Montesquieu, *The Spirit, supra* note 33, book XX.13 (vol. I, 323).
36 *Ibid.*, book XXIC (vol. II, 156).
37 *Ibid.*, book XIX.21 (vol. I, 304–5).
38 *Ibid.*, book I.3 (6).

Hobbes, Grotius and Pufendorf had turned things upside down by suggesting that sovereigns were needed as a rational response to the violence in the state of nature.[39] But humans were not naturally warlike; even as egoists, they did not seek to destroy each other but understood that they had reciprocal need for each other. In producing a justification for state power, the tradition actually created the situation from which it claimed to produce an exit. 'All ran towards their chains believing that they were securing their liberty'.[40] War did not end with the establishment of States, but began with it. As part of the state system the law of nations was powerless: it was followed only to the extent that seemed useful.[41]

Rousseau was not looking for increasingly more sophisticated legislative or governmental techniques. Instead, he suggested to get rid of traditional institutions and find ways of life and natural laws that governed the state of human society before corruption had set in. Natural laws should be allowed to operate spontaneously, and not to be mediated through distorted systems of state and government. Thus Rousseau's theory of legislation made the famous distinction between the 'will of all' that was the name for psychological, momentary wants of individuals – a will that was hopelessly infected by the lives individuals had been compelled to live in a corrupted society – and the 'general will' that was the enlightened, spontaneous sense of order that would realise the interests of everybody as well as those of the society at large.[42]

The expression 'general will' was then expressly taken up by Diderot in his essay on *Droit naturel* in the Encyclopaedia. If the law of nature was universal, and could be found by reasoning, what was it? A person who reasons, Diderot claimed, will find it as the same as the 'general will' of humankind: 'elle serait toujours relative à la volonté générale & au désir commun de l'espèce entière'. 'Of the whole species' – this meant that the 'general will' was not 'voluntary', but instead a scientific statement of what might be useful for the human race. In this form, it was also compatible with d'Alembert's preliminary discourse that strongly put forward the view of human history as a

---

39 In *Du contrat social* Rousseau attacked Grotius' 'characteristic method of reasoning [which] is always to offer fact as proof of right. It is possible to imagine a more logical method, but not one more favourable to tyrants'. See Jean-Jacques Rousseau, *The Social Contract* (first published 1762) (translated by Maurice Cranston with introduction, Penguin, 1958) at 51. The target here was the weight Grotius attached to customs and treaty practices as evidence of the content of the law – his famous '*a posteriori*' method.
40 Jean-Jacques Rousseau, *A Discourse on Inequality* (translated by Maurice Cranston with introduction, Penguin, 1984) part II (122).
41 Jean-Jacques Rousseau, 'Principes du droit de la guerre', in Jean-Jacques Rousseau, *Principes du droit de la guerre: Ecrits sur la paix perpetuelle* (Blaise Bachofen et Céline Spector, dir., Bruno Bernardi et Gabriella Silvestrini, éd., Vrin, 2008) at 70.
42 Rousseau, *Social Contract, supra* note 39 at 80–3. On the role of 'natural rights republicanism' in France and especially in Rousseau, see Dan Edellstein, *The Terror of Natural Law* (Chicago University Press, 2009) at 75–82.

history of utilitarian need-fulfilment. The development of arts and sciences, he had written, emerged from '[t]he necessity of protecting our own bodies from pain and destruction', especially from the effort of the body to provide for 'its endlessly multiplying needs'.[43] To come to know and organise the government of human society by natural law was to learn about natural human needs and the ways of their fulfilment. The analytical-compositive method of the encyclopaedists made them invariably return to individual human nature, to the powers of 'passion' and the urge to avoid pain and to find pleasure, from which they would proceed to a long-term, 'enlightened' sense of self-preservation that would encompass concern for humans not only at home but everywhere.[44] By translating their utilitarianism into the vocabulary of natural rights, and by adopting the view of the natural human being as a rational egoist, the encyclopaedists found the simplest way to defend their programme of reform.[45] The most radical of the group, Baron d'Holbach, for example, produced a fully naturalist structure of universal morality in which all rights and duties were determined in view of the search for happiness, understood as continuous pleasure:

> [O]ur purpose is to found a social science on our physical sensibility, on the passions that constantly animate us, the constant love that each of us has for ourselves, on our real interests.[46]

Legislation had no other task than to lead humans from the pursuit of blind passions to seeing 'the necessity to be useful for those whose assistance is needed for our own felicity'.[47] The social contract and the binding force of laws were received from calculations of long-term utility.[48] There was in d'Holbach no normative difference between natural and positive law at all; the legislator merely declared what natural law said. Only scientific and technical questions remain about how to reach general happiness, interpreted as always compatible with enlightened interests.[49] This was the basis of the law of nations, too:

---

43 Jean Le Rond d'Alembert, *Preliminary Discourse to the Encyclopedia of Diderot* (translated by Richard N. Schwab with an introduction, Chicago University Press, 1995) at 11, 14.
44 See further, Marc Bélissa, *Fraternité universelle et intérêt national (1713–1795): Les cosmopolitiques du droit des gens* (Kimé, 1998) at 23–49 and especially on Hélvetius, see Christian Laval, *L'homme économique: Essai sur les raciness du néoliberalisme* (Gallimard, 2007) at 138–47.
45 Joseph Schumpeter, *Histoire de l'analyse économique* (first pubished 1953) (3 vols, Gallimard, 1983), vol. I, *L'age des fondateurs*, at 196–7. See further Michel Foucault, *Il faut défendre la société: Cours au Collège de France (1975–1976)* (Gallimard, 1997) at 186–7.
46 Baron d'Holbach, *Système social ou principes naturels de la morale et de la politique* (3 vols, Niogret, 1822), vol. 1, at 77.
47 *Ibid.*, at 92.
48 *Ibid.*, at 308.
49 *Ibid.*, at 310–11.

> A nation is obliged, by its own interests to share the same virtues as every individual needs to show to their kind, even foreigners and those unknown.[50]

All nations had a duty of humanity towards each other, none may do to others anything that is not within the boundaries of the equitable: 'Such are the principles of the law of nations that is fundamentally nothing but the moral of the peoples.'[51] Sovereigns did not exist in a state of war with each other; all humans were joined as members of their nations in a moral community where war was only an expression of the vain search for glory. History showed that conquests were rarely useful, that large military forces were economically destructive and wars always created injustice.[52]

d'Holbach may have been extreme as materialist but the political consequences he drew from his naturalism were widely shared among the encyclopaedists. Modern legislative theory needed to adopt a scientific approach to the operation of needs and interests in society. As we have seen, Diderot regarded natural law as a scientific statement of what might be useful for the human race. Diderot rejected pure voluntarism. 'Les volontés particulières sont suspectes; elles peuvent être bonnes ou méchantes, mais la volonté générale est toujours bonne'.[53] The 'general will' was in fact a proposition about the needs of the species, of what was useful for humankind.[54] And to think about humanity as a whole was to understand its ubiquitous opposition to 'nature'. As Diderot wrote: 'C'est la nécessité de lutter contre l'ennemi commun, toujours subsistant, la nature, qui a rassamblé les hommes'.[55] It was by working in, and against, nature that humanity would find its *telos* and its happiness. It would be the function of practical sociability – of government – to produce material goods to satisfy humanity's the ever growing needs.

III

This view eventually became the heart of a new naturalism that integrated the law of nations within a series of assumptions about the operation of the

---

50 Baron d'Holbach, *La morale universelle, ou les devoirs de l'homme, fondés sur la nature* (3 vols, Masson, 1820), vol. II, at 2. This was obviously very close to Montesquieu's formulation, namely that 'different nations ought in time of peace to do one another all the good they can, and in time of war as little injury as possible, without prejudicing their interests', in Montesquieu, *The Spirit, supra* note 33, at 5.
51 d'Holbach, *Morale universelle, supra* note 50, at 4.
52 *Ibid.*, at 2–21. On this point among the philosophes generally, see Bélissa, *Fraternité, supra* note 44, at 79–84.
53 Diderot, 'Droit naturel,' in *Encyclopédie, infra* note 86, vol. 5, at 115–16.
54 Ernst Cassirer, *The Philosophy of the Enlightenment* (Princeton University Press, 1968) at 246–8.
55 Diderot, 'Observations sur le Nakaz' (para. 71) as quoted in Larrère, *L'invention de l'économie, infra* note 57, at 91.

global economic system. In early eighteenth century, 'Colbertism' (legislative centralisation of economic policy) had been undermined by the financial chaos of the last years of the Sun King's reign. New types of policy advice began to emerge from French intellectuals who were often impressed by England's commercial spirit, which they saw as an essential part of the nation's power. It had become evident that to finance their wars, monarchs could not satisfy themselves with domestic resources but needed to turn to international commerce and financing. State power was not only to be conceived in terms of control of domestic resources, but those terms had to take into account the resources that rival states, even foreign individuals, could muster from an international market. In a hugely successful work on the politics of commerce, the jurist and political commentator Jean-Francois Melon emphasised the dangers of economic dependency that would be created by the intensification of commerce – especially commerce on 'necessities' – but also the advantages that would follow for all nations from their specialisation in particular trades. Trade policy, he suggested, was an absolutely central aspect of a nation's foreign relations and '[t]he greatest of all Maxims, and the best understood is, that Commerce requireth only Liberty, and Protection'.[56] This meant liberty for selling the excess product a country had to offer and protection of essential subsistence industries, especially agriculture. As long as the nation could take care of its subsistence, it would have no reason to fear trading with others. On the contrary, as long as it was self-reliant on necessities and could export 'superfluities', it would generate a favourable trade balance that would keep it ahead of its rivals.

What Melon was developing was a novel theory of statehood that situated it in a competitive network where the power of the State would be a function of its ability to operate its economic resources. The 'domain of rationality' of this vision of State power, as Larrère put it, 'was the same as natural law'.[57] Like the latter, it was concerned to grasp the underlying relations of natural sociability in a network of interdependencies within which the State ought to be governed. In the 1750s and 1760s the debate on the relationship between national power, economic wealth and commercial activity intensified owing to the military and economic disasters accompanying the Seven Years' War (1756–1763). Where men like Melon saw economic policymaking in strictly *raison d'état* terms, others were taking inspiration from the *doux commerce* thesis and advocated a closer imitation of the English model of a commercial society. A group of writers around Vincent Gournay, France's influential intendant of commerce during 1751–1758, stressed the good faith of commercial

---

56 Jean-Francois Melon, *Political Essay upon Commerce* (translated by D. Bindon, Crampton, 1738) at 42–3.
57 Catherine Larrère, *L'invention de l'économie au XVIIIe siècle* (Presses Universitaires de France, 1992) at 97.

activities and distinguished between the corrupting effects of trade, especially trade in 'luxuries' (something that had worried many Frenchmen) and luxury trade as stimulating the increase of nation's wealth. Already the early critics of Colbertism such as Pierre le Pesant, Sieur de Boisguilbert and Richard Cantillon had advocated free trade as the best instrument of national strength. Gournay and the men around him now emphasised the 'civilising' effects of commerce in general, and the morality of good faith, loyalty and keeping to agreements that were crucial for mercantile success. They suggested that commerce was an effect of a natural *sociability* that would produce the best outcomes if allowed to develop without excessive state intervention. In particular, Gournay and his associates stressed the extent to which the interests of parties to mercantile transactions were best known to those parties themselves.[58] Supporting those interests was conducive to constancy and predictability of transactions, enabling rational planning and reliable measurement of outcomes.[59]

But others objected to the expansion of a purely commercial ethic. The fate of Holland suggested that it was no guarantee for lasting success. Therefore, a 'patriot political economy' in the 1760s turned attention to agriculture instead, seeking a more openly naturalist approach to economic governance. The most important representatives of this move, Marquis de Mirabeau and Francois Quesnay stressed the imperative need for an efficient agricultural base for a nation's economy. Once France was able to outmanoeuvre its rivals in this respect, its power in the global marketplace would be enhanced, especially in conditions of the free grain trade that they (together with English industrialists) advocated.[60]

These men – the physiocrats – were adherents of natural law, defined by Quesnay as 'the right that every human being has on things they need for happiness' (*jouissance*).[61] In the natural state this right remained only abstract and virtual, becoming concrete by the way humans took things into possession by labour. By then agreeing on a division of labour, they organised the government of their rights (of 'jouissance') and duties (of 'conservation') by positive laws. The *form* of government – monarchical, aristocratic or popular – was not important. What was important was that the liberty of

---

58 See further *ibid.*, at 135–50.
59 Albert O. Hirschmann, *The Passions and the Interests: Political Arguments for Capitalism before its Triumph* (first published 1977) (2nd anniversary edition, Princeton University Press, 1997) at 48–56.
60 See especially John Shovlin, *The Political Economy of Virtue: Luxury, Patriotism, and the Origins of the French Revolution* (Cornell University Press, 2006) at 49–79.
61 François Quesnay, 'Le droit naturel' (first published in 1765) in *Collection des principaux économistes* (15 vols, avec commentaires, notes, et notices par MM. Blanqui et Rossi (de l'Institut); Eugène Daire *et al.*, Guillaumin, 1840–48), vol. II: *Physiocrates* (first published 1846) (edited by Eugène Daire, Zeller, 1966) at 41.

citizens and the security of their property would be guaranteed for without them there could be no profitable or stable society at all ('il ne peut y avoir de gouvernement et de société profitables, ni stables').[62] The task of legislation was simply to expressly establish a society, one that was virtually in existence already, as the optimally profitable configuration of natural rights and duties.

> Positive laws are authentic rules that have been set up by sovereign authority in order to fix the administration of government to assure the defence of society to observe natural laws in a regular manner.[63]

The first and the most important positive law was the one that provided for public instruction on the content of natural law. Without instruction, citizens were unable to realise their rights and duties. Instruction and legislation had the same objective: the realisation of the intrinsic laws of society. Ignorance and evil were just two aspects of the same thing – the failure to ensure the 'most advantageous' operation of society ('l'ordre évidemment le plus avantageux possible aux hommes réunis en société'). Once reason was enlightened of the natural laws, it would immediately discard anything that was not suited for this purpose. Government was the exercise of a kind of trusteeship ('autorité tutélaire') and obedience to the laws did not signify a loss of freedom but realised it. This is why 'human beings could not reasonably decline to obey these laws'.[64]

Society, for Quesnay, was a system that operated by its own laws that government would only declare and enforce. The state was nothing but a mechanism to lift the obstacles that prevented the operation of natural sociability. The task of the new science (of 'political economy') was to show how this could be done in the most efficient fashion. Nothing puts more clearly the ethos of this new science than the brief essay by one of Quesnay's most influential protégés, Pierre Samuel Dupont de Nemours, later Inspector General of Commerce, a tireless propagator of free trade.[65] He began with the anti-Hobbesian dictum that a natural society existed between humans that was formed out of their needs and interests and was prior to any convention between them.

---

62   *Ibid.*, at 51.
63   *Ibid.*, at 53.
64   *Ibid.*, at 55 ('L'homme ne peut se refuser raisonnablement à l'obéissance qu'il doit à ces lois').
65   For a useful discussion, see Martin Giraudeau, 'Performing Physiocracy: Pierre Samuel Dupont de Nemours and the Limits of Political Engineering', 3 *Journal of Cultural Economy* (2008) 225–42.

> In this primitive state human beings have reciprocal rights and obligations of an absolute justice, owing to the fact that they are based on physical and thus absolute necessity for their existence.[66]

It was the task of good government to organise these rights and duties in a harmonious system of relationships. It was also in the nature of those needs and interests that they would increase: humans were constantly looking for more enjoyment; increased production was part of natural society.

In this natural society all humans had the liberty to pursue their welfare; they also had the right of property over things they had achieved through their labour. The rights were anterior to any laws and could not be taken away by legislation, either. In Dupont's dramatic formulation, the human sovereign was incapable of legislating anything new – 'car les lois sont toutes faites par la main de celui qui créa les droits & les devoirs'.[67] Positive laws were powerless to contradict the laws of freedom and property; all they could (and should) do was to declare their content and to enforce them.[68] There was, Dupont wrote, a 'judge' over the sovereign, this being the 'evidence' that showed what was at each moment in accordance with the natural rights and obligations.[69] With these principles, it was clear that '[p]hysiocracy was only meant to actualise a virtual world that was already there as a potentiality'.[70]

The most outspoken member of the Quesnay group was the jurist and former governor of the French Antilles, Paul-Pierre Le Mercier de la Rivière whose main work, *L'Ordre naturel et essentiel des sociétés politiques* (*Natural and Essential order of Political Societies*, 1767), was – at least if we are to believe Adam Smith – the most impressive literary achievement of the group.[71] This work translated Quesnay's economic theories into a political and legal philosophy and a proposal for the constitutional renewal of political communities. The work was in three parts. The first part contained a sketch of a utilitarian political theory that operated on the basis of absolute respect of private property. The second lay out the social and legal philosophy that accompanied Le Mercier's version of the physiocratic theory and the constitutional role of different social institutions in producing the happiness of nation. Here Le Mercier also introduced the unfortunately labelled doctrine of

---

66 Pierre Samuel Dupont de Nemours, *De l'origine et des progrès d'une science nouvelle*, (Desaint, 1768) at 17–18.
67 *Ibid.*, at 30.
68 Hence there was no reason to separate between legislation and enforcement; valid legislation was always also enforcement of the prior system of natural rights and obligations; see *ibid.*, at 31–2.
69 *Ibid.*
70 Martin Giraudeau, 'Performing Physiocracy', 3 *Journal of Cultural Economy* (2008) 225–42 at 228.
71 Paul-Pierre Le Mercier de la Rivière, *L'ordre naturel et essentiel des sociétés politques* (Nourse, 1767). The assessment by Smith is referred to in I Ph. May, *Le Mercier de la Rivière: Aux origines de la science économique* (Centre National de la Recherche Scientifique, 1975) at 66. For a brief biography, see *ibid.*, at 150–3 and *passim*.

'legal despotism' that was to translate the requirements of natural science into positive laws. And the third part contained a detailed elaboration of the operation of this institutional system through which the enlightened monarch would be able to manage State finances in an optimally beneficial way. It contained the controversial view of the monarch as a 'co-proprietor' of all property in the kingdom, as well as the proposal for a peaceful confederation of European nations that, le Mercier assumed, would be a necessary consequence of all nations being guided to organise their productive activities in accordance with the insights of economic science.

There was, Le Mercier claimed, a 'natural order' for all societies; the social world was but an aspect of the physical one.[72] By grasping this, humans could realise the twin objects of all their actions: enjoyment of pleasure and avoidance of pain.[73] The first right of all was the right of self-preservation. This right was *absolute*, as was its concomitant, the right to acquire for oneself whatever was useful. For every right, there was a duty, and society could be articulated in terms of the absolute rights and duties of individuals towards each other.[74] Societies were based on the search of happiness, and greatest happiness was abundance:

> [T]he greatest possible happiness consists for us of the greatest possible abundance of objects of our enjoyment [la plus grande abondance possible d'objets propres à nos jouissances].[75]

To achieve this, production had to increase. This, again, was possible only in a regime of liberty – through the free use of our forces and our properties.[76] Awareness of its laws provided knowledge of *absolute justice and absolute injustice* in the same way that the laws of nature operated in an absolute way.[77] Everything either pointed to increased abundance or it did not; that is, everything was either called upon or prohibited. Private vices turn into public virtue:

> [I]n the system of nature everyone works constantly for their best possible state and in this way they also necessarily contribute to the best state of the whole corpus of society.[78]

The repetition over again of the italicised expression '*absolute*' by Le Mercier

---

72   Le Mercier, *L'ordre naturel*, *supra* note 71, at 37.
73   '[l]a nature ... a voulu que [les hommes] ne connussent que deux mobiles, l'appétit des plaisirs & l'aversion de la douleur', in *ibid.*, at 33.
74   *Ibid.*, at 11–17.
75   *Ibid.*, at 27.
76   *Ibid.*, at 33.
77   *Ibid.*, at 11.
78   *Ibid.*, at 35.

was intended to highlight the necessary character of the natural order of relationships and to justify the despotism of the laws that would express society's natural order in a quasi-scientific vocabulary of natural rights and duties.

This led le Mercier into an authoritarian government under laws that had the absoluteness of physical laws. Quesnay had already written that '[t]he natural laws of the social order are themselves the physical laws of perpetual reproduction of those goods necessary to the subsistence, the conservation, and the convenience of men'.[79] From this, Quesnay had developed a very rigorous notion of the rule of law. His 'legal despotism' was not meant as monarchic absolutism, however. The 'laws' the ruler would enforce were the intrinsic laws of the social order. Their 'absoluteness' meant that they 'had already been written' by nature itself. The only task left for the monarch was to discover them and to 'dictate' them to society at large.[80] Thus there was no basis to distinguish between legislative and executive power either: one was merely the extension of the other. 'Partager l'autorité, c'est l'annuller'[81] A multitude of opinions would create chaos, while the power and correctness of legislation would be guaranteed by the proof of the laws of the social order ('la force intuitive et déterminante d'évidence').[82]

Exactly the same principles were operative at the international level. In the first place, the universal society that preceded the establishment of particular societies was not destroyed by the latter. When visiting distant peoples in peaceful conditions, Le Mercier argued, the same hospitality was found as at home. The expansion of commercial relations relied on a wholly unthinking respect for rights and duties all over the world. Different political societies were not fundamentally different but best seen as branches of the same tree, parts of the universal human society.[83] A federation of Europe was no chimera. In fact, it was already in existence.

> [O]ne needs to suppose that it has been made, or rather that it has always existed without any express agreement to that effect, by the sole force of the necessity that ensures the political security of each particular nation.[84]

Short-sighted passions had driven nations to war in the past. But nature compelled them to regard each other as brothers, possessing the same rights

---

79 Quesnay, 'Despotisme de la Chine', quoted in David McNally, *Political Economy and the Rise of Capitalism: A Reinterpretation* (University of California Press, 1988) at 123.
80 Le Mercier, *L'ordre naturel*, *supra* note 71, at 75–8, 105, 113.
81 *Ibid.*, at 129.
82 *Ibid.*, at 100, 101–4, 130. On the physiocrat doctrine of legal despotism, see further McNally, *Political Economy*, *supra* note 79, 121–9.
83 Le Mercier, *L'ordre naturel*, *supra* note 71, at 318–20.
84 *Ibid.*, at 323.

and duties as individuals possessed at home. The prosperity of nations lay in the way they followed the 'essential order of societies' that called upon respecting the rights of each other. [85]

The physiocrats understood the relations between private economic actors to be governed by the natural laws whose operating principle was private interest and the search for 'jouissance'. The role of the State and of legislation was not to hinder these activities – they were ultimately beneficial – but to lift obstacles from their realisation and, when needed, to channel human activities to the profitable directions. These principles were shared by the most influential of the new economists, Anne-Robert-Jacques Turgot, who worked as Controller-General in France in 1774–1776 and had fundamental mistrust in the regulation of economic activities. Any legislation on 'luxuries' for example, was arbitrary, harmful and above all wrong – there was no justification in imposing ideas about 'corruption' and virtue over the honest pursuit of their interests and 'jouissance' by individuals. Turgot and his colleagues felt that the increase of regulation had been absurdly responsible for the problems it was seeking to alleviate. There were nowhere more publicly kept houses for the poor than in Spain, Turgot wrote in his article '*Fondation*' in the *Encylopédie* – but perversely nowhere the number of the poor was greater. Many travellers have noticed the problem, he claimed: 'to provide for a large number of men to live freely is to underwrite laxity and all the disorders that follow. It is to render the situation of weakness preferable to that of work and consequently to diminish the amount of labour and production of land ... industrious citizens are replaced by a population of the vile, composed of beggars and vagabonds who subject them to all sorts of crimes'.[86]

Turgot and his colleagues agreed that state power was needed for reasons of public utility, 'the supreme law' of all government. But they envisaged wealth-creation and distribution best take place through citizen activity that was independent of the State. The citizens would use their natural rights and freedoms – above all their right of property – in pursuit of their individual happiness. This activity could be articulated in terms of a 'civil society' in which a special type of sociability operated outside State policy. Because the desires and tastes of citizens changed constantly, and nobody knew them better than the individuals themselves, there was no point in seeking to regulate them externally. When everyone followed their own interests and tastes, the laws of commercial sociability would lead to the best result for everyone, including the State. In his important article on '*Fondation*' in the *Encyclopédie* Turgot tried to redress the balance between

---

85   *Ibid.*, at 331–3.
86   *Encyclopédie, ou dictionnaire raisonné des sciences, des arts et des métiers, etc.* (first published 1751–1765) (edited by Denis Diderot and Jean le Rond D'Alembert, 17 vols, Chez Briasson, 1755) made available by the University of Chicago ARTFL Encyclopédie Project at <encyclopedie.uchicago.edu> (Spring 2011 edition) at 73.

the search for 'utility' that was the overriding objective of State policy and the individual right of citizens, in this case, their right to establish and conduct commercial operations:

> Citizens have rights, even sacred rights against the society; they exist independently of the latter but are its necessary elements; citizens enter society for the sole reason to submit their rights under the protection of the very same laws to which they sacrifice their liberty.[87]

The freedom of commerce belonged to all. It was inextricable from the rights of property and personal liberty and it had no other point than the pursuit of individual interests. According to Turgot and his colleagues, this freedom was universal in nature, it belonged to all humans and therefore justified their pursuit of interests beyond state boundaries. The most efficient way to fight famine, for example, was to liberate grain trade, they argued. To the 'civil society' that commercial sociability created within and in juxtaposition to the State corresponded a cosmopolitan world of trade that was outside of and contrasted with the foreign policies of States, their diplomacy, their hopeless search for a balance of power, their wars and their violence.

IV

The physiocrat doctrine of 'legal despotism' was derived from a naturalist notion of legislation as the expression of universal truths ('evidence') about the human condition. The laws were not to be the effects of the will of a more or a less fickle legislator, but similar to statements of the laws of science. This kind of naturalism has a long history in subsequent French social and legal thought ranging from Auguste Comte's 'positivism' to Emile Durkheim's 'conscience collective', Third Republic 'solidarism' and the objectivism of such early-twentieth century public lawyers as Léon Duguit and Georges Scelle. One famous expression of this view is the idea of human beings as being born indebted to the society and of laws as so many expressions of that indebtedness.[88] This would be one translation into legal thought of the view of humans as social animals. The expanse of such views is not, of course, limited to France. It is an expression of the much more widespread idea that there exists outside present political institutions a more 'natural' sphere of sociability where humans already enjoy freedoms and are subjected to duties towards each other, which is the task of positive legislation to uncover and organise in an working whole. This is no place to give an

---

87 *Ibid.*, at 75.
88 For all this, see the current author's *The Gentle Civilizer of Nations: The Rise and Fall of International law 1870–1960* (Cambridge University Press, 2001) at 266–352.

account of the many versions of natural law and natural rights that have expressed and continue to express this faith. Suffice it to say that all of them are united in the view of legislation as not a matter of what we may now 'will' but what it is that we 'know' or should know about the operation of that anterior structure of normative relationships.

Since mid-twentieth century sociology and classical social theory have lost some of their intellectual clout, perhaps owing to their failure to produce powerful statements about how political communities – states and their conglomerates – ought to be ruled. Neither Weberian pessimism nor the usually Left-orientated strictures of legal sociology have fitted well with the ethos of post-war ideas of European and international governance. Despite setbacks, however, an essentially optimistic view still persists concerning the ability of the economic sciences to grasp the intrinsic laws of modern sociability that it has become customary to address through the vocabularies of interdependence, globalisation and 'governance'. This essay has tried to trace the intellectual trajectory that leads from theology, through law to political economy as carriers of such pursuits. They have each tried to bring into consciousness laws that are already given by society itself so that the only task left for legislation would be to apply them. It is as if an enormous puzzle had been thrown in the winds at the beginning of time. The task of governance would be to bring its pieces into place, with the assumption that they all ultimately fit together so as to so as to form an image of the perfect society. Here, there would be no tragic conflict of interest, no fundamental tension between claims of right.

This kind of harmony has been often critiqued but there may not have been sufficient stress on the way its accompanying providentialism has the structure of political theology. Even as historically orientated analysts such as Foucault, Hirschmann, Senellart and Agamben, among others, have pointed to the theological roots of modern economics,[89] the way this is reflected in views about law and legality – including the nature of legislation, especially legislation claiming universal validity – has received only limited attention.[90] Liberal democracy, many have noted, operates in a schizophrenic predicament of simultaneous belief and non-belief, with lapses into cynicism or authoritarianism as never too distant possibilities. Its preferred

---

89 See, e.g., Michel Foucault, *Naissance de la biopolitique: Cours au Collège de France 1978–1979* (Gallimard/Seuil, 2004); Hirschmann, *The Passions and the Interests*, supra note 59; Michel Senellart, *Les arts de gouverner: Du régimen médiéval au concept du gouvernement* (Seuil, 1995); Giorgio Agamben, *Le règne et la gloire: Homo sacer II,2* (Seuil, 2008). See likewise, Jacob Viner, *The Role of Providence in the Social Order* (Princeton University Press, 1972) and, of course, Karl Löwith, *Meaning in History* (Chicago University Press, 1949).

90 One useful exception is Anne Orford, 'Trade, Human Rights, and the Economy of Sacrifice', in Anne Orford (ed.), *International Law and its Others* (Cambridge University Press, 2006) 156–96, where she writes of international law's 'messianic logic' that integrates suffering as a kind of redemptive promise of a better future.

intellectual and political terrain is that of mid-level 'opinion' and parliamentary compromise. This I suppose is what Churchill was in effect pointing to. Avoiding the dangers of perfectionism was more important for him than teasing out its possible truths. But the time of states and those kinds of statesmanship may now be over. Even Weber's old instruction for those with a vocation of politics might appear as to strike an excessively sceptical note in a world enchanted by the spontaneous dynamism of economic governance as a religion of immanence.

3 Legalism and the 'dark' side of global governance

Friedrich Kratochwil

1 Introduction

The debate on globalisation has gone through several stages. The earlier episodes centred more on the nature of the beast, i.e. whether the increasing interdependencies were something unprecedented or not.[1] The later discussions accepted the transformative nature of the changes: here the implications of the information revolution were discussed, which had spawned revolutions in production and trade (intra-firm rather than arms-length trade), had dis-embedded the financial sector from the 'real' economy and had given rise to fundamental ideological shifts. The latter was exemplified by the 'silent revolutions' and the appearance of new actors (non-governmental organisations and members of a 'global' civil society),[2] as well as by new organisational forms (networks)[3] on the political stage and in the law-making processes.[4] To that extent the later debates addressed more the 'responses' to the changes than getting the 'description' right,[5] precisely because the transformations showed that the social world is of our making, which inevitably connects our analysis of what is, with certain political projects.

---

[1] See, for example, the earlier debate among students of interdependence whether or not the growth of interdependencies was a sign of a structural transformation of world politics. Kenneth Waltz, 'The Myth of National Interdependence' in Charles Kindleberger (ed.), *The International Corporation* (MIT Press, 1970). Robert Keohane and Joseph Nye, *Power and Interdependence* (Little Brown, 1977).

[2] On the close connection between the human rights discourse and transnational social movements see Samuel Moyn, *The Last Utopia: Human Rights in History* (Harvard University Press, 2010).

[3] Ann Marie Slaughter, *A New World Order* (Princeton University Press, 2004).

[4] Alan Boyle and Christine Chinkin, *The Making of International Law* (Oxford University Press, 2007).

[5] For a further discussion see Friedrich Kratochwil, 'Global Governance and the Emergence of a World Society' in Nathalie Karagiannis and Peter Wagner (eds), *Varieties of World Making* (Liverpool University Press, 2007) 266–86.

Moreover, the earlier responses concerned largely strategies of 'adaptation' to the inevitable, while the later debates focused on the chances for innovation inherent in the existing 'disorder' that had been caused by the dissolution of the boundaries between the internal and the external dimension of politics, and between the 'public and the 'private' realm. In this way, the 'deficits' created by the de-nationalisation of politics on the one hand and by the development of increasingly 'soft' law-making and 'private' ordering on the other hand, could be used either for pleas of 'constitutionalising' existing international organisations[6] or for advocating a conceptually more radical move from the old notion of 'government' as a specific form of steering (governmentality), to a new mode of rule, such as 'bio-politics'[7] or, more benignly, to a global or 'multi-level' governance.[8]

In this way, cosmopolitans and former functionalists could be brought under one concept that sounded 'neutral' as it promised everything to everybody: the cosmopolitan dream was now reinforced by technical expertise, so dear to former functionalists. But, of course, there were more critical lawyers who saw that the common notion of a 'constitution' and judicial review – where law was allegedly overcoming politics – was already problematic within the state; moving this conceptual baggage to the international arena was certain to create additional problems. Jan Klabbers suggested that only a 'constitutionalism light'[9] was realistic but that did not hinder him from exploring in greater detail constitutional thinking beyond the state.[10]

Other 'legalist' responses were far less circumspect. If special expertise was lacking or contested, as for example in the area of 'development', or the environment, one simply could use the short-cut of assigning responsibilities via 'human rights' without bothering too much about how to bring about the desired goal. Thus despite the fact that the puzzle of (economic) development had proven elusive for the classical economic orthodoxies – it seemed that the only countries that developed had been those that had not taken the (neo)liberal prescriptions too seriously, as exemplified by the 'tiger states' – the creation of a 'human right to development' was, nevertheless, supposed to terminate the endless 'technical' debates by attributing to each person a claim that could serve as a 'trump'.[11] This seemed like a convenient

---

6   See, for example, David Held, *Democracy and the Global Order: From the Modern State to Global Governance* (Stanford University Press, 1996); Daniele Archibugi, *The Global Commonwealth of Citizens: Toward Cosmopolitan Democracy* (Princeton University Press, 2008).
7   See Michel Foucault, *The Birth of Biopolitics: Lectures at the College de France 1978–79* (ed. by Michael Snellart, Palgrave-Macmillan, 2008).
8   See Lisbeth Hooghe and Gary Marks, 'Unravelling the Central State, but How? Types of Multilevel Governance', 97(2) *American Political Science Review* (2003) 233–43.
9   Jan Klabbers, 'Constitutionalism Lite', 1 *International Organization Law Review* (2004) 31–58.
10 See the anthology, Jan Klabbers, Ann Peters and Geir Ulfstein, *The Constitutiuonalization of International Law* (Oxford University Press, 2009).
11 Ronald Dworkin, *Taking Rights Seriously* (Harvard University Press, 1978), ch. 4.

way out: using the rather strong instrument of a claim, taken from the legal armoury, while leaving us in the dark in terms of the implementation and the specific duties.[12] After all, if something is 'good' for people or for human flourishing, why should we not also say that people have a 'right' to it? Since we all want to be happy, there is a right to (the pursuit of) happiness.

However, the seemingly innocent word of 'pursuit' does some heavy work here. Two interrelated problems arise in this context. The first is that the grammar of 'good' and 'right' are wider than that of 'having a right'.[13] From the notion of a universal striving after happiness there is certainly only a small step to calling such a striving 'right' (it is right that). But *having a right* goes farther: neither 'others', nor the government should interfere with our 'pursuit' – even if we are mistaken in our quest – unless other 'important' goods are placed in jeopardy. However, while happiness is an important 'good' (in the sense of *bonum*) it thereby does not create a direct entitlement beyond non-interference. We cannot sue our fellow-men or the government for a dereliction of duty if we are not happy, although we do have a claim against them to leave us alone and let us try. This is of course another gloss on the distinction of negative and positive rights which, in its categorical form, might be mistaken,[14] but which nevertheless points us – quite often inconveniently – to the factual and empirical conditions that come with entitlements and which quickly complicate our neat conceptual frameworks.

Here the connection with a second problem becomes visible, as the proliferation of rights shows. Even if we accept that rights are 'trumps' it is no longer clear which trump 'trumps' which other trump in which circumstances (security *versus* liberty). But this means that the assignment of duties to specific duty-bearers cannot be left hanging, as if 'trumps' were free-standing and did not depend on the game one was playing or on the umpires who decide our actual controversies. It also means that 'judicial' decisions, arrived at after proper 'scrutiny' or weighing of competing rights, presuppose functioning institutions, including those forking out the money for implementing these decisions.

In the case of international law and human rights it is clear that states have to be 'deputised' for that purpose. But the increasing adjudication of competing rights also raises the wider problem that courts now not only exercise legislative powers but also increasingly get involved in policy design and execution, as exemplified by the growth of administrative law. It is

---

12 Onora O'Neill, 'The 'Dark' Side of Human Rights', 81(2) *International Affairs* (2005) 427–39.
13 See Friedrich Kratochwil, *Rules, Norms, and Decisions* (Cambridge University Press, 1989), ch. 6.
14 The distinction between negative and positive rights goes back to the classical distinction Isaiah Berlin popularised in his 'Two Concepts of Liberty', which can be found in Isaiah Berlin, *Four Essays on Liberty* (Oxford University Press, 1958).

therefore not surprising that after the rights revolution we see also in the international arena the advocacy of making certain principles of global administrative law the dominant paradigm rather than on relying on the old props of 'sovereignty', or on the new one of 'human rights'. Needless to say, the 'minor' problem of how such an administrative apparatus could be financed in the absence of a tax-base remains somewhat unclear. It is, nevertheless, somewhat surprising that the 'normative' matters, such as accountability and transparency, get most of the attention as if the nitty-gritty of the wherewithal of the administrative apparatus could be left unattended.

These conceptual difficulties of 'rights' and 'administration' create a certain unease and provide the grounds for another evaluation of 'governance' more along the lines of a Foucauldian 'bio-politics'.[15] In that case the administrative aspect of managing populations and 'risks', subjecting societies to capillary control, has less of a 'functionalist' ring to it, but points to the 'darker sides' of both law and administration as instruments of 'rule'. In other words, Weber's bureaucracy as the iron cage of modernity is just around the corner. But matters are even worse when we consider the following. Precisely because power is now not limited to the exercise of specific actions, as it defines the 'normal', it has become 'structural', or even 'productive'.[16] It escapes the gaze of transparency and circumvents accountability since it works by delineating the bounds of sense. Despite its apparent invisibility, power is pervasive, planned, methodical and non-idiosyncratic, but not necessarily less tyrannical as the power exercised by specific agents. And it certainly is far removed from Smith's benevolent 'hidden hand', as it systematically creates 'winners' and losers. This dystopia has then given rise to resistance to global institutions and national governments alike, since it is the hegemony of the 'politics as usual' that is at issue.

The fortunes of the global movements who have articulated their dissatisfaction along those lines have waxed and waned over time, ranging from the riots in Seattle and Genova to the recent more targeted sanctions of the Attac or the Occupy movements. Meanwhile 'politics as usual' continues, be it in terms of the policy-networks of the 'disaggregated' state, national election campaigns or 'supra-national' meetings and organisational routines that try to 'translate' doctrines like the responsibility to protect (R2P),[17] or those of a common currency area (in the absence of some crucial preconditions), into practice.

Since evidence is easily supplied for either interpretation of governance – the benign one as well as the dystopian one – an assessment is difficult and it certainly cannot be decided by looking harder at the 'facts' since their

---

15 Michel Foucault, *Security, Territory, Population* (Palgrave, 2007).
16 Michael Barnett and Raymond Duvall, 'Power in International Politics', 59(1) *International Organization* (2005) 39–75.
17 See the *Report of the International Commission on Intervention and State Sovereignty* (2 vols, International Development Research Center, 2001).

meaning is under scrutiny. As social facts are not 'natural' but result from actions that are recursively related to the projects people pursue, and to the beliefs and meanings they share (or do not share), they cannot be examined through 'observations' of the 'world out there'. Here the causal arrows no longer fly only from 'the world' to the mind but mainly from the 'mind' to the 'world'. To that extent, the focus of my contribution here is on the conceptual problems of the global domain and on assessing the exhortation of 'embedding the system of governance in a broader global framework of social capacity that did not exist previously'.[18]

On the face of it, global governance seems, at first, to be a good thing and is usually taken an indicator of 'progress'. But before we jump to such conclusions I want, following the suggestion of James Davis,[19] to examine three matters in particular, which are germane for any such assessment: the matter of global collective goods and their provision, questions of regulation, and the emergence and proliferation of human rights. While the findings of these three subject areas might not allow us to draw conclusive inferences for global governance as a whole, it would be pretty surprising if these examinations would not provide us with a rather persuasive plausibility probe, given their strategic position within the governance *problematique*. But before those topics can be taken up in Section 3, I want to address in the next section some common conceptual problems first, which tend to muddy the waters in the governance debate.

2 Conceptual traps

From these preliminary considerations above some further corollaries follow. The first is that the 'growth' of organisational activity should not be identified with 'progress'. After all, given the questionable employment of this biological metaphor, we had better realise that not all growth is beneficial since some forms of growths kill their hosts! Similarly, as the discussion about the fragmentation of the international legal order showed, the existence of 'more' dispute-settlement institutions represents more the embarrassment of riches than a coherent legal process. Forum-shopping, circumvention of the *res judicata* rule and plain inconsistencies among the different 'courts' now replicate the former struggle for territorial hegemony in the form of a struggle for the hegemonic discourse, e.g. treating something as a trade rather than as an environmental or human rights concern.[20]

---

18 John Ruggie, 'Reconstituting the Public Domain: Issues, Actors and Practices', 10(4) *European Journal of International Relations* (2004) 499–531, at 519.
19 See James Davis, 'A Critical View of Global Governance', 18(2) *Swiss Political Science Review* (2012) 272–86.
20 See, for example, Martti Koskenniemi, 'The Fate of Public International Law: Between Technique and Politics', 70 *Modern Law Review* (2007) 1–30.

This observation leads us to the second corollary: the caution with which we should approach 'functionalist' arguments. For one, depending on the framing conditions the notion of what is considered 'functional' changes dramatically. While the dis-embedding of the financial market from the real economy might be 'functional' when measured by the notions of the 'frictionless' markets propagated by the 'efficient market hypothesis', it is certainly not functional for the economy as a whole, as the recent financial crises show. Two, while the existence of some organisations, such as technical bureaus or functional international organisations, might 'respond' to some perceived 'need', we certainly are not entitled to take this as a sufficient condition for their existence or satisfactory performance. The refutation of the latter thesis has supplied generations of students of organisation theory with research topics. The former thesis, exemplified by the 'demand for regimes'[21] argument, is falsified by the many areas that would require a regime, but where no organisational solution has been found. The upshot of this argument is that for the creation and design of institutions nationally and supra-nationally, 'politics' matters[22] as it is here that the historical struggles get inscribed and become afterwards through habituation and hindsight, the 'way in which things are handled' and taken for granted.

The 'obviousness' of an organisational solution gets rattled, such as when we encounter the rather 'strange' phenomenon that e.g. a property rights got placed within the trading regime (as is the case with the Trade-related Aspects of Intellectual Property Rights [TRIPS] agreement of the WTO), while a 'functional' organisation for patents and thus for intellectual property existed and enjoyed considerable support among the members.[23] But this 'oddity' in turn can be explained by further research, which shows that the US successfully drafted the Europeans to support their plans for the WTO regime, and thus that 'politics' mattered more than the ideology of functionalism.

This case can again be interpreted optimistically as well as pessimistically. Optimistically we see how through hegemonic action, or 'k-groups' (privileged groups), or even through clever draftsmanship of a rapporteur (as, for example, in the case of Third United Nations Conference on the Law of the Sea [UNCLOS III]), solutions actually emerge that did not seem reachable, given the diverging interests. Similarly, it might not be the best solution that finally won out, but still it might be better than the existing status quo. This might occur in cases where multiple equilibria with

---

21　Robert Keohane, 'The Demand for Regimes', in Stephen Krasner (ed.), *International Regimes* (Cornell University Press, 1983) 141–71.
22　See Daniel Drezner, *All Politics is Global* (Princeton University Press, 2007).
23　See the analysis of David Bach, 'Varieties of Cooperation: The Domestic Institutional Roots of Global Governance', 36(2) *Review of International Studies* (2010) 561–89.

asymmetric pay-offs exist[24] and the chosen alternative might heavily favour one player or group of players. The pessimistic interpretation, of course, will either focus on the absence of a regime, leaving certain concerns unattended, on the coercive moves by forcing weaker players 'into the boat' (as otherwise their chances 'at sea' are even worse), or on the inequitable outcome it institutionalises as 'normal'. All of these considerations point to the fact that power and historical contingencies do matter and should not be forgotten when assessing international institutions.

But if this is true, then a third corollary is that institutions are embedded in historical understandings and conjunctural configurations, and that 'optimal design' and transferability cannot be assumed. To that extent what worked once need not work in the future, what was 'functional' here, might fail to deliver the desired outcome 'there',[25] all of which makes the recurrent enthusiasm concerning 'best practices' and their codification highly suspect. As a matter of fact, relying on rules without creating further social, epistemic and legitimising support or the inevitable 'discretion' that the application of rules and principles requires, might end up with a governance system that is neither efficient, nor effective, nor as benign as it is made out to be.[26] This, of course does not mean that 'good' outcomes are not possible, but it does mean that they are happy coincidences rather than the result of planning or institutional design, as both logic and experience suggest, thereby reinforcing the more critical take.

Let us begin with logic and with the assumption that 'elements' of regimes are easily separable and transferable, and that the problem reduces itself to finding a proper arrangement of the various parts. Let us further assume that we have created clearly defined regimes and have found for each subject area an optimal solution. But from this apparently ideal state we, nevertheless, cannot infer that all regimes will also work optimally together, fitting like hand in glove. Such an inference would commit the fallacy of composition, since what is true of the parts need not be true of the whole and

---

24 Consider the following matrix of a coordination game which two players (A and B) with three strategies (I, II, III) face:

		B		
		I	II	III
A	I	1,9	0,0	2,1
	II	0,0	1,2	0,0
	III	0,0	0,0	9,1

Although strategies (I, I); (I, III); (II, II) and (III, III) are clearly better than other combinations it is not difficult to see that cooperation is unlikely.
25 A curious example comes from industrial management. Japanese management methods, ironically based on US managerial doctrines, were successful in Japan but failed in the US when applied by Japanese companies there.
26 Laura Zanotti, *Governing Disorder: UN Peace Operations, International Security, and Democratization in the Post Cold-War Era* (University of Pennsylvania Press, 2011).

vice versa. It might very well be true that both ice cream and cucumber salad are 'good', but (unless we are pregnant) cucumber salad *with* ice cream has little appeal. On the other hand, there is also good news since we no longer have to wait, as Plato suggested, that social order is possible only if each individual (soul) is well-ordered and finds its proper place in a society ruled by philosopher-kings.[27] If this were true, Kant's 'republic among devils'[28] would be an impossible project.

It was precisely the insight of setting ambition against ambition and thus using the very 'vices' as instruments for controlling them, which gave the 'republican' project,[29] focusing on institutions, on checks and balances (rather than on individuals and their morals), its bite. While of course such an arrangement presupposes some constitutional ordering, the important point here is that it is a design problem that works with a 'second best solution', i.e. not an optimal one, but instead pays close attention to what is possible given the particular circumstances. This includes the recognition that what worked 'here' need not work 'there', as 'local knowledge' matters. Thus, no 'solution' can claim universal validity, as sequences, history and the formation of 'traditions' matter. Such a realisation is, of course, bad news for 'best practices' and their codification that has become the rage in global governance.

This problem of perverse effect is often (mistakenly) identified with the matter of 'application' of rules and principles, not with the codification of a practice itself. But something is amiss in thinking that the real problem lies in clarifying principles or codifying best practices while leaving their application to the 'practitioners' on the ground. While this separation might seem like a sensible division of labour, it is likely to skew the analysis. Instead of beginning with a problem and trying to formulate the 'right' question, we begin with a 'solution', which is looking for problems to be applied to. Here 'the law of the hammer' exerts a powerful pull, since if you have a hammer, the whole world looks suspiciously like a nail, even if we all know that if the task is fetching water, a hammer is of no avail. Students of organisation theory have analysed this problem in terms of the 'garbage can model' of organisational decision-making.[30] Solutions are in search of problems rather than the other way around. They are more like containers in which various things are thrown rather than specific 'answers' fitting well-thought-out questions.

Proceeding in this fashion when solutions chase 'problems' rather than are conceived as 'answers' raises of course the more general problems of sense or

---

27 Plato, *Republic*, book VI.
28 Immanuel Kant, 'Perpetual Peace', in H. S. Reis (ed.), *Kant's Political Writings* (Cambridge University Press, 1970).
29 Nicholas Onuf, *The Republican Legacy in International Thought* (Cambridge University Press, 1998).
30 See John March and John Olsen, *Ambiguity and Change in Organizations* (Universitetsforlaget, Bergen, 1979).

'non'-sense of 'ideal theory' and of formal modelling based on idealised assumptions (such as complete and costless information) as in Eugene Fama's efficient market, as opting for such a heuristic might be essentially misleading. It cannot be pursued here further. But examples illustrating these points are not hard to find. Take economic development theory of the 1960s and the notion that it could be 'jump started' by transfer of funds and the creation of a labour market.[31] According to this model, Japan should have never developed, since it did not possess a labour market during its periods of expansion. On the other hand, the 'miracle' of European recovery induced by the Marshall plan should have worked everywhere, instead of leading to the well-known pathologies of 'development aid'.

Albert Hirschman was one of the first ones that doubted the appropriateness of our models derived from the European and US experience – whereby even significant variations in the development of capitalism were neglected – for understanding the problems for the developing world. Different from disagreeing only on the strategy, such as Prebisch and much of the former New International Economic Order (NIEO) proposals did, Hirschman pointed to the more general problem of how 'paradigms' are hindrances for our understanding,[32] misdirecting our attention and asking the wrong questions for diagnosing specific problems. This train of thought was later followed up by the studies on the 'sociology' of science,[33] i.e. on what counts as knowledge is powerfully shaped not only by the community of scientists – the epistemic communities regime analysts have examined – but also by the networks that link knowledge production with ruling elites and institutions whose standard operating procedures they inform. Thus a lot of havoc can be wrought upon other societies not only if the wrong lessons are learned and get ensconced in an orthodoxy, but also by transferring even apparently 'right lessons' without much concern for local conditions. Furthermore, it is quite obvious that formulating the respective legal rules that impose obligations or codifying best practices is only a small part of the solution, since drafting skills – the main contribution lawyers can make – are here clearly subordinate to the presumed knowledge upon which these solutions are formulated.

As banal as these 'objections' to ensconced thinking are, they seldom are taken into serious consideration. Take peacekeeping for example. It worked in the Middle East by radically calling into question the orthodoxy of traditional collective security envisaged by the UN Charter. A neutral police

---

31 Walt W. Rostow, *The Stages of Growth* (Cambridge University Press, 1960).
32 See Albert Hirschman, *Essays in Trespassing* (Cambridge University Press, 1981) and also his 'The Search for Paradigms as Hindrance to Understanding', 21 *World Politics* (April 1970) 329–43.
33 Bruno Latour, *Science in Action* (Harvard University Press, 1987); see also Bruno Latour, *Pandora's Hope: Essays on the Reality of Science Studies* (Harvard University Press, 1999); Karin Knorr-Cetina, *The Manufacture of Knowledge* (Pergamon, 1981).

force, keeping the Great Powers *out*, was indeed an answer to the problem of assurance among the conflict parties and the dangers of escalation. But obviously such a solution depended on functioning states and the assent of the parties involved. The latter two conditions no longer prevailed in the Congo, which led to near disaster for both the mission and the UN. There is no need to follow the path of further developments in peacekeeping operations other than to note that it had little to do with the original 'answer': instead of monitoring, 'peacemaking', 'peace enforcement' and even the transformation of both state and society became the 'goals'. Instrumental for these changes was also the concomitant conceptual stretch of the notion of 'humanitarianism'. Conceived originally as a depoliticised move to help the wounded and sick in battle who were no longer as combatants of any value to their respective military commands, Henry Dunant had persuaded some European powers to allow the Red Cross to minister in strict neutrality to those in need, by not taking sides in the question of the 'justice' of their causes. By now humanitarianism has become, however, a justification not only for intervention and the use of force against those engaged in genocidal activities, but increasingly also for purposes of insuring democracy, human rights and freeing markets.

Under such an expansive new doctrine of the causes for a 'just war', the question of neutrality was out of place, as was one of the traditional principles of the 'helping professions', i.e. to enable others, who have agreed to a treatment, to go on with their lives instead of running it. The notion that outsiders can just administer 'help' instead of becoming part of the problem, however, is heroic indeed. The continued adherence to this assumption is all the more surprising given the ample evidence that perverse effects can obtain through structural interdependencies, even when no direct intervention by outsiders occurs. Examples abound: the import of cheap food as 'humanitarian aid' (or as part of an enduring programme of 'feeding the hungry') has nearly always had the effect of ruining the local small farmers, or of making large sectors of the population dependent on charity from abroad. Nowadays we have the additional problem of tying the farmer to a supplier of seeds for which yearly royalty payments are due. The recent gift of Monsanto to Haiti after the last earthquake is just one of the more recent cases of this familiar pattern.

When experts and their helpers actually descend upon a society, the image that such an intervention resembles a 'surgical' procedure, in which a tumour or bullet is just being removed while leaving the body (politic) the same, only better off, is belied by the facts. True, there might be some analogies that fit the medical metaphor, but the similarities are superficial at best. The popularity of 'surgical strikes' by the military shows what is problematic in such an analogy. It suggests precision and minimal invasion that do not rend the social fabric, even though experience tells us that such strikes are hardly ever possible, in spite of the exculpatory euphemism of 'collateral damage'. Of course, helpers and experts are usually aware of such externalities and (disingenuously?) insist on processes and policies that are 'owned' by the local population. But despite the good intentions, there is the dilemma of trade-offs between effectiveness on the one hand and the 'autonomy' on the other.

Finally, given that much of 'help' is at present administered by non-governmental organisations (NGOs), there is now, contrary to the expectation of enhanced legitimacy through the inclusion of global civil society, a serious problem of responsibility and accountability as multiple principal/agent problems arise in such arrangements. While bidding for contracts – which is sometimes blamed for those problems[34] – does not occur in the informal law-making networks and in the public/private partnerships which work out the 'soft law' of governance, similar legitimacy problems arise in determining the stakeholders and in regard to the lack of representativeness of the NGOs involved. The latter might have a certain expertise, but they have also obviously an axe to grind. As in the case of war, which is much too serious a business to be left to the military, it might not be such a good idea to leave it to, say, the bankers, to make the rules under which they operate. As Louis Pauly correctly quipped already some time ago, 'who elected the bankers'?

3 Public goods, regulation and human rights

The debate on global governance also suffers from some of the shortcomings of the predominant neo-liberal approach that serves as its frame. This becomes obvious when we compare these accounts with Weber's broader and more sombre discussion of 'rule' exercised through the bureaucracy, or with Foucault's 'governmentality' and bio-politics. But even within the liberal discourse – when Kant's 'cosmopolitanism' is pressed into its service – some highly consequential gaps are noticeable. There is the matter of a reduction of collective action problems to those of the undersupply of collective goods. The hidden generative grammar suggests that problems of collective life can be solved by two opposing strategies: assignment of subjective rights and governmental regulation. That this narrow focus was not part of the original liberal theory can be seen from Adam Smith's conceptualisation of education as a 'public good' – even the 'public schools' of his time were 'private institutions' while 'turnpikes', always 'public' in his time, should be 'privatised' according to his advice, by making the users pay.

Obviously what is public and private is not akin to identifying natural kinds, but depends on certain choices and so does the answer to *how much* of a public goods is to be procured, given inevitable trade-offs. The changes

---

34 See, for example, Alexander Colley and James Ron, 'The NGO Scramble: Organizational Insecurity and the Political Economy of Transnational Action', 27 *International Security* (Summer 2002) 5–39.

in the semantic field of liberalism need not concern us here further, save to notice that the discourse shifted over time from the central concept of a 'good' (*bonum*, still with ontological and/or ethical overtones) to that of 'procurement' (task, as in 'the duties of the sovereign') and then it changed back within a considerably more restricted field, to the 'nature' of the 'good' (collective *versus* private good), although as part of a considerably more restricted semantic field. The good is now seen only as a commodity, which the market can(not) adequately provide. Within this narrowed focus on supply, questions the assignment of property rights or governmental regulation take then the pride of place. Supply questions inspired the debates about enclosure in England and later Hardin's discussion of the 'Tragedy of the Commons'.[35] Although that article has spawned an enormous literature on the under-procurement of global public goods it is, ironically, not a classical public goods problem, since the overgrazing of the commons can only occur because the good is *not* characterised by non-rivalrous consumption.

Again confusion abounds and, as the subsequent debate on resource regimes showed, no 'one size fits all' solution is in the offing.[36] Thus casting the net wider and examining a bit closer the conceptual framework seems not only prudent but necessary, especially when a brief reflection shows that there are virtually no 'public goods'[37] – perhaps street lighting being one of the few exceptions. All the other examples, such as national defence or free air, are either 'club goods' (they do not satisfy the public goods criterion of non-exclusivity), or are goods which were traditionally *in ample* supply. Thus defence might be for alliance-members a public good, but the whole point of making alliances is to distinguish between those one will defend from those who are either enemies or 'outsiders' who cannot claim protection (save perhaps incidentally). Similarly, if air is a public good and public goods cannot be supplied by the market because of market failure, why would we bother to institutionalise now 'pollution markets' where certificates can be traded?

Strange as it sounds, what is entirely missing in these debates is the question of the 'public' for whom and by whom these goods are supposed to be supplied. This is in a way the result of a gap in liberal theory, where questions of membership were hardly ever explicitly addressed. Thus even contemporary theorists like Rawls in his *Theory of Justice*[38] 'assumes' an existing community in which it is rather clear as to who is 'in' and who is 'out'. It thereby nicely sidesteps the underlying political problem of whom I have to listen to, and who can outvote me. Even in Rawls' later attempt to

---

35 Garret Hardin, 'The Tragedy of the Commons', 162 *Science* (1968) 1243–8.
36 See Todd Sandler, *Global Collective Action* (Cambridge University Press, 2004).
37 Mancur Olson, *Theory of Collective Action* (Harvard University Press, 1965).
38 John Rawls, *Theory of Justice* (Harvard University Press, 1970).

answer to global problems in his *The Law of Peoples*,[39] the matter of membership – concretely experienced by mass migrations and streams of refugees – remains strangle outside his vision. But if neither the nature of the good is given – as education has become virtually everywhere a public good and a 'task' for the state[40] – and if the 'public' needs a specific definition in the absence of an encompassing imperial order, then these concerns cannot be left unaddressed.

Liberal theory has attempted to deal with these issues only obliquely via an 'interest' theory of rights and – when transposed to the international arena – through a proliferation of human rights. This has led not only to some strange constructions, such as the 'right to a promotion',[41] which will come as a great surprise to, say, practicing doctors or lawyers, but also to an alleged 'right to the internet',[42] to 'clean water' or to 'democracy', all of which are allegedly human rights of the 'third' or 'fourth' generation. While all of these alleged 'rights' are *goods* in the sense of specifying desirable goals and protecting certain interests, the question is rather whether their formulation as quasi free-standing subjective rights (human rights) can solve the political problems when discussions about membership, and the question of who is entitled to decide upon priorities among competing rights, are on the agenda.[43]

Again it is easy to find a 'legalistic' answer by kicking these problems into the 'courts'. But courts can do their jobs only if they are part of a system of institutions that translate decisions into effective outcomes. This, in turn, assumes that the resources against which those claims are made are available and/or can be legitimately distributed. This is most obvious in the cases where material entitlements are at stake. But how is the right to food – which might require a substantial increase in production and thus the use of pesticides, fertiliser and water – to be squared with the right to a 'clean environment'? How much clean water is to be procured when these demands have to weighted against the 'best available health care', or against rights to 'education'? These questions can hardly be decided legitimately by courts alone, unless judges are ready to rely on their personal preferences and to subvert, thereby, the rule of law by becoming the 'benevolent despots' Kant so

---

39   John Rawls, *The Law of Peoples* (Harvard University Press, 1999).
40   For a further discussion see Friedrich Kratochwil, 'El fracaso de la "falla de mercado": vuelta a, pensar en bienes "públicos" y "privados" con base en "La riqueza de las naciones" de Adam Smith y el derecho romano', 50(200) *Foro Internacional* (2010) 422–45.
41   See Additional Protocol to the American Convention on Human Rights in the Area of Economic, Social and Cultural Rights, Organization of American States, 17 November 1988, in force 16 November 1999, OAS Treaty Series No. 69, Article 7(c), which James Griffin considers a case of unacceptable extension: James Griffin, 'Discrepancies between the best philosophical Account of Human Rights and the International Law of Human Rights', 101 *Proceedings of the Aristotelian Society* (2001) 1–28, at 23.
42   See the Report of the Human Rights Council, UN Doc. A/HRC/17/27, 16 May 2011.
43   See Davis, 'A Critical View of Global Governance', *supra* note 19.

abhorred. Similarly, one need not be an adherent of Carl Schmitt to see that membership questions are 'political'[44] in nature and that the conceptualisation of corporate rights as individual rights is hardly tenable. As a matter of fact, the whole point of assigning rights to corporations is not only to shield members – the famous corporate veil that can be lifted only in special circumstances as suggested by the *Barcelona Traction*[45] case – but to enable a body thus constituted to do things that no individual could do singly or even together.

Thus only universities can give degrees, even if professors decide on pass or fail of students. Only states can send ambassadors and this right cannot be understood as a 'delegation' of some subjective 'human' right to the state, because it cannot exist prior to the existence of a body politic. Similarly, there cannot be a 'human right' to democracy as desirable as this form of government might be.[46] 'Democracy' refers to a way in which public power is constituted and its exercise is legitimised. It concerns, therefore, a specific institutional arrangement that cannot be conceptualised as an individual 'human' right that belongs to individuals in virtue of their being part of a species and of the assigned status as free agents. Here the rights discourse runs up against some of its conceptual limitations.

The individualistic focus of a 'liberal' theory of rights becomes even more problematic when it is tied also to a strict notion of 'methodological individualism', i.e. that all 'collective' phenomena must be explainable as aggregations of individual properties.[47] That this position is untenable becomes clear when we consider, e.g. emergent properties,[48] or deal with collective intentions[49] or cultural phenomena, such as language that cannot be reduced to the aggregation of individual utterances. The upshot of this argument is that the proliferation of rights can neither dispense with more 'wholistic' problems such as, e.g. a theory of justice, nor with many of the practical problems that arise out of our interferences or common projects in social life.[50] There cannot be a subjective 'right' to go downtown on Lexington Avenue (because it is one-way uptown), as even Dworkin admitted as such regulations fall under the police powers of the community that cannot be construed as an aggregation and transfer of individual rights.

---

44 Carl Schmitt, *The Concept of the Political* (University of Chicago Press, 1996).
45 *Barcelona Traction, Light and Power Company, Limited (Belgium v. Spain) (Second Phase)*, ICJ Reports (1970) 3.
46 See the resolutions of the Commission on Human Rights: CHR Res. 2000/47, 25 April 2000, and CHR Res. 2002/46, 23 April 2002.
47 Methodological individualism was originally advocated by the economists of the Austrian school, see Ludwig von Mises, *Human Action* (Henry Regenry, 1963), ch. 2, meanwhile even economists have a problem with that position, see Mark Blaug, *The Methodology of Economics* (Cambridge University Press, 1992) at 45f.
48 Thus water has properties that neither of its elements exhibits.
49 Michael Bratman, *Intentions, Plans and Practical Reason* (Harvard University Press, 1987).
50 For a further discussion see my 'The Burden and Limits of Rights', in *The Status of Law in World Society: Meditations on the Role and Rule of Law* (Cambridge University Press, forthcoming), ch. 8.

It is therefore not surprising that we can observe everywhere the growth of administrative law and of 'agencies',[51] which, as part of the disaggregated state, are also cooperating trans-nationally in inter-governmental networks. But the latter often include non-state actors in their law-making activities.[52] The results are largely only 'soft laws'[53] but this is for practical purposes of lesser importance since the prescriptions are frequently accepted by national agencies or courts and thus 'incorporated' into the respective legal systems.

Two hopes are usually connected with these new practices. One is that that the arbitrary exercise of power, which administrative law was to check nationally, could now also be achieved transnationally if we were able to identify a set of administrative principles that could command assent by having become part of 'custom'. Various tribunals nationally or internationally could then rely on them. The other hope is that a transnational regulation that, in a way, relies on a surrogate political process by including all stakeholders irrespective of their public or private status, could enhance the legitimacy of the norms emerging from such deliberations. In short, the quality of law-making could be improved by tapping into the expertise of the stakeholders and it also could alleviate the legitimacy problem[54] as both, politics and law-making, no longer can be sequestered into the old institutional framework of national legislation or classical treaty making.

Although we can consider these expectations an open question, I think the high hopes placed on a global administrative law and on the participation of global civil society are unjustified. Thus even if we were able to provide a set of norms for a global administrative law, such as publicity, non-retroactivity, proportionality, the giving of reasons for decisions, information and notice requirements, there would remain several problems. The first is whether these principles are sufficiently freestanding so that they can be separated from their constitutional context and can have the same or quite similar effects when transplanted to a different arena. But since administrative law crucially interacts with constitutional law this would be a tall order to fill in the case of the international realm which has no overarching 'constitution'.

---

51   See Benedict Kingsbury, Nico Krisch, Richard B. Stewart, 'The Emergence of Global Administrative Law', 68 *Law and Contemporary Problems* (2005) 1–63

52   See, for example, the Codex Alimentarius, or the standards developed by the International Organization for Standardization (ISO).

53   See the original debate between Joseph Gold, 'Strengthening the Soft International Law of Exchange Agreements' and Prosper Weil, 'Towards Relative Normativity in Law', 77 *American Journal of International Law* (1983) 443–89 and 413–42, respectively; for a more recent controversial intervention in this ongoing debate, see Jan Klabbers, 'The Redundancy of Soft Law', 65 *Nordic Journal of International Law* (1996) 167–82.

54   See in this respect the White Paper on European Governance, COM (2001) 428 final, 25 July 2001, OJ 2001 C 287/1.

A second difficulty, which every student of comparative law encounters,[55] is that these terms are not exactly free standing and interchangeable, as much of their meaning derives from the semantic and institutional field, as well as from the 'tradition' in which they are embedded.[56] Thus 'due process' is well understood and parallels can be found in virtually all legal orders. But this does not mean that they work in the same way.[57] The role of courts and judicial review differs markedly among common law systems and within civil law systems one can identify quite distinctive traditions concerning 'discretion' accorded to the agencies and of the provided remedies (ombudsman *versus* tort action). Connected with this is a third difficulty to which Antje Wiener[58] has called attention. Even if norms are relatively clear and uncontested and thus also resonate in a society and its institutions, their 'perlocutionary effect' is likely to differ as existing traditions emphasise different aspects. This 'normative baggage' can even be seen in the European context at Brussels, whose Brusselisation process has been noted,[59] but which apparently does not lead to the expected homogenisation in the understanding of norms. If this is true – and Wiener's empirical work makes a good *prima facie* case – the prospects for a transcultural convergence are not good. If a convergence occurred it is more likely to be the result of the growth of largely US-based transnational law firms and of litigation through forum shopping than through the emergence of common understandings and practices.

The last point leads us directly to the second 'hope' mentioned above, i.e. enhancing the legitimacy of law-making and of decisions so that they can marshal assent and enhance compliance. Here of course 'outcome legitimacy' and *de facto* acceptance are usually stressed, while freely admitting that the criteria of input-legitimacy might not be safeguarded in multi-level governance arrangements.[60] There is, of course, something to this, but *de facto* acceptance seems clearly too thin a reed on which to hang one's hat. It

---

55 See Pierre Legrand, 'European Legal Systems are not Converging', 34 *International & Comparative Law Quarterly* (1996) 52–82.
56 Martin Krygier, 'Law as a Tradition', 5(2) *Law & Philosophy* (1986) 237–62.
57 Carol Harlow, 'Voices of Differences in a Plural Community', 50 *American Journal of Comparative Law* (2002) 339–67.
58 Antje Wiener, *The Invisible Constitution of Politics: Contested Norms and International Encounters* (Cambridge University Press, 2008).
59 Aside from architecture where Brusselisation means the mindless building of high-rises in a historical city escape, Brusselisation in law means the successive development of an EU legal order after the 'depillarisation' in the Lisbon treaty. Of course the overtones also cover the attitudinal shift of policy elite interacting on a daily basis in and around the European institutions. See Ramses Wessel, 'The Dynamics of the European Union Legal Order', 5 *European Constitiutional Law Review* (2009) 117–42.
60 Due to the complexity in modern systems of governance, Fritz Scharpf has stressed the need for effectiveness as complicated governance structures might lead to decision traps and stalemate. See Fritz Scharpf, *Governing in Europe* (Oxford University Press, 1999).

not only comes close to 'decisionism', i.e. that the decision-maker or agency 'knows' best, but also to defeatism, since the acceptance of an option that one has no power to change or even influence is magically transformed into an 'approval'. While political reality has of course frequently resembled this state of passive acquiescence, it is hard to consider this a 'democracy-enhancing' feature.[61]

Similarly 'publicity', although essential, is certainly not enough. Placing the agenda for a meeting of an inter-governmental organisation or some position papers in the net, and marching some largely self-appointed 'representatives' of 'civil society' into a meeting room for an 'exchange' of ideas, is not tantamount to granting them a 'hearing'.[62] Their concerns can be ignored as soon as they are asked to leave the room and the actual 'business' starts. But even if these civil society groups become part of a public/private partnership and are involved in law-making activities, serious problems remain. The main one is that attaching greater legitimacy to decisions or 'laws' made with civil society participation is flawed since most of these organisations are one-issue organisations. They lack therefore the 'publicness' of having to make decisions in the light of, and with the responsibility for trade-offs among all other issues that a group or society has to face.

The same can be said about 'voting' in the net, which is sometimes being touted as a new form of 'e-democracy'. Indeed we are constantly asked to give our opinion and register our likes. But the fact that Facebook has no 'dislike' button shows the problem with such a conception of 'voting'. As Cass Sunstein[63] has pointed out, people checking in and out of chat rooms can do so at their pleasure. They need not inform themselves about alternatives, and they usually prefer to talk to those with the same likes and causes. Thus the picture is one of dispersion, showing even a tendency towards radicalisation, rather than one of a convergence on some 'common thing' – the *res publica* of old – whereby, of course, the *common thing* presupposes a trans-generational commitment and a capacity of making binding decisions on all issues. The 'debates' on the net have neither the requisite variety, which genuine deliberation requires, nor the seriousness with which voice and loyalty have to be exercised since only the 'exit' option predominates.[64]

Thus the legitimising potential of public/private law-making and global administrative law seems rather limited, with obvious consequences for global governance. Those with established interests are part of the 'functionalist' club, have their interests ensconced in transnational institutions. They

---

61 See Benedict Kingsbury, Nico Krisch and Richard B. Stewart, 'The Emergence of Global Administrative Law', 68 *Law & Contemporary Problems* (2004/2005) 14–62.
62 See David Kennedy, 'The Politics of the Invisible College: International Governance and the Politics of Expertise', 5 *European Human Rights Law Review* (2001) 463–97.
63 Cass Sunstein, *Republic.com 2.0* (Princeton University Press, 2009).
64 Albert O. Hirschman, *Exit, Voice, and Loyalty* (Cambridge University Press, 1970).

are also able to prevent any serious discussion of 'peaceful change' *i.e.* a change in the agendas or of foregrounding other concerns – and here the history of the General Agreement on Tariffs and Trade (GATT) and the WTO is instructive – since they also possess the ability to dominate the further development through the interpretation of 'the law'.[65] Finally, coming back to courts and putting one's trust in administrative law principles is problematic. After all, administrative law partakes both in the shortcomings of functionalism – as if functions were natural, free-standing kinds – and of corporatism, as the stakeholders are assembled in order to shore up support. Thus both the 'citizen' and the 'public' at large have disappeared, and this is the 'dark' side of global governance.

---

65 For a reform proposal see Joost Pauwelyn, 'New Trade Politics for the 21st Century', 11 *Journal of International Economic Law* (2008) 559–73, at 572f.

4 Global legislation and its discontents

Gianluigi Palombella

1 Premises and frames

There is an inherent uneasiness in furthering the idea and prospect of 'legislation' in the international and supranational environment, typically lacking a common central authority, endowed with final say and representative legitimation. Nonetheless, it is plain fact that norms-production has been a massive and persistent reality, in a variety of forms as well as from a large number of sources.

Relatively recent international law transformations have been building on general *community interest* as well as revolving around *regulatory governance*. The post-war trend from 1948 has actually shaped a *super partes law*,[1] beyond the bilateral interests of States. Moreover, transnational/supranational *governance*, through regulatory rule-making[2] and administrative regimes, emerged intensively. This last occurrence shows an overwhelming weight shaping the realm of global intercourses.

It is now mainly the latter transformation to trigger theoretical attempts at reconceiving the scope and rationale of legislation, especially under the label of a 'global administrative law': invoked at the same time as a reality and a project itself, centred upon the aspiration to grant *accountability* of a

---

1 Antonio Cassese, *International Law* (2nd edn, Oxford University Press, 2005), at 217. Cf. Antonio Cassese, *The Human Dimension of international law* (Oxford University Press, 2008). Anne Peters, 'Humanity as the A and Ω of Sovereignty', 20 *European Journal of International Law* (2009) 513–44; Ruti Teitel, *Humanity's Law* (Oxford University Press, 2011); Bruno Simma and Andreas L. Paulus, 'The "International Community": Facing the Challenge of Globalization', 9 *European Journal of International Law* (1998) 266–77.

2 J. H. H. Weiler, 'The Geology of International Law: Governance, Democracy and Legitimacy', 64 *Zeitschrift für ausländisches öffentliches Recht und Völkerrecht* (2004) 547–62; on global administrative law (GAL), see Benedict Kingsbury, Nico Krisch and Richard B. Stewart, 'The Emergence of Global Administrative Law', 68 *Law & Contemporary Problems* (2005) 15–61; Sabino Cassese, 'Administrative Law Without the State? The Challenge of Global Regulation', 37 *NYU Journal of International Law & Politics* (2005) 663–94; Sabino Cassese, Bruno Carotti, Lorenzo Casini, Eleonora Cavalieri, and Euan MacDonald (eds), *Global Administrative Law: The Casebook* (3rd edn., IRPA and IIJL, 2012).

plethora of dispersed global deciders through procedural provisions, intended to foster transparency, revisability, reason-giving, hearing.[3] In the project vein, that is tantamount to *taming massive substantive rule-making power through further (independent) rule-making.* The latter is held to grant and legitimise the legislative quality of the former.

Eventually, the reframing of a new dimension of 'global' legislation underpins the recurrent attempt at 'constitutionalising' the entire setting, one that reflects an ideal of ordering most times reminiscent of State-system's archetypes. It points to the construction of some 'global' reassuring borders: either by forging a hierarchical, Kelsenian structure of norm-delegations, or by enhancing universal values-principles, that should control rules' validity on a content-dependent basis (i.e. as a matter of 'material' coherence). A new *constitutional adventure*,[4] if any, should thereby recompose disparate changes, sources/authorities, rules, structures, under some common criteria. There is quite an oscillation over the import of naming such an endeavour in constitutional terms: a potential candidate is a weak form of constitutionalism,[5] which revolves around principles widely accepted, from due process to reasonableness, from hearing to reasons giving, from subsidiarity to proportionality and respect for human rights. Constitutionalisation is often hoped for as compensation for the fading of States' constitutional control over global intercourses.[6] But these or other principles in larger or thinner list tend to be invoked however also outside constitutional thinking,

---

3   For example Simon Chesterman, 'Globalisation Rules: Accountability, Power and the Prospects for Global Administrative Law', 14 *Global Governance* (2008) 39–52; Andrew D. Mitchell and John Farnik, 'Global Administrative Law: Can it Bring Global Governance to Account?', 37 *Federal Law Review* (2009) 237–261.

4   Cf. Ulrich K. Preuss, 'Disconnecting Constitutions from Statehood', Mattias Kumm, 'The Best of Times and the Worst of Times', and Neil Walker, 'Beyond the Holistic Constitution?' in Petra Dobner and Martin Loughlin (eds), *The Twilight of Constitutionalism* (Oxford University Press, 2010), chs 2, 11 and 16. Critical stances are taken by Martin Loughlin, 'What is Constitutionalisation?' and by Dieter Grimm, 'The Achievement of Constitutionalism and its Prospects in a Changed World', *ibid.*, chs 3 and 1. See also Dieter Grimm, 'The Constitution in the Process of Denationalizaton', 12 *Constellations* (2005) 447–63.

5   Constitutionalism as a shared set of values versus traditional 'document-based' constitutionalism; likewise the option between a 'big C' and a 'small c' constitutionalism. In a supranational setting, see Neil Walker, 'Big "C" or small "c"?' 12 *European Law Journal* (2006) 12–14; in the American bibliography, see Larry Alexander (ed.), *Constitutionalism: Philosophical Foundations* (Cambridge University Press, 1998), especially ch. 3 by Michael J. Perry, 'What Is "the Constitution"? (and other fundamental questions)'.

6   Anne Peters, 'Compensatory Constitutionalism: The Function and Potential of Fundamental International Norms and Structures', 19 *Leiden Journal of International Law* (2006) 579–610.

as necessary for the very *legality* of global *rule-making*.[7] The importance of *law* as a requisite-dependent notion is seen to both qualify and constrain entities as lawmakers – be they of private, public or hybrid nature.

At any rate, the quest for *legality* (and *'legislation'*) has to respond to important questions itself, starting from the existing state of the art: the absence of global government and power's organisation, the matter of the mediation between rule-giving and the political sources of public autonomy, the need for new criteria shaping the relation between constituencies and decision-making. In the absence of a central *Grundnorm*, on the forefront of the question about 'legislation' are decentralised entities-institutions developing their regulatory nature, whether the Security Council or the WTO, the Codex Alimentarius Commission or the Internet Corporation for Assigned Names and Numbers (ICANN), the Convention for the Law of the Sea and so forth. Although it should be said that they take care of the *community* interest on a *global* scale, paradoxically they would do so by pursuing their own separate and segmented rationalities. They are seen to forge a *global* stage, beyond the *inter-national* one, and they appear to be co-ordinative, 'universal' players, whose borders are not defined by territoriality but through thematic, issue-specific, that is, functional limits.

If one takes this perspective, the wider notion of 'global' law surfaces, one that re-conceives and enlarges the inter-States processes focused upon by more traditional international law.[8]

2 The recognition of legality

2.1. As a consequence, the legislating capacity developed in global governance, including a non-treaty law mode, is hardly recognised as included in some other pre-existing 'system'. Thus, questions do not arise as to its sheer *validity* (i.e., an intra-systemic matter), but more radically about its basic legality. From this angle, it should suggest a wider notion of legality that neither international law nor national law encompasses.

According to the answer that Benedict Kingsbury has proposed, the notion of *law* can be restated as one requiring a practised rule of recognition (concerning sources), plus further criteria of 'publicness' that have to be met. The rule of recognition admits a varied typology of very diverse source entities, states or not states (including those producing specialised rule-

---

7   Tellingly, Richard Stewart and Michelle Ratton Sanchez Badin, 'The World Trade Organisation and Global Administrative Law', *IILJ Working Paper* 2009/7, at 2, write that aside from 'a constitutionalist paradigm' nonetheless 'current conditions ... are compatible with and indeed call for development of a global administrative law'.
8   Nico Krisch and Benedict Kingsbury, 'Introduction: Global Governance and Global Administrative Law in the International Legal Order', 17 *European Journal of International Law* (2006) 1–13.

making, and of an administrative nature), provided that, however, they comply with the principles of publicness, which embody the general legality principle, rationality, proportionality, the Rule of law and respect for basic human rights.[9] The reasoning partakes both of a *principle*-based acknowledgment of law and of a *source*-based delimitation of it. As a matter of fact, and unsurprisingly, the view from global administrative law theory ends up however proffering this definition not only as an answer to the question about *legality*, but also as one drawing the border of a legal *order in itinere:* that is, shaped incrementally in so far as common criteria of recognition are progressively shared and practiced by judicial authorities and other relevant actors. Such a legality is thus seen since the start as more than a loose set of rules.[10] The dual, descriptive and normative, stances of the discourse, are inherent in a state of affairs that is ever evolving.

Addressing a similar concern, Jan Klabbers has enriched the picture of law, himself selecting the conditions of *legality* in order to make sense of the complexities and thickness that the notion has reached in the extra-state transformations.

Thus, even if, as we can agree upon, a generalised conviction *(i)* that some norm is law (a socio-legal criterion) is considered in itself a decisive threshold of legality,[11] effectiveness must be integrated with *(ii)* the authentication *via procedural* requirements enunciated by Lon Fuller:[12] a guarantee of legality in its very *nature*, one that does not depend on sheer attitudes and contingent behaviour of the people. Third, being law different from morality, it is relevant *(iii)* that it is posited by a legitimate *authority*. Here the Hartian–Razian conundrum resurfaces, that is, the question of *sources* is raised: but for an authority's rule-making recognition, evidence of an even indirect *consent* is recommended, one that can be somehow traced back to those affected, the interested people, registered in some participatory mode, either through States themselves or otherwise outside their representative channels.

Each of these three paths has been claimed elsewhere as separately self-sufficient, epistemically ultimate and mutually exclusive. Klabbers does not concede much to such a self-understanding of the respective underlying legal theories. As I would grasp the argument, they can function separately only as one ground to cast a *presumption* of legality on issued norms. Thus,

---

9   Benedict Kingsbury, 'The Concept of "Law" in Global Administrative Law', 20 *European Journal of International Law* (2009) 23–57, esp. at 31 ff. Moreover, 'what it means to be a "public" entity would routinely be evaluated by reference to the relevant entity's legal and political arrangements, which may derive from national law, inter-state agreement, self-constitution, or delegation by other entities.' *Ibid.*, at 56.
10 See H. L. A Hart, *The Concept of Law* (2nd edn, Oxford University Press, 1994) at 233.
11 *Contra* Roger Cotterell, 'Transnational Community and the Concept of Law', 21 *Ratio Juris* (2008) 1–18 (against legality being reduced to social belief).
12 Lon Fuller, *The Morality of Law* (revised edn, Yale University Press, 1969), at 33–8.

a Security Council resolution should be presumed to be binding; any agreement between states, whether given the name 'treaty', 'convention' or anything else, should be presumed to be binding between them; standards adopted by the ISO should be presumed to be law; decisions of the G7 or G8 are presumed to create law; the *lex mercatoria* is presumed to be law; even resolutions of the General Assembly are presumed to be law.[13]

That points to inverting the burden of proof: what Klabbers calls *presumptive legality* means to me that different parameters of legality work as provisional validation, but are thereafter expected to actually concur or converge. In fact, when such an eclectic assessment of legality is to be made, the outcome would depend on the *resistance* of a *presumption* of legality *vis-à-vis* a potential rebuttal, due to the good reasons that countervailing approaches[14] can provide.

It must be noted that diverse theoretical efforts on the identification of legality – through paths transcending States' legal order – unsurprisingly resolve (or conflate) two questions into one: the requirements of *legality* are implicitly at the same time requirements of *validity* of a normative utterance. In truth, as to its nature, legality can be identified through necessarily typological, and relatively abstract criteria: legality may be made to depend on (whatever) social sources claiming legitimate authority, or on requisites of justice, and the like. But validity, which cannot be predicated of a system in its entirety, *presupposes the borders of one order* and refers to a 'candidate' norm, in relation to it. The more the specific contents of a rule of recognition are determined ('what the Queen enacts is law', 'what the Treatise decides is law'), the more such a definition holds – not as a parameter of legality, of whatever norm in whichever realm, but as a parameter of validity (that is, *within* a certain order).

Now, as we have seen, the theoretical insights mentioned in the foregoing, while widening the definition of legality (opening the door to formal and informal, public and private, State and non-State norms) end up proposing their features also as requisites of *validity:* as the argument goes, ISO standards can be presumed of legal nature and due to the same requirements, they are considered as *valid* law within an international/global (administrative) *legal order*. This means that the question of some new all-encompassing unitary rule of recognition is being addressed as well, for a realm still far from being 'ordered' like a system.

---

13 Jan Klabbers, 'Law-making and Constitutionalism', in Jan Klabbers, Anne Peters and Geir Ulfstein, *The Constitutionalisation of International Law* (Oxford University Press, 2009) ch. 3, at 115–16.
14 Otherwise we would need autonomous theory of the grounds of rebuttals. However, Klabbers considers contents, context, origins, procedures and topics (from the recognisability of the issuing authority to its connection to the addressees, to respect for procedural Fullerian requisites to the nature of contents etc.). *Ibid.,* at 116–21. In my opinion, the list of exemplifications is relatively open.

Invariably, this 'new' international/global legal order, in its either constitutional or publicness-focused forms, can only be described as itself *in progress*: resulting mainly from the dual descriptive-interpretive efforts of theorists, legal experts, judges and variable further actors. As a consequence, the vocabulary of presumption has to be extended, as I think, not only as regards *normative utterances*, to be presumed law, but also to a *legal order*,[15] thus, itself *presumptive*.

2.2. Much in the endeavour enlarging the requisites of legality beyond those recognisable within the State-based legal theory, includes an implicit relaxing of the cultural/logical, presupposition, according to which making sense of law is tantamount to making sense of it as a 'system'. And most attempts to 'constitutionalise' the global law try and compensate for the uninvited system's obsolescence.

Yet, questions such as those concerning transnational rule of law and justice, the plurality of regulatory regimes, the segmentation of international law, the emergence of non-State rulemakers on a massive scale, interdependence among legal orders could not be[16] reflected upon in the lessons of the most influential legal theorists of the last century, such as Kelsen or Hart. Whether reducing the law to the State or *vice versa*, the concept of law was essentially connected with the 'hardware' notion of 'a system'.[17]

The connection between legislation and the *hard structure*[18] of a 'system' showed its significance and after all, in both Kelsenian and Hartian representations, it marks at least the passage from primitive to mature law. It allows for identity and stability, and the unending effort of border drawing.

What characterises global legislation is thus the interruption of the virtuous circle between *legality* and *validity*, until the frame of something like a global legal *order* is clearly defined and practiced. Somehow, the former (legality) gets to an autonomous life, despite the latter (system/validity) is wanting. The legal *software*–global legislation flourishes on the lack of its *hardware*, the system, a structured machine that once upon a time was intended to serve and made to work.

---

15   For global law as a specific layer-incremental legal order, see my 'The Rule of Law in Global Governance: Its Normative Construction, Function and Import', *Straus Institute for the Advanced Study of Law & Justice Working Paper* 2010/5.

16   Similarly William Twining, 'Schauer on Hart', 119 *Harvard Law Review Forum* (2006) 122–30.

17   'The compulsory nature of the rules in force, whatever their remote origin may be, appears henceforth as the effect of th[at] centralizing will ... a true and proper subject ... the State', granting for itself 'exclusiveness rendered necessary in order to assure the unity of the system'. Giorgio del Vecchio, 'On the Statuality of Law', 19 *Journal of Comparative Legislation & International Law* (1937) 1–20, at 8 and 9.

18   For this, I am drawing on my 'Global Threads: The Rule of Law and the Balance of Legal Software', in Filippo Fontanelli, Giuseppe Martinico and Paolo Carrozza (eds), *Shaping the Rule of Law through Dialogue* (Europa Law Publisher, 2009) 413–30.

Such a legal *software*, which thrives on an elusive design, is increasing, differentiating and perfecting itself around the kernel of many distinctive rationalities; as repeatedly noted, it flourishes in multi-centred spaces, and enables to perform, in diverse 'windows', highly complex regulations, assessments and dispute resolutions, from trade to environment, from the law of the sea to internet domains, from labour to telecommunications, energy, human rights, security.

In coping with these coupled phenomena, that is, system fading and regulatory proliferation, we are thus witnessing *software* self-expansion at the expense of some final *hardware* capability. We cannot proceed from the available (state) system structure (the *hardware*) to the permissible law and rules (the *software*) as it was in nineteenth and twentieth century legal positivism. We run after the spreading of norms-generation instead, come to terms with it, assess their legality and then presuppose some suited and so far 'presumptive' frame.

In such a state of affairs, through diverse avenues (the idea of 'publicness',[19] the ideal of the 'rule of law',[20] the architecture of common 'principles'[21]) legality is re-launched because of its basically constitutive function,[22] as I will restate later on, vis-à-vis a state of nature: i.e. a state of affairs merely devoid of law and thus, in a Kantian vein, of the very transcendental possibility of justice.[23]

Whereas the 'system' might be out of sight, nonetheless the implicit expectation is that the *rule of law* might increase its relevance and role, up to becoming the closest thing to a post-'Babel' legal understanding.[24]

---

19 Benedict Kingsbury, 'International Law as Inter-Public Law' in *NOMOS XLIX: Moral Universalism and Pluralism* (Henry R. Richardson and Melissa S. Williams, eds, New York University Press, 2009) 167–204.

20 This is the path in my 'The Rule of Law as an Institutional Ideal', in Leonardo Morlino and Gianluigi Palombella (eds), *Rule of Law and Democracy: Internal and External Issues* (Brill, 2010), ch. 1.

21 For example Armin von Bogdandy, 'General Principles of International Public Authority: Sketching a Research Field', 9 *German Law Journal* (2008) 1909–1938.

22 For a constitutive function of law and inherent public nature, at length in my 'The (re)Constitution of the Public in a Global Arena', in Claudio Michelon and Neil Walker (eds), *After Public Law?* (Oxford University Press, 2013), ch. 14. Significantly, though in a different 'constitutional' sense, Klabbers writes: 'if the label "constitutional" is to have any meaning beyond the rhetorical, it stands for placing a premium on law, over power, but also over other normative orders'. Klabbers, 'Law-making and Constitutionalism', *supra* note 13, at 124.

23 For Kant, the state of nature being devoid of justice, law must be resorted to conceptually in order to avoid that condition in which the abuse of personal liberty and possession is *unobjectionable*. Immanuel Kant, 'Metaphysical First Principles of the Doctrine of Right', in *The Metaphysics of Morals* (Mary Gregor trans., Cambridge University Press, 1996 [1797]) 33, 42, at 86.

24 The metaphor was recalled both in Rosalyn Higgins, 'A Babel of Judicial Voices? Ruminations from the Bench', 55 *International & Comparative Law Quarterly* (2006) 791–804 and in Sabino Cassese, *I Tribunali di Babele* (Donzelli, 2009).

3 Introducing the further issues of legislation

Despite the appealing implication of a common code or shared pre-understanding of law, new questions are ahead, which inhere in the nature of such a 'legislation', its features and its discontents. The background question is how can the couple law and legislation respond to the uneasiness generated by its redefinition in the 'new' environment.

Through plenty of global administrative (and 'self-observing') regimes,[25] a kind of managerialism[26] surfaces, whose efficiency-driven imperatives miss a vital root-connection with political realities in ordinary social life and with some coherent vision of the well-being of any situated 'community'.[27] Kingsbury wrote that the 'real question might be whether it is possible to identify a determinate public at all',[28] and even if the (global) law claims 'in the name of the whole society', here it is unpredictable 'how far the whole society extends'.[29]

A few aspects/discontents under stress here are not among those that we reframe only by 'readjusting' our criteria of legality: not detracting from the above efforts around legality's notion, some matters cannot be managed through definitional revisions, as the following suggests: 'if international law does not fit the criteria of the concept of law used at the domestic level, it may not (only) be a problem for the legality of international law, but (also) for those criteria themselves and hence for a given legal theory'.[30] The structure of the restated legality – beyond States and inter-States law – detaches from the rationale and scope of legislation as we know it.

4 Legislating goods

A peculiar trait throughout governance-style 'legislation' concerns the ready-made appearance of fixed goals (whether entrusted to global regimes, regional authorities, supranational organisations) dictated as objectives to

---

25 See also Andreas Fischer-Lescano and Gunther Teubner, 'Regime Collision: The Vain Search for Legal Unity in the Fragmentation of Global Law', 25 *Michigan Journal of International Law* (2004) 999–1046; and Andreas Paulus, 'Commentary', *ibid.*, 1047–58.

26 On *managerialism* (and instrumentalism) Martti Koskenniemi focuses in his book, *The Politics of International Law* (Hart, 2011), esp. chs 13 and 14.

27 Theorisations of the global law respond somehow by recommending accountability devices, between interested parties and decision-makers.

28 Benedict Kingsbury and Megan Donaldson, 'From Bilateralism to Publicness in International Law', in Ulrich Fastenrath, Rudolf Geiger, Daniel-Erasmus Khan, Andreas Paulus, Sabine von Schorlemer and Christoph Vedder (eds), *From Bilateralism to Community Interest: Essays in Honour of Bruno Simma* (Oxford University Press, 2011) ch. 7, at 85.

29 *Ibid.*, referring to the ban on shrimps, affecting India without previous communication, and to all WTO decisions intruding into an unpredictable number of peoples, groups and interests.

30 Samantha Besson and John Tasioulas, 'Introduction', in Samantha Besson and John Tasioulas (eds), *The Philosophy of International Law* (Oxford University Press, 2011) at 8.

'lower' level orders and politically elected governments. This holds true for World Bank's prescriptions concerning rule of law requisites as well as for EU conditionality strategies to access/establish partnership of candidate countries, and extends to fiscal/economic measures imposed by 'external' orders: dramatically reducing self-determination in the allocation of social priorities in a country. Along these lines, the distinctive feature of legislation here is not best represented by the much-celebrated characters of 'soft law', but by looking at its self-authorised paternalism of the 'good goals', one that characterises much of this 'legislative governance' style: namely, norm-making is exposed into end-setting, standards and benchmarks. Accordingly, *indicators*[31] surface at the core of normative enterprise.

As known, starting from the European experience, this governance develops by defining *goods*, rather than envisioning a politically elaborated (all-encompassing) notion of the *good*. In the European scene, that stems mainly from the Commission's work furthering EU interventionism and effectiveness, given the difficulties of political cohesion: thus mirroring precisely what is often complained about, i.e. the permanent shift from *politics* to *policies*. Despite its unparalleled peculiarities, the EU can still represent an advanced template of an increasingly global regulatory style: politics is replaced by creating 'levels of criticism', by problem-solving pragmatism, involving those 'interested' (or pre-chosen as such), experts, fragments of peripheral public administrations, etc. When what is 'an informed consumer choice' is 'technically' defined as well as, say, a healthier style of life, it becomes a rather incontrovertible 'end'. The selection of the *means* is left free for institutional actors required to take provisions pursuing established policies.[32]

It has been aptly said that this is a European *Eudaimonia*, and one that relies on a Durkheimian *organic*, not mechanical, solidarity:[33] i.e. the model of equilibrium of *inter*dependence, the division of labour among mutually functional parts.[34] If we take this *Eudaimonia* seriously, it is then *legislation by goals* that surfaces as its norms-building arm.

It is hard to discover however which sovereign dictates or underpins this administrative drive. From the perspective of institutional subsequent actors, such as national legal orders, governments and addressees, this generates a chain of double-edged consequences: empowerment, towards further rule-giving, as well as limitation and disempowerment *vis-à-vis* frameworks/goals

---

31 Lastly, Kevin E. Davis, Benedict Kingsbury and Sally Engle Merry, 'Indicators as a Technology of Global Governance', 46 *Law & Society Review* (2012) 71–104.
32 It generates self-corrective standards internalising criticisms through recurrent assessments and manages risk-related anxiety: a claim founded 'partly on the authority of expertise' and the limits of scientific knowledge: Damian Chalmers, 'Gauging the Cumbersomeness of EU Law', *LSE 'Europe in Question' Discussion Paper* 2/2009, at 31.
33 *Ibid.*, at 18 ff.
34 Chalmers stresses rightly this point as to EU governance. *Ibid.*, at 19.

largely presupposed. Policymaking *without politics*[35] as well as 'governance without government' are flags of the new legislation.

Despite the many narratives evoking mutual learning, the participatory, revisable nature of this experimental new world,[36] I am inclined to agree that even 'participation within the governance-paradigm is no sufficient guarantee against the tyranny of goals'.[37] The emphasis upon construction of consensus on 'substantive values and aims' often recognises the centrality of the point, but significantly 'it is assumed that if the right information is provided and if the right context is created for ongoing discussion, consensus on goals and values may gradually emerge'.[38] Likewise proportionality, subsidiarity, transparency and accountability are, so to speak, frame-dependent: they work properly only within a predefined spectrum of granted ends, one that in the global setting is ultimately up to and rests on the discrete field-related regimes. The latter, again, are hopefully committed to reasonableness, investigation, discussion, of course within – in coherence with – their self-referential ambit 'devoted to a specific goal or aim'.[39]

If one may add a further presumption, beyond those regarding the *legality* of normative utterances, and as I suggested, the existence of a further legal *order*, one can turn to goals: to be themselves presumed by those asked to take them for granted.

5 Law, administration and legitimacy

5.1. The core 'good goals' of United Nations Convention on the Law of the Sea (UNCLOS), the European Convention on Human Rights (ECHR), WTO, the UN Security Council and so forth are far from being objectionable and hardly open to contestation; apparently these and other issuing authorities remain politically deracinated from ordinary life-worlds and devoid of location.

Somehow global legislation thrives on blurring the line that States, in the experience of the nineteenth and twentieth centuries,[40] had drawn between (political) *legislation* and (technical-discretionary) *administration*. First, while administration within the State kept a means-related, implementing function,

---

35 I am not endorsing some apolitical nature of policy choices, but the elusiveness of such choices from the perspective of the political communities.
36 Charles F. Sabel and Jonathan Zeitlin, 'Learning from Difference: The New Architecture of Experimentalist Governance in the EU', 14 *European Law Journal* (2008) 271–327.
37 Pauline Westerman, 'Governing by Goals: Governance as a Legal Style', 1 *Legisprudence* (2007) 51–72, at 68.
38 *Ibid.*, at 60.
39 '[H]ealth care organizations might still struggle between competing interests ... but they are not fighting over the priority of hospitals versus the standing army or of a clean environment versus the national symphonic orchestra'. *Ibid.*, at 62.
40 Think of the development of the 'administrative state' and works such as Otto Mayer, *Deutsches Verwaltungsrecht* (2 Bd, 1895) (Kessinger Legacy Reprints, 2010).

in the globalised scenario instead it is political legislation (eminently State-based) that must yield to the requests of global administration, now raised to independent, self-standing level. Second, global jurisgenerative authorities can hardly speak for a compact political community, but ironically expose their *raison d'etre* as unencumbered with sheer particularism or localisms; they can resort to principles of impartial administration that displace the 'political question' from the global management of power.

Through the prospect of constitutionalisation and of common general principles,[41] some may attempt at recasting the equilibrium between administration and politics; however, global legislation works with more success in removing decision-making from the reviled quicksand of the political arenas.[42]

5.2. Here comes the delicate matter of legitimacy, and subsequently the role of 'legality' in furthering its prospect.

The increasing desire for a more stable ethical floor on which the action of international organisations should rest points to better support the *acceptability* of power exercise, be it of public or private origin.[43] Yet, the matter of legitimacy inevitably resurfaces through new peculiarities.

We need to recall our received views about legitimacy though. They have been modelled in conjunction to law, on a State perspective, and in *two* moves: the first is centred upon the very form of legality; the second on substantive consensus. The first is based on the inherent service of *formal* rationality that law provides in vesting the exercise of power (as taught by the analyses of Max Weber). The second in turn conveys the importance of *material* soundness of legislation, the pursuit of shared substantive values.

According to Weber, 'material' scrutiny and the quest for substantive consensus could have only weakened the legitimating strength of legal

---

41   Carol Harlow, 'Global Administrative Law: The Quest for Principles and Values', 17 *European Journal of International Law* (2006) 187–214.

42   That conviction underpins Majone's 'regulatory Europe'. Cf. Giandomenico Majone, 'Nonmajoritarian Institutions and the Limits of Democratic Governance: A Political Transaction-Cost Approach', 157 *Journal of Institutional & Theoretical Economics* (2001) 57–78. See also Gary Miller, 'Above Politics: Credible Commitment and Efficiency in the Design of Public Agencies', 10 *Journal of Public Administration Research & Theory* (2000) 289–328. Political criticism of Kingsbury's requirements of publicness, dubbed 'privatization of the 'public', Ming–Sung Kuo, 'Taming Governance with Legality? Critical Reflections upon Global Administrative Law as Small-c Global Constitutionalism', 44 *NYU Journal of International Law & Politics* (2011) 55–102. In truth, even legal institutions possibly translate politics into the 'politics of procedure, a struggle for the power to define, for jurisdiction: the question is not so much whether a weighing of interests has to take place, but rather which authority in the final analysis is empowered to make the weighing'. Martti Koskenniemi, 'The Effects of Rights on Political Culture' in Philip Alston (ed.), *The European Union and Human Rights* (Oxford University Press, 1999) ch. 3, at 114.

43   Peter Muchlinski, 'International Business Regulation: An Ethical Discourse in the Making?' in Tom Campbell and Seumas Miller (eds), *Human Rights and the Moral Responsibilities of Corporate and Public Sector Organisations* (Kluwer, 2004) ch. 5, at 99.

formality,[44] undermining the grounds achieved by the modern state, dispersing its unity under law and making its order prey to values' polytheism.[45]

Certainly legality/rationality of power in the modern State had become the ultimate reason why it was obeyed. However, such a reason for obedience was increasingly superseded in subsequent times: the State of the twentieth century needed to nurture the belief of its legitimacy also by responding to material/normative demands.

Now, it is known that legitimacy, as in the Weberian narrative, has nothing to do with truth: it works regardless of whether the spread of belief can be founded on something being 'true'. Likewise it turns to be right that ultimately, as Koskenniemi noticed, 'legitimacy is not about normative substance. Its point is to avoid such substance but nonetheless to uphold a *semblance* of substance'.[46] And yes, this objective is tantamount to accepting 'Hobbes but sound like Grotius': this being the function of legitimacy, in such a context, that is, 'to ensure a warm feeling in the audience'.[47] As I shall submit, this note bears on the legitimacy problem of 'global legislation' as well.

5.3. If something more ought to be included in the same picture, it is the costs of the global *Eudaimonia*, be it either a sheer production of the 'semblance of substance', or the paternalism of the good. Can legitimacy be generated by global 'juridification', in the top-down mode, using the legal form[48] as an *instrument for producing* social ordering?

In truth, one can reflect upon this by way of similitude. It reminds us the 'dilemmatic structure' that Habermas attributed to legalised interventionist policies of last century: 'juridification' by the Welfare State, as he wrote, introduced into previously free domains of social life *both* pervasive regulation *and* new opportunities (rights and other entitlements). Nonetheless, its irruption into life spheres overwrote the pre-existing contents of social interactions.[49] Policies obeying functional imperatives (of economic or administrative nature) and implementing regulatory measures, jeopardised

---

44 With Max Weber 'formal rationality' maintains an absolute indifference 'towards all substantive postulates'. Max Weber, *Economy and Society* (Günther Roth and Claus Wittich, eds, University of California Press, 1978) vol. I, at 108. The *material* rationality of law instead refers to ethical aims rather than legal principles. Cf. *ibid.*, vol. II, at 656 ff.
45 For Weber it is a question 'not only of alternatives between values but of an irreconcilable death-struggle, like that between "God" and the "Devil" '. Max Weber, 'The Meaning of "Ethical Neutrality" in Sociology and Economics', in Max Weber, *On the Methodology of the Social Sciences* (Edward A. Shils and Henry A. Finch, trans. and eds, Free Press, 1949) at 17.
46 Koskenniemi, *The Politics of International Law, supra* note 26 at 322.
47 *Ibid.*, at 322 and 323.
48 I reconstructed the *non-instrumental* side of law as a predicate of the *rule of law*, in my 'The Rule of Law as an Institutional Ideal', *supra* note 20.
49 Jürgen Habermas, 'Law as Medium and Law as Institution', in Günther Teubner (ed.), *Dilemmas of Law in the Welfare State* (Walter de Gruyter, 1986), at 209–11. As Habermas noted, law deeply enters the personal and social sphere once left outside of legal control, in order to accompany an assisted individual life from birth to death. *Ibid.*, at 203–20.

the realms of 'life-world', by re-interpreting their internal relations through the lens of external rationalities and imposing one-sided ideas of the good. But only the 'life-world', where basic social links are woven, is the 'reservoir' and source of meaning for human individuals.[50]

For Habermas, the 'point' was

> to protect areas of life that are functionally dependent on social integration through values, norms and consensus formation: and to protect them from falling prey to the system imperatives of economic and administrative subsystems that grow with dynamics of their own. And finally to defend them from becoming converted, through the steering medium of the law, to a principle of socialization which is for them dysfunctional.[51]

In other words, the risk of 'colonisation': the dilemma whether an external legal imperative offers in case a better 'guarantee' or a 'withdrawal' of freedom, can be responded only 'from the viewpoint of the life-world'.[52]

Now, *mutatis mutandis*, in the scope of equally top-down global legislation, and its pursuit of the good(s), the deep question of legitimacy remains attached to the shortcomings of a similarly dilemmatic structure.

6 The spectrum of legislation

However, legality and legislation are affected by a further fundamental change. Legislation – in the State context – revolved around modern law felt as all-encompassing device, coping with complexity and covering the *full circle* of human activities. Global legislation downplays this venerable profile, it increasingly weakens the *holistic character of law* that represented the public interest under political control.

Turning to the WTO 'regime' can explain such a point: no serious questions undermine its authority, it is universally recognised the capacity to 'speak in the name of the whole society' of its members at least, and in the interests that they have subscribed to. State legislation has occasionally – depending on places and times – worked with even less authoritativeness. Nonetheless, something is missing. It is ambiguous, as noted, which or whose public should be relevant, given the chain of side effects affecting people so far from the core deciders. Even leaving this aside, we would not call the WTO, nor would we name the Security Council, the 'global legislator', despite their global reach and effectiveness.

---

50 *Ibid.*, at 206. All the more so in the domain of 'autonomous' relations (that is, the realms of school law, social security, cultural reproduction, fields of moral sensitivity that extend to legal areas, such as criminal or constitutional law).
51 *Ibid.*, at 220.
52 *Ibid.*, at 214.

Contrariwise, we entrust instead the State in its own right, and within its domain, as the legislator. The contrast does not rise from the chronic democracy deficit of supranational organisations. At stake is not the albeit dramatic lack of political reflexivity in legislation outside the State, the absence of one demos and the like. At stake, rather than a matter of democracy, is the even earlier question of the *public* nature of law:[53] the pre-understanding that 'law', as far as we trust it, deals with the *totality* of concerns related to what is of 'public interest'.

Legislation should – *à la* Rousseau – concern the generality of the people (the *subjective side*).[54] This requirement is not a necessary condition for each legislative acts or rules.[55] The quality of generality/universality is referred to as a property of a *sum* of laws[56] as well as its *orientation* to the common, general interest.

Our received understanding of legislation includes an inherent connection to this latter *objective side* – i.e. the comprehensive fate and ends of the community.[57] We are used to thinking that however disparate and divergent the goals, all are to be (politically) organised or resolved *along the diachronic axis of a full-blown development* of *legislative* decision-making; and the latter in its entirety remains an interpretation of the *whole* life of the public, its constituencies and addressees.

Of course, the WTO can instead decide about trade in its own 'segmented' mode: matters of, say, security, are beyond its power and purview, and under some other's responsibility. Accordingly, we can hardly deny that the decoupling of State/legislation has brought us before a new figure of legislative power, let us call it legislation 'with limited responsibility'.

7 Responsibility versus accountability

That shift is substantive, and as far as I see, it cannot be compensated by improving requisites of accountability.[58] There is in truth a conceptual

---

53 More at length in my 'The (re-)Constitution of the Public in a Global Arena', *supra* note 22.
54 Benedict Kingsbury forfeited the requirement of generality: 'Generality is not a necessary requirement for a general concept of law applicable to all law as such, and as indicated above there are good reasons why it is not necessarily part of the particular jurisprudence of the law of global administration'. Kingsbury, 'The Concept of "Law"', *supra* note 9, at 52.
55 Otherwise it would exclude not only most of minute administrative rule-making, but also a certain amount of statute-law.
56 The same in Immanuel Kant, 'Metaphysical First Principles of the Doctrine of Right', *supra* note 23, § 42 ff., at 86 ff.
57 And we shall see, the ultimate responsibility for it.
58 Ruth W. Grant and Robert O. Keohane, 'Accountability and Abuses of Power in World Politics', 99 *American Political Science Review* (2005) 29–43; Erika de Wet, 'Holding International Institutions Accountable: The Complementary Role of Non-Judicial Oversight Mechanisms and Judicial Review', in Armin von Bogdandy *et al.* (eds), *The Exercise of Public Authority by International Institutions* (Springer, 2010) 855–82.

watershed between accountability and responsibility that is worth of a brief clarification. Put concisely, 'responsibility' (evoked, for example, with a 'responsible person') projects a sensible and self-involving consideration of as many relevant factors (be they facts, interests, intentions, consequences) and personal expectations, as possible. It exceeds the view of a required task (which is self-limiting and leaves aside any concern beyond the task itself). As Hans Jonas once aptly defined it, responsibility, like the one we associate with the figure of a statesman, bears a significant relation with the notions of *totality, continuity* and *future:* because the responsible person (here, bearing in mind the State) cares for the 'total being' of its object, with no possible interruption in time, and 'beyond its immediate present'.[59]

Although responsibility is mainly related to virtue and ethics, the notion sheds light on our understanding of the State as a 'general ends' entity. Within a State's borders, on the one hand, the law protects the domain of a polity's social practices; on the other, it is so because the State is not just any 'public' entity whatsoever, but the fullest image/archetype of the existent 'public' and – what is highly defining its very nature – the only public entity entitled to all encompassing reach; the one that can by definition embody the entirety of potential ends:[60] what requires the State to be conceived of as the ultimate shelter for any sort of common objectives 'deserving' care, protection, regulation, control. Thus, law as (State) legislation factually entails as well the *responsibility* to cover the full circle of *publicness* and public problems. The background belief of those subject to law-making presupposes some coherence as to its 'general' result and importantly an implicit responsibility for the 'whole'. This last presupposition is the simple objective *raison d'etre* of the State, thereby affecting our idea of law and legislation.

The perceived fading of the ultimate connection between law and the burden of the *whole* in the extra-state environment is inevitable. Regardless of the difficulty to circumscribe its precise borders, the notion of 'being responsible' points, unlike accountability, to the overall state of affairs, and the problematic equilibrium among separate rationalities. Such a notion is premised on a general interpretation of ideas, needs, values, and priorities, dictated by a situated perception, encumbered with a kind of meta-concern (so to speak) that is not institutionally required through the perspective of holding 'accountable' organs, entities, powers acting within discrete fields and under circumscribed, predefined imperatives.

In principle, accountability can work effectively as much as the imperatives to be accountable for are well indicated, limited and feasible. However 'accountable', that is, transparent and revisable, communicative

---

59 Hans Jonas, *The Imperative of Responsibility* (University of Chicago Press, 1984), at 98–105.
60 However, the misunderstanding should be avoided that for the State to embrace 'general ends' means that 'law be general': the concepts are possibly linkable, but different.

and consented on, WTO rule-making can become,[61] this shall be working with reference to the provided tasks, already embedded in the *raison d'etre* of a trade regime.[62] The separate allocation of functional control over thematic issues is a basic and valued strategy of coping with complexity: a *divide et impera* that gives us some chance to disentangle necessarily interconnected matters. And it would be rather fancy, if not illusory, to hold each in the array of global norms producers, accountable for indeterminate and further ideals, from human rights[63] to environmental protection, security and the like.

On the contrary, if we think back to legislation in the State-based self-understanding, the pregnant point that qualifies it, had – and still has – much to do with such a irreducible mutuality between the *subjective* (generality) and the *objective* (the whole of potential aspects deserving care) side, between the capacity to speak *in the name of the public*, and the capacity to represent some interpretation – *in their entirety* – of the concerns at stake in the comprehensive well-being of a community. The two traits are hardly met in the *global* legislation 'circumstances': respectively, because of the elusive and unseizable nature of its '*public*' and because of its field-related pursuit of *special goods*. The combined consequences make the *universality* of legislation strikingly absent despite the global capacity of the 'legislator': a matter that has further aspects as well.

8 'Globality'[64] versus 'universality' (and the relation among orders)

The emergence of a wider legality, distinctively 'global', adds to the already rich plurality of levels of law, such as national, regional, international, transnational and private ordering.

Peculiarities, limits, discontents, in the appearance of a specifically 'global' legislation not necessarily detract from the worthiness of pursuing its 'legality'. At the same time though, they should prompt a further reflection – to be only hinted at in this concluding section – over the *relation among legalities* that interact on the globe. As the topic can be concisely outlined, the reason why the relationships between different legal orders, regimes and,

---

61 Richard Stewart and Mary Ratton Sanchez Badin, 'The World Trade Organisation and Global Administrative Law, *IILJ Working Paper*, 2009/7, and also Ngaire Woods, 'Holding Intergovernmental Institutions to Account', 17 *Journal of Ethics & International Affairs* (2003) 69–80.
62 To take into account other factors, reducing the un-conditionality of precepts, shall not be mistaken for the pursuit of different or external-goals. Some analyses are in Stephan Griller (ed.), *International Economic Governance and Non-Economic Concerns* (Springer, 2003).
63 The metaphysical elevation of market autonomy as a human right, through the lens of the new economic liberties of free trade, is sometimes endorsed.
64 I use the term drawing simply on 'a state or condition of worldwide relevance or impact'.

generally, 'legalities', should themselves be arbitrated by the guarantee of legal means, lies in the fact that on the one hand, *global legislation* is just one among the legalities competing on the globe; and on the other that, as I shall submit below, 'globality' and 'universality' do not match.

Unlike in the domestic setting, the 'global' law does only work through impinging upon other legalities, otherwise persisting, and requires mostly States' cooperation. Its goal-orientated pretensions ironically must rely on *polities' independent existence*[65] but penetrate them. When global law works as transmission belt of efficiency imperatives (through benchmarking, debt control, rules for 'undistorted competition' and the like) it often alters domestic equilibrium, replaces rights interpretations and overwrites 'internal' meanings within the polities it regulates. Nonetheless, it remains incommensurably distant from their social and political allegiance.[66]

The notion *supra* reminded, i.e. *presumptive* normativity, might actually be the case here: the vantage point of *global* regimes, general coordination's entities, beyond localism and national self-interest, claims just a *presumptive*, or *prima facie* authority: one that cannot pretend *unconditional* primacy. For something being 'global' is just a matter of fact, related to its scope and reach. Contrariwise, its *universalisability (-universality)* can only result from a value judgement, and should depend upon satisfaction of *normative* conditions.[67]

The present experience in the relations among supranational, regional, national orders and Courts, reveals the resilience of legal notions and argumentative tools that work to the effect of attenuating the unobjectionable power of 'global' legislation (Not necessarily to the effect of weakening other substantive achievements, say, of common international law). Arguments of subsidiarity, proportionality, margin of appreciation, equivalent protection, scope of manoeuvre, rule of law (and more) have been widely allowed and resorted to.[68] Such arguments are not necessarily

---

65 In the mode once described as holding (even) for the EU, that is, a suprastate unity for which it was true that 'it does not do, it does cause others to do'. Sabino Cassese, 'Democrazia e Unione Europea', *Giornale di storia costituzionale* (2002) no. 3, 9–16, at 11.

66 In some instances a similar trend is seen to reflect the fading (or 'the liberal undermining') of 'republican legitimacy'. Fritz Scharpf, 'Legitimacy in the Multi-level European Polity', in Petra Dobner and Martin Loughlin (eds), *The Twilight of Constitutionalism?* (Oxford University Press, 2010), ch. 5, at 111.

67 As I would take it, Jan Klabber's suggestion about 'presumptive legality' can be located at the intersection between *globality* and *universality*, it expresses the tension (rather than the coincidence) between the two.

68 In truth, on the one hand, States or regional authorities resorting to them are often suspected of instrumental strategy, serving protectionist objectives (e.g. resisting world trade regulations), or of avoiding some more 'internationalist' deference by the pretext of internal democracy (e.g. making reservations to human rights regimes, ignoring supranational Courts' decisions). On the other hand, the duplicity of the matter is apparent, and the difference has a *normative* quality.

'miserable comforters', at least within the limits of what the service of law offers in favor of non-unilateral, non-arbitrary legal scrutiny. Their space originates because of the space that separates/distinguishes the 'global' and the 'universal'. Appealing to legality and confronting juridical arguments ought to work in keeping that gap visible.[69] *Legality* with its albeit procedural and argumentative tools, includes the chance of normative, substantive confrontation, even in the global stage, thereby justifying the Kantian idea that it can bring about the 'possibility of justice', out of a sheer state of nature.[70]

In explaining the legitimacy of the modern State, Weber himself undervalued a further import that his recognition of *formal/rational* law embodied. Law does not *only* entail the possibility of 'legal' domination:[71] it allows – along with governing means – for an inherent invocation of practical reason, the reverse, 'moral' face of the instrumental, formal law.

Such a *duality* of law is still of value.[72] If a confrontational stage can be established where the normative conditions of *universalisability* can be discussed and made to matter (as they should), that shall depend firstly on our ideal about the rule of law, and the recognition of that dual potential.

A picture of legislation needs to consider the pluralism of legalities on the globe, without ignoring either questions of 'weight', difference in social embeddedness, political legitimacy or substantive justice, and providing a legally generated guarantee of voice and standing. As in the Kantian peroration of the 'imperative of public law' (or the reason for abiding by the law), even in the extra-State environment the point is overcoming a state (of nature) where abuse and domination of one-sided ideas *cannot* be discussed or objected against. The problem of the relations among legalities and the function of the *rule of law* in this very conjunction are an inevitable consequence of the new frontiers of legislation(s).

---

69 And to make it possible for parties involved to advance normative arguments, basing either in international law achievements or in constitutionalism, and so forth.
70 See *supra* note 22.
71 Habermas wrote that, regarding the formal rationality of law in the western states as source of (legitimacy and) 'legal' domination, Weber sidelined the inherent potential of the 'positivity' of law, its moral – albeit thin – service of non-arbitrariness. Jürgen Habermas, *Law and Morality: The Tanner Lectures on Human Values (1986)* (University of Utah Press, 1988), vol. VIII, 217–79, esp. § 3.
72 This statement does not entail a dismissal of legal positivism, precisely as the Kantian philosophy of law does not. Such a view, in fact, does not impinge upon the criteria of legal validity. An elaboration of the 'duality of law' within a reconstruction of the rule of law ideal is in my *The Rule of Law as an Institutional Ideal*, *supra* note 20.

5 Informal international law as presumptive law

Exploring new modes of law-making

Joost Pauwelyn, Ramses A. Wessel and Jan Wouters

1 Introduction

In the past decade, international lawyers started to show an increased interest in normative processes that traditionally sit uneasily with international law. To name just a few (main) examples: Anne-Marie Slaughter drew our attention to 'transgovernmental regulatory networks';[1] Benedict Kingsbury and others pointed to an emerging 'global administrative law';[2] José Alvarez noted that more and more technocratic international bodies 'appear to be engaging in legislative or regulatory activity in ways and for reasons that might be more readily explained by students of bureaucracy than by scholars of the traditional forms for making customary law or engaging in treaty-making';[3] Armin von Bogdandy and others argued that international public authority may have different sources;[4] the project on 'Private Transnational Regulatory Regimes' draws attention to transnational private actors;[5] and all of this returns in the project on 'The Architecture of Postnational Rulemaking'.[6] In doing this, lawyers increasingly seem to be able to set aside their traditional hesitations by accepting a reality of many different forms, actors and processes in the formation of international norms. Obviously, to political scientists and international relations theorists, the existence of 'transnational' normative

---

1 Anne-Marie Slaughter, *A New World Order* (Princeton University Press, 2004), ch. 6.
2 Benedict Kingsbury, Nico Krisch and Richard B. Stewart, 'The Emergence of Global Administrative Law', 68 *Law & Contemporary Problems* (2005) 15–61.
3 Jose Alvarez, *International Organizations as Law-Makers* (Oxford University Press, 2005) at 217.
4 Armin von Bogdandy, Rüdiger Wolfrum, Jochen von Bernstorff, Philipp Dann, Matthias Goldmann (eds), *The Exercise of Public Authority by International Institutions: Advancing International Institutional Law* (Springer, 2010).
5 See 'Private Transnational Regulatory Regimes', <privateregulation.eu> and Fabrizio Cafaggi (ed.), *Enforcement of Transnational Private Regulation* (Edward Elgar, 2012).
6 See 'The Architecture of Postnational Rulemaking: Views from International Public Law, European Public Law and European Private Law', <www.uva.nl/architecture>.

processes does not come as a surprise and, in a way, always formed part of their 'reality of global governance'.[7]

Indeed, lawyers continue to struggle with the new and extensive normative output in global governance: 'we continue to pour an increasingly rich normative output into old bottles labelled "treaty", "custom", or (much more rarely) "general principles"'.[8] At the same time it is increasingly recognised that we may not be able to capture all new developments by holding on to our traditional notions. One solution is to simply disregard all normative output that cannot be traced back to any of the traditional sources of international law. This approach, however, runs the risk of placing international legal analysis (even more) outside the 'real world' or, and perhaps even more frighteningly, 'to reduce law to a sub-branch of the social sciences',[9] as there would not be much left for lawyers to deal with.[10] After all, in many cases the non-traditional normative processes *de facto* have similar effects as traditional legal norms. Do lawyers then simply have to accept a pluralisation of international norm- and law-making processes,[11] or perhaps even a retreat from formal law-ascertainment?[12] Or, does some of the 'non-traditional normative output' actually fit within existing sources of international law or is it at least part of the process of law creation (including custom and treaty interpretation), given the absence of formal criteria for an agreement to constitute a treaty or legally binding commitment, as well as the accessible nature of customary law (broadly defined in Article 38 of the ICJ Statute as 'evidence of a general practice accepted as law')?

---

[7] Jonathan G. S. Koppell, *World Rule: Accountability, Legitimacy, and the Design of Global Governance* (University of Chicago Press, 2010), ch. 1. Koppell sketched both empirically and conceptually the 'organization of global rulemaking'. Even in the absence of a centralised global state, the population of Global Governance Organizations (GGOs) is not a completely atomised collection of entities: 'They interact, formally and informally on a regular basis. In recent years, their programs are more tied together, creating linkages that begin to weave a web of transnational rules and regulations'.

[8] Alvarez, *International Organizations as Law-Makers, supra* note 3.

[9] Jan Klabbers, 'Law-making and Constitutionalism' in Jan Klabbers, Anne Peters and Geir Ulfstein, *The Constitutionalization of International Law* (Oxford University Press, 2009) 81–125, at 97.

[10] The possible demise of international law is described in Joost Pauwelyn, Ramses A. Wessel and Jan Wouters, 'The Stagnation of International Law', Leuven Centre for Global Governance Studies Working Paper No. 97, October 2012, <ghum.kuleuven.be/ggs/publications/working_papers/new_series/wp91-100/wp-97-pauwelyn-wessel-wouters-revjp.pdf>.

[11] Cf. Nico Krisch, *Beyond Constitutionalism: The Pluralist Structure of Postnational Law* (Oxford University Press, 2010).

[12] As eloquently argued by Jean d'Aspremont, *Formalism and the Sources of International Law: A Theory of the Ascertainment of Legal Rules* (Oxford University Press, 2011). d'Aspremont even claims that there is a 'growing acceptance of the idea of a penumbra between law and non-law [which] has provoked a move away from questions of law-ascertainment, [which are] increasingly perceived as irrelevant.' *Ibid.*, at 1.

The 'informal international law-making' (IN-LAW) project – which forms the basis for the present contribution – sits comfortably with the current trend in international law to look at other manifestations of normativity.[13] Its scope may be broader than some of the related projects as it looks for the source of informality in different aspects: actor informality, process informality and output informality (see section 2).[14] Yet, it has a specific focus (and perhaps objective): it starts from the assumption that we are at least dealing with *law*-making.[15] Would this not be the case, then – for most lawyers – psychologically, the project would be very difficult to handle. Given this starting point, the work of Jan Klabbers in particular is helpful to assess the legal nature of the normative output generated by less traditional actors or through informal processes. In this contribution we will use notions that are central in his work (such as the broad concept of international agreement and the notion of 'presumptive law') to shed more light on the legal nature and the accountability of the phenomenon that we termed 'informal international law-making'. In a recent and extensive study, this phenomenon was introduced;[16] yet, it became clear that by simply placing something under the term 'law-making', not all questions related to the nature of the norms or the accountability of the actors are answered. In fact, the distinction between law and non-law[17] is at the heart of the informal international law project, which is characterised by a struggle to come to grips with normative processes and outcomes that most would not consider to be law while in many cases the norms are perceived or implemented as (if they were) mandatory, restrict freedom the way law does and were (in many but not all cases) elaborated in line with rules of procedural integrity we expect from law. In the present contribution, we hope to take an extra step in arguing why lawyers should not ignore IN-LAW. Starting with *prima facie* non-

---

13 'Informal international lawmaking' was a two-year research project, involving over forty scholars and thirty case studies. See for the main results: Joost Pauwelyn, Ramses A. Wessel and Jan Wouters (eds), *Informal International Lawmaking* (Oxford University Press, 2012); and Ayelet Berman, Sanderijn Duquet, Joost Pauwelyn, Ramses A. Wessel, and Jan Wouters, (eds), *Informal International Lawmaking: Case Studies* (TOAEP, 2012).
14 Cf. Philipp Dann and Marie von Engelhardt, 'Legal Approaches to Global Governance and Accountability: Informal Lawmaking, International Public Authority, and Global Administrative Law Compared', in Pauwelyn, Wessel and Wouters (eds), *Informal International Lawmaking, supra* note 13, 106–21.
15 Cf. Dick W. P. Ruiter and Ramses A. Wessel, 'The Legal Nature of Informal International Law: A Legal Theoretical Exercise', in Pauwelyn, Wessel and Wouters (eds), *Informal International Lawmaking, supra* note 13, 162-184.
16 Pauwelyn, Wessel and Wouters (eds), *Informal International Lawmaking, supra* note 13.
17 The scope of this contribution does not allow us to refer to the large debate on the question how to differentiate 'law' from 'non-law'. See further Jack Goldsmith and Eric Posner, *The Limits of International Law* (Oxford University Press, 2005); d'Aspremont, *Formalism and the Sources of International Law, supra* note 12; Laszlo Blutman, 'In the Trap of a Legal Metaphor: International Soft Law', 93 *International & Comparative Law Quarterly* (2010) 605-24.

legal norms to study law-making is less strange than it may seem. After all, 'once a system accepts that law can be distinct from non-law, it can start to think about how exactly law can come into being (the basis of obligation), and what forms it can possibly take (the sources issues)'.[18]

Indeed, this book offers an excellent opportunity to highlight a number of insights offered by the rich and influential academic output generated by Jan Klabbers over the years. In this chapter, we first introduce the notion of IN-LAW (section 2). We then aim to confront a number of open questions related to informal international law with some of the insights developed and applied by Jan Klabbers (section 3). The outcome of this will be presented in a concluding section (section 4).

2 Defining informal international law-making

We use the term 'informal' international law-making in contrast and opposition to 'traditional' international law-making. Informal law is 'informal' in the sense that it dispenses with certain formalities traditionally linked to international law. These formalities may have to do with *output, process* or the *actors involved*.[19] It is exactly this 'circumvention' of formalities under international and/or domestic procedures that generated the claim that informal law is not sufficiently accountable.[20] At the same time, escaping these same formalities is also what is said to make informal law more desirable and effective. Lipson, for example, explains that 'informality is best understood as a device for minimizing the impediments to cooperation, at both the domestic and international levels'.[21] Indeed, in today's increasingly complex

---

18   Klabbers, 'Law-making and Constitutionalism', *supra* note 9, 81–125.
19   Informal law was extensively defined by Joost Pauwelyn, who deserves full credit for the main concepts in this section. Joost Pauwelyn, 'Informal International Law-making: Framing the Concept and Research Questions', in Pauwelyn, Wessel and Wouters (eds), *Informal International Lawmaking, supra* note 13, 13–33.
20   See, for example, Eyal Benvenisti, 'Coalitions of the Willing' and the Evolution of Informal International Law' in Christian Calliess, Georg Nolte and Peter-Tobias Stoll (eds), *Coalitions of the Willing: Avantgarde or Threat?* (Carl Heymanns Verlag, 2007); Benedict Kingsbury and Richard Stewart, 'Legitimacy and Accountability in Global Regulatory Governance: The Emerging Global Administrative Law and the Design and Operation of Administrative Tribunals of International Organizations', in Spyridon Flogaitis (ed.), *International Administrative Tribunals in a Changing World* (Esperia, 2008) 1–20, at 5, framed this critique as follows:

> Even in the case of treaty-based international organizations, much norm creation and implementation is carried out by subsidiary bodies of an administrative character that operate informally with a considerable degree of autonomy. Other global regulatory bodies including networks of domestic officials and private and hybrid bodies operate wholly outside the traditional international law conception and are either not subject to domestic political and legal accountability mechanisms at all, or only to a very limited degree.

21   Charles Lipson, 'Why Are Some International Agreements Informal?', 45 *International Organization* (1991) 495–538, at 500.

and fast-paced world, informality may not only be the less costly option – with new technologies cutting down communication costs, the participation of diverse stakeholders through novel processes has become less costly – it may also be the more effective option, in that a treaty or formal international organisation can be too rigid and states may not be able to do it alone (due to limited resources, knowledge or implementation capacity).

2.1 Output informality

First, in terms of *output*, international cooperation may be 'informal' in the sense that it does not lead to a formal treaty or any other traditional source of international law,[22] but rather to a guideline, standard, declaration or even more informal policy coordination or exchange. Aust defines an 'informal international instrument' as 'an instrument which is not a treaty because the parties to it do not intend it to be legally binding'.[23] Our definition, however, does not necessarily equate output informality with not being legally binding. We focus on lack of certain formalities; not lack of legal bindingness *per se*.

This, indeed, seems to bring us back to the extensive debates on 'soft law' (although soft law is fundamentally different from IN-LAW as we defined it above). As Klabbers held,

> underneath the broad consensus concerning the utility of soft law resides an element of discomfort, which manifests itself in a variety of ways. For one thing, in its effects soft law is often indistinguishable from hard law. It is drafted in similar ways; it comes, like hard law, with its own loopholes and exceptions, and indeed, when applied by courts and tribunals it typically gets to be applied as if it were hard law (as a treaty provision or a rule of customary international law). This then provokes the obvious question: if soft law and hard law are really indistinguishable, then what is the point of differentiating between them? It is here then that doubts creep in: the most obvious point where they differ relates to their acceptance by domestic democratic bodies. Typically, treaties need to be approved by parliaments under domestic treaty making rules; equally typically, governments have a free hand when it comes to concluding instruments that are not, formally, treaties, such as soft law instruments.[24]

---

22 That is, sources of international law as described in Article 38 of the Statute of the International Court of Justice, 26 June 1945, in force 24 October 1945 (conventions, custom, general principles of law).
23 Anthony Aust, 'The Theory and Practice of Informal International Instruments', 35 *International & Comparative Law Quarterly* (1986) 787–812, at 787.
24 Jan Klabbers, 'Reflections on Soft International Law in a Privatized World', 16 *Finnish Yearbook of International Law* (2005) 313–18, at 316.

The IN-LAW project emerged out of a similar discomfort. Yet, we do not use the term here, to allow for a more comprehensive analysis of informal law, in which not only the output but also the actors (not only states but also other public and private actors – see below) and the process are different from formal law-making.[25]

At the *domestic* level, output informality may, at least in some situations, lead to weaker forms of domestic oversight, e.g. little or no internal coordination, notice and comment procedures, parliamentary approval or obligation of publication. In the US, for example, Circular 175 and its coordinating role for the US State Department and obligation of publication and transmittal to Congress, 'does not apply to documents that are not binding under international law'.[26] Similarly, in the UK, the formalities that surround treaty making do not apply to so-called Memoranda of Understanding (MOU) which the UK defines as 'international commitments' that are 'not legally binding' and are, moreover, not usually published.[27] In Germany, an internal instruction directed at all federal ministries stipulates that ministries must always inquire whether an international agreement is really needed or whether 'the same goal may also be attained through other means, especially through understandings which are below the threshold of an international agreement'.[28] Given the real-life impact of informal international law-making, this carve-out from domestic oversight for instruments that are not strictly speaking 'binding' is hard to justify.

At the *international* level, output informality raises the fundamental question of whether informal law-making is even part of what we call

---

[25] See, however, another contribution to the project, where informal international law-making is placed within the broader debates: Joost Pauwelyn, 'Is It International Law or Not and Does it Even Matter?', in Pauwelyn, Wessel and Wouters (eds), *Informal International Lawmaking, supra* note 13, 125–61.

[26] See US State Department, 'Circular 175 Procedure', <www.state.gov/s/l/treaty/c175/>. Similarly, the US constitutional rule that 'treaties' must be adopted in the Senate by a two-third majority does not apply to what in US law are known as 'international agreements' (distinguished from 'treaties'). This explains why today the large majority of US international cooperation takes the form of 'executive agreements' rather than 'treaties' (to avoid the hurdle of two-third majority in the Senate). Such 'international agreements' are, however, subject to Circular 175. That said, if a document is not legally binding (i.e. not an 'international agreement' under the specific criteria of Circular 175), even the limited obligations in Circular 175 do not apply.

[27] UK Foreign and Commonwealth Office, *Treaties and MOUs: Guidance on Practice and Procedures* (2nd edn, rev'd, 2004) at 1. Note, however, that the United Nations, *Treaty Handbook* (2006) does consider MOUs as legally binding: 'The term memorandum of understanding (M.O.U.) is often used to denote a less formal international instrument than a typical treaty or international agreement ... The United Nations considers M.O.U.s to be binding and registers them if submitted by a party or if the United Nations is a party'. *Ibid.*, at 61.

[28] Gemeinsame Geschäftsordnung der Bundesministerien, § 72, <www.verwaltungsvorschriften-im-internet.de/bsvwvbund_21072009_O113120018.htm>

'international law' (be it traditionally defined or under some modern, evolutionary definition) and whether informal law is, as a result, subject to the normative structures and consequences that normally come hand in hand with being part of international law. Such structures and consequences include the basic rule that no state can be bound without its consent, applicability before international courts or tribunals, hierarchy and systemic relation to other norms of international law including basic human rights and *jus cogens*, registration with the UN Secretariat,[29] etc. We leave the matter of whether informal law-making and/or its output is regulated under, part of, or even (partly) binding under, international law open for case-by-case scrutiny. The reason to use the term 'law-making' is exactly meant to find out whether the normative processes under review can somehow lead to 'law'. At the same time it forces lawyers to reassess the foundations of their discipline in view of emerging forms of global governance.

2.2 *Process informality*

Second, in terms of *process*, international cooperation may be 'informal' in the sense that it occurs in a loosely organised network or forum rather than a traditional international organisation (intergovernmental organisation [IGO]). Think of the G20, Basel Committee on Banking Supervision or the Financial Action Task Force, versus the UN or the WTO. Such process or forum informality does, however, not prevent the existence of detailed procedural norms (as exist, for example, in the Internet Engineering Task Force), permanent staff or a physical headquarter. Nor does process informality exclude informal law-making in the context or under the broader auspices of a more formal organisation (a lot of informal law-making occurs, for example, under the auspices of the Organisation for Economic Co-operation and Development [OECD]).

Process informality, on top of output informality, may, in certain situations, further limit normative structures or control under both domestic and international law. As Slaughter phrased it, '[t]he essence of a network is a *process* rather than an *entity*; thus it cannot be captured or controlled in the ways that typically structure formal legitimacy in a democratic polity'.[30]

---

29   Article 102 of the UN Charter provides:

> 1. Every treaty and every international agreement entered into by any Member of the United Nations after the present Charter comes into force shall as soon as possible be registered with the Secretariat and published by it.
> 2. No party to any such treaty or international agreement, which has not been registered in accordance with the provisions of paragraph 1 of this Article, may invoke that treaty or agreement before any organ of the United Nations.

30   Anne-Marie Slaughter, 'Agencies on the Loose? Holding Government Networks Accountable', in George Bermann, Matthias Herdegen and Peter Lindseth (eds), *Transatlantic Regulatory Cooperation, Legal Problems and Political Prospects* (Oxford University Press, 2000) 521–46, at 525.

For example, regulators may face fewer domestic constraints when operating in a loose network abroad with foreign partners compared with when they act purely domestically or in contrast to formal delegates to an IGO. As a result, process informality raises additional questions and trade-offs between effectiveness and accountability both at the domestic and at the international level.

As we did above in respect of informal output and the question of whether such output is part of international law, we do not want to prejudge the matter of whether an informal law-making grouping or network can be a subject of international law or have legal personality of its own, although there is clearly something to say on that.[31] A possible advantage of being a subject or having legal personality may be that some informal law-making bodies can be held accountable as separate entities and may fall under the control (albeit partly) of international law. A possible drawback of such independent status may, however, be that it enhances the power of the body and may, in turn, make it more difficult rather than easier to hold the informal law-making body accountable (participating national actors may, for example, hide behind the informal nature as a legal person when it comes to responsibility; independent international status may enhance the power of the body and reduce the need for domestic implementation and the domestic control that comes with it).

Indeed, as much as process or forum informality may enhance fears of lack of accountability, as Anne-Marie Slaughter has argued, 'transgovernmental regulatory networks' (one particular kind of informal law-making) may also be *more* accountable to domestic constituencies than traditional IGOs. Slaughter's argument is that in transgovernmental networks input and output is channelled directly through domestic actors with a shorter accountability chain back to the people, and no independent international body exists to which authority has been delegated or which could impose its will on participants.[32]

That said, even where accountable to domestic constituencies and, in this sense, accountable to *internal* stakeholders, the question remains whether informal law-making bodies are sufficiently accountable to *external* actors including broader societal interests and countries outside the body (say where network output is *de facto* implemented, as is the case of ICH[33] guidelines in many non-ICH member countries). As Richard Stewart pointed

---

31 Ayelet Berman and Ramses A. Wessel, 'The International Legal Status of Informal International Law-making Bodies: Consequences for Accountability', in Pauwelyn, Wessel and Wouters (eds), *Informal International Lawmaking, supra* note 13, 35–62.
32 Slaughter, *A New World Order, supra* note 1.
33 ICH stands for International Conference on Harmonization of Technical Requirement for Registration of Pharmaceuticals for Human Use.

out, 'the problem is often not lack of accountability, but disproportionate accountability to some interests and inadequate responsiveness to others'.[34]

2.3 Actor informality

Third, in terms of *actors involved* international cooperation may be 'informal' in the sense that it does not engage traditional diplomatic actors (such as heads of state, foreign ministers or embassies) but rather other ministries, domestic regulators, independent or semi-independent agencies (such as food safety authorities or central banks), sub-federal entities (such as provinces or cities) or the legislative or judicial branch.[35] Under Article 7 of the Vienna Convention on the Law of Treaties,[36] for example, only heads of state, heads of government, foreign ministers, heads of diplomatic missions or specifically accredited representatives are presumed to have so-called full powers to represent and bind a state.

The non-traditional nature of the actors involved in IN-LAW may be further accentuated with the participation of private actors (besides public actors) and/or international organisations. In some cases, informal lawmaking may even consist exclusively of a network of IOs (think of the UN System Chief Executive Board of Coordination).

The fact that regulators or agencies – rather than diplomats – are involved further complicates the question of whether informal law-making is part of *international* law (e.g. can such regulators or agencies bind their state; are they 'subjects' of international law?). Under US law, for example, 'agency agreements' *do* constitute international agreements.[37] For France, by contrast,

---

34 Richard Stewart, 'Accountability, Participation, and the Problem of Disregard in Global Regulatory Governance', paper presented at the IILJ International Legal Theory Colloquium *Interpretation and Judgment in International Law* (January 2008) <www.iilj.org/courses/documents/2008Colloquium.Session4.Stewart.pdf>, at 27, adding that 'policies are often strongly influenced by well organized financial, business, and other economic actors, which operate more effectively and exert greater sway in the informal, opaque, negotiation-driven networks of national-global regulatory decision making than more weakly organized general societal interests'.
35 That the actors involved may make international law-making (including its domestic angle) more or less formal is confirmed in the distinction made under French practice between 'accords en forme solennelle' (Article 52 of the Constitution), concluded by the French President and subject to 'ratification', and 'accords en forme simplifié', concluded at the level of the government by the Minister of Foreign Affairs and subject to 'approbation'. Circulaire du 30 mai 1997 relative à l'élaboration et à la conclusion des accords internationaux, Journal Officiel de la République Française n° 125 du 31 mai 1997 page 8415.
36 23 May 1969, in force 27 January 1980, 1155 UNTS 331.
37 1 USC §§ 112a, 112b; 22 CFR § 181.2(b):

> *Agency-level agreements.* Agency-level agreements are international agreements within the meaning of the Act and of 1 USC 112a if they satisfy the criteria discussed in paragraph (a) of this section. The fact that an agreement is concluded by and on behalf of a particular agency of the United States Government, rather than the United States Government, does not mean that the agreement is not an international agreement. Determinations are made on the basis of the substance of the agency-level agreement in question.

'arrangements administratifs' are *not* recognised under international law, are not even registered by the French Ministry of Foreign Affairs and should, according to a 1997 Circular of the Prime Minister, only be resorted to in exceptional circumstances given, *inter alia*, their uncertain effects.[38]

Besides creating uncertainty under international law, actor informality may also reduce *domestic* oversight and coordination (e.g. through the ministry of foreign affairs). At the same time, non-traditional actors (such as regulators and agencies) do remain subject to domestic administrative law, internal bureaucratic controls, ministerial responsibility and any parliamentary-oversight or limited mandate that may be in place under domestic law. In this respect, the question arises whether an ambassador or diplomat (traditionally engaged in international cooperation) is more accountable, more legitimately exercising authority or subject to a shorter delegation chain than, for example, a regulator or agency, or *vice versa*.

3 The validity criterion in informal international law-making

3.1 Presumptive law

The above analysis reveals that one of the most difficult questions in relation to IN-LAW concerns the legal nature of the norms. It is well accepted that not all law or legal norms impose or proscribe specific behaviour or legally binding rights and obligations. Normativity must not be confused with imperativity.[39] As we will see, this notion lies at the back of our analysis as well. Indeed, the debate between those who argue in favour of a bright line between law and non-law, like Jan Klabbers,[40] and those arguing for the existence of a grey zone[41] is well-known. In practice the divide may not always

---

38 French Ministry of Foreign Affairs, 'Archives et patrimoine: Base des Traités et Accords et de la France' <www.doc.diplomatie.gouv.fr/pacte/index.html>:

> Les arrangements administratifs conclus par un ministre français avec son homologue étranger ne sont pas répertoriés dans la base de données documentaire. En effet, il ne s'agit pas de traités ou d'accords internationaux ... Cette catégorie n'est pas reconnue par le droit international. La circulaire du 30 mai 1997 relative à l'élaboration et à la conclusion des accords internationaux recommande aux négociateurs français de ne recourir à ce type d'arrangements qu'exceptionnellement et souligne que les effets qu'ils produisent sont incertains.

39 André Lalande, *Vocabulaire technique et critique de la philosophie* (Presses Universitaires de France, 1993), *sub verbo* 'Normatif'.
40 For example, Prosper Weil, 'Towards Relative Normativity in International Law?', 77 *American Journal of International Law* (1983) 413–42, at 417–8; Jan Klabbers, 'The Redundancy of Soft Law', 65 *Nordic Journal of International Law* (1996) 167–82, at 181; and Jan Klabbers 'The Undesirability of Soft Law', 67 *Nordic Journal of International Law* (1998) 381–91.
41 For example, Richard R. Baxter, 'International Law in "Her Infinite Variety" ', 29 *International & Comparative Law Quarterly* (1980) 549–566; and Oscar Schachter 'The Twilight Existence of Nonbinding International Agreements', 71 *American Journal of International Law* (1997) 296–304.

be clearly visible: 'for the bright line school something may be law; for the grey zone school it may not be law (or fall in the grey zone between law and non-law) but still have legal effects, with little practical difference between the two approaches'.[42] Yet, large parts of the debate have been devoted to the establishment of one or more criteria to decide what makes an instrument law (be it sanctions, formalities, intent, effect, substance or belief). Thus, depending on how one distinguishes between law and non-law, informal output may or may not be part of international law. If formalities or intent matter, a lot of the informal output would not be law. If, by contrast, effect or substantive factors decide, a lot would be law.

Taking a somewhat different stance, d'Aspremont points to the fact that the empiricism of the IN-LAW project and similar projects 'has impelled their promoters to loosen their legal concepts and abandon a strict delineation of their field of study. In that sense … confronted with a pluralisation of norm-making at the international level, international legal scholars have come to pluralise their concept of international law'.[43] It is the normative impact of the variety of informal output that has led to perhaps a 'legal overstretch'. However, such a deformalisation does come at a price and it is not made clear, argues d'Aspremont, why lawyers so desperately wish to capture the new phenomena as international law. '[W]hy not coming to terms with the interdisciplinary aspects of such an endeavour and recognize that, even as international legal scholars, we can zero in on non-legal phenomena without feeling a need to label them law?'

Yet, the question in the present contribution is whether it is not possible (or perhaps even more logical) to view these *prima facie* non-legal phenomena as law. After all, as Jan Klabbers taught us – in particular in presenting his 'concept of treaty'[44] – one would need good reasons not to consider international commitments as law, or at least as legally relevant:

> Although several normative orders may govern international relations, none of them is capable of serving as a viable alternative to the international legal order, for they cannot be utilized intentionally. Courtesy and morality develop over time, through the aggregate conduct of actors; and neither can be created intentionally (except, perhaps, by legal instrument). It follows, that an agreement cannot be concluded with the intention of becoming courteously bound, or morally bound. Politics moreover, perhaps the most popular alternative to law, is really no alternative. Rather, law is the normative order governing politics,

---

42 Pauwelyn, 'Framing the Concept and Research Questions', *supra* note 19.
43 Jean d'Aspremont, 'From a Pluralization of International Norm-making Processes to a Pluralization of the Concept of International Law', in Pauwelyn, Wessel and Wouters (eds), *Informal International Lawmaking, supra* note 13, 185–99. See more extensively his book *Formalism and the Sources of International Law, supra* note 12.
44 Jan Klabbers, *The Concept of Treaty in International Law* (Kluwer Law International, 1996).

and in that sense at least, law and politics are one and the same. Again, it follows that one cannot intend to become politically bound without at the same time also becoming legally bound.[45]

Obviously, for lawyers this is a very attractive quote and acceptance by the present authors (for legal theoretical reasons or simply because of the festive occasion that lies behind the present collection of contributions) would imply that part of informal law-making indeed needs to be considered 'law'. Yet, Jan Klabbers' arguments were drafted in relation to treaties and other forms of inter-governmental cooperation. While the reasons may therefore hold for informal law-making that is carried out by formal actors producing informal output, it does not necessarily help us out in the case of actor informality.

A major element here may be the notion of 'presumptive law'. This notion was developed by Klabbers in his important publication 'Law-making and Constitutionalism'.[46] In building his argument, Klabbers departs from the more or less pragmatic concept of law developed by Tamanaha: law is 'whatever people recognize and treat as law through their social practices'.[47] Indeed, as Klabbers holds, this is less open-ended than it seems as people generally do not regard all norms they live by as 'law' (recall the Article 38 definition of custom quoted above: custom is 'evidence of a general practice *accepted as law*'). The validity problem that would emerge out of this approach could be solved by including Fuller's eight desiderata to ensure that the law would be both morally acceptable and procedurally sound.[48] Yet, as Klabbers rightfully concludes: in the end we cannot escape the need for a formal criterion. And this may bring us back to familiar territory: 'It is difficult to imagine the formal validity criterion to be anything other than a consent-like criterion, whether consent be expressed directly or indirectly, as is the case when it comes to binding [sic] majority decisions within international organisations'.[49] Yet, we need to be able to establish whether the actors

---

45 *Ibid.*, at 247.
46 Klabbers, 'Law-making and Constitutionalism', *supra* note 9. See also Jan Klabbers, 'International Courts and Informal International Law', in Pauwelyn, Wessel and Wouters (eds), *Informal International Lawmaking*, *supra* note 13, 217–40.
47 Brian Tamanaha, *A General Jusrisprudence of Law and Society* (Oxford University Press, 2001), at 67.
48 Summarised: 1. Law must consist of norms; 2. Law ought be made public; 3. Law should not made retroactively; 4. Law should be made understandable; 5. Laws should not be made to contradict each other; 6. It should be possible to obey the law; 7. The law should not change so frequently as to become unpredictable; and 8. There should be a reasonable measure of congruence between the rules and the way they are applied by officials. See Lon L. Fuller, *The Morality of Law* (Yale University Press, 1969). See also Jan Klabbers, 'Constitutionalism and the Making of International Law: Fuller's Procedural Natural Law', 5 *No Foundations: Journal of Extreme Legal Positivism* (2008) 84–112.
49 Klabbers, 'Law-making and Constitutionalism', *supra* note 9, at 114.

expressing their consent (democratically, legitimately) represent the subjects of the new norms. This is where Klabbers proposes to focus on how the norms are received by their possible addressees:[50] 'One possible approach might be to propose what can be labelled "presumptive law": normative utterances should be presumed to give rise to law, unless and until the opposite can somehow be proven'.[51] Obviously, this presumption could be rebutted, but the idea is to reverse the burden of proof.

3.2 The source of authority

This is where the notion of 'presumptive law' may be helpful to solve a dilemma underlying the IN-LAW project. In particular in the case of *actor informality*, the norms are not enacted by states or state representatives, but by persons sitting in international/transnational boards and councils because of their specific expertise or because they represent particular stakeholders or interests. Everything that is produced can be labelled under the heading 'normative utterances', but the fact that in many cases we are not dealing with formal international organisations, or with state representatives with a national public mandate, makes it difficult to square with the traditional sources doctrine. Yet, it is clear that, irrespective of their 'informal' nature, the norms may be hard and do play a role in legal orders.[52]

Solutions have been sought by the 'public authority' project as well in accepting that new manifestations of normativity may play an import role in global governance. Following the notion that 'governance' is about creating (public) order,[53] the 'public authority' avenue may indeed be helpful. The notion was studied in the framework of the Max Planck project on the 'Exercise of International Public Authority'.[54] Large parts of international cooperation (including some of the forms mentioned above) could be considered as merely affecting the private legal relationships between actors. In particular when non-governmental actors are involved, we would argue that the 'public' dimension is essential whenever we wish to see international

---

50 While not referring to it, this approach comes close to the debate on 'output legitimacy', initiated by Fritz Scharpf. See further Fritz W. Scharpf, *Governing in Europe: Effective and Democratic?* (Oxford University Press, 1999).
51 Klabbers, 'Law-making and Constitutionalism', *supra* note 9, at 115.
52 Klabbers, 'International Courts and Informal International Law', *supra* note 46.
53 For example: Guy Peters, 'Introducing the Topic', in Guy Peters and Donald J. Savoie (eds), *Governance in a Changing Environment* (Canadian Centre for Management Development, 1995) 3–19.
54 See von Bogdandy *et al.* (eds), *The Exercise of Public Authority by International Institutions*, *supra* note 4. See in the same volume also Matthias Goldmann, 'Inside Relative Normativity: From Sources to Standards Instruments for the Exercise of International Public Authority', 661–711; and Armin von Bogdandy, Philipp Dann and Matthias Goldmann, 'Developing the Publicness of Public International Law: Towards a Legal Framework for Global Governance Activities', 3–32.

norm-setting as 'law-making'. Von Bogdandy, Dann and Goldmann define the 'exercise of international public authority' in the following terms: 'any kind of governance activity by international institutions, be it administrative or intergovernmental, should be considered as an exercise of international public authority *if* it determines individuals, private associations, enterprises, states, or other public institutions'.[55] 'Authority' is defined as 'the legal capacity to *determine* others and to reduce their freedom, i.e. to unilaterally shape their legal or factual situation'.[56] And in many cases, IN-LAW does have that capacity and impact. Also important is the fact that the determination may or may be not legally obligating: 'It is binding if an act *modifies the legal situation* of a different legal subject without its consent. A modification takes place if a subsequent action which contravenes that act is illegal.'[57] The authors believe that this concept enables the identification of all those governance phenomena that public lawyers should study.

In subsequent studies, the notion of 'exercise of public authority' was further developed. What remains important is that a traditional conception of public authority based on coercion has become, if it has not always been, inadequate: 'In an era of influential institutions of global governance, it should rather include other ways of exercising power that is no less decisive and incisive than coercive enforcement'.[58] At the same time it became clear that it is not so much about *determining* individuals, private associations, enterprises, states or other public institutions, but rather about *shaping* and *constraining* their freedom. This calls for considering the activities in 'a public law perspective'. Or, phrasing it the other way around: 'If an activity of international institutions does not affect liberty or human rights significantly, it does not need to be conceptualized in a public law perspective'.[59]

Similarly, 'normative utterances' are also quite easily regarded as 'law' by institutional legal theorists. 'Institutional legal theory' (ILT) led to a broader picture of what could count as 'law'. What ILT basically does is combine legal positivism with the institutionalism that can be found in the linguistic philosophy of John Searle. According to Searle, speaking is more than just uttering sounds; it is both a regulated and a regulating activity.[60] This is reflected in the possible relations between, what he calls, 'word' and 'world'.

---

55   *Ibid.*, at 5 (original italics).
56   *Ibid.*, at 11 (original italics).
57   *Ibid.*, at 11–12 (original italics).
58   Armin von Bogdandy and Ingo Venzke, 'In Whose Name? An Investigation of International Courts' Public Authority and its Democratic Justification', 23 *European Journal of International Law* (2012) 7–41.
59   Armin von Bogdandy and Matthias Goldmann, 'The Exercise of International Public Authority through National Policy Assessment: The OECD's PISA Policy as a Paradigm for a New International Standard Instrument', 5 *International Organizations Law Review* (2008) 241–98, at 261.
60   John Searle, *Speech Acts: An Essay in the Philosophy of Language* (Cambridge University Press, 1969).

Depending on the type of 'speech act' the 'world' adapts itself to the words that are uttered in its context, or *vice versa*. But, it is equally possible that there is no relation between word and world or even that there exists a mutual adaptation. This way language does not merely convey content, but the speaker also performs an action in saying something. Translated to legal theory this means that this latter act consists of the creation of legal rights and duties, once it is performed by a competent actor. The legal acts that are the result of these utterances can take different shapes and the idea is that they form part of the legal order even if they are not 'binding' someone to take a certain course or action, but simply because they may change the legal situation. Thus the aim of ILT is to classify legal acts and to reveal that the distinction between 'binding' and 'non-binding' may be less helpful in determining what belongs to the legal order.[61]

This comes close to the arguments underlying the 'presumptive law' notion. Klabbers argues that to come to terms with the idea that somehow 'consent' should be at the basis of 'law', we may need to rethink representative decision-making. Again, this could be achieved by focusing not so much on the input, but rather on the output: 'rethink the way law is recognized'.[62] Obviously this can lead to an acceptance as law of a large (indefinite?) number of normative utterances, and only when the presumption is rebutted this would lead to the conclusion that we are dealing with a non-legal phenomenon. Klabbers came up with possible situations which would/could all by themselves lead to such a rebuttal:[63]

- an instrument that leaves everything to the discretion of the addressee;
- no one ever thought of making law (note that this seems to start from the idea that recognition by the addressee could be decisive);
- procedural guarantees are not met (e.g. norms are impossible, secret, in the end not accepted, conflicting higher norms, or – indeed – not democratic); and
- the topic may be too trivial to be regulated by law.

In the following section we will confront these criteria with the practice of informal international law-making. In doing so, we may indeed have to focus more on the actual effects and the acceptance of the norms as playing a role in legal orders, but we feel that acceptance cannot be decoupled from the origin of the norms both in terms of the authority (or authorities) they emanate from and their procedural pedigree. Many of the case studies in the IN-LAW project indicate that the acceptance of the norms – and perhaps their

---

61 See more extensively Ruiter and Wessel, 'The Legal Nature of Informal International Law', *supra* note 15.
62 Klabbers, 'Law-making and Constitutionalism', *supra* note 9, at 115.
63 Obviously, this short summary does in no way do justice to the rich analysis: *ibid.*, at 117–21.

legitimacy – is based on the fact that they are created by people who know what they are talking about and in such a way that takes account of many (if not always all) affected stakeholders. 'Expertise-based legitimacy' or 'executive authority' are not new phenomena but may very well form a key to a more inclusive understanding of international legal norms. Again, this is not groundbreaking. As argued by Paul Craig, in national polities also, law-making is legitimated in three ways: 'through legislative oversight/imprimatur from the top; through participation from the bottom by input from those affected by the rules; or through executive authority combined with technocratic expertise'.[64] While the second way (participation) is relevant for IN-LAW as well, the fact that only a limited number of stakeholders may be involved renders the third possibility (executive authority) equally relevant. However, 'executive authority' is usually used to describe (or promote) the role of 'the executive' in situations of secondary rule-making in (domestic) constitutional systems.[65] In the case of informal international law-making, however, it is not about authority to make secondary norms on the basis of primary legislation, it is in fact about primary norms. This may make it difficult to apply the 'executive authority' argument in our case.

In addition, the technocratic (rather than the bureaucratic) version of executive authority seems to suffer from a changing societal attitude towards technocratic expertise. As argued by Craig:

> There is less trust in technocracy than there was a generation ago. The idea that we should trust in those who know best, and that those with technical expertise should be regarded as primus inter pares in this respect, is now viewed with greater scepticism. The related idea that science provides 'objective' answers to certain problems that have to be dealt with in the political arena, has likewise come under strain. It has been recognized that the 'answer' may be contentious in scientific terms, and that any one version of the scientific solution may embody value judgments of a social, moral or political nature, even if such factors are not immediately apparent on the face of the decision.[66]

This, obviously, may have consequences for the extent to which the norm-setters can actually be seen as representing the final addressees of the

---

64 Paul Craig, 'Postnational Rulemaking: Conceptions of Legitimacy', paper presented at the conference *Postnational Rulemaking between Authority and Autonomy*, University of Amsterdam, 20–1 September 2012.
65 Cf. Paul Craig and Adam Tomkins (eds), *The Executive and Public Law: Power and Accountability in Comparative Perspective* (Oxford University Press, 2005); and, with regard to the EU, Deirdre Curtin, *Executive Power of the European Union: Law, Practices and the Living Constitution* (Oxford University Press, 2009).
66 Craig, 'Postnational Rulemaking', *supra* note 64, at 25.

norms.[67] On the basis of which (procedural and substantive) criteria do we select the actors in informal international law-making?

We are aware of the debates on the relation between legitimacy and expertise and of the critique, which was so well summarised by Laski in 1931: 'The expert tends ... to make his subject the measure of life, instead of making life the measure of his subject'.[68] In Laski's view,

> [i]t is one thing to argue the need for expert consultation at every stage in making policy; it is another thing, and a very different thing, to insist that the expert's judgment must be final. For special knowledge and the highly trained mind produce their own limitations which, in the realm of statesmanship, are of decisive importance. *Expertise*, it may be argued, sacrifices the insight of common sense to intensity of experience. It breeds an inability to accept new views from the very depth of its preoccupation with its own conclusions. It too often fails to see round its subject. It sees its results out of perspective by making them the centre of relevance to which all other results must be related. Too often, also, it lacks humility; and this breeds in its possessors a failure in proportion which makes them fail to see the obvious which is before their very noses. It has, also, a certain caste-spirit about it, so that experts tend do neglect all evidence which does not come from those who belong to their own ranks. Above all, perhaps, and this most urgently where human problems are concerned, the expert fails to see that every judgment he makes not purely factual in nature brings with it a scheme of values which has no special validity about it. He tends to confuse the importance of his facts which the importance of what he proposes to do about them.[69]

While the debate on the role of experts continued ever since,[70] this lengthy quote still reflects the main sources of concern and relates to the

---

67 William Wallace and Julie Smith, 'Democracy or Technocracy? European Integration and the Problem of Popular Consent', in Jack Hayward (ed.), *The Crisis of Representation in Europe* (Frank Cass, 1995) 137–57, at 140.
68 Harold J. Laski, *The Limitations of the Expert* (The Fabian Society, 1931), at 8.
69 *Ibid.*, at 4 (original italics).
70 See for recent contributions in various policy fields: Alberto Alemanno, 'Science and EU Risk Regulation: The Role of Experts in Decision-Making and Judicial Review' in Ellen Vos, *European Risk Governance: Its Science, its Inclusiveness and its Effectiveness* (Connex Report Series, 2008); Jacqueline Peel, *Science and Risk Regulation in International Law* (Cambridge University Press, 2010); Mark A. Pollack and Gregory C. Shaffer, *When Cooperation Fails: The International Law and Politics of Genetically Modified Foods* (Oxford University Press, 2009); Lukasz A. Gruszczynski, 'The Role of Experts in Environmental and Health Related Trade Disputes in the WTO: Deconstructing Decision-Making Processes', in Monika Ambrus, Karin Arts, Helena Raulus and Ellen Hey (eds), *Irrelevant, Advisors or Decision-Makers? The Role of 'Experts' in International Decision-Making* (Cambridge University Press, forthcoming).

importance of 'consent' dealt with above. We feel that, today perhaps more than ever, these concerns are valid and should guide our assessments of 'experts-based legitimacy'. As Jan Klabbers recently contended, the debate on the legitimate role of experts seems to be stimulated by the emerged 'audit society': in the absence of democratically elected experts, the establishment of public audit bodies seems to have become the panacea for democratic legitimacy. Klabbers argues, that in order to prevent the emergence of even a 'global audit society', we may need to get back to the (Aristotelian) tradition of virtue ethics. On this view, what matters is not so much the existence of external standards and accountability mechanisms, but whether actors' behaviour displays virtuous character traits. Thus, honesty, temperance, humility, fortitude, empathy, sympathy and justice are virtues that possibly may have some application when it comes to evaluating the work of experts engaged in the exercise of global governance.[71]

Rather than participating directly in this debate, in this contribution we attempt to find some answers on the basis of the cases that informed the idea of informal international law-making.

4 Informal international law-making as law? Confronting theory and practice

In the present contribution we – admittedly – are somewhat sloppy when we use terms such as law and public authority. The argument we try to build is that the informal law phenomena could (and perhaps should) be regarded 'legal' because they form an expression of public authority. When we would follow the presumption that the outcome of informal law-making is law, then it would *not* be law when the presumption could be rebutted on the basis of the four mentioned factors. Let's take a look at these factors one by one.

4.1 *The instrument leaves everything to the discretion of the addressee*

In the more than thirty cases that were addressed in the IN-LAW project, we did not easily find examples of completely open norms. This should not come as a surprise. Most bodies and networks involved in informal law-

---

71 Jan Klabbers, 'The Virtues of Expertise', in Ambrus *et al.* (eds), *Irrelevant, Advisors or Decision-Makers?*, *supra* note 70. See also: Jan Klabbers, 'Changing Futures? Science and International Law', 20 *Finnish Yearbook of International Law* (2009) 211-13.

making[72] were in fact created for one reason only: to produce concrete norms and standards. Frequently these norms are extremely precise (think of most ISO standards) and little is left to the discretion of the addressee. In fact, because of the fact that the norms are created 'informally', with experts rather than politicians in leading roles, the result is often less watered-down than in the case of a political compromise. Thus, the guidance documents of the Global Harmonization Task Force (GHTF) on medical devices,[73] for example, list very concrete standards that are to be met before a product can be marketed.[74] In general, discretion seems to be less of a concern than in formal law-making.

4.2 No one ever thought of making law

This may very well be the trickiest factor. After all, this is usually the reason not to consider any informal norm-setting as law.[75] Returning to our example of the GHTF, the 2005 Essential Principles of Safety and Performance of Medical Devices itself states that '[t]he document is intended to provide *non-binding* guidance to regulatory authorities for use in the regulation of

---

[72] The project addressed the G-20, the Asia Pacific Economic Cooperation, financial institutions (Basel Committee, the International Organisation of Securities Commissions, the OECD's Committee on Corporate Governance, the Financial Stability Board, the Financial Action Task Force, and the International Swaps and Derivatives Association), the International Forum of Sovereign Wealth Funds, medical products regulation bodies (the International Conference on the Harmonization of Technical Requirements for Registration of Pharmaceuticals for Human Use, the International Cooperation on Harmonization of Technical Requirements for Registration of Veterinary Medicinal Products, the Global Harmonization Task Force, the International Medical Devices Regulators Forum), bodies involved in food safety standards (Mercosur, the EU, the Codex Alimentarius Commission, the World Health Organization's International Code on Marketing of Breastmilk Substitutes, the Global Partnership for Good Agricultural Practice, the Global Food Safety Institute), the International Organization for Standardisation (ISO), the Kimberly Process on 'blood diamonds', the International Strategy for Disaster Reduction (ISDR), competition networks (the Central American Group of Competition and the Andean Committee for the Defense of Competition), United Nations Principles for Responsible Investment, and bodies regulating the internet (the Internet Corporation for Assigned Names and Numbers, the Internet Governance Forum, the Internet Engineering Task Force, and the Internet Society).

[73] Ayelet Berman, 'Informal International Lawmaking in Medical Products Regulation', in Berman *et al.* (eds), *Informal International Lawmaking*, supra note 13, 353–94.

[74] Essential Principles of Safety and Performance of Medical Devices, Doc. GHTF/SG1/N41R9:2005, 20 May 2005, section 5.12.3: 'Devices where the safety of the patients depends on an external power supply should include an alarm system to signal any power failure.' With many thanks to Dick W. P. Ruiter for finding and analysing these examples. See further Ruiter and Wessel, 'The Legal Nature of Informal International Law', *supra* note 16.

[75] For possible reasons for actors to opt for informal rather than formal law, see Pauwelyn, 'Is It International Law or Not and Does it Even Matter?', *supra* note 25.

medical devices'.[76] While 'non-binding' by itself may not form a reason to list it under 'non-legal', one may safely assume that the drafters indeed had the intention to prevent going to have to go to court in case of a violation of the norms. Moreover, in most cases 'should' rather than 'shall' is used in the description of what is expected of the addressees. This is in line with many other areas that have been researched. Yet, there are as many differences as there are cases. Some informal norms merely aim to be a source of subsequent domestic legislation. In that sense they would *contribute* to law-making, rather than being law themselves (although one may argue that the law-making process did already start at the international/transnational regulatory body/network, in particular when the only thing domestic law does is refer to an established norm or standard). In many other cases, however, the norms themselves aim to 'determine individuals, private associations, enterprises, states, or other public institutions' (see section 3.2) from the outset. In these many cases, the norms are to be followed directly, without interference by a domestic legislator.

In fact, there are reasons to argue that the 'informal' norms are perceived by the addresses as committing them in their activities.[77] This then, according to Klabbers, could do the trick: as we have seen, in his view, the fact that people may actually perceive the norms as committing could be decisive. And, there may obviously also be cases where people don't recognise law as law, in which case it still may be applied, as 'in the end ... it is eventually the law which determines which consequences to attach to which acts.'[78] The question then would be whether informal law is perceived as law or committing by its addressees. This is a psychological rather than a legal question and, frankly, it would be somewhat strange to make the emergence of law depended on people's state of mind. Klabbers relies on Fuller's eight desiderata[79] to help him out, but, indeed, the distinction between law and non-law was not as important for Fuller as it is for others and, irrespective of the impressive analysis, one is again left with a need for clear decisive criteria.

The informal law-making project was confronted with similar questions. When we argue that it is above all the actors, the process and the output that distinguishes informal from formal law, we may perhaps solve the procedural questions along Fuller's lines, but we are still left with the sources question. In many cases, the norms are made not by state representatives, but by

---

76 Essential Principles of Safety and Performance of Medical Devices, *supra* note 74, at Preface (italics added).
77 See Ruiter and Wessel, 'The Legal Nature of Informal International Law', *supra* note 15, at 165; Alexandre Flückiger, 'Keeping Domestic Soft Law Accountable: Towards a Gradual Formalization', in Pauwelyn, Wessel and Wouters (eds), *Informal International Lawmaking*, *supra* note 13, 409–36, at 415; Pauwelyn, Wessel and Wouters, 'The Stagnation of International Law', *supra* note 10, at 13.
78 Klabbers, 'Law-making and Constitutionalism', *supra* note 9, at 118–19.
79 See Fuller, *The Morality of Law*, *supra* note 48; Klabbers, 'Constitutionalism and the Making of International Law', *supra* note 48.

experts, administrators, civil society actors or business organisations. Yet – and this may lead in the direction of a possible way out – there is a reason why experts decide on the content of the norms: it is because they are the experts. In fact, this brings us back to the question of authority: the case studies in the IN-LAW project revealed that in most cases the authority of the experts or stakeholders that will be involved in the implementation of the norms lay at the basis of the acceptance of the norms, which are often quite technical in nature. Indeed, 'technical necessity' as a source of public authority.[80] This does not at all contradict Klabbers' starting points, as he argues that '[i]t might be wiser to focus on material evidence of authority: actors who are usually heard or followed will be deemed to have some prima facie law-making capacity'.[81]

Following this line of reasoning, one would not only need to be able to accept expertise or stakeholder consensus as a source of authority, but also to establish a consensus on who can be regarded the expert or to otherwise legitimately exercise certain authority (e.g. because one is representing certain stakeholders or has proceeded in a transparent and open manner allowing all interested parties to provide input). For instance, the authority of a formal advice of a medical examiner to declare a person disabled depends above all on his recognised knowledge and expertise as a specialised physician and only derivatively on his formal position as a medical officer. It seems that the authority of all formal advice, recommendations and the like are in the final analysis reducible to their foundations in forms of special knowledge or expertise that addressees do not have themselves but need for making proper choices. In advice and recommendations coming from advisory boards the notion of personal knowledge and expertise is replaced by that of consensus on the best available knowledge and expertise where a difference of opinions proves to be possible.

Here we touch possibly on the key term indicating the answer to the question of how to found a legal power in informal international law-making: consensus on the best available knowledge and expertise established in an open and transparent manner allowing for input by all affected stakeholders. Returning to our earlier example: where can we find the best available knowledge and expertise for designing and manufacturing medical devices? The answer is: within the professional community consisting of the medical device manufacturers and regulatory authorities themselves, debated in an open and transparent manner that allows for input also be other affected stakeholders, such as consumer and patient organisations.

---

80 Matthias Hartwich, 'ICANN – Governance by Technical Necessity', in von Bogdandy *et al.* (eds), *The Exercise of Public Authority by International Institutions, supra* note 4, 575–605. It has been argued that not only 'expertise', but also 'information' that could form the starting point: 'governance by information'. See von Bogdandy and Goldmann, 'The Exercise of International Public Authority through National Policy Assessment', *supra* note 59.
81 Klabbers, 'Law-making and Constitutionalism', *supra* note 9, at 119.

And how can consensus be reached? We may answer: that was what the GHTF was created for. However, attractive as this direction for finding a solution to the main problem dealt with in this contribution may appear to us, we are well aware of the fact that these two positive answers are still a far distance from really grounding a legal power of the GHTF to issue exhortations that are directly valid under international law.[82]

The past decade a similar debate took place in political science and international relations theory. Less concerned about the sources of law, these scholars attempted to construe a source of legitimacy for the emerging (or at least suddenly visible) forms of transnational governance and regulation. Empirical findings revealed that 'transnational governance bodies do indeed refer to participation, expertise and procedural fairness as sources of their claims to be legitimate regulators, though they vary in the degree of attention given to each dimension and the mix between them. The same is true of the legitimacy beliefs in terms of which audiences evaluate and validate these claims'. At the same time, these studies show that consensus on who is the expert or who is to have a voice and at what level is essential. 'Expertise-based legitimacy' runs the risk of being claimed by market powers that may not only have an eye for public needs.[83]

So, even when 'no one thought of making law', it may be perceived as law by its addressees. The reason for that may be that expertise or stakeholder consensus as the source of the norms reflects material evidence of authority.

4.3 Procedural guarantees are not met

IN-LAW will not be law when procedural guarantees are not met (e.g. norms are impossible, secret, in the end not accepted, conflicting higher norms or not democratic). This threshold thus contains 'substantive' procedural norms. While occasionally the absence of the guarantees may indeed bar informal law from becoming law, the project does not give reasons to argue that IN-LAW is impossible, secret, not accepted, conflicting higher norms or undemocratic (there are, of course, exceptions, where for example more openness or inclusiveness is called for, as in the ICH which was recently reformed to include the voices of a greater diversity of countries and stakeholders, and reduced the power of the pharmaceutical industry). On

---

82 For a more elaborate discussion, see Ruiter and Wessel, 'The Legal Nature of Informal International Law', *supra* note 15.

83 Sigrid Quack, 'Law, Expertise and Legitimacy in Transnational Economic Governance: An Introduction', 8 *Socio-Economic Review* (2010) 3–10, as well as the references in this article. A similar discussion runs in relation to risk regulations. See for instance Olivier Borraz, 'From Risk to the Government of Uncertainty: The Case of Mobile Telephony', 14 *Journal of Risk Research* (2011) 969–82, at 969: 'Scientific procedures define how expertise should be organized so that its claims will be seen as legitimate by authorities and the public.'

the contrary, the extensive use of informal law in various areas of transnational and global cooperation reveals that it is possible, and in fact, that it works. Some have even argued that it is gradually replacing traditional international law.[84] Furthermore, the involvement of many actors with clear links to civil society guarantees that the norms are not secret: in most cases, both the decision-making process is transparent and the outcome is made known to the actors in the field, be it the producers of medical devices, banks, the internet society or food producers.

While 'non-acceptance' in the end would be possible, it remains hard to see this as a helpful criterion to establish whether or not the norm is legal. After all, and despite a traditional stream in legal theory arguing otherwise, using acceptance as a criterion would deprive many international norms from their legal character. A similar problem relates to the demand that the norm does not conflict with higher norms. Presumably these should then be higher legal norms, but accepting the possibility of conflict in the legal order implies the acceptance of all norms involved as being legal.

The most problematic criterion may indeed be democracy. Traditional international law would generally become valid in domestic legal orders only after (prior or *ad hoc*) approval by a parliament. In informal international law-making, democratic legitimacy would be at stake. Yet, we argue that this could well be compensated by other procedural meta-norms against which new cooperation forms ought to be checked. We will refer to this as 'thick stakeholder consensus', imposing limits in respect of actors (authority), process and output. Intriguingly, this benchmark may be normatively superior (rather than inferior) to the validation requirements of traditional international law, coined here as 'thin state consent'.

In the context of the rather thin validation requirements of traditional international law, the charge that new forms of cooperation circumvent the formal structures of *international law* or are 'devoid of the guarantees that come with law'[85] rings rather hollow. What are these guarantees that come with international law? What are the structures of formal international lawmaking that these new forms of cooperation circumvent? Other than state consent, there are none. In contrast to this, thin consent at the international level supplemented, at the domestic level, with what often amounts to rubber-stamping by domestic parliaments, the emerging code of good practice for the development of standards or new forms of cooperation outside international law is normatively thicker.[86] In many (though not all) cases, the process is more inclusive, transparent and predictable. The actors

---

84　Gralf-Peter Calliess and Peer Zumbansen, *Rough Consensus and Running Code: A Theory of Transnational Private Law* (Hart Publishing, 2010); Pauwelyn, Wessel and Wouters, 'The Stagnation of International Law', *supra* note 10, at 12.
85　Klabbers, *The Concept of Treaty*, *supra* note 44, at 79.
86　See International Social and Environmental Accreditation and Labeling (ISEAL) Alliance, Code of Good Practice for Setting Social and Environmental Standards, Version 5.0, January 2010 <www.isealalliance.org/sites/default/files/Standard-Setting%20Code%20v5.0_0.pdf>

involved are more diverse and expert. The output, finally, is elaborated more carefully and coherently, supported by a broader consensus (both *ex ante* when the norm is developed, and *ex post* when the norm is accepted because it works) and continuously questioned and adapted to practical, real-world developments and needs[87] (the so-called 'rough consensus and running code',[88] without veto or opting-out power for any given actor, contrary to traditional international law). Whereas traditional international law is driven by thin (state) consent, new forms of cooperation are increasingly based on thick (stakeholder) consensus.[89]

Arguably, the circumvention of *domestic* formalities linked to law-making must be taken more seriously. In most countries, for a treaty to become binding it must receive consent from Parliament or Congress. Certain new forms of cooperation may avoid this legitimising step. That said, the domestic approval of treaties is often a mere rubber-stamping of a *fait accompli* anyhow.[90] Yet, to secure domestic democratic legitimacy,[91] a mini-

---

87 See, in the field of intellectual property, Graeme Dinwoodie, 'The International Intellectual Property Law System: New Actors, New Institutions, New Sources', 10 *Marquette Intellectual Property Law Review* (2006) 205–14, at 211 (urging to 'resist the effort to feed these developments [in non-traditional processes and fora] back toward the multilateral treaty system, because it is inevitable that the non-treaty based system will effect internationalization more efficiently than the further development of TRIPs').

88 Calliess and Zumbansen, *Rough Consensus and Running Code*, supra note 84.

89 Harm Schepel, 'Private Regulators IN-LAW', in Pauwelyn, Wessel and Wouters (eds), *Informal International Lawmaking*, supra note 13, 356–67, clarifies the notion of 'consensus' in the standards world as follows:

> 'Consensus' is best understood as shorthand for the near universal procedural core of private standard setting: elaboration of a draft by consensus in a technical committee with a composition representing a balance of interests, a round of public notice-and-comment of that draft with the obligation on the committee to take received comments into account, a ratification vote with a requirement of consensus, not just a majority, among the constituent members of the standards body, and an obligation to review standards periodically. The codes, manuals and 'standards for standards' where these rules are laid out are impressive tomes of private administrative law.

> See, for example, American National Standards Institute, *ANSI Essential Requirements: Due Process Requirements for American National Standards* (2010); *CEN/CENELEC Internal Regulations Part 2: Common Rules for Standardization Work* (2012); DIN 820 (2009); British Standards Institute, *BS 0:2011, A Standard for Standards: Principles of Standardization* (2011).

90 See David Y. Livshiz, 'Updating American Administrative Law: WTO, International Standards, Domestic Implementation and Public Participation', 24 *Wisconsin International Law Journal* (2007) 961–1016; Richard Mulgan, *Holding Power to Account, Accountability in Modern Democracies* (Palgrave, 2003) at 12 ('In modern representative democracies, little direct power remains to the people who must rely almost entirely on professional politicians and bureaucrats. Specialist institutions of accountability thus become increasingly important as means by which the public can try to keep governments in line').

91 For an analytical framework to assess the democratic legitimacy of private standard-setting, see Nicolas Hachez and Jan Wouters, 'A Glimpse at the Democratic Legitimacy of Private Standards: Assessing the Public Accountability of GlobalG.A.P.', 14 *Journal of International Economic Law* (2011) 677–710, at 679–95, with a subsequent application to GLOBALG.A.P. at 695–709.

mum degree of parliamentary or congressional oversight (not necessarily formal consent) of all international cooperation that affects public policy-making or individual freedom – treaty or not – must be available. To the extent law-making powers are delegated to administrative agencies, transparency, reason-giving and notice-and-comment procedures should apply to both the domestic *and* international activities and norm-making of these agencies, whether norms are binding under international law or not. A general guideline along these lines is already in place in Canada.[92] Requirements under domestic administrative law of one (important) member may then *de facto* also apply to the operation of the entire international network. When it comes to private standards or norms, competition law may play a controlling role.[93] Finally, judicial review must be available before domestic courts to protect fundamental rights of individuals and to ensure checks and balances between the legislature, executive and administrative agencies. Examples of such court control can be found in the EU,[94] The Netherlands,[95]

---

92 Ayelet Berman, 'The Role of Domestic Administrative Law in the Accountability of Transnational Regulatory Networks: The Case of ICH', IRPA GAL Working Paper 2012/1.
93 See Harm Schepel, 'Delegation of Regulatory Powers to Private Parties under EC Competition Law: Towards a Procedural Public Interest Test', 39 *Common Market Law Review* (2002) 31–51. In the US, so-called *Parker* immunity protects government action from antitrust scrutiny on the theory that the political process should be left alone to determine 'the public interest'. See *Parker v. Brown*, 317 US 341 (1943).
94 In the EU context, only very few agencies have been allotted formal and binding decision-making powers. Such powers are, in accordance with the *Meroni* doctrine, strictly circumscribed executive powers, mainly relating to the registration of trademarks and certain chemicals, and the issuance of certificates. Cases 9/56 and 10/56 *Meroni v. High Authority* [1957–1958] ECR 133. See recently Stefan Griller and Andreas Orator, 'Everything under Control? The 'Way Forward' for European Agencies in the Footsteps of the Meroni Doctrine', 35 *European Law Review* (2010) 3–35. For other examples of judicial review, see Case C-327/91, *France v. Commission* [1994] ECR I-3641, where the European Court of Justice declared void an act of the Commission whereby the Commission had sought to conclude a cooperation agreement with US anti-trust authorities. The Court was of the view that this agreement would bind the EU under international law but found that the Commission did not have the power to conclude such agreement. In Case C-233/02 *France v. Commission* [2004] ECR I-2759, France challenged guidelines on technical barriers to trade negotiated between the Commission and the US Trade Representative and US Department of Commerce, within the framework of the Transatlantic Economic Partnership. France argued that the guidelines formed a legally binding treaty, which in the constitutional framework of the EU should have been concluded by the Council. The Court disagreed: since the parties had agreed to apply the guidelines 'on a voluntary basis', the Court concluded that no legally binding agreement had been intended and, hence, none had been concluded.
95 See Leonard F. M. Besselink, 'Informal International Lawmaking: Elaboration and Implementation in The Netherlands', in Berman *et al.* (eds), *Case Studies, supra* note 13, 95–138 (referring to cases of legislative referral to an informally set norm or standard where the question arose whether this standard itself acquires a legislative character and, if so, whether it must live up to constitutional requirements for legislative acts, in particular as regards its publication and public availability; e.g. Gerechtshof [Court of Appeal] of The Hague, 16 November 2010, LJN: BO4175; Raad van State, 2 February 2011, LJN: BP2750).

US,[96] Canada[97] and Brazil.[98] Also, international courts and tribunals can play a controlling role, and, as Klabbers held, '[international] courts by and large tend to approach [informal international law-making] as they would approach regular law: while the drafters of informal law typically will want to escape both democratic and judicial accountability, courts are not too keen on letting them do so'.[99] It is not that traditional international law is legitimate and new forms of cooperation are not, or *vice versa*. Both require close scrutiny and vigilance.[100] Both can be more, or less, democratically legitimate depending on the circumstances.[101]

---

96   See, for example, *Free Enterprise Fund v. Public Company Accounting Oversight Board*, 561 US 1 (2010) (where the US Supreme Court struck down a provision requiring 'good cause' before the US SEC could fire Public Company Accounting Oversight Board [PCAOB] board members, arguing that this would undermine executive control by the US President over the PCAOB). The PCAOB is heavily involved in international standard-setting through bilateral agreements with foreign authorities as well as membership in international networks such as the International Forum of Independent Audit Regulators. See <pcaobus.org/International/Pages/default.aspx>.

97   See, for example, *A. v. Ontario Securities Commission* [2006] CanLII 14414 (OSC), where the Ontario Superior Court of Justice evaluated the constitutional legitimacy of the investigations carried out by the Ontario Securities Commission in execution of a MoU between this Canadian authority and the US SEC.

98   See, for example, Superior Court of Justice (Superior Tribunal de Justiça – STJ) (Preliminary Injunction (Medida Cautelar) n. 17.350-RJ, October 7, 2010, upholding a lower court finding that the implementation in Brazil of certain International Organization of Securities Commissions (IOSCO) guidelines on the remuneration of administrators violated the legality principle, discussed in Salem H. Nasser and Ana Mara França Machado, 'Implementation of IN-LAW and Accountability in Brazil BASEL – IOSCO – ICH', in Berman *et al.* (eds), *Case Studies, supra* note 13.

99   See Klabbers, 'International Courts and Informal International Law', *supra* note 47. In this respect, Scott and Sturm have advocated a role for courts (including international tribunals) beyond rule enforcement or formal adjudication, namely: courts as 'catalysts' which 'facilitate the realization of process values and principles that are crucial to new governance's legitimacy and efficacy by the institutional actors responsible for norm elaboration within new governance'. Joanne Scott and Susan Sturm, 'Courts as Catalysts: Rethinking the Judicial Role in New Governance', 13 *Columbia Journal of European Law* (2007) 565–94, at 567; in the specific context of the WTO, see Joanne Scott, 'International Trade and Environmental Governance: Relating Rules (and Standards) in the EU and the WTO', 15 *European Journal of International Law* (2004) 307–54.

100 See Jürgen Habermas, *Between Facts and Norms: Contributions to a Discourse Theory of Law and Democracy* (Polity Press, 1995) at 441–2: 'the only thing that serves as a "palladium of liberty" against the growth of independent, illegitimate power is a suspicious, mobile, alert, and informed public sphere that affects the parliamentary complex and secures *the sources from which legitimate law can arise*' (emphasis in original).

101 Louis L. Jaffe, 'An Essay on Delegation of Legislative Power', 47 *Columbia Law Review* (1947) 359–76, at 360:

> We must not take lightly the objection to indiscriminate and ill-defined delegation. It expresses a fundamental democratic concern. But neither should we insist that 'law-making' as such is the exclusive province of the legislature. The aim of government is to gain acceptance for objectives demonstrated as desirable and to realize them as fully as possible. We should recognize that legislation and administration are complementary rather than opposed processes; and that delegation is the formal term and method for their interplay.

4.4 The topic may be too trivial to be regulated by law

The examples given by Klabbers under this heading include: an agreement between political leaders to have a photo session during a summit meeting, or an agreement reached at a conference to have a coffee break at 11.00.[102] The argument that 'the presumption of law shall be rebutted by the circumstance that such an agreement is simply too trivial' is convincing and, yet, makes clear that it would be hard to rebut the legal presumption underlying informal international law on these grounds. IN-LAW is not about this type of agreements, but rather about setting norms on topics such as financial stability, food safety, medical products, climate change or trade matters.

5 Concluding observations

This contribution has sought to build bridges between the approaches taken in the literature on classifying and defining alternative methods to generate international agreement, using the writings of Jan Klabbers as a point of departure and possible guiding principles. The study of non-traditional forms of international law has not only been carried out in the IN-LAW project and in other international research efforts, but has also benefitted greatly from the research of our colleague and friend Jan Klabbers. His insights in the constitutionalisation of international law, the institutions involved in it and the legal nature of norms have been helpful in assessing international law-making in its very diverse appearances.

In the cross-fertilisation exercise carried out in this contribution, we have focused in particular on the relationship between validity, legitimacy and authority in law-making processes. To do so, first, we drafted a conceptual basis to determine the scope of international public policy instruments. The IN-LAW framework has been helpful in this since it focuses on instruments characterised by informality in the way they come into being, with regard to the actors involved or in its outcomes. The latter, the output of processes of law-making, has in turn been analysed in light of the sometimes unclear divide between law and non-law. Here, the introduction of the validity criterion in IN-LAW provided for interesting synergies. The inescapable need for a formal criterion to determine a legal nature – which may very well be the consent expressed by actors or a benchmark in the form of 'everything that actors adhere to' – has been central in analysing an instrument's possible legal nature. Furthermore, it has proved impossible to judge the legal nature of international agreement when not taking into consideration sources of authority. The exercise of authority was revealed across the informal international landscape. Informal processes form an expression of public authority and can therefore be regarded as legal. It was, in addition, concluded that the exercise of authority also clearly triggers

---

102 Klabbers, 'Law-making and Constitutionalism', *supra* note 9, at 121.

questions related to the accountability of informal mechanisms. Finally, the arguments underlying the notion of presumptive law were confronted with the practice of informal international law-making. Maybe not to much surprise, it turned out that Jan Klabbers' 'presumptive law' theory fitted well in the informal practice. As such, four criteria were outlined that may rebut a presumption that informal law-making processes are law. It was found that, in general, informal law-making's output is concrete and well-defined, procedurally and substantively sound, developed out of (technical) necessity and that compliance with these norms is, in many cases, extremely high.

In conclusion, there is nothing new in arguing that 'regulation beyond the state' seems to have pushed traditional forms of law-making to the background. Yet, scholarship is still in the process of assessing these phenomena. The importance of continuing the study of norm-setting beyond the traditional channels cannot be overstressed. We would suggest that a legal approach in this is needful, because of the fundamental legal nature of norms that only in specific cases can be rebutted. This will obviously further impact on the discussed constitutionalisation of international law and the rethinking of representative decision-making. It may even result in a complete redefinition of the sources doctrine in public international law.

6 Mankind's territory and the limits of international law-making

Wouter G. Werner

Introduction

Since the Second World War, the concept of 'mankind' has proliferated in international treaty law. In areas such as the law of the sea, the regulation of outer space or the preservation of cultural heritage, states have acknowledged that 'mankind' has interests that are worth protecting through international law-making. The invocation of 'mankind' within the traditional paradigm of treaty-law, however, is somewhat of an oxymoron. Since the concept appears in international treaties, its validity, scope of application and meaning derives largely from the express or tacit consent of states. The *pacta tertiis* formula, for example, would stand in the way of attempts to create world-wide obligations for the sake of mankind through treaty provisions. At the same time, including terms such as 'mankind' in international treaties seeks to do exactly that; to go beyond the rights and interests of individual states by presenting an encompassing world community or set of core values that transcend the confines of state sovereignty. The invocation of these concepts in international law-making thus reflects the foundational paradox that has informed many parts of Jan Klabbers' work: international law is unstably situated in-between state sovereignty and world community, state consent and objective norms.[1]

A study into the concept of mankind in international law is therefore unavoidably also a study into the limits of international law-making and the idea that international legal rules are not pre-given, but produced through acts of will. In this chapter, I will illustrate this point by means of a comparison between two rather different ways in which 'mankind' has been invoked in international law. In the *first* place, I will study how writers such as Vitoria, Grotius and Vattel, notwithstanding their tremendous differences on some fundamental points, all rooted 'mankind' in natural law, used it to bar claims to sovereignty and to identify enemies of mankind (section 1). In

---

[1] See, for example, his widely used textbook on the law of international organisations: Jan Klabbers, *An Introduction to International Institutional Law* (2nd edn, Cambridge University Press, 2009).

the *second* place, I will study how the concept of mankind appears in the modern law of the sea, the law of outer space and the Antarctica regime (section 2). I will show how the modern way of invoking mankind differs from earlier invocations in at least three respects: (a) the nature and role of international law-making, (b) the nature of the global community whose interests are at stake and (c) the existence or absence of enemies of mankind in legal reasoning.

A final note on terminology. This chapter focuses on the concept of 'mankind'. Although the concept is seldom precisely defined and its use varies across contexts, 'mankind' is generally used to refer to a global community that includes, yet transcends sovereign states; to a community that is more inclusive than a society of sovereign, independent states.[2] The concept of 'mankind' is sometimes used interchangeably with the concept of 'humanity'. However, 'humanity' is a more ambiguous term, as it can be used to refer to the totality of all human beings ('humankind'), but also to that what makes us humane ('humaneness'), to 'human dignity' or to what makes us human ('humanness').[3] Since the focus of this chapter is on the regulation of territories that belong to a global community and not on questions of humaneness or what constitutes a human being I will primarily discuss the concept of 'mankind' in the following sections.

1 Mankind's Territory: Vitoria, Grotius and Vattel

This section studies the concept of 'mankind' in the work of Vitoria, Grotius and Vattel. Although these three writers operated in different historical contexts and worked on sometimes radically diverging assumptions, there are three structural similarities in the way in which they invoked the concept of mankind. First, all three root the concept of mankind in natural law, or in a state of nature from which humankind has evolved. In this sense, 'mankind' is not perceived as the product of law-making, but rather as the precondition for and a limitation on the creation of positive law. Second, the concept of mankind is initially invoked to set limits to sovereign rule and to bar attempts at appropriation; not so much in attempts to bring nations actively together for a common cause. Third, the concept of mankind plays a crucial role in the justification of wars; those who violate or refuse to recognise the rights that are common to all turn into an enemies of mankind against whom enforcement measures may be taken.

---

2   In terms of the English School this would signify a turn from 'international society' to 'world society'. Barry Buzan, *From International Society to World Society: English School Theory and the Social Structure of Globalization* (Cambridge University Press, 2004).

3   For a discussion see Britta van Beers, Luigi Corrias and Wouter Werner (eds), *Humanity Across International Law and Bio-Law* (Cambridge University Press, forthcoming).

1.1 Vitoria

According to Vitoria, the ultimate foundation of legal and political authority was a global community which had organised itself in sub-communities of independent peoples (the so called 'perfect communities').[4] As Grewe summarises the basic assumption of the Spanish school: 'The world community of the human race was conceived by Vitoria and the other Spanish theorists of his era as an organised community of peoples which were themselves constituted politically as states'.[5] The concept of mankind thus went hand in hand with the obligation to respect the integrity and right to self-determination of other perfect communities. Such obligations did not derive from the sovereign will of princes or from imperial rule, but from dictates of natural law. For Vitoria, this also implied that most justifications that had been offered for the conquest of the Americas lacked normative basis; the Native Americans had organised themselves in political communities that were part of the global community of mankind. Neither the Pope nor the Spanish Empire had direct jurisdiction over the Native American communities and the fact that native communities were guilty of sins and violations of the law of nature did not *as such* give the Spaniards a right to wage war or occupy native land.[6]

However, alongside the duty of peaceful co-existence of political communities, Vitoria also identified the so-called *ius communicationis*, the universal right to communicate. The right to communicate is not only grounded in a conception of mankind, but in a more general sense to the idea of 'humanity'. In the first place, Vitoria argues that communication is what makes us 'human'; what sets us apart from (other) animals. The right to communicate is thus rooted in the idea of 'humanness'. Second, the *ius communicationis* is linked to the interests of humanity as a whole; to what binds mankind together. The right to communication implies three obligations for political communities: they cannot set aside the right to travel, to trade and to preach the Christian faith. Vitoria grounds the *ius communicatonis* in the 'natural' condition of man, before the idea of property and exclusive jurisdiction was introduced:

> it was permissible from the beginning of the world (when everything was in common) for anyone to set forth and travel whithersoever he would. Now this was not taken away by the division of property, for it

---

4 Vitoria described perfect communities as follows: 'A perfect State or community, therefore, is one which is complete in itself, that is, which is not a part of another community, but has its own laws and its own council and its own magistrates, such as is the Kingdom of Castile and Aragon and the Republic of Venice and other the like'. *Vitoria: Political Writings* (Anthony Pagden and Jeremy Lawrance, eds, Cambridge University Press, 1991), at 301.
5 Wilhelm Grewe, *Epochs of International Law* (Michael Byers, transl., De Gruyter, 2000), at 146.
6 Vitoria dismisses the different grounds offered for the Spanish conquest, including the difference of religion, enlargement of empire, personal glory of the prince. *Vitoria, supra* note 4, at 302–3.

was never the intention of peoples to destroy by that division the reciprocity and common uses which prevailed among men, and indeed in the days of Noah it would have been inhumane to do so.[7]

The right to travel, trade and preach also extended to rivers, harbours and the sea, which Vitoria considered to be 'common to all ... and public things ... by natural law'.[8] Of course, Vitoria's *ius communicationis* should not be misread as a liberal-cosmopolitan ideal that applies equally to all. While Vitoria accepted the right to travel, trade and preach, as well as the common nature of harbours and waterways, he did make an important qualification. If it would be in the interest of the propagation of Christianity, Vitoria argued, '[t]he Pope could entrust to the Spaniards alone the task of converting the Indian aborigines and could forbid to all others not only preaching, but trade too'.[9]

Those that hinder the harmless exercise of the *ius communicationis* violate natural law, the interests of mankind and the rights of other political communities. They could become the targets of a just war, provided no other means are available and waging a war helps to effectively vindicate the rights of the injured party.[10] For Vitoria, this would indeed be a justification for the use of force against Native American communities and the occupation of their land and property: 'when the Indians deny the Spaniards their rights under the law of nations they do them a wrong. Therefore, if it be necessary, in order to preserve their right, that they should go to war, they may lawfully do so'.[11] Mankind thus works as a double-edged sword for the Native Americans: it protects them against interferences based on a universal right to rule by the Spaniards and the Pope, but also puts them under an obligation to accept foreigners on their territories. If they frustrate the

---

7   The so-called *relectiones* on the 'Indians lately discovered' are published online at <www.constitution.org/victoria/victoria_4.htm>. The *relectiones* are divided up in three parts. Below I will refer to this source as Vitoria, *De Indes*. The quote here is taken from *De Indes*, pt. III, para. 1.
8   *Ibid.*, pt. III, para. 1.
9   *Ibid.*, pt. III, second proposition. Vitoria adds:

> as it is the Pope's concern to bestow especial care on the propagation of the Gospel over the whole world, he can entrust it to the Spaniards to the exclusion of all others, if the sovereigns of Spain could render more effective help in the spread of the Gospel in those parts; and not only could the Pope forbid others to preach, but also to trade there, if this would further the propagation of Christianity, for he can order temporal matters in the manner which is most helpful to spiritual matters.

> Another clear signal that Vitoria should not be read in liberal cosmopolitan terms is his denial of the right to fight just wars to Saracens (and by implication to Native Americans). For an analysis, see Anthony Anghie, *Imperialism, Sovereignty and International Law* (Cambridge University Press, 2005), at 26.

10 The argument regarding the criteria for waging war against the Native Americans is set out throughout Vitoria, *De Indes, supra* note 7, pt. III.
11 *Ibid.*, pt. III, fifth proposition.

peaceful exercise of the *ius communicationis*, Native American communities could become the target of just war and have their lands occupied.[12]

1.2 Grotius

The concept of mankind figures prominently in Grotius' defense of the freedom of the high seas. For Grotius, areas such as the air and the sea 'lie open unto all'[13] and therefore belong to the 'whole of society of mankind'.[14] Grotius brought forward three main arguments to underpin the idea that the sea belonged to the commons of mankind.

The *first* is that it is impossible to effectively acquire and possess the sea. While land could be 'worked and improved upon through cultivation and construction, the sea cannot be altered by man and is therefore incapable of ever being owned'.[15] The freedom of the high seas is here derived from a labour theory of acquisition; only through mixing one's labour with the fruits of the earth and through occupation it is possible to obtain property or exclusive jurisdiction.[16] Since Grotius believed it to be impossible to occupy or mix one's labour with the seas, these waters should remain open for everyone – the domain of mankind.

The *second*, and related, argument is that the high seas are what we would nowadays call 'public goods'; goods that are non-rival and non-excludable.[17] Public goods are goods 'which all enjoy in common in the sense that each individual's consumption of such a good leads to no subtractions from any other individual's consumption of that good'.[18] In similar fashion, Grotius defended the freedom of the high seas as rooted in the idea that by nature some goods are composed in such a way that they make exclusive property impossible: 'all those things which have been so constituted by nature that, even when used by a specific individual, they nevertheless suffice for general use by other persons without discrimination, retain to-day and should retain for all time that status which characterised them when they first sprang from

---

12 For a more elaborate discussion of the different faces of Vitoria's work see Anghie, *Imperialism*, *supra* note 9.
13 Hugo Grotius, *The Freedom of the High Seas* (Ralph Van Deman Magoffin, Oxford University Press 1916 [1933]), at 26, <socserv.mcmaster.ca/econ/ugcm/3ll3/grotius/Seas.pdf>.
14 *Ibid.*, at 55.
15 Dan Lynch, 'The VOC, the EIC and the Free Sea: The Rhetoric and Reality of Free Trade in Early Modern World Economy', NEH Seminar (2005), at 29, <www1.umassd.edu/euro/2005papers/lynch.pdf>.
16 The acquisition theory of property is central to the work of John Locke, who assumed that 'one justly appropriates the fruits of the Earth by laboring on those things' – 'mixing one's labor with them'. John Locke, *Two Treatises of Government* (P. Laslett, ed., Cambridge University Press, 1960 [1690]), § 27.
17 Paul Samuelsson, 'The Pure Theory of Public Expenditure', 36 *Review of Economics and Statistics* (1954) 387–9.
18 *Ibid.*, at 387.

nature'.[19] While Grotius acknowledged that in principle the stock of fish in the ocean was exhaustible, the idea of over-exploitation of the oceans was regarded as a mere theoretical option at the time. In addition, Grotius realised that in practice it had proven possible to exclude others from navigating the high seas. After all, it was exactly the arrogation of exclusive jurisdiction over the oceans by Spain and Portugal that formed the background of Grotius' treatises. The assumption of such powers against the law of nature, however, was for Grotius a sign of 'monstrous cupidity'[20] that undermined the laws of mankind.

Third, the freedom of the high seas is rooted in the natural right to global travel and trade, in mankind's liberty of 'going hither and thither and trading'.[21] Harking back to the work of Vitoria (but not accepting his claims about Papal authority, of course),[22] Grotius defends the existence of a *ius communicationis*: a right to travel and trade globally and a corresponding obligation for others not to hinder the exercise of this right. This right is even rooted in God's will, Grotius contends:

> For God has not willed that nature shall supply every region with all the necessities of life; and furthermore, He has granted pre-eminence in different arts to different nations. Why are these things so, if not because it was His Will that human friendships should be fostered by mutual needs and resources.[23]

Global travel and trade are thus conceived as ways to reunite a diversified global society and to gain peace through commerce.

Ironically, however, these were the very same arguments that Grotius used to defend the right to use force, even by private companies, against the Spaniards and the Portuguese. His defence of the freedom of the high seas did exactly what critics of concepts such as 'mankind' would expect: it turned adversaries into violators of the laws of nature and into enemies of mankind.[24] The seizure of the *Santa Catarina* by Van Heemskerck[25] could

---

19 Grotius, *Freedom of the High Seas*, supra note 13, at 60–1; quoted in Ellen Hey, 'Interdependencies, Conceptualizations of Humanity and Regulatory Regimes', in van Beers, Corrias and Werner (eds), *Humanity across International Law and Bio-Law*, supra note 3.
20 Grotius, *Freedom of the High Seas*, supra note 13, at 83.
21 *Ibid.*, at 6.
22 For an analysis of the relation between Grotius and Vitoria on the matter of free trade see Johannes Thumfahrt, 'On Grotius's *Mare Liberum* and Vitoria's *De Indis*, Following Agamben and Schmitt', 30 *Grotiana* (2009) 65–87.
23 Grotius, *Freedom of the High Seas*, supra note 13, at 12.
24 The classical critique can be found in the work of Carl Schmitt, *The Concept of the Political* (University of Chicago Press, 2007).
25 As may be recalled the Portuguese ship *Santa Catarina* was captured by the Dutch East Indies Company in 1605. The capture of the *Santa Catarina* not only roughly doubled the capital of the Company, it also raised fundamental questions regarding the rights of private (or public-private) companies to seize foreign ships.

now be defended as the exercise of a natural right to free trade and travel, against those that stand in the way of the dictates of nature, the laws of mankind and the establishment of peace through commerce. Grotius would even go so far as to label those that blockade the seas and hinder global trade as 'pirates', thus making it possible to brand the Portuguese as *hostes humani generis*.

1.3 Vattel

Emerich de Vattel is generally known for his rejection of Wolff's idea of the *Civitas Maxima*; the idea of an overarching political community that binds the world together.[26] Instead, Vattel positioned the sovereign state as the sole subject of international law, emphasising its free and independent nature and putting it under an obligation to 'preserve and perfect its own nature'.[27] This is not to say that Vattel denied the existence of a larger community of which sovereign states form part. As Koskenniemi points out, however, Vattel conceived of this society primarily as a 'system', in which states 'by looking to their (enlightened) self-interest, … would be able to contribute to the good of the whole'.[28] Within this system, each state 'possesses the right of judging, what conduct she is to pursue' – when states use this right to preserve and perfect themselves, the net result is akin to what the invisible hand accomplishes at the free market: 'at least externally … a perfect equality of rights between nations … in the pursuit of their pretensions, without regard to the intrinsic justice of their conduct, of which others have no right to form a definitive judgement'.[29] Notwithstanding the pivotal position of each state's right to judge and strive for perfection, Vattel left room for legal rules that follow from non-consensual sources. Alongside the positive law of nations, Vattel recognised the existence of so-called voluntary law, based on the *presumed* consent of sovereigns (i.e. those rules that states would agree to if they could see their enlightened long-term self-interests clearly) and rules stemming from natural law. Vattel's notion of the law of nations thus combined two aspects that do not always go together easily: pre-given rules in the form of voluntary and natural law together with the right of each states to judge what conduct she is to pursue.

---

26 Martti Koskenniemi, ' "International Community" from Dante to Vattel', in Vincent Chetail and Peter Haggenmacher (eds), *Vattel's International Law from a XXIst Century Perspective* (Martinus Nijhoff, 2011) 51–76, at 51.
27 Emerich de Vattel, *The Law of Nations, or Principles of the Law of Nature Applied to the Conduct and Affairs of Nations and Sovereigns* (T. & J. W. Johnson & Co., 1883 [1852]), at para. 14, <www.constitution.org/vattel/vattel.htm>.
28 Koskenniemi, 'International Community', *supra* note 26, at 24.
29 Vattel, *Law of Nations*, *supra* note 27, at para. 21; quoted in Tony Carty and Zhang Xiaoshi, 'From Freedom and Equality to Domination and Subordination: Feminist and Anti-Colonialist Critiques of the Vattelian Heritage', 43 *Netherlands Yearbook of International Law* (2013) 53–82.

The tension between these two aspects can also be found in Vattel's treatment of mankind. It is interesting to find that Vattel, some 150 years after Grotius defended the freedom of the high seas in terms of natural law, comes up with arguments that to a large extent overlap with Grotius' approach.[30] For Vattel, the freedom of the open seas follows from two interrelated elements: the nature of property rights and the public nature of the open sea. The right to property, Vattel contends, was introduced because nature itself provided insufficient means for the ever-expanding population of the earth ('the human race, who were extremely multiplied').[31] In order to deal with the scarcity dominating primitive life,

> it became necessary to introduce the right of property, in order that each might apply himself with more success to the cultivation of what had fallen to his share, and multiply by his labour the necessaries and conveniences of life. It is for this reason the law of nature approves the rights of dominion and property.[32]

The right to property, in other words, is grounded in a functional logic that justifies the acquisition of the earth and its fruits that would otherwise belong to mankind in general. Vattel denies that the same functional logic can be applied to public goods; to goods that are unlimitedly available and whose use by one person does not affect the possibilities of others to consume the same good. In these cases, 'nature does not give to man a right of appropriating to himself things that may be innocently used, and that are inexhaustible, and sufficient for all'.[33] Acting under the assumption that the open sea indeed provides inexhaustible resources, Vattel regarded this to be a prime example of such a public good that cannot be appropriated. When nations nevertheless claim exclusive rights to the open sea, they violate the natural law that holds the community of nations together. Thereby they not only violate another state's subjective right to navigate and fish on the open sea, they also disrespect the laws and interests of human society as such and become the enemies of mankind. Such a state 'infringes their common right' giving other states the right or even obligation 'to rise up against him; and, by uniting their forces to chastise the common enemy, they will discharge their duty towards themselves, and towards human society'.[34]

The existence of rights of mankind are thus connected to the duty of each state to unite against transgressors; a duty that is rooted in the obligation of each state to strive for preservation and perfection as well as its right to judge

---

30 For an analysis of non-consensual arguments in Vattel's work see also Koskenniemi, 'International Community', *supra* note 26.
31 Vattel, *Law of Nations*, *supra* note 27, at para. 281.
32 *Ibid.*
33 *Ibid.*
34 *Ibid.*, at para. 283.

for itself what conduct to pursue. In other words: 'mankind' in Vattel's work goes back and forth between pre-given natural law and the right to judgement of individual nations, between the freedom of states and their common duties to rise up against enemies of mankind.

2 Mankind enacted

From the 1960s on, the concept of 'mankind' was rediscovered in the law regulating territories beyond sovereign rule. Against the backdrop of rapid technological developments and increasing concerns about the gap between rich and poor countries, the concept of mankind was introduced to prevent over-exploitation and to ensure that the use of territories such as the seabed, the ocean floor, Antarctica or outer space would not only benefit powerful nations. Following the ideas of the Maltese representative Arvid Pardo,[35] the seabed and ocean floor were declared 'common heritage of mankind' in the 1982 Law of the Sea Convention, which also set out that 'all rights in the resources of the Area are vested in mankind as a whole'.[36] In order to ensure that the exploitation of the seabed and ocean floor would take place for the benefit of humanity, a specific authority was created – the International Seabed Authority.[37] The idea that areas beyond sovereign jurisdiction should be exploited for the benefit of mankind as a whole was taken up in other branches of international law as well. The Outer Space Treaty, for example, states that the 'exploration and use of outer space, … shall be carried out for the benefit and in the interests of all countries, … and shall be the province of all mankind',[38] with astronauts being elevated to the status of 'envoys of mankind'.[39] The preamble of the Antarctic Treaty speaks of the 'interests of all mankind' that are at stake in ensuring that Antarctica is used solely for peaceful purposes.[40] Notions such as the 'common heritage of mankind'

---

35 See declaration and treaty concerning the reservation exclusively for peaceful purposes of the seabed and the ocean floor underlying the seas beyond the limits of present national jurisdiction, and the use of the resources in the interest of mankind, UN Doc. A/6695 (1967).
36 United Nations Convention on the Law of the Sea (UNCLOS), 10 December 1982, in force 16 November 1994, 1833 UNTS 3, Articles 136–7.
37 For more information on the authority see <www.isa.org.jm/en/home>.
38 Treaty on Principles governing the Activities of States in the Exploration and Use of Outer Space, including the Moon and Other Celestial Bodies, 27 January 1967, in force 10 October 1967, 610 UNTS 205, Article 1.
39 *Ibid.*, Article 5. See also Agreement Governing the Activities of States on the Moon and Other Celestial Bodies, GA Res. 34/68, 5 December 1979, in force 11 July 1984, 1363 UNTS 3, Article 4, ensuring that the exploration and use of outer space, including the moon and other celestial bodies, shall be carried out for the benefit and in the interests of all countries, irrespective of their degree of economic or scientific development, and shall be the province of all mankind.
40 Antarctic Treaty, 1 December 1959, in force 23 June 1961, 402 UNTS 71, Preamble.

even gained a foothold in areas other than the law of non-sovereign territory. The World Heritage Convention, for example, regards parts of the cultural or natural heritage as 'part of the world heritage of mankind as a whole'[41] and seeks to protect it accordingly, while in the field of bio-law attempts have been made to protect the human genome as the 'common heritage of humanity'.[42]

The above-mentioned examples overlap in at least two ways with the way in which Vitoria, Grotius and Vattel used the concept of mankind. At the most general level, certain territories are presented as belonging to something that transcends a society of individual states, namely mankind (with post-1945 treaties increasingly also including future generations).[43] Although there is controversy whether 'mankind' can be regarded, properly speaking, a subject of international law,[44] the above-mentioned treaties do yield legally valid presentations of an entity ('mankind') that are invoked in legal discourse, which form the ground for rights and obligations of states and are acted upon by a variety of actors. Second, the concept of mankind is generally used to exclude appropriation by private or public actors, not unlike the way in which mankind was invoked by Vitoria, Grotius and Vattel. Treaties such as the Outer Space Treaty, the Moon Treaty or the Law of the Sea Convention typically invoke 'mankind' to bar claims to sovereignty and ownership.

However, the use of mankind in post-1945 treaties also differs significantly from its invocation by Vitoria, Grotius and Vattel. From the perspective of international law-making, three differences stand out in particular: *first*, differences regarding the epistemological assumptions underlying legal reasoning; *second* differences concerning the nature of the commons of mankind; *third* differences relating to legitimate responses to violations of the regime regulating the commons of mankind.

---

41   Convention Concerning the Protection of the World Cultural and Natural Heritage, 16 November 1972, in force 17 December 1975, 1037 UNTS 151, Preamble.

42   The idea of a common heritage was even invoked in the non-binding Universal Declaration on the Human Genome and Human Rights, which was adopted unanimously and by acclamation at UNESCO's 29th General Conference on 11 November 1997 (UNESCO Doc. 29 C/Res.16) and endorsed by the United Nations General Assembly in the following year (GA Res. 53/152, 9 December 1998). The declaration expresses the belief that 'the human genome underlies the fundamental unity of all members of the human family, as well as the recognition of their inherent dignity and diversity. In a symbolic sense, it is the heritage of humanity' (Article 1). Note that the invocation of the human genome as underlying the unity of mankind as well as human dignity constitutes an interesting reinvention of natural law as the basis for a cosmopolitan community.

43   For overviews, see Emanuel Agius and Salvino Busuttil (eds), *Future Generations and International Law* (Earthscan, 1998); Laura Westra, *Environmental Justice and the Rights of Unborn and Future Generations: Law, Environmental Harm and the Right to Health* (Earthscan, 2006).

44   This topic was debated mainly in the late 1970s and 1980s. See, for example, Rüdiger Wolfrum, 'The Principle of the Common Heritage of Mankind', 43 *Zeitschrift für ausländisches öffentliches Recht und Völkerrecht* (1983) 312–337, at 318 and the references mentioned there.

2.1 Mankind as treaty provision

As was set out above, early modern scholars discussed the concept of mankind as part of natural law; often in the context of a state of nature where private property and sovereign rule had not yet entered the stage. Even Vattel, whose writings put the sovereign state in the centre of the international legal order, used the concept of mankind in the context of a discussion of natural common rights and a state of nature before the introduction of private property and exclusive jurisdiction. The invocation of mankind in post-1945 treaties, however, often takes place in a different epistemological context.

When the concept of 'mankind' appears in provisions of treaty-law (or, for that matter, in customary law) it can be read in at least two ways. One interpretation would be that the invocation of 'mankind' is merely a confirmation of something already existing; the normative force of a pre-given 'mankind'. The legal force of 'mankind' would then derive, *not* from the consent of states, but from its own normative status. This reading would fit theories of international law that ground the international legal order on sources such as 'social interdependence' and the 'common will' of the global community,[45] 'world public order',[46] 'humanity'[47] or the 'well being of individuals'.[48] Under this reading, 'mankind' would not be the *product* of law-making, but rather the ultimate ground that makes law-making by states possible and legitimate. As was set out above, this is exactly how writers such as Vitoria, Grotius and, even to some extent, Vattel understood the concept of mankind.

By contrast, the second reading would follow the more standard account of contemporary international law in terms of relatively well-defined sources that validate legal rules and help to set legal arguments apart from non-legal arguments.[49] These sources are then generally presented as reflecting the will of states, either in explicit or in some tacit form.[50] Rosalyn Higgins, for example, states that 'we have in international law a system in which norms emerge either through express consent or because there is no opposition …

---

45 *Corfu Channel (UK v. Albania)*, ICJ Reports (1949) 4, Individual Opinion by Judge Alvarez, at 43.
46 Myres McDougal, Harold Lasswell and Michael Reisman, 'The World Constitutive Process of Authoritative Decision', 19 *Journal of Legal Education* (1967) 243–300.
47 Ruti Teitel, *Humanity's Law* (Oxford University Press, 2011).
48 *Prosecutor v. Tadić*, Case no. IT-94-1, ICTY Appeals Chamber, Decision on the Defence Motion for Interlocutory Appeal on Jurisdiction, 2 October 1995, para. 97.
49 The clearest example can be found in Ian Brownlie's textbook which starts right away with the sources of international law as 'fundamental' to the entire legal system. Ian Brownlie, *Principles of Public International Law* (7th edn, Oxford University Press, 2008).
50 As Koskenniemi has set out, there exists an unbridgeable gap between reliance on formal sources and reliance on state will as the foundation of international law. Martti Koskenniemi, *From Apology to Utopia: The Structure of International Legal Argument* (Cambridge University Press, 2002).

to obligations being imposed in the absence of such specific consent'.[51] In similar fashion, Catherine Sweetser regards consent 'as constitutive of the international legal order; treaties and even customary international law are based on norms of state consent, whether explicit or tacit'.[52] Even when authors readily admit the limits of the consensual paradigm, they often fall back on consent as the *sine qua non* for the existence of international law. Malcolm Shaw, for example, while admitting the existence of some legal obligations that do not rest on state consent, still contends that '[i]n a broad sense, states accept or consent to the general system of international law, for in reality without that no such system could possibly operate'.[53] In similar terms, Prosper Weil argues that, '[a]bsent voluntarism, international law would no longer be performing its functions'.[54] The constitutive value or functional necessity of consent is reaffirmed in several general introductions to international law.[55]

The presentation of international law as rooted in the will of states has far-reaching consequences for the validity and meaning of concepts such as 'mankind'. Where for writers such as Grotius 'mankind' was a category of natural law that could be discovered through reason, for consensualism 'mankind' can only derive its legal existence and legal force from state consent. In other words, rather than treating 'mankind' as a foundational category, it is now conceived as the product of international law-making; as the product of acts of will by states that could as well have been otherwise.

A consensual reading would thus derive the legal meaning and validity of 'mankind' from its acceptance by sovereign states, either expressly or through tacit consent. At the same time, however, through their voluntary acceptance of obligations that serve the interest of 'mankind', states are turned into members of a global community, where they actively work together in the name of the common good. While the interests of mankind still bar sovereign rule or private property of global commons, they now also require states not to over-exploit resources and to ensure that their activities

[51] Rosalyn Higgins, *Problems and Process: International Law and How We Use It* (Oxford University Press, 1994), at 16
[52] 'Humanity as the A and Ω of Sovereignty: Four Replies to Anne Peters', 20 *European Journal of International Law* (2009) 545–67, at 550 (Catherine Sweetser).
[53] Malcolm N. Shaw, *International Law* (Cambridge University Press, 2003), at 10. While Shaw discusses several legal obligations that bind states without their consent, he still uses consensualism as a foundational principle for the international legal order as a whole.
[54] Prosper Weil, 'Towards Relative Normativity in International Law?', 77 *American Journal of International Law* (1983) 413–42, at 420.
[55] For an overview see Andrew Guzman, 'The Consent Problem in International Law', Berkeley Program in Law and Economics Working Paper (2011), at notes 1 and 2 <www.escholarship.org/uc/item/04x8x174.pdf>. O. A. Elias and C. L. Lim, while acknowledging the paradoxical nature of state consent, still hold on to consensualism: 'seeking to impose some conception of the law as being distinct from the actual claims of states fails for a number of reasons' including because '[t]here is no better evidence of international law doctrine than that which is expressed by States as a reflection of their legal expectations'. *The Paradox of Consensualism in International Law* (Kluwer, 1998), at xi.

benefit mankind as a whole. A consensual reading of 'mankind', therefore, seeks to ground a thick and solidaristic global community on arbitrary acts of will by sovereign states.

However, it is questionable whether it is possible at all to ground the concept of mankind in the free will of states. If 'mankind' would be nothing but the cumulative will and interests of individual sovereign states, the concept would have no independent meaning of its own. It would at best be a shorthand for 'that what states happen to agree upon at a certain point in time'. Not surprisingly, this is not how the concept has been used in international practice so far. The aim of invoking concepts such as the 'common heritage of mankind' is exactly to go beyond the freedom and interests of states. The concept of 'mankind' is generally used to refer to a global community that transcends individual sovereigns, as is evidenced by terms such as 'the heritage of humanity', 'the interests of future generations' and 'envoys of mankind'. Grounding such a more encompassing global community solely on the will of individual states yields what Jürgen Habermas called a 'performative contradiction': a statement whose propositional content contradicts the presuppositions on which it rests.[56] An example of a performative contradiction would be the sentence 'I don't believe what I am saying now'. If 'mankind' indeed stands for a more encompassing community in which states operate, its validity and meaning cannot at the same time be derived from the will of states only.

2.2 *The commons of mankind as benefit and burden*

The idea that international law is created through will went hand in hand with the assumption that law could be used to change political life. As David Kennedy has argued, post-1945 international law was viewed as 'primarily the instrument for building the institutions to *transform* the political order – not for articulating the normative boundaries and limits of sovereign power'.[57] The above-mentioned treaties on the deep seabed, the ocean floor or outer space constitute examples of this belief in 'transformation through law'. Introducing concepts such as the 'common heritage of mankind', and setting up supervisory procedures and authorities, were considered important steps in the creation of a more just and sustainable world order. Where, for example, Grotius invoked 'mankind' to argue for an obligation not to interfere with the freedom of others, modern treaties also use the concept of mankind to bring states actively together in a common effort to tackle global

---

56   Jürgen Habermas, *Philosophical Discourse on Modernity: Twelve Lectures* (MIT Press, 1990).
57   David Kennedy, *Of War and Law* (Princeton University Press, 2006), at 75 (italics added). Not surprisingly, such ambitious efforts are not always successful; the attempts to make the world a better place through law-making are often frustrated by the very same power-structures they seek to transform. The prime example in this context is the difficulties of taking action against powerful states that violate the cornerstone of the UN Charter system, the prohibition on the use of force.

problems. Concepts such as the 'common heritage of mankind' not only bar claims to sovereignty and private property; they also put powerful states under an obligation to exploit common resources and to transfer technology in the interest of mankind and to the benefit of poor countries.

The focus on cooperation in post-1945 treaties not only derives from ideals of international solidarity, but should also be understood in light of changing conceptions of the nature of the commons of mankind. For Vitoria, Grotius and Vattel the commons of mankind were regarded as public goods that were available to all because of their non-exclusionary and non-exhaustible nature. What the commons had to offer was abundance and freedom. Nowadays, the conception of the commons of mankind is more ambiguous. Areas such as Antarctica, the moon or the deep seabed hold promises of scientific and economic progress when exploited properly.[58] At the same time, they are seen as vulnerable and exhaustible. The commons of mankind, in other words, are as much a burden as a potential benefit. Both the promises and the vulnerability of the commons spur calls for cooperation and supervision, as to make sure that mankind's territories will sustainably benefit humanity at large.

2.3 Enemies of mankind

In the work of Vitoria, Grotius and Vattel, matters of enmity and the commons of mankind were intrinsically linked. For Vitoria, the use of force against the Native Americans could be justified if they broke the rules of the *ius communicationis*, being the law of humanity. For his part, Grotius sought to defend the use of force by the East India Company against the Portuguese and Spaniards as measures against the enemies of mankind, even making attempts to put them on a par with pirates. Finally, Vattel advocated collective military measures against enemies of human society that failed to respect the open nature of the commons of the world. In contemporary international law, the link between legal regimes regulating the commons of mankind and enmity is much less prominent. Nowadays, the term 'enemies of mankind' is mainly reserved for those that violate core provisions of the laws of armed conflict and international human rights norms, not for those that fail to respect the integrity of the common territories of mankind. The only exception is the pirate, who is still regarded a *hostis humanis generis* over whom all nations can exercise jurisdiction on the high seas and to arrest suspects, seize ships and aircraft, as well as property on board.[59]

---

58   Although these promises are not always fulfilled, as the saga of the deep seabed exploitation attests.
59   UNCLOS, *supra* note 36, Article 105. See also the extension of these rights to the exclusive economic zone (EEZ) in Article 58, as long as they are compatible with the other provisions regarding the EEZ. For a discussion on the relevance of the pirate for international law in general see Gerry Simpson, *Law, War & Crime: War Crime Trials and the Reinvention of International Law* (Polity, 2007).

When it comes to other legal regimes regulating non-sovereign territories, however, the link between mankind and enmity seems to have disappeared. The starting point of regimes on the deep seabed, Antarctica or outer space is that areas belonging to 'mankind' cannot be used for military purposes. Apparently, military usages are seen as beneficial to individual states or coalitions of states at best, but not to mankind as such. The main focus of the treaties in question is on cooperation, exchange of information, reporting and so forth; not on measures that should be taken against those who disrespect the commons of mankind. Of course, this does not mean that the subject of norm violation has become totally irrelevant. Sometimes the treaties explicitly identify those who are responsible (liable) for injuries[60] and the general rules on state responsibility still apply to breaches of treaty obligations. All this, however, does not turn the violators of the rules pertaining to the commons of mankind into *hostes humanis generis* against whom military force may be used. While the ambitions of contemporary international law are much greater, the means to discipline those that violate mankind's law are much more limited.

Conclusion

The concept of mankind is frequently invoked in international law-making. The concept plays a pivotal role in treaties regulating territories beyond sovereign control, such as the deep seabed, outer space, the moon or Antarctica. At first sight, these treaties seem to stand in an age-old tradition in international law, where 'mankind' is invoked in the regulation of non-sovereign territories. Thinkers such as Vitoria, Grotius or Vattel relied on the concept of 'mankind' to advocate the freedom of the seas and the right to trade and travel globally. However, in post-1945 international law the concept of 'mankind' underwent some significant transformations. Vitoria, Grotius or Vattel rooted 'mankind' in natural law, used it to ground negative freedoms as well as to identify 'enemies of mankind'. By contrast, post-1945 international law is often read predominantly through the lens of consensualism, uses 'mankind' also to bring states actively together for the common good and has only very limited room for the idea that spoilers of the commons of mankind are *hostes humanis generis*. The invocation of 'mankind' in contemporary international law-making thereby produces paradoxical results. If 'mankind' is read through the prism of consensualism, its meaning and force is dependent on the will of sovereign states. This dependency on state consent is difficult to square with the very nature of the argumentative claims that are based on the concept of mankind. After all, the concept of

---

60 See for example the Outer Space Treaty, *supra* note 38, Articles 6 and 7, as well as the Convention on International Liability for Damage Caused by Space Objects, GA Res. 2777 (XXVI), 29 November 1971, in force 1 September 1972, 961 UNTS 187.

'mankind' signifies a community that is more inclusive than a society of individual, sovereign states. Moreover, contemporary international law seeks to ground a much thicker conception of a global community on a much thinner epistemological basis. For Vitoria, Grotius and Vattel 'mankind' was a category of natural law that basically grounded the freedom to travel, exploit and navigate. Nowadays, 'mankind' is the product of the free will of states that seeks to ground a global community where states actively work together for the common good, international solidarity and the protection of the interests of future generations. Finally, the idea that mankind has enemies against whom just wars could be waged was one of the driving forces, especially of the work of Vitoria and Grotius. In contemporary international law, the notion of enemies of mankind has moved to the area of international criminal law and the fight against piracy. The ambitions of the regimes regulating the deep seabed, outer space or Antarctica have to be realised without the notion of an enemy – through international cooperation, managerialism, some liability provisions and the rules of state responsibility.

Part II
Domestic and international

7 (International) Law!

Inger Österdahl

1 The argument

In this contribution it is argued that the distinction will disappear between international law and non-international law, most often referred to as domestic law, due to a number of current developments involving the globalisation or de-nationalisation of law-making.

It will be argued further that, in contradistinction to the divide between international and non-international law, the distinction between law and non-law will stay intact. 'Law' will not disappear as relevant category, whereas ' "international" law' arguably will; all law will be more or less international, but it will still be 'law'.

'Law' on the other hand may be more or less binding and the role of soft law is bound to increase, despite Jan Klabbers' pronouncements to the contrary.[1] The globalisation of law-making coupled with the continuing relevance of 'law' as such will result in an increasing amount of soft law. Soft law is easier and quicker to produce than hard law and it is more amenable to adaption and transformation in relation to different legal settings. These are essential characteristics of any 'law' that wishes to survive in the increasingly fuzzy, fluid and global legal milieu of tomorrow.

The constitution of global law-making is changing; law is being produced along new organisational principles and the resulting legal outcome will be increasingly softer. Still, 'law' is the preferred normative language here, not virtue as recently promoted by Klabbers as a substitute for law altogether.[2] Even, or perhaps in particular, in an increasingly turbulent world we must

---

1   Jan Klabbers, *The Concept of Treaty in International Law* (Kluwer, 1996) at 157–64; Jan Klabbers, 'The Redundancy of Soft Law', 65 *Nordic Journal of International Law* (1996) 167–82; Jan Klabbers, 'The Undesirability of Soft Law', 67 *Nordic Journal of International Law* (1998) 381–91.
2   Jan Klabbers, 'Kadi Justice at the Security Council?', 4 *International Organizations Law Review* (2007) 1–12; 'Controlling International Organizations: A Virtue Ethics Approach', 8 *International Organizations Law Review* (2011) 285–9; 'The European Union in the Global Constitutional Mosaic', in Neil Walker, Jo Shaw and Stephen Tierney (eds), *Europe's Constitutional Mosaic* (Hart, 2011) 287–307.

stick to 'law' – even soft law – with the minimum of security and predictability that this notion contains.

2 International versus non-international law

The distinction in theory and practice between international and non-international law is slowly but steadily eroding; and not even so slowly any longer. The nation-state heretofore has been regarded as the principal reference point for law-making and a principal distinction has been made between domestic, or non-international, law on the one hand and international law on the other.

There have been different approaches to linking the two worlds of law-making. The two main ways of uniting the law produced domestically – or non-internationally – and the law produced internationally, have been labelled monism and dualism, respectively.[3] Monism presumes that the domestic and international legal systems are ultimately one whereas dualism presumes that domestic law-making and international law-making make up two distinct, self-contained systems without any natural link between them.

There are variations to the two main approaches for linking international and domestic law. In particular, there are varying degrees of superiority in the monist model for international law in relation to the domestic law, including the domestic constitution, and varying degrees of impermeability in the dualist model. A monist approach stipulating the superiority of international law even to the domestic constitutional provisions would be at one end of the spectrum of openness and superiority whereas a dualist model closed to international law – in treaty form as well as in the form of customary law – would find itself at the other end of the spectrum.

This is on the level of principle. In practice, the actual implementation and carrying through of international legal obligations turns on the degree to which international legal undertakings are taken seriously and are actually transformed into living domestic law by and through the domestic public administration.[4] The actual implementation may speak a language radically different from the position of principle of the domestic legal system: a monist state may ignore its international legal obligations in practice while a dualist state might meticulously implement each and every one of its obligations.

---

3   See further, for instance, Hans Kelsen, *Pure Theory of Law* (Max Knight trans., University of California Press, 1967) chapter VII; Dinah Shelton, 'Introduction', in Dinah Shelton (ed.), *International Law and Domestic Legal Systems: Incorporation, Transformation, and Persuasion* (Oxford University Press, 2011) 1–22, at 2–5.

4   See generally the comprehensive empirical study of the handling of international law in different countries contained in Shelton (ed.), *International Law and Domestic Legal Systems*, *supra* note 3.

If we take a step back from the monist and dualist schools, it can be observed that both schools still presume that there will be distinct law-making internationally and non-internationally and that these two broad types of law-making will have to be linked somehow, i.e. that there is a relationship between the international and the non-international that has to be handled. Both schools could be said to presume the existence of states that make law both within themselves and between themselves.

This contribution argues that the role of the nation-state as a law-maker will diminish as a result of law-making carried on by others and in other forms than intra- or inter-state legislative procedures. The state, a primarily territorially grounded entity for law-making, will be phased out and other kinds of law-making entities, not necessarily territorially defined, will arise.[5] Also, law will be produced according to different organisational principles than today. In short, law-making will be pluralised both in terms of law-making fora and law-making forms and the state's role as the supreme vehicle for law-making will disappear.[6]

Therefore, the relevance of the respective stances of monism and dualism will disappear as well since there will no longer be any relationship between the international and the non-international to handle. There will be a plurality of law-makers and a plurality of legal outcomes, and the relationships between these legal systems and their legal acts will have to be handled differently from the relatively simple dichotomous relationship between international and domestic law caught by the concepts of monism and dualism.

There are already such signs of change through the increasing amount of law-making taking place in supranational fora. The role of international organisations as loci of law-making is constantly growing. For example, the EU has taken over large parts of the law-making earlier performed in domestic institutions, basically reducing the role of the domestic legislative assemblies to one of reacting to and ultimately accepting the legislation adopted on the level of the EU.

The question of law-making by international organisations is not limited to the situations where the organisations have been given the mandate to produce legislative acts binding for the members of the organisation (which,

---

5   See further Catherine Brölmann, 'Deterritorialization in International Law: Moving Away from the Divide Between National and International Law', in Janne Nijman and André Nollkaemper (eds), *New Perspectives on the Divide Between National and International Law* (Oxford University Press, 2007) 84–109.

6   On the partial disappearance of the nation-states in the European community, see Bruno de Witte, 'The Emergence of a European System of Public International Law: The EU and its Member States as Strange Subjects', in Jan Wouters, André Nollkaemper and Erika de Wet (eds), *The Europeanisation of International Law: The Status of International Law in the EU and its Member States* (T.M.C. Asser Press, 2008) 39–54; see further Janne Nijman and André Nollkaemper (eds), *New Perspectives on the Divide Between National and International Law* (Oxford University Press, 2007).

in fact, is still rather unusual). Even if the international organisations – and, of course, even more so the informal but important groupings of states such as the G20 – lack the capacity to issue law that is formally binding for the member states, the sheer quantity of norms flowing from the international organisations will outweigh their qualitative weaknesses in terms of lacking binding form and specific, demanding contents. The states cannot shield themselves against this flood of international norm-making even if they wanted to.

The soft law flowing out from the international organisations may even be more effective as far as law goes, or at least more attractive from the point of view of the states. Its very softness gives such law-making an air of voluntariness and creates the consequent impression that states can choose whether and how to domestically implement the internationally produced soft law. Thus, soft law creates the appearance of retained domestic control, which may paradoxically reassure the citizens. It can perhaps even reassure the states as well to the extent that the latter believe that there still is a choice and they wish to have such a choice. Then the states may voluntarily choose to implement what has been agreed in non-binding form.

Non-binding international law will not have to be ratified by the domestic legislative assemblies making it easier to implement than binding law, such as treaties. Thus international soft law may end up being more effective than hard law since it is easier to adopt, it is generally more attractive to the states and it is easier to implement. The formally and substantively soft law-making also has the advantage, from the point of view of the powers that be, of being impossible to check by outsiders until it necessitates changes in domestic law, in which case the domestic legislative assembly must become involved. Thus, this is a very powerful form of international law-making, which is already influencing, and will continue to influence, domestic law-making.

In addition to the more traditional inter-state and the less traditional supra-state arenas for law-making, there is the emerging field of transnational or sub-national law-making, where public authorities from different states cooperate on a level inferior to the central government.[7] 'Subnational' might also in the future signify functional entities not necessarily originating from the public administration of the state, but entities independent of the public administration making agreements across the increasingly porous territorial borders.

International legal instruments are agreed on the sub-national level too and this contributes to the permeation of the domestic legal system by international law. The horizontal relationship and cooperation between the agencies originating from different territorially based states becomes more important than the vertical relationship between the public authorities and their own domestic central government. From the point of international

---

7   Cf. Anne-Marie Slaughter, *A New World Order* (Princeton University Press, 2004).

law-making this may be a more effective way of making law despite the fact that the law is agreed on a lower political and legal level than would be the case if the central governments were the parties to the agreement. The increased effectiveness may be due to the fact that the law is technical, close to reality and makes up a more living part of the day-to-day practice of the respective domestic agencies than the grand international agreements adopted by the central governments. The increased effectiveness may also be due exactly to the fact that international law-making in this case is carried out on lower levels of public administration. The trans-nationally made law will be directly applied by the lower levels of the domestic administration to which it otherwise might take some time for the international law to trickle down.

Trans-nationally the law is injected directly into the domestic system and, due to its more technical character, will be more easily applied by the officials concerned. Since they were themselves involved in the trans-national agreement they will feel less resistance to such law compared with the law emanating from the central government – in our case a hypothetical international agreement.

Thus we can expect an increase both in the amount of soft law, which may paradoxically be more effective than binding law, and in the amount of transnational law which, also a bit paradoxically considering its lower status, may also potentially turn out to be more effective than higher level international agreements.

The pluralism of international law-making is increased further by institutions that include as their members both public and private actors, persons representing different groupings, as well as individuals in their own right. The most evident example, which is also very significant, is ICANN – Internet Corporation for Assisgned Names and Numbers, a private, Californian non-profit corporation with ties to the US Government – producing the fundamental norms governing the internet.[8] The internet is the very manifestation of internationalisation and it is potentially very powerful as a medium. Thus, the tendencies described earlier concerning international law-making – in particular the increasing pluralism and deformalisation – can be expected to be many times reinforced both in the law regulating the internet and through the internet itself with the effect it is having on practically all aspects of society. In the context of the internet the very difference between international and non-international breaks down. The law regulating the internet can only reasonably be international, or global, or just law.

International practice and international legal doctrine increasingly view the relationship between the international and non-international legal orders as flexible and organic, and this relationship is often expressed in

---

8   <www.icann.org>.

terms of a dialogue taking place between different legal systems.[9] There is also a tendency not to distinguish as carefully as before between different law-making fora (such as different international organisations, or international fora as opposed to domestic fora) and not to look at their respective legal orders as original and self-contained. Rather, acts originating from different law-making systems and organs are linked and balanced in an open and reasoned way. Legal acts and norms originating from one international organisation are not viewed as alien within the context of another international organisation or a domestic legal system, even a dualist one. The role of formalism can be said to be decreasing and the role of finding substantive solutions to legal problems increasing. Finding substantive solutions might involve a dialogue with other legal systems and balancing own norms against other norms rather than either entirely rejecting or entirely embracing the other legal systems and their norms on formal grounds. The way the EU Court of Justice (ECJ) entirely rejected the UN Charter system in the *Kadi I* case would constitute an exception to the emerging substantive balancing trend.[10]

Substantive balancing of international and non-international law contributes to breaking down the difference between the two just as it would break down the difference between any other legal systems involved in the making and application of the law. The relationship between the international and non-international legal orders is becoming more pluralistic: the two systems are amalgamating and sources of law originating from the one or the other are not kept apart as carefully as before by those who apply the law, but are more easily used across legal boundaries in order to contribute to the finding of solutions to substantive problems. This also increasingly applies to legal inspiration flowing across borders between domestic national systems of law. The international and domestic legal systems are more and more interwoven.

What is argued here goes further than the constitutionalisation of international law as discussed by Klabbers, Peters and Ulfstein.[11] The constitutionalisation of international law may be a first step towards the amalgamation of the international and domestic legal orders, but not necessarily for constitutionalisation may halt in the international sphere.

---

9   See, for instance, Filippo Fontanelli, Giuseppe Martinico and Paolo Carrozza (eds), *Shaping Rule of Law Through Dialogue: International and Supranational Experiences* (Europa, 2010); Joost Pauwelyn, 'Europe, America and the 'Unity' of International Law', in Wouters, Nollkaemper and de Wet (eds), *The Europeanisation of International Law, supra* note 6, 205–25.

10 Joined Cases C-402/05 P and C-415/05 P *Yassin Abdullah Kadi* and *Al Barakaat International Foundation v Council of the European Union and Commission of the European Communities* [2008] ECR I-6351; cf. Erika de Wet and Jure Vidmar, 'Conclusions', in Erika de Wet and Jure Vidmar (eds), *Hierarchy in International Law: The Place of Human Rights* (Oxford University Press, 2012) 300–10, at 309.

11 Jan Klabbers, Anne Peters and Geir Ulfstein, *The Constitutionalization of International Law* (Oxford University Press, 2009).

The discussion in this contribution, however, addresses international and domestic law at once.

The state will no longer be the guardian specifically of the territorially based domestic legal system, but of a legal system that is applied in domestic courts among other fora. Domestic courts, by increasingly applying international law, will also have an impact on the international law, resulting in a two-way flow between international law and domestic law, contributing to the erosion of the border between the two systems.[12] The domestic legal system will be the channel for different non-territorially based legal systems to flow into the domestic sphere – domestic lawyers will have to take not only domestic law but different kinds of international law into their argument. Since the domestic handling of non-domestic law will affect international law, the domestic application of the law will take place in conscious or subconscious dialogue with the domestic application of the law in other jurisdictions. Moreover, courts on the international level will presumably also be involved in a two-way communication with the domestic courts.

In short, the territorially based nation-state would be the vehicle for the application of the law, but no longer for the making of the law. Whether new state-like formations will assemble around new, functional rather than territorial legal systems is a question worth asking, but for the time being impossible to answer. The process so far is breaking down the existing territorially based nation-state structures as concerns in particular the idea of a self-contained domestic legal system, but the possible eventual appearance of state-like legal systems or organisational entities based on other than territorial grounds is far away in the future. The tendency now is the erosion of the difference between the international and the non-international legal systems still taking place within the infrastructure of territorially based public administrations and courts.

Domestic application of the law, according to this line of thought, would be taking a step back on the road towards the *dédoublement fonctionnel* launched by George Scelle – it would mean a return to a unidimensional position where the application of one and only one law would be concerned.[13] In this situation, the realisation of the (international) legal order through the domestic system is increasing in importance whereas the assertion of the domestic legal order *vis-à-vis* the international one is decreasing in importance since there is only one law. In the context of

---

12 On domestic input into the international law-making, and *vice versa*, see Ole Kristian Fauchald and André Nollkaemper (eds), *The Practice of International and National Courts and the (De-)Fragmentation of International Law* (Hart, 2012); Yuval Shany, *Regulating Jurisdictional Relations Between National and International Courts* (Oxford University Press, 2007); André Nollkaemper, *National Courts and the International Rule of Law* (Oxford University Press, 2011).
13 Cf. Henry G. Schermers and Niels M. Blokker, *International Institutional Law* (5th edn, Martinus Nijhoff, 2011), at paras. 919, 1886, 1900.

international organisations, the stress on the doubled-faced position of states as constituent parts of organs of the organisation on the one hand, and, on the other, as counterparts of the organisation, will similarly diminish. If there is no duality there will be no need for *dédoublement fonctionnel*.[14] The emergence of an alternative new entirely de-territorialised legal system is yet to come. What is not likely to come back is the (modern) historic organisation of the structures of law-making exclusively through nation-state units.

If pushed one step further, the current reorganisation of law-making might also imply the erosion of the border between the public and the private. This potential erosion would currently seem to be most pronounced as concerns law-making for the internet where the fundamental organisational unit is a private entity – the ICANN – and the principal actors tend to be private companies. If the eroding public/private distinction is added to the eroding international/non-international distinction the reorganisation of law-making on the global level will be all the more revolutionary.

3 Law versus non-law

Whereas the distinction between international and non-international law is breaking down, the same is not happening to the distinction between law and non-law. The globalisation of law is discussed in precisely those terms – the globalisation of *law*. In the growing literature on the relationship between international and domestic law and their mutual influence on each other, the matter of the legal quality of the norms being discussed – their quality as law – has not been the subject of debate. It is not assumed that the closer links between the international and domestic legal systems will efface the particular character of law from the law. Or, for instance, that the amalgamation of the legal systems will diminish the strength of law generally and thus that the de-nationalisation would constitute a danger to the strength of the law as a whole.

It is presumed that the law will remain, but that it will be created, applied and interpreted differently due to the current internationalising or globalising tendencies. The continued existence of law as something different and possibly more significant than other normative systems is taken for granted, even in the quickly transforming normative world of interaction between the international and domestic spheres. Intuitively, this presumption in the doctrine that law will remain law makes sense since law is a concept with a much longer history than the concepts of the state and the national and international respectively.

---

14 See also Yuval Shany, '*Dédoublement fonctionnel* and the Mixed Loyalties of National and International Judges', in Fontanelli, Martinico and Carrozza (eds), *Shaping Rule of Law through Dialogue, supra* note 9, 29–44.

The literature on the relationship between different international *regimes* is already extensive and thematically related to the literature on the relationship between international and domestic law.[15] Some issues and problems that emerge when different international regimes are supposed to be linked are also present when the international legal system and the domestic legal systems are linked together. The primary focus in this contribution is the relationship between the international and the domestic legal systems, however, i.e. the international/non-international divide and not the international/international divide.

The international/international divide becomes relevant at a later stage when, within the de-nationalised legal system, different substantive norms of divergent content will have to be linked and mutually adjusted. If the de-nationalised legal system – where the international and domestic legal systems have more or less amalgamated – contains substantive norms of divergent content, which find themselves on an identical level in the hierarchy of norms, the same factors will emerge as between different regimes in the current international legal system where, due to the lack of a normative hierarchy, different general principles of law have to be used in order to prioritise between competing substantive norms.

In the current international legal system, the existence, or lack, of institutions – in particular judicial institutions – contributes in practice to the prioritisation between the competing legal regimes.[16] The situation will not be the same if the de-nationalised law is applied domestically since it can be presumed that judicial institutions exist across the substantive board on the level of the state. The judicial institutions may be of varying quality in different jurisdictions of course, but a state can be presumed in principle to have a comprehensive legal system and the corresponding judicial institutions. On the international level, as is well known, there is no default judicial system.

The amalgamation of the international and the domestic legal systems may well affect the normative hierarchy in the resulting 'law', the influence of international law making it more horizontal or the impact of domestic law making it more vertical.[17] At the same time, the legal systems resulting from the creation of international organisations tend to more vertical than the traditional horizontal international legal system. Thus, the constantly increasing significance of international organisations may reinforce the domestic vertical influence on the 'law'.

---

15   See, for instance, Margaret A. Young (ed.), *Regime Interaction in International Law: Facing Fragmentation* (Cambridge University Press, 2012); and, for regime interaction expressed as treaty conflict, Jan Klabbers, *Treaty Conflict and the European Union* (Cambridge University Press, 2009).
16   See further Yuval Shany, *The Competing Jurisdictions of International Courts and Tribunals* (Oxford University Press, 2003).
17   Cf. de Wet and Vidmar (eds), *Hierarchy in International Law, supra* note 10.

The amalgamated de-nationalised law might also be differently applied in the national public administration and judicial institutions than in the international judicial institutions. The same substantive body of rules may thus be applied in a horizontal, non-hierarchical paradigm in the international judicial sphere and in a vertical, hierarchical fashion within the domestic institutional legal apparatus. This would create a confusing picture of the law. It is more likely that, as international and domestic substantive law amalgamates, the respective constitutional visions of the law, including the vision of normative hierarchy, will also converge.

A sign of the continued relevance of law at least on the conceptual level was the decision of the Conference of the Parties to the UN Framework Convention on Climate Change in Durban in 2011 to launch a process to 'develop a protocol, another legal instrument or an agreed outcome with legal force under the Convention applicable to all Parties'.[18] The third option, 'agreed outcome with legal force', was supposed to denote something somehow legal, but less binding than 'law'. It was a compromise formula necessary in order to make all states parties agree to the decision because not all states were prepared to take on the serious kind of obligations that 'law' entails. Judging from the Durban decision, the particular quality of law is significant, which is encouraging to the law and the lawyers, but which can also have the effect that the law is avoided because it is significant. The context of this decision is also important because climate change represents a completely globalised concern of the kind that we will see more of as other areas of society become internationalised. The global character of climate change is extreme in the sense that the problem truly cannot be locked in behind national borders – the solutions can be found in no other place than on the global level. Even the internet, which would seem almost as global a factor as climate change, could still possibly be controlled domestically somehow, whereas weather is entirely borderless.

The compromise formula in the Durban decision – 'agreed outcome with legal force' – could indicate that there are different degrees of law in the minds of states, with some being more legal or binding than others. 'With legal force' could indicate several things: ordinary, binding law; less binding than ordinary law but still legally binding; or even non-binding soft law that could still be labelled somehow 'legal' (although the concept of soft law may seem difficult to reconcile with the phrase 'with legal force', even though 'soft power' is an emerging concept in political science).

As is well known, Jan Klabbers has persistently criticised the notion of 'soft law'. It would seem as if time has, if not proven Klabbers' argument wrong, still shown that his criticism has not gained many followers – at least not in the world of international practice. This should come as no surprise since soft law, according to Klabbers, basically serves the interests of the states who

---

18   UNFCCC Decision 1/CP.17, 2007, in UN Doc. FCCC/CP/2011/9/Add.1, operative para. 2.

want to exercise their power as freely and arbitrarily as possible and thus unconstrained by 'hard law'.

Klabbers' argument begins by declaring soft law redundant, then continues by declaring it not only redundant but detrimental and thus undesirable, and lastly, at least so it seems, Klabbers ends up by giving up law altogether in favour of virtue.[19] Klabbers' critique of soft law is apposite and pertinent, but slightly misdirected. Klabbers is probably right: soft law is redundant and potentially even bad, but then the real world is neither as neat nor as pure as the world of legal logic would like to have it. In the world of legal logic the dichotomy of (binding) law and (non-binding) non-law makes sense and hard law is sufficient to grasp what is legal. States are either bound or not bound and cannot hide behind 'soft law' in order to pretend to be bound, while they in reality are not, or pretend not to be bound, while in reality they are.

As a phenomenon and as a generic term, however, soft law has not diminished in importance since Klabbers launched his devastating critique. In fact, the trend is rather the opposite. Somehow there seems to be a demand for 'soft law' and even actors more benign than power-hungry unscrupulous states make frequent use of soft law instruments. Perhaps 'soft law' may also serve useful and benign purposes and not only be an instrument of evil.

The question is how one should handle the fact that the practical world does not manage to live up to the strict requirements of purity and simplicity postulated in the legal world according to Klabbers. Instead of disregarding soft law – or, even worse, turning one's back to the law, altogether soiled and weakened by 'soft' thinking – one should accept reality as it is and adjust the theoretical scheme. The values of fairness and checks on power should continue to be struggled for in the context formed by real practice. Law can still be useful in this context even though it might not be as pure and simple as Klabbers and many others would wish. The law and the values inherent in the 'rule of law' must be upheld while in constant negotiation with countervailing forces on all levels. This is a messy and fuzzy business but, as lawyers, we should do our best to inject as much 'law' into it as possible and rather muddle through than give up if our preconceived theoretical notions do not fit reality. If you cannot beat soft law then make it part of the empire of law, embrace it and use it for good purposes. The world can do without elegant intellectual constructs, even if theoretically and logically pertinent, but it cannot or should not be able to do without law. And 'law' apparently cannot be contained in the hard law/non-law dichotomy propagated by Klabbers, however much we would wish this to be the case.

---

19   *See supra* notes 1 and 2.

4 Law!

Even though the idea of the law will not disappear when the distinction between international and non-international law erodes, the de-nationalisation process may still affect the structure of the law in other ways. It is likely that the amount of soft law will increase relative to the amount of hard law. We can discuss whether soft law is redundant or even undesirable from a theoretical point of view, but from the point of view of actual practice, in the world of eroding hinders and thus increasing communication between the international and domestic legal systems, the occurrence and thereby the importance of soft law is likely to grow. In the more pluralistic milieu that will inevitably emerge when the international and domestic legal systems are not kept apart, soft law will be ever more necessary in order to find agreement among the greater plurality of actors who participate in the making of the law and the applying of the law in an increasing variety of environments. The law will become softer in order to cater to the differing needs of the pluralistic de-nationalised world. The law-making will become softer also because the need for law will develop so quickly that there will not be time for traditional law-making either in the form of earlier domestic legislation or in the form of international treaty-making. The internationalised, de-nationalised or globalised legal milieu will be more fluid, fast-changing and pluralistic compared with that based on the relatively self-contained nation-states and a clearly maintained difference between international and domestic law.

There will of necessity be less formalism in the law-making and in the fluid kaleidoscopic flickering legal world of de-nationalisation; it might even be tempting to abandon the law for other values, since the other values may be even more flexible than the law. Virtue could be such a value. For different reasons, however, virtue will not and, more importantly, should not be allowed to replace the law. Klabbers' unfortunate turn to virtue seems originally to have been meant as a solution to conflicts between international (treaty) regimes, for which, according to Klabbers, there is no law to turn to. At stake was the apparently insoluble conflict between, on the one hand, decisions taken by the UN Security Council under Chapter VII, in particular decisions on targeted sanctions against suspected terrorists, and, on the other hand, the rules on human rights contained, for instance, in the European Convention on Human Rights. Most immediately, it was the *Kadi I* case in the ECJ which apparently gave rise to Klabbers' turn to virtue, out of frustration with the law presumably.

The turn to virtue gives evidence of a rather resigned stance towards the potential of the law and it also gives evidence of a rather narrow view of what can be included in the notion of the law.[20] True, even in a world where

---

20 Interestingly, the younger Jan Klabbers favours a very wide and inclusive notion of law, see his *Concept of Treaty*, *supra* note 1, at 257–9, and 'Redundancy of Soft Law', *supra* note 1, at 179, 181–2.

international and domestic law become more and more amalgamated, linking and mutually adapting diverging and even contradictory rules originating from different (international) regimes will remain difficult, as long as no constitutional rules on how to judge conflicts between regimes will develop. One solution to the dilemma of conflicting treaties or regimes might be the constitutional effects of domestic law: the law that has an international origin may become more verticalised and constitutional rules on normative hierarchy may develop also with respect to norms that would earlier have been strictly horizontally organised.[21]

Another possibility hinted earlier is that a more flexible relationship between legal systems – based on dialogue, balancing and so on – can lead to a greater emphasis on the substance of norms, rather than on their formal relationship. In consequence, the idea of self-contained legal regimes will lose importance and substantive norms will be allowed to flow in and out of regimes, which will have a constructive effect on the efforts to solve conflicts between regimes.

Substantive norms – even if agreed in very different fields and even if considered fundamentally different from the point of view of the matters they are supposed to regulate – will no longer be confined to their respective legal systems, but will find their way into other legal systems as well. The free-flowing (substantive legal) norms will fill up the alleged legal void between the formal legal regimes.

Also, even if a formal constitutional ordering of norms does not develop for the amalgamated de-nationalised law, and even if the alleged void between regimes is not filled with free-flowing substantive norms, the European Court of Human Rights (ECtHR) showed in the *Al-Jedda* case that it is possible to solve apparently insoluble conflicts between treaties within the framework of the law and legal argumentation.[22] Moreover, the ECtHR did not apply the blunt formalistic method of rejecting the entire UN Charter system, as the ECJ did in the *Kadi I* case.[23] Through and interpretative technique, the ECtHR managed to turn upside down the presumptive normative hierarchy with the UN Charter at the apex. The ECtHR managed to inject into the very UN Charter system a human rights component, which was not obviously there before, at least not to such a prominent extent: '[T]he Court considers that, in interpreting its resolutions, there must be a presumption that the Security Council does not intend to impose any obligation on Member States to breach fundamental principles of human rights.'[24] The ECtHR came to this conclusion among other things '[i]n the

---

21 Cf. de Wet and Vidmar, 'Conclusions', *supra* note 10, at 309.
22 *Al-Jedda v. UK*, Application no. 27021/08, Judgment of 7 July 2011.
23 *Supra* note 10. Still, but perhaps less bluntly, Joined Cases C-584/10 P, C-593/10 P and C-595/10 P *Commission v. Kadi*, Judgment of 18 July 2013 (not yet reported).
24 *Al-Jedda v. UK*, *supra* note 23, at para. 102.

light of the United Nations' important role in promoting and encouraging respect for human rights'.[25]

From our point of view, this would seem to show that if the creativity of those applying the law is let loose, solutions can be found to problems by constructively linking different international legal regimes. The legal void would become relative and only exist to the extent that lawyers themselves would not be able to make up solutions that could be labelled 'legal'.

While it may take time for the matter of the legal void between different treaty regimes to diminish or disappear, it is a bad idea to turn away from the law and seek solutions in other normative bodies. Rather, the efforts to expand the frontiers of what is possible within the law should be strengthened. In the volatile context of de-nationalisation, it is more important than ever to maintain as many of the values inherent in the concept of the 'law' as possible. One of such values is equality, i.e. the equal application of the law in equal cases. 'Law' also carries with it a certain rationality based on reason and consistency in decision-making, which can be contrasted to the arbitrariness that would easily ensue if values other than those embodied in the law would be turned to in order to find solutions to normative conflicts. Trusting virtue, for instance, intuitively feels less secure than trusting law. If the presumption is correct, furthermore, that the eroding difference between international and domestic law will lead to an increasing incidence of soft law, whose legal nature is open to questioning in the first place, it will be all the more important to stick as much as possible to the virtues inherent in the law. Soft law in itself constitutes a move away from true traditional (hard) law in the direction of something more amorphous and less predictable.

The decreasing formalism in combination with a turn to soft law will constitute a serious challenge to the idea of law as a whole but, in order to meet the challenge, the 'law' in soft law should be guarded carefully. Instead of emphasising the distinction between binding and non-binding legal acts, the quality of 'law' should be emphasised in what we have. Even 'soft law' means something in this perspective and is important as one form of law indeed. It is more important than ever to contain as much normative stuff as possible within the realm of the 'law' and to have an expansive notion of the law and an expansive notion of what kind of considerations might be contained within a legal argumentation, rather than giving norm-makers the considerably freer reins that they would have within systems of norms other than 'law'. When the form is becoming increasingly non-binding, it becomes all the more important to make the substance as binding as possible through the appeal to values inherent in the very notion of 'law'.

---

25 *Ibid.* The ECtHR also showed a similarly large measure of creativity in the recent case of *Nada v. Switzerland*, Application no. 10593/08, Grand Chamber, Judgment of 12 September 2012.

There are also important legal policy concerns at stake here. When in many parts of the world the term 'law' and the idea of the 'rule of law' are values fervently strived for by oppressed populations it would seem irresponsible and unwise on the part of respected researchers in international law to actively propagate the abandonment of 'law' altogether. A turn to virtue, for instance, would manifest a certain condescension or contempt *vis-à-vis* populations less fortunate than ourselves who are living in societies where the 'law' in any meaningful sense has not yet arrived, let alone matured to a stage where the population can take its existence for granted. The perspective of throwing out the law would probably scare all those who have for long been subjected to 'virtue'-based justice and are now longing for the more orderly 'law'. Law is relative and indeterminate, it is true, but virtue would be even worse.

It is important to speak the language of the law in the fluid global normative milieu we see coming. For the time being it is rather the traditional state institutions that are being broken down by the sweeping globalising influences – it is too soon to tell what is actually taking form. The law is one of the few checks on the exercise of power that exists in the current internationalising and de-formalising norm-making environment. The mechanisms to check the exercise of power – potentially inherent in the organisation of the world into territorially based nation-states – are challenged by globalisation. This development will not be stopped and reality cannot be pushed back. So the best strategy will be to try to keep at least some of the formerly state-based checks on the exercise of power and thus to strengthen the law and the role of law-making in all the emerging law- and policy-making contexts. In the future, new organisational units may form where mechanisms corresponding to the ones inherent in the (democratic) nation-state can be reinstituted. In the short term it would seem as if law will have to partly replace (state-based) democracy as the primary check on power since the democratic institutions for popular control on the nation-state level are being overridden by the law-making power emanating from other fora. The world of norm-making will have to be reconquered. The globalised political community – whatever its fundamental units might be and even before such units form – will have to contain as many corresponding elements as possible to the checks and balances through the rule of law formerly contained in the nation-state, but now irrevocably evaporating into the global de-nationalised normative commons.[26]

---

26 See further Nicolás Carrillo-Santarelli and Carlos Espósito, 'The Protection of Humanitarian Legal Goods by National Judges', 23 *European Journal of International Law* (2012) 67–96; Gianluigi Palombella, 'Global Threads: Weaving the Rule of Law and the Balance of Legal Software', in Fontanelli, Martinico and Carrozza (eds), *Shaping Rule of Law through Dialogue, supra* note 9, at 413–33.

8 Perspectivism in law

*Kaarlo Tuori**

1 Contemporary black-box models

International lawyers, constitutional lawyers and EU lawyers seem to be engaged in a perpetual academic turf war over the legal categorisation of the EU and its law. Is the EU an international organisation under public international law and is what EU lawyers call 'EU law' merely an offspring of international law? Should we characterise the founding treaties of the EU merely as international agreements or do they amount to a constitutional charter of a transnational polity, standing at the apex of a transnational legal order? Was the abortive Constitutional Treaty[1] an international agreement or a constitution? Disagreements extend to assessing the case law of the ECJ. Was *Kadi*[2] a worrying questioning of the authority of general international law or a consequent and legitimate application of an EU-law perspective to international law? Jan Klabbers, who started as an EU lawyer and switched over to international law, is exceptionally sensitive to questions like these.

Every lawyer – or at least every legal scholar – is familiar with the distinction between the internal and external point of view, famously introduced by H. L. A. Hart, although not all agree on it. The perspectivism that the above questions manifest is different in character: it is inherent to the law, but it can be approached from both an internal and an external point of view. According to a popular contemporary account, almost approaching a new orthodoxy, perspectivism in law results from the institutional and professional, maybe even personal, biases of legal actors and participants in legal discourse, engaged in legal power games. The stake in these power games is high: the privilege to say the law, to determine its contents. Whether they are aware of it or not, legal actors are prisoners of

---

* The chapter has been written within the research programme of the Centre of Excellence (CoE) in Foundations of European Law and Polity, financed by the Academy of Finland.
1 Treaty establishing a Constitution for Europe, 29 October 2004, not in force, OJ 2004/C 310/01.
2 Joined Cases C-402/05 P and C-415/05 P *Kadi and Al Barakaat International Foundation v. Council and Commission*, [2008] ECR I-6351.

their institutional and professional interests that dictate how they approach and define legal issues and what position they take on these. Thus, the views of international environmental lawyers and WTO lawyers on whale meat trade are bound to conflict; international lawyers, constitutional lawyers and EU lawyers cannot but differ in how they categorise the EU and its law; and as regards the *Kompetenz-Kompetenz* of EU law and the reach of its jurisdiction, the judges of the constitutional courts of the member states inevitably come to conclusions contrary to those adopted by their Luxembourg colleagues. No neutral position immune to particular interests exists nor are objective solutions to conflicts of interpretation possible; the winner of legal power game is the one who is able to impose as universal a particular interest-based view.

Such *legal strategism* is perhaps the dominant view of perspectivism in law, at least among 'critical' international lawyers; the seeming (temporary?) winner of the legal power game in international law. It represents a view on legal perspectivism from an external perspective: legal speech acts are examined as strategic acts with perlocutionary objectives and consequences. This gives us, so I shall argue, but a one-sided picture of law and its workings. When applied to the relationships between legal orders or legal systems – or legal regimes, as the term goes – it is an example of radical legal pluralism and of what I would call a 'new black-box model'; a contemporary successor to the state-sovereigntist black-box model of mutually closed national legal orders complemented by a distinct international legal order.[3]

The external view I have sketched may be the dominant one, but it is not the only version of radical pluralism. As the constitutional and legal theoretical debates on the relationship between EU law and national legal orders prove, the *Kelsenian* variant has its contemporary supporters as well. The strategic model has all-embracing pretensions: it purports to elucidate the workings of law and legal discourse in general and not merely the pluralism of legal orders and systems. In this respect, the Kelsenian alternative is more modest in its claims: its focus is on the relationship between distinct legal orders. The conclusion the Kelsenians draw with regard to conflicts of authority between legal orders – say, EU law and the municipal legal order of a member state – is similar to the one adopted by those who claim monopoly over the critical position for their strategic perspective. But diverging from the Kelsenians, the latter approach the perspectivism in law from an external point of view.

Let us try to unravel the Kelsenian argument. Each of the conflicting legal orders displays its specific *Grundnorm*, constituting its ultimate basis of authority (validity); contests of authority receive a different solution depending on the legal order whose perspective one adopts. Institutional legal actors, such as judges or legislators, are bound to assume the viewpoint

---

3   William Twining, *Globalisation and Legal Theory* (Nothwestern University Press, 2000).

of the legal order under which the institution they serve has been established and its powers defined. Following this line of thinking, it is inevitable that the constitutional courts of the member states review EU law's claims of authority in light of the domestic constitutions, whereas the ECJ clings to the claim of EU law as an independent legal order and employs criteria of validity internal to this order. No legal bridge leads over the gulf between the perspectives of self-contained legal orders.[4] Hence, the Kelsenians find themselves in the camp of radical pluralists. Kelsenians and 'crits' might seem to be odd bed-fellows. Yet, in fact, it is no wonder that Martti Koskenniemi, perhaps the most prominent exponent of legal strategism, has great respect for Kelsen's writings in international law and cites approvingly Kelsen's comment of the solipsism and imperialism of especially those municipal legal orders that have adopted the monistic position.[5] Solipsism and imperialism are quite apt descriptions of rival legal regimes, such as they appear in Koskenniemi's portrayal, as well.

The Kelsenian approach is a radical version of the internal point of view. As is well known, multiple interpretations of the *Grundnorm* exist, and there is variation even in Kelsen's own accounts of its role. But a Kantian-transcendental aspect, at least, is crucial to an understanding of the function of the *Grundnorm* in the pure theory of law: for Kelsen, the (tacit) assumption of a *Grundnorm* is a necessary precondition of all legal cognition and all judgements of legal validity. To put it in Gadamerian terms: the supposition of a *Grundnorm* is a necessary and integral element of the *Vorverständnis* of legal actors.

A reconstruction of legal actors' normative *Vorverständnis* is wholly alien to legal strategists' approach. Koskenniemi, for example, shuns any discussion of the normative presuppositions or implications of legal speech acts; for him, the grand concerns of normatively orientated legal theory – validity and meaning – do not possess any intrinsic significance. Instead of legal speech acts' illocutionary dimension, where normative credentials are appraised, Koskenniemi focuses on the perlocutionary, strategic aspect; the former is subordinated to the latter.[6] Conflicts of jurisdiction are irresolvable not because of divergent *Grundnorms*, but because of diverse institutional biases and the irreconcilability of the strategic interests which the institutional actors of different regimes – say, the WTO and the international environmental-law regime or, EU law (the ECJ) and national law (constitutional courts) – are pursuing.

---

4   MacCormick's path-breaking articles from the 1990s, which in fact launched the still continuing debate on constitutional pluralism, largely adhered to the Kelsenian approach. See Neil MacCormick, *Questioning Sovereignty* (Oxford University Press, 1999). As a representative example of the approach, see also Theodor Schilling, 'Autonomy of the Community Legal Order: An Analysis of Possible Foundations', 37 *Harvard International Law Journal* (1996) 389–410.
5   Martti Koskenniemi, 'International Law: Constitutionalism, Managerialism and the Ethos of Legal Education', 1 *European Journal of Legal Studies* (2007).
6   See the discussion in my *Ratio and Voluntas* (Ashgate, 2011), at 24 ff.

Theorists drawing from Niklas Luhmann's autopoietic systems theory deny Koskenniemi's interpretation of the intractability of inter-regime conflicts. Gunther Teubner and Andreas Fischer-Lescano[7] argue that ultimately, inter-regime conflicts do not derive from policy divergences and conflicting strategic interests of institutional actors; they originate from the self-contained, autopoietic character of the global social sub-systems that have given rise to transnational law. Nothing can be done to the very source of the problem, the evolutionary accomplishment of (global) social differentiation. Teubner and Fischer-Lescano's favourite citation from the Master is the following: 'The sin of differentiation cannot be undone. Paradise is lost.'[8] At the most, we are entitled to hope that some of the consequences of transnational legal fragmentation can be managed, through, for instance, conflict rules focusing on legal issues' functional location; mutual observation of systems of transnational law; and a striving for compatibility of the respective claims and criteria of validity. But instances of transnational law are bound to the particular rationality of the respective global social system – economy, health, sports, etc. – and each instance produces its own functionally orientated conflict rules and reactions to problems of compatibility. The source of the problems remains, and nothing can guarantee the congruence of the treatment of inter-regime disputes in each legal subsystem exists. What we have here is a third variant of radical pluralism.

In sum, the three variants of radical pluralism condemn legal orders (Kelsenians), systems (autopoietical systems theorists) or regimes (legal strategists) to their respective solipsist perspectives, without hope of boundary-breaking, cross-perspective contacts. These all end up advocating a new version of the black-box model of legal universe. The boxes are defined differently from the traditional model and the emergence of transnational law beyond the dichotomy of national and international law is acknowledged. But the self-contained legal orders, systems or regimes remain shut in their respective boxes.

2 A new start: Perspectivism of the legal Vorverständnis

But radical pluralism with its new black-box models evidently conveys a one-sided and distorted picture of our contemporary legal landscape. True, hegemonistic turf-wars among legal orders, systems and regimes occur; institutional and professional interests influence legal speech acts; legal actors are committed to their legal order of affiliation; and functionally

---

7 Andreas Fischer-Lescano and Gunter Teubner, 'Regime-Collisions: The Vain Search for Legal Unity in the Fragmentation of Global Law', 25 *Michigan Journal of International Law* (2004) 999–1046.

8 *Ibid.*, at 1007. The citation is from Niklas Luhmann, *Die Wirtschaft der Gesellschaft* (Suhrkamp, 1994), at 344.

differentiated legal orders follow their divergent rationalities. But this is not all there is: co-operative relations, cross-boundary dialogue, mutual learning, overlapping and interpenetration exist as well. Perspectivism in law is inevitable, solipsism is not. What Boaventura de Sousa Santos has called 'interlegality' offers is an alternative to radical pluralisms' solipsism. Instead of the either/or logic of dichotomisation, characteristic of radical pluralism, interlegality follows rather the logic of both/and. In Sousa Santos' account, typical of interlegality are 'different legal spaces superimposed, interpenetrated and mixed in our minds, as much as in our actions'. He argues that 'we live in a time of porous legality or of legal porosity, multiple networks of legal orders forcing us to constant transitions and trespassing. Our legal life is constituted by an intersection of different legal orders, that is, by interlegality.'[9]

Thus, in the mirror of interlegality, plural legal orders, systems or regimes do not appear as self-contained entities; they are seen as mutually overlapping and maintaining a dialogue with each other. Obviously, this is how the pluralism of European law, for instance, should be conceived; this holds for relations between EU law and national legal orders, between these and the Council of Europe law-making and, increasingly, even for the reciprocal relations between national legal orders.

Existing interlegality warrants a new approach to the plurality and perspectivism of legal orders, systems and regimes. Instead of confining ourselves to conflicts of authority, hegemonistic turf war or mutual misunderstandings – which do exist! – we should reformulate our problem. Given the inevitable perspectivism, how are cross-border co-operation and dialogue, as well as interlegality in general, possible?

I shall sketch my solution to the reformulated problem by giving the Kelsenian reading of perpectivism a legal cultural twist. Kelsenian perspectivism revolves around the notion of *Grundnorm*. In Kelsen's pure theory of law, this notion is supposed to capture the fundamental presuppositions that make legal knowledge possible in the first place: legal cognition is premised on the general validity of the legal order, and this validity ultimately flows from a hypothetical, transcendental *Grundnorm*. Let us restate Kelsen's point in a way that allows for its immanent criticism and further development. Kelsen could perhaps have agreed with the following formulation: the normative claims of legal speech acts are always made with reference to a specific legal order. This leads to the perspectivism that Kelsenians have emphasised in the context of EU law: the multiplicity of alternative referential legal orders inevitably entails a multiplicity of views on the validity of EU law.

---

9   Boaventura de Sousa Santos, *Toward a New Legal Common Sense* (2nd edn, Butterworths, 2002), at 347.

In the debate on the allegedly irresolvable conflict of authority between EU law and the municipal law of the member states, the perspective of EU law is usually attached to the ECJ and that of national legal orders to national courts. But this may be a too simplistic and straightforward equation: the national courts are organs of not only the national but also the EU legal system. Why should they, in cases involving both national and EU law, necessarily use the national legal order as the referential framework? Could they not instead adopt the perspective of EU law or of European law at large (comprising EU law, domestic legal orders and the Council of Europe law-making)?

The answer depends on how we answer another question: what does it actually mean to adopt a particular legal order as one's normative framework and point of reference? For Kelsenians, this amounts to adherence to the *Grundnorm* of the legal order in question, and this adherence accounts for the different views that the ECJ and national constitutional courts hold of the ultimate criteria of EU law's validity (authority). The courts have no choice, at least not legally speaking: a court is bound to take the perspective of the legal order under which it has been set up; the assumption of another *Grundnorm* would amount to – again legally speaking – a revolution. Thus, the only alternative legally available to both national courts and the ECJ is the perspective and the *Grundnorm* of the legal order under which it has been established. A similar Kelsenian radical pluralist view is applicable to all conflicts of ultimate authority between legal orders: between national law and other instances of transnational law or among the latter.

Another reformulation of Kelsen's position may help us to see its inherent flaws. Kelsen draws our attention to the significance of legal actors' implicit pre-understanding (*Vorverständnis*) in legal practices and legal discourse. But he tries to reconstruct this pre-understanding in a-historical, transcendental terms: he claims that the assumption of a *Grundnorm* and the concomitant hierarchical understanding of the legal order are transcendental presuppositions, necessarily involved in all legal cognition and reasoning. However, legal *Vorverständnis* is not transcendentally fixed for all times and places; legal actors draw the pre-understanding they need for engaging in legal reasoning and for tackling the legal problems confronting them from the available, temporally and spatially variable reservoir of legal culture.

Arguably, a legal order does not consist merely of such explicit norms that would be organisable in a Kelsenian hierarchical *Stufenbau* under the crowning apex of a *Grundnorm*. In the framework of Kelsenian positivism, a legal order is composed of posited (*gestellte*) norms, deriving their validity (authority) from a pre-posited (*vor-gestellte*) *Grundnorm*. In addition to such explicit legal normative material, a legal order also includes elements of legal culture, without which 'surface-level' norms could not be applied, interpreted or systematised. The layers of legal culture provide legal actors' *Vorverständnis* with contents that reach far beyond anything compressible to a Kelsenian *Grundnorm*. The legal culture does include a doctrine of legal sources which determines what counts as valid law and as a legal argument, but it also includes much else; for instance, general legal concepts and principles employed in legal interpretation and decision-making. And in addition, it is historically and culturally contingent whether the doctrine of legal sources adopts the hierarchical view implicit in both Kelsen's *Grundnorm* and Hart's rule of recognition.

Legal actors assess the validity of legal norms in accordance with the doctrine of legal sources inherent in the legal culture of the referential legal order. In routine legal practices, this transpires in a quasi-automatic, unconscious way. The prevailing doctrine of legal sources is part of the legal actors' tacitly functioning pre-understanding or – in Anthony Giddens' terms – practical knowledge.[10] Only in hard cases are they forced to articulate this knowledge, to spell out the exact contents of the doctrine and to ponder its implications in the case at hand. This is how other cultural elements of legal actors' pre-understanding – such as legal concepts, principles and theories – function as well.

Thus, to sum up, we should understand the legal actors' dependence on a referential legal order in broader terms than just surface-level normative material or the doctrine of legal sources determining the legal validity of this material. We should also be aware of the general role of the legal culture in legal practices, of the functioning of legal concepts, principles and theories as a filter through which surface-level legal material is cognised and interpreted. The rejection of the Kelsenian reading of legal perspectivism does not imply denying the fact that national courts remain in an important way bound to their national legal order. Legal culture is internalised in the course of legal socialisation: during university studies and subsequent professional activities. Judges in national courts have received their legal education in national universities and have accumulated their professional experience in the national judiciary; consequently, their pre-understanding is imbued by the national legal culture. We are entitled to assume that judges in national courts approach and interpret EU law through their national legal culture: through the legal concepts, principles and theories inherent in this culture. And, recalling the thesis of legal culture as part of any legal order, we can speak, not only of divergent views to European law, but also of different European laws, cast in different moulds of legal culture.

As regards the specific matter of ultimate authority, the Kelsenian radical pluralist position on the relations between EU law and national law, too, is in need of revision. By no means is it a self-evident truth or an axiomatic fact that national courts are animated by a doctrine of legal sources that reserves the ultimate and incontestable authority to the national constitution. It may well be that the doctrine of EU law's supremacy has sedimented into the legal culture of not only EU law but also of national legal orders, and that

---

10   Anthony Giddens, *Central Problems in Social Theory* (MacMillan, 1979), at 24–5.

this doctrine gives precedence to EU law even in the exceptional, hard cases where the claims of authority of EU law and national law clash. Moreover, hard cases are not necessarily representative of the legal practice as a whole: most of the cases are routine cases, and in such cases the doctrine of legal sources, like other elements of the legal culture, unravel their effects in an unconscious way, through the legal actors' tacit pre-understanding.

Again, our conclusions are generalisable: they do not concern merely the relations between national law and EU law, but also other instances where actors of a particular legal system appraise claims of authority raised by a legal order that is not the referential legal order.

It takes time before a budding legal order manages to develop a legal culture that supports the explicit surface-level norms. Legal practices are inconceivable without means of interpretation and argumentation embedded in the legal culture. In emergent transnational legal systems, legal actors are likely to bring with them the *Vorverständnis* their national legal culture has equipped them with. This, of course, is bound to cause misunderstandings between actors coming from different formative legal cultures. It is only through transnational legal practices that transnational legal culture(s) can develop. If we acknowledge law's multi-layered nature, we may argue that the independence of a legal order requires not only a rule of recognition capable of delineating its surface-level norms but also the development of a legal culture supporting these norms. At least in its core areas of free movement and competition law, EU law has perhaps reached a stage where a particular EU legal culture informs the pre-understanding of EU legal actors. And, consequently – to return the intractable perspectivism in EU law – a distinct EU-law understanding of EU law should be added to the versions of EU law, coloured by the particularities of Member-State legal cultures.

But have we, through our reformulation and immanent criticism of the Kelsenian position, made any progress in overcoming the closures of the black-box model? Have we not merely given Kelsenian perspectivism a wider twist, relating it to broader, but culturally diverging, contents of legal *Vorverständnis*? Arguably, more than that has been achieved: our restatement of the inevitable perspectivism in law also indicates the way out of the solipsist consequences inherent in the Kelsenian stance.

If the idea of legal orders as self-contained normative entities with sharply definable contours – an idea implicit in Kelsen's pure theory as well as Hart's conception of law – is in general of any assistance in mapping our present legal landscape, its potential applicability is confined to the surface-level of explicit norms. When we turn to the layers of legal culture supporting surface-level regulations, boundaries of legal orders turn out to be much more porous; no rule of recognition or *Grundnorm* exist that would allow us to draw exact borderlines. Ever since the reception of Roman law took off in the twelth century, legal culture has been a transnational affair, breaking the exclusiveness of *leges propria*. Medieval *ius commune* gave expression to transnational legal culture, shared and spread by a transnational, university-educated corps of learned lawyers; this legal culture also influenced the application and interpretation of *leges propria*. Contemporary interlegality, too, is primarily about overlaps and interaction of legal cultures. Indeed, EU law is, in a crucial sense, premised on such interlegality. Legal traditions common to member states are an important source of general principles of EU law, and Article 6(3) of the Treaty on European Union even explicitly refers to shared constitutional traditions as a basis of fundamental-rights principles.[11] And in spite of the perspectivism induced by legal culture, EU law is still interpreted and applied in a sufficiently uniform manner across the borders to guarantee, for instance, the functioning of the internal market. This would not be possible without similarities, interfaces and overlapping in the typical legal *Vorverständnis* among legal actors in the diverse member states.

In international-law debates, opponents to Koskenniemi's radical pluralist view have pointed to the role that general international law still plays in such 'self-contained' regimes as, say, human-rights, WTO or international environmental law.[12] The argument perhaps gains in cogency when transferred to the legal cultural level and detached from, say, the jurisdiction of the International Court of Justice and the reach of its rulings' precedent effect: the perspectivism of the semi-independent regimes – or, expressed in another conceptual framework, instances of transnational law – is tempered by affinities in the *Vorverständnis* of the jurists serving in them. Indeed, as Klaus Günther has remarked, much of transnational law – even when it has its origin in international-law treaties – is *Juristenrecht*, lawyers' law. And lawyers as primary legal actors seem to be in possession of a common language that enables them to engage in inter-systemic dialogues; here Günther introduces the notion of a 'universal code of legality'.[13] Relations between legal systems do not consist merely of contests over jurisdiction, the privilege to state the law; they also involve dialogue and co-operative strivings for normative coherence. All this is made possible by common legal language, shared features in the legal culture informing legal actors' *Vorverständnis*.

So, to sum up, our late-modern de-nationalised legal landscape displays not only signs of fragmentation and disputes of authority but also counter-tendencies of consensus-orientated dialogue and overlapping and interpenetration, in particular at the level of legal culture. Phenomena such as the spread of human-rights talk – and its incursion also into transnational

---

11   Consolidated Version of the Treaty on European Union, OJ 2010/C 83/01.
12   See, for example, Pierre-Marie Dupuy, 'A Doctrinal Debate in the Globalisation Era: On the "Fragmentation" of International Law', 1 *European Journal of Legal Studies* (2007) 1–18.
13   Klaus Günther, 'Rechtspluralismus und universaler Code der Legalität: Globalisierung als rechtstheoretisches Problem', in Lutz Wingert and Klaus Günther (eds), *Die Öffentlichkeit der Vernunft und die Vernunft der Öffentlichkeit* (Suhrkamp, 2001) 539–67.

legal systems not specialised in human-rights monitoring – even lend credence to the claim that the most fundamental processes of globalisation or de-nationalisation are occurring in the sub-surface, cultural layers of law. This does not equal a universalist claim of a fundamental normative unity in law. It is debatable whether it is meaningful in general to speak of a new master-principle, replacing state-sovereigntism and creating an 'order of orders' in a legal world where national law is overlain by functionally delineated and mutually overlapping instances of transnational law. But, if it is, such a meta-principle would not be of a substantive but of a *discursive* nature. It could not, though, work without sufficient congruence at the level of legal culture; that is, without the existence of a common legal language.

3 The perspectivism of legal roles and disciplines

So I would paint the picture of global legal landscape in quite different colours from radical pluralists. Which aspect of legal development dominates in one's account is obviously a matter of perspective as well. It is no coincidence that sociologically orientated observers have, from their external perspective, been prone to emphasise the fragmentation of law. Legal anthropologists and sociologists originally coined the very notion of legal pluralism, and in contemporary debates scholars drawing their inspiration from Niklas Luhmann's sociological theory of autopoietic social systems adhere to a radical pluralist position. It should not come as a surprise that, among legal scholars, the legal strategists have joined forces with sociologists in their depiction of the relationships among legal systems and regimes; they, too, tend to ignore the internal point of view and, for instance, refuse doctrinal research the status of science. The 'crits' extend their external, reductionist account from conflicts among legal regimes to other instances of perspectivism of law; to legal discourse in general. We are familiar with the narrative of international, constitutional and EU lawyers being engaged in a strategic contestation over the vocabulary which should be applied to EU law. No neutral linguistic ground exists; the conceptual apparatus that the discussants employ is unavoidably tainted by their positions in the field of law and academic scholarship, which provides the setting for the power game over the privilege of stating the law (*juris-diction*).

The dependence of legal actors' *Vorverständnis* on the legal culture of a referential legal order is not the only epitome of perspectivism in law. Here at least two other typical manifestations deserve mention: the perspectivism of legal roles and the perspectivism of legal disciplines. The approach to law of legal actors such as the legislator, the judge, the counsellor (the practicing lawyer) and the scholar displays important differences. The legislator sees in law primarily a means for achieving politically defined social objectives, and the practicing lawyer looks at it through her client's extra-legal interests that she is supposed to promote; both the legislator and the legal counsellor focus on the perlocutionary effects of legal speech acts, such as statutes and court decisions. Both of them participate in the legal discourse and are players in the game of law, but the prizes they are seeking are of an extra-legal character; consequently, they are prone to subordinate legal speech acts' illocutionary aspect to the perlocutionary one.

Judges, by contrast, privilege the illocutionary dimension where such criteria as argumentative cogency and normative correctness hold sway. As Klaus Günther has argued, an aspiration to comprehensive normative coherence is inherent in judicial interpretation and decision-making.[14] In contemporary law, this desire increasingly demonstrates cross-boundary implications, and it is here that mechanisms that enable a 'host' legal order to allow for the influence of a 'foreign' one show their potential. Let me refer to the analyses presented by Neil Walker, Rolf Michaels and Paul Schiff Berman.[15] Of course, 'foreign' impacts are always filtered and translated through the legal cultural perspectivism of the 'host' legal order. Yet, as I have argued, this does not necessarily prevent the commensurability of the respective reconstructions of law.

What about, then, legal scholars? What is their typical perspective on law? Doctrinal scholars – 'legal dogmaticians' – assist other legal actors through interpretation recommendations and systematisation proposals. Their focus is clearly on the illocutionary aspect; they appraise the normative credentials of the speech acts of other legal actors and claim normative correctness for their own contributions. Arguably, the perspective of a doctrinal scholar is close to that of a judge. By contrast, legal theory is a meta-level legal practice or discourse – producing second-order observations, as a Luhmannian systems-theorist would put it – which, consciously or unconsciously, relates to a particular first-order perspective and gives it a reflexive twist. The first-order perspective may be the normatively (illocutionarily) orientated perspective of a judge or a doctrinal scholar, as is the case both in Kelsenian and Hartian legal positivism and in the principle jurisprudence of, say, Ronald Dworkin or Robert Alexy. But legal theory may also approach the law from a legislator- or counsellor-related meta-perspective. The former may not be so common, but it has animated contemporary endeavours in 'legisprudence' or *Gesetzgebungslehre*.[16] The point of view of a practicing lawyer was in turn the main gateway to law for American realists, as it is for their successors in the critical legal studies school. It is this perspective that

---

14 Klaus Günther, *The Sense of Appropriateness* (State University of New York Press, 1993).
15 Neil Walker, 'Beyond Boundary Disputes and Basic Grids: Mapping the Global Disorder of Normative Orders', 6 *International Journal of Constitutional Law* (2008) 373–396; Ralf Michaels, 'The Re-State-Ment of Non-State Law: The State, Choice of Law, and the Challenge from Global Legal Pluralism', 51 *Wayne Law Review* (2005) 1209–1259; Paul Schiff Berman, 'Global Legal Pluralism', 80 *Southern California Law Review* (2007) 1155–1237.
16 As a representative example, see Luc Wintgens, *Legisprudence: Practical Reason in Legislation* (Ashgate, 2012).

leads a legal strategists to focus on strategic interests and biases, and to neglect the illocutionary aspect of law.

Finally, there is the perspectivism of distinct branches of law and corresponding academic disciplines: international law, constitutional law, criminal law, private law and so forth. Many debaters have noted that EU law as well as other instances of transnational law tend to ignore the traditional divisions which we are used to apply to municipal law. Yet, this does not mean that these divisions would have lost their significance in the discourse on transnational law. Most lawyers, including legal scholars, are specialised in a certain field of law and have developed their professional identity within that field; coming to terms with phenomena of transnational law may thus cause problems. This is manifest in, for instance, the never-ending succession of *legal hybrids* that legal scholarship marches before us. There are no legal hybrids as such but only as seen through a particular conceptual and systematising framework. What we today call legal hybrids are legal phenomena that cannot be caught by the traditional systematisation and conceptual ordering of national law or the complementary black-box model of the relations among national legal orders and international law.

An external sociological observer is prone to explain the variation in the accounts of different legal disciplines by strategic disciplinary interests and by the stakes involved in the power game of the legal field. A similar view, focusing on the perlocutionary aspect of legal discourse, is also cherished by the critical legal scholarship Koskenniemi represents. An international lawyer privileges the language of international law; consequently, she stresses the international-law qualities of EU law, such as the power of member states over the founding treaties of the EU. Correspondingly, a scholar of constitutional law defends the institutional and academic status of her discipline, and depicts European law in constitutional terms.

Again, an account focusing on legal actors' strategic, perlocutionary aims has its justification. But, again, it catches but one side of the coin. The participants in, say, the EU-law discourse make normative claims, too, and the illocutionary edge of their speech acts is affected by their pre-understanding based on legal culture. Not only is there variation in the legal cultures of the member states; the legal culture is also differentiated in accordance with the divisions of law. Different branches of law and corresponding legal disciplines possess their particular concepts, principles and theories; what in German legal theory is called *allgemeine Lehren*, general doctrines. A distinct disciplinary perspective entails the employment of the concepts, principles and theories of the discipline in question. And, to return to EU law as an epitome of transnational law, we are confronted by a new variety of EU laws: a variety produced by divergent disciplinary approaches. If we can already speak of a specific EU law culture, with its specific conceptual, normative and methodological elements, one of these disciplinarily differentiated EU laws consists of the EU law of EU lawyers. And yet another of them is the EU law of international lawyers!

The perspectivism of branches of law and corresponding academic disciplines is likely to affect one's view of the interrelations among legal orders, legal systems and regimes. Arguably, Koskenniemi's emphasis on adversarialism, the role of particular strategic interests and the ensuing fragmentation is associated with his doctrinal identity as an international lawyer. International law is intimately linked with politics, which makes it particularly conflictual by nature and confers a more obviously strategic label upon its argumentation than is usual in other fields of law. In international law, adjudication is still quite underdeveloped; as a rule, the jurisdiction of courts or other dispute-resolving bodies depends on the consent of the parties. These distinct features probably impregnate the *Vorverständnis* of international lawyers and leave an imprint on their legal theoretical views.

But as is the case when examining the relationships among legal orders, systems and regimes, the effects of the perspectivism of legal roles or disciples should not be exaggerated, either. Again, solipsist generalisations overstate their case. Legislators, judges, practicing lawyers and scholars adopt divergent perspectives on law but usually they get each other's points and are able to engage in joint legal argument. The same goes for representatives of diverse branches of law. Private and public lawyers or international and constitutional lawyers may offer different conceptualisations of, say, regulatory private law or the EU's foundational treaties but they are still ready to acknowledge that the interlocutor, too, is talking law and that there might be something to be learned from the other discipline. Branch-specific idioms exist, but the fundamentals of legal language – both basic concepts as the vocabulary of law and basic patterns of legal argumentation as its grammar – are shared across disciplinary boundaries.

So, Jan, debate goes on!

9 Law-making through comparative international law?

Rethinking the role of domestic law in the international legal system

René Urueña

The last couple of decades have seen the emergence of novel forms of global political decision-making, which result in norms akin to treaties or international custom, and yet are undertaken away from the traditional expression of state consent, or the well-known landscape of international organisations. Regulatory networks (such as the Basel Committee on Banking Supervision),[1] public–private entities (think the ISO),[2] purely private governance (such as the Fédération Internationale de Football Association [FIFA],[3] or privatised public utilities[4]) and regional/domestic agencies (e.g. the European Commission or United States Environmental Protection Agency [EPA]), among many others, have become crucial players in determining who wins and who loses in the distribution of power today.

Such transformations reveal a transformed political landscape, and the traditional doctrine of international legal sources (as featured, for example, in Article 38 of the ICJ Statute) seems to be a particularly unreliable map to navigate it. Hence the renewed interest of some international legal scholars in the problem of international law-making – if the map that we have today is unreliable, let's draw a new, better, map. Just like a cartographer who has recently discovered Global Positioning System (GPS) technology and tries to include new islands or straits in ever-more accurate maps, recent academic projects try to factor in new forms of law-making in their ever-expanding

---

1   See Anne-Marie Slaughter and David Zaring, 'Networking Goes International: An Update', 2 *Annual Review of Law & Social Sciences* (2006) 211–29 (arguing that regulatory networks form the new fabric of global governance).
2   See Jan Klabbers, 'Reflections on Soft International Law in a Privatized World', 16 *Finnish Yearbook of International Law* (2005 [2008]) 313–28 (exploring soft law regulation by the ISO).
3   See Lorenzo Casini, *Il diritto globale dello sport* (Giuffrè, 2010).
4   See Bronwen Morgan, *Water on Tap: Rights and Regulation in the Transnational Governance of Urban Water Services* (Cambridge University Press, 2011).

maps of international law, pondering their risks and opportunities, and suggesting ways to make them more democratic or more accountable.[5]

Part of this new cartography has also turned to *domestic* law. Indeed, as power shifts from traditional governments to a decentralised network of global governance, featuring international organisations, regulatory networks and public-private regulators, the role of domestic law in the international legal systems becomes of crucial importance. Thus, part of the effort today is to factor domestic law into our map of international law. To do so, international legal scholarship, both recent and some less so, has proposed a dual model featuring a vertical (cosmopolitan) axis, where domestic courts serve as enforcer of the international rule of law, and a horizontal (comparative) axis, where courts act as organs of their respective state. Even though this model was inspired by the stability needs of the Cold War, most recent efforts to think about the role of domestic courts in international law replay its basic structure, over and over again.

This chapter argues that this way of thinking obscures more than it enlightens. It was designed to maintain a peaceful coexistence between hegemons, and ignore all the rest. It is based upon a narrative that presupposes a single vantage point that fails to consider radical differences of power between the subjects of international law. And yet, the point *is* power, to begin with: the distribution of power and institutional competences along the domestic/international matrix is, increasingly, the main question defining the political landscape that we are trying to map. Ultimately, we lack good tools to think about power in the interaction between domestic and international law. This contribution is an effort to fill that void, by offering an alternative to the dominant dual model.

To do so, the chapter sets the scene by presenting first the classic international legal theory of domestic law (the 'factual' approach), and then explores its critiques. The dual model is then presented, and contextualised as an intellectual offspring of the Cold War. The early 1990s, though, brought a hiatus to the model's influence, which was retaken 15 years later, in early years of this century. And yet, this post-national version of the dual model suffers from the same blind spots as its predecessor. Therefore, an alternative way of thinking is needed, the basic elements of which are presented in the last section of this paper, under the general label of 'law-making interaction'. Finally, some conclusions are drawn.

---

5   See, for example, Joost Pauwelyn, Ramses A. Wessel and Jan Wouters, 'An Introduction to Informal International Lawmaking', in Joost Pauwelyn, Ramses Wessel and Jan Wouters (eds), *Informal International Lawmaking* (Oxford University Press, 2012) 13–34. See also Armin von Bogdandy and Ingo Venzke, 'Beyond Dispute: International Judicial Institutions as Lawmakers', in Armin von Bogdandy and Ingo Venzke (eds), *International Judicial Lawmaking: On Public Authority and Democratic Legitimation in Global Governance* (Springer, 2012) 3–34.

1 The traditional view: Domestic law as a fact, and its discontents

As any international law student knows after a couple of lessons, the textbook account of the role played by domestic law in the international legal system is something of a paradox (or, at least, a clever-sounding game of words): for international law, domestic laws are actually facts.[6] Such was the famous *dictum* by the Permanent Court of International Justice (PCIJ) in the *Certain German Interests in Polish Upper Silesia*,[7] and such is the standard version held traditionally by other instances of international adjudication. Since then, the ICJ,[8] the WTO[9] and some arbitration awards have confirmed this approach.[10]

---

6 For example, see Ian Brownlie, *Principles of Public International Law* (7th edn, Oxford University Press, 2008), at 39.
7 *Certain German Interests in Polish Upper Silesia (Germany v. Poland)*, *PCIJ Reports* (1925) Ser. A, No. 7, at para. 52 (stating that from the standpoint of International Law and of the Court which is its organ, municipal laws are merely facts which express the will and constitute the activities of States, in the same manner as do legal decisions and administrative measures)
8 See *Fisheries (UK v. Norway)*, ICJ Reports (1951) 116, at 132 (stating that, with regard to other States, the validity of maritime limitation adopted in domestic law depends upon international law); *Nottebohm (Liechtenstein v. Guatemala) (Second Phase)*, ICJ Reports (1955) 4, at 20–1 (holding that, even if a state is free to grant nationality to an individual under its domestic law, the matter of exercising protection is one of international law) (see also Guggenheim's dissenting opinion, para. 4, arguing that the international Court can merely enquire into the application of municipal law as a question of fact); *Applicability of the Obligation to Arbitrate under Section 21 of the United Nations Headquarters Agreement of 26 June 1947 (Advisory Opinion)*, ICJ Reports (1988) 12, at para. 57 (quoting the *Alabama* award, and recalling the principle that international law prevails over domestic law); *LaGrand (Germany v. US)*, ICJ Reports (2001) 466, at para. 52 (stating that examining the actions of domestic courts does not convert the Court into a court of appeal of national proceeding); *Avena and Other Mexican Nationals (Mexico v. US)*, ICJ Reports (2004) 12, at para. 28 (recalling that it has the jurisdiction to examine the actions of domestic courts in the light of international law); *Frontier Dispute (Benin/Niger)*, ICJ Reports (2005) 90, at para. 28 (arguing that the fact the Court refers to domestic law does not imply the existence of 'continuum juris', a legal relay between such law and international law). See generally André Nollkaemper, 'The Role of Domestic Courts in the Case Law of the International Court of Justice', 5 *Chinese Journal of International Law* (2006) 301–22, at 311–14.
9 See Appellate Body Report, *India – Patent Protection for Pharmaceutical and Agricultural Chemical Products*, WT/DS50/AB/R, 19 December 1997, para. 66 (quoting from the PCIJ's Upper Silesia case, and stating that the Panel was not interpreting Indian law 'as such'); Panel Report, *United States – Sections 301–310 of the Trade Act of 1974*, WT/DS152/R, 22 December 1999, para. 7.18 (holding that the Panel is called to establish the meaning of domestic law as a factual element). See generally Sharif Bhuiyan, National Law in WTO Law: Effectiveness and Good Governance in the World Trading System (Cambridge: Cambridge University Press, 2007), at 207–38.
10 See *Nykomb Synergetics Technology Holding AB v. Latvia*, SCC Case No. 118/2001, Award of 16 December 2003, 11 International Centre for Settlement of Investment Disputes (ICSID) Reports 158, at 187, at sect. 3.7 (holding that there is no need for the Tribunal to embark on any interpretation or application of Latvian national law on its own); *Azurix Corp. v. Argentina*, ICSID Case No. ARB/01/12, Award of 14 July 2006, at para. 259–260 (applying the principle of *exceptio non adimpleti contractus* to Argentine domestic law).

As traditional as the traditional factual approach is its critique, which features two basic lines. The first one is pragmatically inspired, and argues that, for better or for worse, international courts do engage on a permanent basis with domestic law. In this sense, courts and scholars need not delve too deeply in theoretical considerations, but rather aim at being practical and in accord with the majority of state practice and international judicial decisions.[11] And practice, in this case, is that domestic law is part of the legal landscape that international courts and practitioners inhabit – part of their bread and butter, if one wills.

The pragmatic critique can be read from two perspectives. The first one is to take at face value its non-theoretical aspirations. From this perspective, international lawyers asking to take domestic law seriously are not making an argument about the structure of the international legal system. Instead, they are more akin to legal professionals concerned with the latest developments in adjacent disciplines, which could make legal practice more relevant for achieving its goals – the adjacent discipline, in this case, being domestic law. In this sense, the pragmatic view is really not a critique of the 'factual' version of domestic law, but rather a call for a better understanding of domestic law as a fact: in order to do a good job, the international judge needs to take seriously, say, Argentinean law, just as the realist judge had to take seriously, for example, demographic variables. For the pragmatic critique, domestic law is no less a 'fact' (as opposed to a 'norm') – instead, it is an important reality that needs to be approached and understood by the international judge.

One can also be sceptical of the pragmatist's scepticism towards theory, and ask: what is the underlying theory that informs the pragmatist's critique? If thought of this way, the pragmatic approach merges with the second line of critique of the 'factual' version of domestic law. In 1964, Jenks deployed a complete attack on the idea by showing how both the PCIJ and the ICJ, as well as other adjudicative bodies, had in fact engaged in interpreting and applying domestic law.[12] His was, though, not only a description of international adjudication, but also a clear normative prescription: for Jenks, international law's function was to promote the rule of law both within and among nations, and this task would be better served if international courts interpret and apply domestic law as a 'normal and necessary incident of international adjudication'.[13] In this sense, Jenks' law was not a social fact, but rather a normative standard that must be applied by international courts as *law*, and not as facts.

The idea of an 'international rule of law' was not unknown for Jenks: in 1958, he had argued for a common law of mankind,[14] where international

---

11 See for example, Malcolm N. Shaw, *International Law* (6th edn, Cambridge University Press, 2008), at 133 (arguing the pragmatic approach to domestic law).
12 C. Wilfred Jenks, *The Prospects of International Adjudication* (Stevens, 1964), at 547–603.
13 *Ibid.*, at 547.
14 C. Wilfred Jenks, *The Common Law of Mankind* (Stevens, 1958).

law was a 'universal formal order'[15] that could include (that had to include) domestic law: 'can we', asks Jenks, 'deduce a sufficient consensus of general principles from legal systems as varied as the common law with its own variants of the Islamic law, Hindu law, Jewish law, Chinese law, African law in its varied forms and Soviet law to give us the basic foundation of a universal system of international law?'[16] For Jenks, the answer was yes: it was possible to distil certain principles that were common to all domestic systems, and such principles would in turn inspire a universal rule of law, for the international community as a whole.[17] Indeed, for Jenks, 'the world community is not a club of the mutually congenial but an experiment in the organised government of all mankind'.[18]

2 Introducing the dual model: The Cold War and the interaction between domestic and international law

Jenks' approach links the matter of the 'factual' view of domestic law to a wider mindset of international relations. Jenks can be read as sharing the cosmopolitan *ethos* of the 1960s that found a new home in welfare-orientated international organisations and human rights institutions.[19] To be sure, as Jenks own personal experience also proves, the Cold War was the main obstacle: and yet, the cosmopolitan outlook was always there. In this context, the question was hardly whether domestic law was indeed a 'fact' in any significant sense. The question was rather one of political economy: how can we recruit domestic courts in order to advance the international rule of law we want? How should domestic courts help maintain it? To be sure, the pragmatist will not explicitly go as far – and yet, if pressed, she would accept that the ultimate goal of their craft is some kind of rule of law.[20] Rediscovering the role of domestic law in international law becomes, then, a proxy for mapping the structure of the international legal system.

---

15 *Ibid.*, at 74–89.
16 *Ibid.*, at 3.
17 This agenda seems influenced by a parallel project developed by MacDougal in the early 1950s. See M. Myres MacDougal, 'The Comparative Study of Law for Policy Purposes: Value Clarification as an Instrument of World Democratic Order', 1 *American Journal of Comparative Law* (1952) 24–57.
18 C. Wilfred Jenks, *Universality and Ideology in the ILO* (Graduate Institute of International Studies, 1969) at 7, quoted in 'Clarence Wilfred Jenks', 46 *British Year Book of International Law* (1973–1972) xi, at xviii.
19 Martti Koskenniemi, 'The Fate of Public International Law: Between Technique and Politics', 70 *Modern Law Review* (2007) 1–30, at 3. David Kennedy, in turn, speaks of the 'liberal cosmopolitan' international lawyers who remained in the 1960s marginalised from the US foreign policy establishment, which was controlled by the very Cold Warriors that attacked Jenks: David Kennedy, 'The Disciplines of International Law and Policy', 12 *Leiden Journal of International Law* (1999) 9–133, at 24.
20 See Zachary Douglas, *The International Law of Investment Claims* (Cambridge University Press, 2009), at 72 (recalling that respect for the integrity of the law of the host state is also a critical part of development and a concern of international investment law).

The complement of this view comes from domestic courts. For Jenks, writing from an international law perspective, domestic courts are crucial for the building of a universal rule of law. For this to actually happen, it seems necessary that domestic courts play their part. Enter thus Richard Falk's 1964 exploration of the role of courts in the international legal order,[21] where he tackles the famous *Sabbatino* case, in which US courts had to decide whether they could assess the propriety of an alleged expropriation by the Cuban government. Falk writes after the 1961 and 1962 decisions of the lower federal courts,[22] and before the 1964 decision of the US Supreme Court.[23] The lower courts had decided that the Act of State doctrine was not applicable; that is, that it was appropriate for a US domestic court to review whether the Cuban decision was a violation of international law. Falk disagreed with that conclusion, and engaged with the court's reasoning in terms of the Act of State doctrine under US constitutional law, a discussion that carried on after the book, when the Supreme Court's decision was adopted.[24]

Interestingly for us, Falk's reasoning in his 1964 book starts off from the premise that law and politics should be clearly distinguished: international law should be distinguished from foreign policy. Domestic courts should avoid being 'politicised' in the sense of becoming instruments of their state foreign policy;[25] instead, they should understand themselves as actors of an emerging international legal order. This move, however, does not exclude national courts from being organs of a state. Thus, for Falk, national courts have a double role:

> Domestic courts are agents of a developing international legal order, as well as servants of various national interests; this double role helps to overcome the institutional deficiencies on a supranational level.[26]

Falk thus sets the basis for what could be called a *dual* model of the role of domestic courts in the international law. On the one hand, it is a cosmopolitan model that neatly complements Jenks' prescription for a universal rule of law, and argues that domestic courts should understand themselves as agents of the international legal order. On other hand, though, Falk is

---

21 Richard A. Falk, *The Role of Domestic Courts in the International Legal Order* (Syracuse University Press, 1964).
22 *Banco Nacional de Cuba v. Sabbatino*, 193 F Supp 375 (US District Court for the Southern District of New York, 1961); *Banco Nacional de Cuba v. Sabbatino*, 307 F 2d 845 (US Court of Appeals for the Second Circuit, 1962).
23 See *Banco Nacional de Cuba v. Sabbatino*, 376 US 398 (US Supreme Court, 1964).
24 Richard A. Falk, 'The Complexity of Sabbatino', 58 *American Journal of International Law* (1964) 935–51.
25 Falk, *The Role of Domestic Courts*, *supra* note 21, at 11 ('the operation of courts should be governed by the structural characteristics of international society rather than by transient foreign policy considerations').
26 *Ibid.*, at 65.

keenly aware of the political limitations of writing during the Cold War. Courts are 'servants' of their national interest. Domestic courts will need to recognise that the national interest of other courts is as legitimate as their own, and the development of international law needs to somehow factor this political reality into the equation. For Falk,

> In a divided world, there will be a divided law. Under such conditions, rules of deference applied by domestic courts advance the development of international law faster than does an indiscriminate insistence upon applying challenged substantive norms in order to determine the validity of the official acts of foreign states.[27]

Taken as a whole, the dual model describes two processes of interaction between domestic and international law: the first one, which I will call the *vertical* axis of the model, describes the fact that there are universal norms that will be enforced by domestic courts as agents of the international legal order (these norms could be distilled from comparing domestic legal systems – *à la* Jenks – or can be adopted in a top-down matter, this matters not for the model). And second, the *horizontal* axis of the model, where one observes a legitimate diversity of approaches towards other international norms (for example, the Act of State Doctrine in *Sabbatino*) and where domestic courts should show deference towards their peers, as each of them acts not only as an agent of the international legal order, but also as an actor reacting to its own (domestic) political and legal contexts.

It was in the horizontal axis of the model that the notion of 'comparative international law' originally made sense. Comparing notes in the midst of the legitimate diversity of approaches by domestic courts seemed like a worthwhile occupation: how did a Soviet court approach a certain international legal doctrine? How did that compare with the approach taken by a US court to the same doctrine?[28]

An example of these concerns is the work of William E. Butler, a well-known expert on Russian and Soviet Law, who gave his lectures at The Hague on the subject of 'comparative approaches to international law'.[29] Butler was not speaking the language of Jenks' common law of humanity. Butler's was an effort of understanding, of bridging the differences: comparative law provided the international lawyer with a toolkit to better understand their craft. Indeed, he argued, international lawyers were already

---

27 *Ibid.*, at 6.
28 According to Mattei and Mamlyuk, the notion of comparative international law can be in fact traced to Falk himself, in a 1966 work on Soviet approaches to international law: see Boris N. Mamlyuk and Ugo Mattei, 'Comparative International Law', 36 *Brooklyn Journal of International Law* (2011) 385–452, at 388.
29 William Butler, 'Comparative Approaches to International Law', 190 *Recueil des Cours* (1985) 9–89.

carrying out comparative analysis, sometimes in fields that seem to foreshadow some of salient concerns of legal scholarship: international legal historians engage in comparisons to create their narrative from different perspectives,[30] and New Haven School scholars use comparative law to develop their policy arguments.[31] International institutional law implies comparison among the regimes of different international organisations,[32] and international adjudication demands that international judges undertake comparative legal analysis in order to understand the domestic laws involved in an international dispute.[33] Butler even spoke of comparison among subsystems of international law (which, for him, are the defined by region and not by functional specialisation).[34]

All these were elements that the method of comparative law could benefit the international lawyer. Finally, Butler moved to substantive questions that comparative lawyers ask as a matter of principle, yet international lawyers fail to consider: how are international legal professionals formed? How is that profession influenced by domestic legal systems and education systems? Who are considered as experts in the international legal profession?[35]

3 Goodbye to all that: The liberal promise

So, whatever happened to all of this? What happened to the comparative international law agenda, to the dual model of domestic courts in international law? Two things happened: the first was the end of the Cold War; the second was the proliferation of international courts and tribunals.

With the collapse of the Soviet Union and the end of *détente*, the idea of comparing approaches with international law became less and less appealing. After all, why would one want to compare different approaches to international law, when whole point was that we lived in in an era when history was over, and liberalism had finally triumphed?[36] In an era such as that, the question was hardly one of Falk's legitimate approaches to international law, and neither was it one of Butler's efforts to bridge the differences. Quite on the contrary, the point was that there were no more differences: international law, especially in its human rights and trade law incarnations, was the standard to be followed by domestic systems.

---

30 *Ibid.*, at 33–5.
31 *Ibid.*, at 36–7.
32 *Ibid.*, at 38–9.
33 *Ibid.*, at 39–41.
34 *Ibid.*, at 41–2.
35 *Ibid.*, at 77–83.
36 See generally Francis Fukuyama, *The End of History and the Last Man* (Free Press, 1992) (arguing that the late 1980s brought not just the end of the Cold War, but the end of history as such: the end point of ideological evolution and the universalisation of Western liberal democracy as the final form of government).

On the human rights front, perhaps the clearest example of this transformation was the debate on the so-called international right to democratic governance. Until the late 1980s, domestic structures of governance (and especially whether and how elections were held) were widely identified with 'internal affairs' of sovereign states.[37] These were factors that would deserve a place in Falk's legitimate variety of approaches. However, in the early 1990s, this changed fundamentally. In 1992, Thomas M. Franck wrote a ground-breaking article where he argued that, as the Cold War ended, we entered a 'new world in which the citizens of each state will look to international law and organisation to guarantee their democratic entitlement'.[38] From then on, debate ensued.[39] The bottom line, though, is that the discussion was structured around a single international normative node (international rule of democratic governance) towards which domestic systems should (or should not) converge. The era of non-democracy as a legitimate approach to international law was officially over. Comparison of domestic approaches to the international norm of democracy was therefore not only fruitless, but politically (and perhaps normatively) undesirable, as it would legitimise as 'normal' regimes that were 'abnormal' in their lack of democracy.

International trade law evidenced a parallel process. The times of the New International Economic Order, with its modest ambitions of global redistribution, were long gone.[40] Gone also was the idea of alternative paths to development, if there were ever any.[41] The Washington Consensus meant, as is well known by now, aggressive one-size-fits-all policies (often in the form of structural adjustment), which rendered moot the question of comparing different approaches to international law. Comparison in the sense of understanding difference was beyond the point. In this context, the interaction between domestic and international law, and the comparison of approaches to international law, were not priorities high in the list; rather, the buzzwords were 'adjustment' and 'reform', and the newly adopted

---

37 See for example, *Military and Paramilitary Activities in and against Nicaragua (Nicaragua v. US)*, ICJ Reports (1986) 14, at para. 261 (holding that Nicaragua had no international legal obligations in respect of the principle or methods of holding elections).

38 Thomas M. Franck, 'The Emerging Right to Democratic Governance', 86 *American Journal of International Law* (1992) 46–91, at 50.

39 A single volume introduction to the debate, including some important contributions is Gregory H. Fox and Brad R. Roth (eds), *Democratic Governance and International Law* (Cambridge University Press, 2000).

40 See David Kennedy, 'The "Rule of Law," Political Choices, and Development Common Sense', in David M. Trubek and Alvaro Santos (eds), *The New Law and Economic Development: A Critical Appraisal* (Cambridge University Press, 2006) 95–173, at 116–124 (describing the NIEO and arguing it was generally ineffectual, despite all the attention focused on it).

41 See generally William Easterly, *Elusive Quest of Growth: Economists' Adventures and Misadventures in the Tropics* (MIT Press, 2002) (explaining that prior waves of consensus include the Harrod–Domar model, the Rostow model, some elements of the Prebischean centre–periphery model and a quite long etc.)

standards at the WTO, together with troops of legal experts flying from one newly independent country to the other, were the order of the day.

This process was underscored by the rapid proliferation of international courts and tribunals in the 1990s.[42] From the ICJ and a couple of human rights tribunals in Europe and the Americas, international law now had the dispute settlement body at WTO, *ad hoc* criminal international criminal tribunals, the first North American Free Trade Agreement (NAFTA) litigations, etc. This process meant that the answers to what international law meant could be, once again, found in the work of some international court or the other. And the problem of enforcement seemed to be, finally, in the hands of international tribunals. No more, or so it seemed, was it necessary to rely on domestic courts enforcing international law. At last, we had international courts to do the job. So, it seemed silly to worry about diverging domestic approaches to international law. What was interesting was how closely (not even whether) domestic courts would follow the decision of their international equivalents.

All in all, the end of the Cold War meant a blow to each element of the dual model explaining the role of domestic law in the international legal system. On the one hand, with regards to the comparative (horizontal) axis, new talk about 'humanity', the 'end of history' and the like, made deference to competing domestic legal system a bit quaint. And there were the international legal instruments (human rights and trade law, for example) that proved so: one single legal standard leading to international justice, to economic development, to end impunity, etc. Moreover, the cosmopolitan (vertical) axis that focused on enforcement of international law seemed also old fashioned. Now, international tribunals existed to do the heavy lifting. In the 1990s, it seemed unnecessary to rely on domestic courts to enforce international law.

4 Failed expectations, and the return of the vertical axis

And yet, here we are. Neo-liberalism has failed as well. The brave new world of liberal states, international justice and enduring peace that the end of history promised never materialised. The post-Cold War liberal agreement seems to have failed: for some to win, apparently others necessarily have to lose. The uniform legal standards of convergence that the post-Cold War dream announced were replaced by a fragmented landscape of overlapping norms regimes. The promise of international tribunals failed to live up to its promises of enforcement, and rather got stuck into this fragmented

---

42 See Benedict Kingsbury, 'Foreword: Is the Proliferation of International Courts and Tribunals a Systemic Problem', 31 *New York University Journal of International Law & Politics* (1999) 679–96 (reviewing literature on proliferation of international courts).

landscape.[43] Global governance institutions are not doing any better, as some of the power that was delegated to them has been misused, begging the question of (legal) controls to global power.

As a result, domestic courts increasingly refer to and apply international law,[44] or have to adjudicate on conflicts that emerge from its application – and do so not as Jenks' agents of a universal legal regime, but an often strategic fashion, trying to defend their relative autonomy *vis-à-vis* other branches of domestic power.[45] Much of the reconstructive agendas of imposing legal control to global power are also, one way or the other, inspired in domestic law (global constitutionalism or global administrative law,[46] to name just a couple, but also legal pluralism).[47] The transnational political agendas that were once focused solely on international institutions now focus increasingly in domestic courts, deploying international legal arguments – for example, in the case of *Pinochet*[48] or the feminist struggle in Colombia.[49]

Faced with these challenges, the 'factual' approach to domestic law sounds completely unworkable, and fails to register the changes described above. In this context, the vertical axis of the dual model seems to be experiencing something of a comeback, in a post-national version of itself, and with new labels. Its Cold War structure, though, seems to be still underlying the discipline's traditional understanding of domestic law in international law.

Indeed, the vertical (cosmopolitan) axis of the model is being rediscovered by pragmatists who see in domestic courts, either a platform of enforcement for an international rule of law, or at the very least a mechanism for bypassing international law's endemic (and to some, worrisome) lack of enforcement. Much of the literature being produced about 'international law in domestic courts' goes in that direction. The very interesting work of André Nollkaemper is a case in point. For Nollkaemper, the rule of law requires

---

43 See Robert Howse and Ruti G. Teitel, 'Cross-Judging: Tribunalization in a Fragmented but Interconnected Global Order', 36 *New York University Journal of International Law & Politics* (2010) 101–29.

44 For more examples of recent domestic decision, see André Nollkaemper, *National Courts and the International Rule of Law* (Oxford University Press, 2011).

45 See Eyal Benvenisti, 'Reclaiming Democracy: The Strategic Uses of Foreign and International Law by National Courts', 102 *American Journal of International Law* (2008) 241–74.

46 See my *No Citizens Here: Global Subjects and Participation in International* Law (Martinus Nijhoff, 2012), at 128–39 (mapping global constitutionalism and global administrative law as two species of a distinctively liberal mindset trying to infuse legal regulation back intro global governance).

47 William Burke-White, 'International Legal Pluralism', 25 *Michigan Journal of International Law* (2005) 963–979 (generally applying pluralism to the international legal landscape).

48 *R. v. Bow Street Metropolitan Stipendiary Magistrate, ex parte Pinochet Ugarte (No.3)* [1999] UKHL 17, [2000] 1 AC 147.

49 Julieta Lemaitre Ripoll, *El Derecho Como Conjuro: Fetichismo Legal, Violencia y Movimientos Sociales* (Siglo del Hombre Editores: 2009), at 197–237 (describing ways in which the domestic women's movement in Colombia deployed international human rights arguments to advance their position before domestic courts).

'accountability' (in the sense that public powers that contravene their legal obligations, whether international or national, are accountable on the basis of the law).[50] This accountability may be provided by international and by domestic courts. However, states are reluctant to subject themselves to international justice. So, 'in some states and under some conditions, national courts can fill the missing link in the international rule of law by providing relief when public powers act in contravention of their international obligations'.[51] For this to happen, one needs to let go of 'dualist' reveries and realise that international and domestic law are complementary – this, of course, requires that international law holds supremacy over domestic law.[52]

Now: this new wave of thinking about domestic courts in international law features one difference with its predecessors. Unlike Jenks, who saw that domestic courts had a role to play in merely enforcing role, Nollkaemper sees they play their part in an 'internationalised' rule of law.[53] This idea appears repeatedly in the literature, in this new version of vertical axis: in the interaction between international and domestic law, the former is somehow 'domesticated' and becomes a species of 'hybrid' law.[54] Not here, nor really there, international law is translated by domestic courts.[55] This idea, though, seems to be more of an intuition than a general questioning of the role of domestic courts in international law-making. While both Roberts and Knop seem to conclude to the effect that is important to take seriously the rule-making role of domestic courts in international law,[56] their efforts seem closer to proposing a productive judicial dialogue that enriches our understanding of international law, along the lines of Slaughter's judicial networks.[57]

5 The limits of the dual model

This way of thinking obscures more than it enlightens. It was designed to

---

50   Nollkaemper, *National Courts and the International Rule of Law*, supra note 44, at 5.
51   *Ibid.*, at 6.
52   See André Nollkaemper, 'Rethinking the Supremacy of International Law', 65 *Zeitschrift für Öffentliches Recht* (2010) 65–85, at 65–7 (elaborating on the implication of the principle of supremacy of international law over domestic systems).
53   André Nollkaemper, 'The Bifurcation of International Law: Two Futures for the International Rule of Law', ACIL Research Paper No. 2011-04 (2011), at 3.
54   See Anthea Roberts, 'Comparative International Law? The Role of National Courts in Creating and Enforcing International Law', 60 *International & Comparative Law Quarterly* (2011) 57–92, at 74 (describing the process of hybridising international and national law).
55   Karen Knop, 'Here and There: International Law in Domestic Courts', 32 *New York University Journal of International Law & Politics* (2000) 501–536, at 505 (explaining that domestic interpretation of international law is not simply a conveyor belt that delivers international law to the people, but instead implies a process of translation).
56   See Roberts, 'Comparative International Law?', *supra* note 54, at 91, and Knop, 'Here and There', *supra* note 56, at 535.
57   Anne-Marie Slaughter, *A New World Order* (Princeton University Press, 2004), at 65–103 (discussing the role of judicial networks as part of the emergence of a global legal system).

maintain peaceful coexistence between hegemons, and ignore all the rest. It is based upon a narrative that presupposes a single vantage point that fails to consider the radical differences of power among the subjects of international law – states, of course, but also individuals. And this blind spot makes it, especially in its post-national version, a conceptual apparatus that fails to provide the vocabulary necessary for thinking critically about the rearrangement of global power that we observe today, and the role that international law plays therein. Instead, it is merely restating inherited wisdom that has been around for decades – and which was created in order to guarantee stability and not social chance, peace and not necessarily justice. Going beyond the dual model requires that we ponder some of its limitations. This section explores two: presuming that each regime is static, and lacking a double sensibility that considers the always changing role of both domestic and international laws in law-making.

5.1 Presuming that each regime is static

The dual model presumes that each regime is static. For its vertical axis, international law is static, its meaning is perfectly determinate, and is applied as such by domestic courts. In turn, the horizontal axis presumes that domestic laws are static, and define their own approach to international law without any regard to what the latter says. Neither of these suppositions is true: international law has multiple meanings that are strategically deployed by domestic courts, and domestic laws change as they interact with international law.

Presuming that each regime is static has a way of making power less visible. If international law and domestic laws are reified and thought of as 'objects', then their interphase is not a matter of political choice and resource redistribution, but rather a technical undertaking with little room for debate. Indeed, due to its presumption of stability, the dual model fails to reflect the differences of power between the subjects of international law, in two different senses:

It argues that some international norms should be enforced by domestic courts, and others may be the matter of a legitimate variety of perspective. And yet, how one norm goes from being a part of the 'universal legal order' to being subject to a 'legitimate variety of approaches' is something that the model fails to explain. And it cannot, because the basic reason for this transformation is the relative power of the actor with an interest in the norm. A powerful actor with little interest in a norm results in the dual model's legitimate variety of approaches. A powerful actor with a strong interest in a norm results in it becoming part of the universal legal order. Thus, norms of investment protection could be read as being subject to a legitimate different 'approach' in the Cold War context of the *Sabbatino* case,[58] but they

---

58   Falk, *The Role of Domestic Courts, supra* note 21, at 65.

are certainly part of the international rule of law as defined by today's bilateral investment treaties and investment tribunals.

In its post-national version, the argument becomes that domestic courts will enforce a 'domesticated' version of the international rule of law. But this approach begs the question: domesticated by whom? If we are talking about the rule of law in any meaningful sense, it is clearly the case that some line has to be drawn between acceptable domestic contributions to this transnational legal dialogue, and domestic contribution that ultimately undermine the international rule of law. For example, it is possible to see how a domestic decision that uses the language of international law in order to, say, protect minorities, amounts to a contribution to the international rule of law. However, it is hard to see that contribution if the domestic judicial decision reinforces prejudice and discrimination on the basis of domestic idiosyncratic values.

The post-national version of the model provides no answer to these questions, because the line is drawn on the basis of the relative power of those setting the ultimate filter to enter the dialogue. Otherwise, the international rule of law would risk being undermined from below. That is why transnational judicial dialogues are really not serendipitous conversations of like-minded gentlemen, but rather reproduce patterns of hierarchy and complex transnational political agendas that are pushed precisely through such dialogues.[59] Not only does knowledge and inspiration circulate in these dialogues, but also power.[60] Building a 'domesticated' rule of international law is bound to rely on political power to define its external frontier, but requires that such intervention be obscured – otherwise, the very idea of a rule of law would be in question.

5.2 A double sensibility

The law that is being applied in each of these cases is both national and international, at the same time. Of course, each of them can be correctly described as national *or* international: doubtlessly, Article 13 of the Colombian Constitution[61] protecting the right to equality is a domestic

---

59 See Víctor Navarrete, 'Judicial Globalisation: A New Model of North-South Relations for the 21st Century', 8 *Anuario Mexicano De Derecho Internacional* (2010) 361–97 (building a critique of Slaughter, Keohane and Moravscik's approach, arguing that their theories of transnational judicial dialogues respond to a particular political agenda).

60 Another context in which informal transnational network of knowledge have been seen as an expression of wider struggles for power is structural reform in Latin America in the 1990s. See Yves Dezalay and Bryant G. Garth, *The Internationalization of Palace Wars: Lawyers, Economists, and the Contest to Transform Latin American States* (University of Chicago Press, 2002) (describing the rise to power of competing elites of lawyers and economists in Latin America, as part of the diffusion of neo-liberalism in the region).

61 English translation available at <confinder.richmond.edu/admin/docs/colombia_const 2.pdf>

norm, and Article 23 of the International Covenant of Civil and Political Rights (ICCPR)[62] protecting the same right is an international one. But that is hardly the end of the discussion. It is as if each of these norms had a double life, which is ignored by the dual model. A first life, their 'day job', if one wills, is the one that is recognised by the dual model, even in its post-national version. Article 13 of the Colombian Constitution has a domestic life, and it is possible to make sense of it without considering international law (which is, in fact, what happens most of the time in domestic courts). Article 23 of the ICCPR, in turn, has an international life where it is interpreted without pondering domestic legal systems.[63]

It often gets more complex than that, all within each norm's traditional role. Sometimes, the domestic life of the Colombian Article 13 will be made a bit more interesting by seeking inspiration in the international legal system. At this point, we hear domestic constitutional law scholars speaking of the 'internationalisation' of domestic law.[64] But this is rhetorical: in fact, domestic law is not changing at all, but is rather drawing inspiration from other legal systems. This may be labelled once again as judicial or legal dialogue,[65] but it is not a reappraisal of the relation between domestic and international law. This is all part of the domestic life of domestic norms. In turn, Article 23 of the ICCPR may have some brushes with domestic law in its international life. Domestic courts may even apply Article 23 of the ICCPR, which may be a source of inspiration and dialogue for international courts – that is, the 'domesticated' version of the international rule of law that we discussed earlier. But all of this is still part of the international life of Article 23, which is the version that is recognised by the dual model.

However, these norms have also a 'night job', overlooked by the traditional approach. When they interact, they transform what we understand, in our example, by right to equality as a whole. This right is different from the

---

62 UNGA Res. 2200A (XXI), 16 December 1966, in force 23 March 1976, 999 UNTS 171.
63 In this sense, the double sensibility that will be discussed in the following paragraphs is not connected to Scelle's *dedoublement fonctionnel*, as the latter theory failed to consider the role of international courts in enforcing international law, but rather contended that this task is fulfilled by the domestic courts of the various states settling conflict of law issues. For this reading of Scelle's theory, see Antonio Cassese, 'Remarks on Scelle's Theory of Role Splitting (*Dédoublement Fonctionnel*) in International Law', 1 *European Journal of International Law* (1990) 212–31, at 217–18.
64 See Marco Gerardo Monroy Cabra, 'El Derecho Internacional Como Fuente Del Derecho Constitucional', 1 *Anuario Colombiano De Derecho Internacional* (2008) 107–38 (proposing that Colombian constitutional has been 'internationalized', as international law is a 'source' of domestic law).
65 For the Colombian case, see Alejandra Azuero, 'Redes De Diálogo Judicial Trasnacional: Una Aproximación Empírica Al Caso De La Corte Constitucional', 22 *Revista De Derecho Publico – Universidad De Los Andes* (2009) 1–22 (discussing empirical evidence of different models of transnational judidicial where Colombian judges are involved, and presenting a critique of Slaughter's model).

domestic or international norms, but is rather a space of contestation that produces new laws – which results from the existence of domestic and international law. Thus, the Colombian right to equality is different because of the existence of Article 23 of the ICCPR – not because Colombian courts apply the international norm, but because Article 23 of the ICCPR frames the frontier of possibilities for the domestic court. The very existence of the international norm creates a magnetic field that bends domestic law, even if it never enters in contact with it, as the dual model would require. The same happens with international law. It is transformed as it interacts with domestic law: for example, Article 36(1)(b) of the 1963 Vienna Convention on Consular Relations[66] looks different after it has interacted with the law as put forward by the US Supreme Court[67] – and it looks different not only for the US justice that applies it, but for all of us. The parts, in this case, only give us some of the elements that we need to understand the whole. The dual model lacks a sensibility to this double life of norms. It is therefore unable to see that the very same rule can be different and change as a function of its interactions. We cannot focus on the US Supreme Court, or on the Vienna Convention, but rather on the line that connects them. This line is not a conveyor belt, nor is it just a sum of the parts. This line *is* international law-making.

6 Towards law-making interaction

Considering such limitations, one way forward is to reject the idea that domestic and international laws are static, but rather to think of them as dynamic; that is, to think that the interphase is in fact a law-making interaction, in which domestic law is transformed by international law, which is in turn transformed by the former, in a never-ending loop. My point is not that there is a third regime, but rather that international law-making is in fact the product of the interaction between domestic and international law. From this perspective, the question is not whether domestic courts enforce an international rule of law, but rather to inquire about the new forms of law that emerge from the interaction. This implies that an understanding of the units (international law and domestic law) is not sufficient to understand the whole. Admittedly, this is a distinctively descriptive enterprise: it is not intended to propose the means to achieve the 'international rule of law' in the sense that has been discussed above, but rather to offer an alternative to the dominant dual model. Its inspiration is, precisely, that all the talk about the international rule of law obscures the power asymmetries that are built into our current understanding of the relation between domestic and international law.

---

66   24 April 1963, in force 19 March 1967, 596 UNTS 261.
67   *Medellín v. Texas*, 552 US 491 (US Supreme Court, 2008).

In order to think in terms of law-making interaction, a fruitful staring point may be some of the lessons learned from the debate of fragmentation in international law; i.e. the emergence of specialised and relatively autonomous rules or rule-complexes, legal institutions and spheres of legal practice at the international level.[68] It is well documented that international law has been suffering from 'fragmentation anxiety', and that such a topic has stirred one of the central debates taking place in contemporary legal scholarship – I will not dwell further on such a debate.[69]

Why are these specialised regimes relevant to our discussion? Because each of them includes both domestic and international law, and it is within them that interaction occurs. Indeed, international lawyers have to compare among specialised regimes. Several specialised regimes are applicable at the same time, to the same subject – hence, the challenges of fragmentation. It is an exercise of comparative law to understand the relative advantages and disadvantages of framing one topic as, say, a human rights concern and not as an investment law matter.[70] An analysis of this sort will consider international norms and institutions, and also the domestic law aspect of the specialised regimes. Therefore, expertise in each of these functionally specialised regimes supposes the knowledge and comparison of different domestic approaches to international norms. Hence, the human rights expert needs to know international human rights, domestic human rights laws, and the way in which the interaction between the two affect her client's case. This is not to say that, institutionally, courts simple belong to one regime or the other. The Supreme Court of Canada does not belong to the human rights, nor the trade regime – most probably, it will decide on those issues and many more. However, as it decides cases that relate to international law, each of these domestic decisions is connected to one or several of the global specialised regimes, and the law-making interaction approach reads them in reference to their specialised regime.

Adopting specialised regimes as analytical units to understand the interaction has important advantages over starting the discussion with the

---

68 Fragmentation of International Law: Difficulties arising from the Diversification and Expansion of International Law (finalised by Martti Koskenniemi), UN Doc. A/CN.4/L.682, 13 April 2006, para. 8.

69 My own take can be found in *No Citizens Here*, supra note 46, at 36–43 and accompanying footnotes (arguing that the 'problem' of fragmentation is both quite real and quite moot, but the real part is necessarily connected to subjectivity and subjectivation, and not abstract regimes and *Kollisionrecht á la* Teubner and Fischer–Lescano).

70 For example, in a case initiated under NAFTA, *Mondev International Ltd. v. US*, ICSID Case No. ARB(AF)/99/2, Award of 11 October 2002, part of the discussion was whether granting an immunity to a certain urban development authority in Boston amounted to a violation of the fair and equitable treatment standard. The Tribunal saw that the issue could be reasonably framed as a problem connected to the 'human right to a court', and went on to seek inspiration in the case law of the European Court of Human Rights to reach its decision (at paras 142–54).

domestic/international law dichotomy. However, it also carries some costs that need to be discussed. Perhaps the main challenge is the issue of 'tunnel vision'.[71] By definition, specialised international regimes exist in order to regulate a certain area of global politics or production: that is, they are only concerned with that specific subject, and not with wider societal concerns. The climate change lobby will be concerned with that climate change and not with the rights of women. And the human rights regime will be focused on that specific issue, and not with economic development, or the environment. Using specialised regimes as an analytical unit risks losing sight of an overarching narrative of a 'good' society.

Moreover, specialised regimes are not static objects to be found in nature. Just as domestic and international law cannot be reified, specialised regimes cannot be understood to be something 'out there'. Instead, they are put together in order to achieve a goal that is not given by the specialised regime itself, but rather by external political forces that see international law as one more of their tools to achieve their needs.[72] In this sense, a specialised regime will most likely play the part intended by the powerful. What is more, regimes themselves may have hegemonic ambitions, in the sense that they would seek to expand their world-view, placing their goal as more important (or universal) in detriment of the goals of other regimes.[73] Adopting such unit of analysis could obscure important differences of power and, in fact, could perpetuate as neutral the structure of 'specialised regimes', which is a specific creation of the powerful.

This move, in turn, could end up empowering the narrowly defined experts that decide what the objective of the regime is. Indeed, because the mindset of these regimes is wholly instrumental, a certain transnational elite, which may act outside democratic or legal checks of accountability, may end up being empowered by global specialised regimes.[74] Thus, the law-making interaction approach could play into this expert-power base, legitimising as 'law-making' what is only the result of the (functional) agenda of domination.

---

71 Gunther Teubner and Peter Korth (eds), 'Two Kind of Legal Pluralism: Collision of Transnational in the Double Fragmentation of the World Society', in Margaret A. Young, *Regime Interaction in International Law: Facing Fragmentation* (Cambridge University Press, 2012) 23–54, at 37 (introducing the problem of 'tunnel vision').

72 See, generally, Koskenniemi, 'The Fate of Public International Law', *supra* note 19 (discussing the challenge of managerialism, which undermines the idea of an inherent normative pull of international law). See also Urueña, *No Citizens Here*, *supra* note 46, at 74–7 (describing as managerial the approach taken by critical legal studies as well).

73 Martti Koskenniemi, 'Hegemonic Regimes', in Margaret A. Young (ed.), *Regime Interaction in International Law: Facing Fragmentation* (Cambridge University Press, 2012) 305–23 (discussing regimes as hegemons that seek to expand their sphere of influence).

74 See René Urueña, 'Expertise and Global Water Governance: How to Start Thinking about Power over Water Resources', 9 *Anuario Mexicano De Derecho Internacional* (2010) 117–52 (exploring expertise as a technology of governance in the specialised regime of global water governance).

All of these are important challenges. The law-making interaction approach, though, does not see specialised regimes as objects whose characteristics exist outside political choices. Quite on the contrary, this approach embraces the fact that the tunnel vision of specialised regimes is able to obscure differences of power. However, these differences of power may be foregrounded through four strategies. First, the inclusion of domestic law as a part of specialised regimes, and as more than mere facts, may provide elements to compensate the 'tunnel vision' problem. It is may allow for other variables, closer to domestic interests, to creep into process of specialised legal reasoning, thus providing the decision-maker with more 'contextualising elements' when they adopt a decision. This strategy may not go too far, as domestic interests may in fact be represented by domestic elites seeking to favour specialised decision-making, instead of grass-root movements seeking to democratise governance.[75]

A second strategy may prove more productive. Law-making interaction is not predicable only of the contact between domestic and international law within specialised regimes, but also of the contact between specialised regimes. Thus, new regulation appears not only when domestic law of property interacts with international law of investment protection, but also when the regime of investment protection interacts with the regime of environmental protection. And in this 'external' interaction, tunnel vision may diminish and contestation may appear.

The most evident arena of contestation is, of course, definition. Such is the third strategy of foregrounding power in the context of specialised regimes. The law-making interaction approach understands specialised regimes as ductile and porous, because their definition includes no act of formal public authority, but rather the decision of experts defining a specific area as 'specialised'. Thus, the definition of an issue (say, an environmental regulation) as a matter of investment law, environmental law, or human rights can be contested. In fact, this definition is the necessary first step of resistance, as it prevents the deployment of the structural bias implicit in the regime that is not desired. This move is well-known in comparative law, where the frontal attack on functionalism was inspired by the need to question the 'function' of the law as a neutral definition. Moreover, this process of contested definition may imply that regimes are transformed as they interact: there is no reason why investment protection cannot become a regime of investment–environment protection, or that the climate change regime includes the interest of forcefully displaced population.

---

[75] For this problem in the context of judicial reform in Colombia, César Rodríguez-Garavito, 'Towards a Sociology of the Global Rule of Law Field: Neoliberalism, Neoconstitutionalism, and the Contest over Judicial Reform in Latin America', in Yves Dezalay and Bryant Garth (eds), *Lawyers and the Rule of Law in an Era of Globalization* (Routledge, 2011) 155–81.

Finally, the use of specialised regimes does not necessarily lead to further unaccountable empowerment of experts. Rather, if the role of experts in defining the regimes and the factors that fall inside and outside a certain specialised regime is highlighted, then the possibility of discussing these choices actually increases – unlike the strategy of merely asking for legal formal coherence or celebrating judicial dialogues that empower global experts even further. All of this is, of course, a political struggle – the point is that using specialised regimes as an analytical unit does not leave us without a vocabulary to speak about it.

Conclusion

The renewed interest in the role of domestic law in the international legal system echoes some of the themes that have preoccupied the discipline for decades. It replays also the framework that defined the international approach to domestic law during the Cold War. This framework, though, fails to consider some of the important transformations in the distribution of global power that have occurred since the 1990s. In particular, it is in the interphase between international and domestic laws where much of the global redistribution of power seems to be taking place. It is therefore important to start thinking about alternative vocabularies to describe this interaction – a vocabulary that, beyond mere the mere rhetoric of domestic law as 'facts', enables scholars in both the developed and the developing world to map the flows of power that influence the regulation that affects them. This article is an effort to that effect.

Part III
Institutions and participants

10 International responsibility and problematic law-making

Katja Creutz

1 Introduction: Problematising international responsibility

Responsibility is one of the fields of international law where extensive development and law-making has taken place.[1] Although state practice has been the prime mover behind the development of responsibility matters, the International Law Commission (ILC) has played a prominent role in the completion of responsibility regimes that display system-building functions beyond the classic reparative or punitive role inherent in the idea of responsibility. The ILC has both codified and progressively developed the law of the responsibility of states, it has contributed to the development and manifestation of international criminal law and hence the principle of individual criminal responsibility, and most recently it has finalised rules concerning the responsibility of international organisations. Generally, this development has been praised; the different responsibility regimes are understood to form a tool-box that gives the international community different mechanisms to deal with violations of international law. State responsibility, international criminal law and the responsibility of international organisations are thus assumed to complement each other. The underlying (and often unspelt) idea is that by having multiple responsibility regimes in international law, one is better able to deal with the infinite variety of cases that emerge and thus one ends up with 'increased' responsibility in international law.

Lately a revived interest in responsibility matters can be discerned, pointing to the fact that this branch of international law needs further

---

1 The term 'international responsibility' has traditionally been understood to refer to state responsibility only. This still holds true today, see, e.g., James Crawford, Alain Pellet and Simon Olleson (eds), *Oxford Commentaries on International Law: The Law of International Responsibility* (Oxford University Press, 2010). However, with the existence of several responsibility regimes at the international level, a change in usage can be discerned. See, e.g., André Nollkaemper and Harmen van der Wilt (eds), *System Criminality in International Law* (Cambridge University Press, 2009), at vii. In this chapter the term will be used to denote the various regimes that currently exist (unless a different meaning is expressly stated).

exploration. The modest aim of this essay is indeed to contribute to the discourse on international responsibility by way of challenging the orthodox tool-box or complementarity view.[2] It will be argued that there is nothing clear about how the two regimes are used and consequently how they would complement each other. No rules exist that would regulate when to use which regime – or even both – and the two responsibility regimes increasingly seem to be unequal in attractiveness. The analysis below will therefore present and discuss two fundamental but overlooked difficulties with the tool-box view: (1) the lack of rules governing when to apply what regime opens the door for randomness and may even lead to dilution of responsibility altogether; and (2) the responsibility regimes are not equally resorted to, i.e. there is an order of precedence to be discerned in international practice. It is consequently argued here that despite normative development in the field of international responsibility many problems remain to be dealt with. Not only societal transformations, such as globalisation, pose problems to the law of international responsibility, but also the way responsibility matters were dealt with and codified by the ILC.

2 Fragmented law-making in responsibility issues

2.1 Separation of responsibilities by the International Law Commission

Vast normative and institutional development has taken place with respect to international responsibility in the last decades. State responsibility – the traditional legal paradigm in international responsibility – was subject to codification and progressive development for almost 50 years by the ILC, a work that ended with the adoption of the Articles on State responsibility in 2001.[3] A few years before, the corresponding work of the ILC in terms of the responsibility of individuals had come to conclusion, reaching its high point in the creation of a permanent International Criminal Court (ICC) in 1998.[4] Moreover, the increased importance of international organisations in international affairs brought the topic of the responsibility of international organisations on the Commission's agenda in 2002, and to completion in

---

2   The analysis in this essay will be limited to state responsibility and the principle of individual criminal responsibility as embodied in international criminal law with respect to wrongdoings covered by both regimes. The responsibility of international organisations will largely be left out.
3   Draft Articles on the Responsibility of States for Internationally Wrongful Acts, in Report of the International Law Commission on the Work of its Fifty-third session, UN Doc A/56/10 (2001), ch. IV. The General Assembly took note of the Articles in GA Res. 56/83, 12 December 2001.
4   Draft Statute for an ICC, in Report of the International Law Commission on the Work of its Forty-sixth Session (1994), UN Doc. A/49/10, ch. II; Draft Code of Crimes against the Peace and Security of Mankind, in Report of the International Law Commission on the Work of its Forty-eight Session, UN Doc. A/51/10, ch. II.

2011.[5] Thus, two characteristics of law-making in the field of international responsibility can be discerned: first, the significant role played by the ILC, and second, the Commission's fragmented approach to responsibility.

Without dwelling in this context on the law-making capabilities of the ILC, one can easily claim that the Commission can be regarded as a *de facto* law-maker in addition to its formal credentials to codify and progressively develop international law.[6] With respect to the issue of international responsibility, the Commission was mandated separately to work on state responsibility and individual criminal responsibility (and later the responsibility of international organisations). Thus, it can be argued that already the mandates steered the Commission upon the path of separation. The piecemeal approach to responsibility within the ILC follows its approach in other general fields of international law such as the law of treaties, in which the Commission first dealt with inter-state treaties only and later expanded the law of treaties to cover treaties between states and international organisations or between international organisations. The Commission's work is by necessity constrained by prevailing understandings of general international law which may explain in part why it has chosen to deal with responsibility concerns one legal subject a time.

The Commission clearly intended to develop and maintain state responsibility and international criminal law separate from each other. Within the ILC, most members favoured the two-track approach during the codification work on state responsibility. It appears that one reason behind the method of separation was the reluctance of many ILC members to have any kind of criminality included within the purview of state responsibility:

> The Special Rapporteur retained the firm conviction that, in the future, the international system might develop a genuine form of corporate criminal liability for entities, including States. Most members of the Commission had refused to envisage that hypothesis and had spoken out in favour of a two-track approach which entailed developing the notion of individual criminal liability through the mechanism of ad hoc tribunals and the future international criminal court ... and developing within the field of State responsibility the notion of responsibility for breaches of the most serious norms of concern to the international community as a whole.[7]

---

5   The ILC was mandated to work on the subject in GA Res. 56/82, 12 December 2001, at para. 8. The final outcome, i.e. the Draft Articles on the Responsibility of International Organizations, was presented in the Report of the International Law Commission on the Work of its Sixty-third session (2011), UN Doc. A/66/10, ch. V. The General Assembly took note of the Articles in GA Res. 66/100, 9 December 2011.
6   On the functions of the Commission, see Statute of the ILC, GA Res. 174 (II), 21 November 1947, ch. II.
7   Report of the International Law Commission on the Work of its Fiftieth Session (1998), UN Doc. A/53/10, at para. 329.

As a consequence of keeping the two responsibility regimes separate, no rules were developed on their relationship except for a mutual recognition of the existence and independence of the respective regimes. The 2001 ILC Articles on State Responsibility expressly state in Article 58 on the question of individual responsibility that: 'these articles [on state responsibility] are without prejudice to any question of the individual responsibility under international law of any person acting on behalf of the State'.[8]

The function of the saving clause has been described as a 'dividing wall[s] between the different systems.'[9] The inclusion of the rule in question was motivated by the desire to assure that any findings relating to state responsibility does not *ipso facto* equal to decisions on individual responsibility. It was thought important to separately point this out, since many international crimes are committed by individuals acting as state officials. The ILC Commentary opens up the connection by further stating that the state cannot escape its international responsibility by prosecuting and punishing state officials who committed the wrongful act. The Commission further explained with respect to the provision:

> Where crimes against international law are committed by State Officials, it will often be the case that the State itself is responsible for the acts in question or for failure to prevent or punish them. In certain cases, in particular aggression, the State will by definition be involved. Even so, the question of individual responsibility is in principle distinct from the question of State responsibility. The State is not exempted from its own responsibility for internationally wrongful conduct by the prosecution and punishment of the State officials who carried it out.[10]

In the reverse, state officials cannot 'hide behind the State in respect of their own responsibility for conduct of theirs which is contrary to the rules of international law which are applicable to them'.[11]

The drafting history of the rule separating the two responsibility regimes is scarce. In the first reading there was no equivalent provision in the draft articles approved by the ILC. In the provisional adoption of the second reading in 2000 the rule had found its way into the totality with a slightly

---

8   A similar saving clause is found in the Draft Articles on the Responsibility of International Organizations, *supra* note 5. Article 57 states: '[t]hese articles are without prejudice to any question of the responsibility under international law of an international organization, or of any State for the conduct of an international organization.'
9   Daniel Bodansky and John R. Crook, 'Symposium: The ILC's State Responsibility Articles – Introduction and Overview', 96 *American Journal of International Law* (2002) 773–91, at 788.
10 Draft Articles on the Responsibility of States for Internationally Wrongful Acts, *supra* note 3, Commentary on Article 58, para. 3.
11 *Ibid.*

different formulation than the final adoption: '[t]hese articles are without prejudice to any question of the individual responsibility under international law of any person acting in the capacity of an organ or agent of the State'.[12] One plausible reason for the insertion of Article 58 at such a late stage may be the development and manifestation of international criminal law in the late 1990s when the ILC was finalising its Articles on State Responsibility. During this time, the *ad hoc* international criminal tribunals had in addition to developing a practice of their own also paved way for the adoption of the Rome Statute for an ICC. Most importantly, their practice had targeted many state officials, and hence the saving clause was needed to clarify that a verdict on the individual criminal responsibility of state officials did not amount to findings with respect to state responsibility.[13] Thus, it had become necessary to take account of international criminal law's cementation, although technically Article 58 is not limited to an individual's criminal responsibility only, but also includes individual civil responsibility.

2.2 The making of the Rome Statute

The corresponding saving clause in international criminal law keeping the two responsibility regimes apart is found under the general principles of criminal law in the Rome Statute of the ICC.[14] The Statute's legislative history can be divided into work performed by the ILC, the Preparatory Committee and the Conference of the plenipotentiaries amounting to the final adopted statute in 1998.[15]

The draft statute adopted by the ILC in 1994 contains no reference to state responsibility.[16] Although general principles of criminal law were introduced into the discussion with the *Ad Hoc* Committee created by the General Assembly in the aftermath of the ILC's Draft statute,[17] the connection to state responsibility was still left out.[18] Attention to the

---

12 International Law Commission, State Responsibility: Draft Articles Provisionally Adopted by the Drafting Committee on Second Reading, A/CN.4/L.600, 21 August 2000, p. 16.
13 Draft Articles on the Responsibility of States for Internationally Wrongful Acts, *supra* note 3, Commentary on Article 58, para. 3.
14 Rome Statute of the International Criminal Court, 17 July 1998, entered into force 1 July 2002, 2187 UNTS 3, Article 25(4): 'No provision in this Statute relating to individual criminal responsibility shall affect the responsibility of States under international law.'
15 For the drafting history of particularly the general principles of international criminal law, see, e.g., William A. Schabas, 'General Principles of Criminal Law in the ICC Statute (Part III), 6 *European Journal of Crime, Criminal Law & Criminal Justice* (1998) 84–112, at 85.
16 Draft Statute for an ICC, *supra* note 4.
17 GA Res. 49/53, 9 December 1994, at para. 2. See Report of the *Ad Hoc* Committee on the Establishment of an ICC, UN Doc. A/50/22, 6 September 1995. The *Ad Hoc* Committee had in turn established a working group to work on, *inter alia*, general principles of criminal law, see, *ibid.*, at para. 9.
18 Report of the *Ad Hoc* Committee, *supra* note 17, Annex II, at para. B.1.

relationship between individual criminal responsibility and state responsibility was paid only with the work of the Preparatory Committee. In the Preparatory Committee the relationship between state responsibility and individual criminal responsibility was raised by several delegations. They demanded an insertion of the effect that a finding on individual responsibility would have on the responsibility of the state. Accordingly the 'statute should clarify whether the assigning of individual responsibility in any way vacated the responsibility of a State'.[19]

The delegations of the Preparatory Committee urged models to be taken from the Statute of the International Criminal Tribunal for Former Yugoslavia (ICTY) and that of the International Criminal Tribunal for Rwanda (ICTR) which both state the irrelevance of the official position regarding individual criminal responsibility.[20] During the Third Preparatory Committee in February 1997, a Working Group on General Principles of Criminal Law and Penalties was established.[21] Its Chairman suggested a formulation of the principle of individual criminal responsibility which included a subsection stating that 'the criminal responsibility for individuals does not affect the responsibility of States under international law'.[22] This formulation was recommended to the Preparatory Committee by the Working Group, which raised no objections to the proposal.[23] The international conference that convened with the purpose to adopt the Statute of the ICC was therefore presented with Draft Article 23(6) reading: 'The fact that the present Statute provides criminal responsibility for individuals does not affect the responsibility of States under international law'.[24]

At the diplomatic conference of plenipotentiaries, the work on general principles of criminal law was continued in a same named working group. No further elaboration on state responsibility *per se* was provided by the working group, although its criminal aspect was touched upon in the discussions on whether or not to include corporate criminal responsibility in the Statute. It was suggested in the working group that the future ICC should also have jurisdiction over juridical persons. A 'juridical person' was defined as 'a corporation whose concrete, real or dominant objective is seeking

---

19 Preparatory Committee on Establishment of ICC, 'Preparatory Committee on International Criminal Court Concludes First Session', Doc. L/2787, 12 April 1996; See also Preparatory Committee on the Establishment of an ICC, 'Summary of the Proceedings of the Preparatory Committee During the Period 25 March–12 April 1996', UN Doc. A/AC.249/1, 7 May 1996, at para. 89.
20 See Article 7 in the ICTY Statute and Article 6 in the ICTR Statute.
21 Schabas, 'General Principles of Criminal Law', *supra* note 15, at 85.
22 Preparatory Committee on the Establishment of an ICC, A/AC.249/1997/WG.2/CRP.2, 13 February 1997.
23 Preparatory Committee on the Establishment of an ICC, A/AC.249/1997/L.5, 12 March 1997.
24 Report of the Preparatory Committee on the Establishment of an ICC, A/CONF. 183/2/Add.1, 14 April 1998.

private profit or benefit, and not a State or other public body in the exercise of State authority, a public international body, or an organisation registered under national law of a State as a non-profit organisation'.[25] A possible criminal responsibility of states was hence left outside the deliberations, interestingly so in a time when the ILC was pondering on what to do with the infamous Draft Article 19 which it had adopted during its first reading of the Draft Articles on State Responsibility in 1996. What is worth mentioning here is nevertheless the explicit connection that was made between natural and juridical persons within the working group: the Prosecutor could file charges against a juridical person and the Court could render a judgement over a juridical person only if, among other conditions, '[t]he natural person has been convicted of the crime charged'.[26] The principle of corporate criminal responsibility was, however, dropped due to the continued firm resistance by a number of states whose national legal systems do not recognise the principle. Hence, the Draft Statute of the Diplomatic Conference as adopted by the Committee of the Whole in which all participating states were represented contained in Draft Article 23(4) a slightly amended formulation to that already adopted by the Preparatory Committee. It now read: 'No provision in this Statute relating to individual criminal responsibility, shall affect the responsibility of States under international law.'[27] This version later became the one adopted as Article 25(4) in the final act of the conference and in the plenary sessions of the conference the subject was not debated.

The discussion in the drafting of the Rome Statute on the separation between state responsibility and individual criminal responsibility was equally limited as that in the ILC regarding state responsibility. However, in two respects the preparation of the saving clause in the Rome Statute has more to offer. First, the delegations of states expressly required clarity in how a finding on individual criminal responsibility affects state responsibility, if at all. This means that the possibility of an interconnection between the two regimes was not *prima facie* ruled out. Second, there was a proposal which linked different principles of responsibility together. Although it did not link individual criminal responsibility with state responsibility but instead with corporate criminal responsibility, the idea that there is interplay

---

25 Working Group on General Principles of Criminal Law, 'Working Paper on article 23, paragraphs 5 and 6', UN Doc. A/CONF.183/C.1/WGGP/L.5/REV.2, 3 July 1998, in United Nations Diplomatic Conference of Plenipotentiaries on the Establishment of an ICC, Rome, 15 June–17 July 1998: Official Records ('Rome Conference Official Records'), vol. III, at 251–2.
26 *Ibid.*, at 252.
27 The version now read: 'No provision in this Statute relating to individual criminal responsibility, shall affect the responsibility of States under international law.' Report of the Committee of the Whole, Doc. A/CONF.183/8, 17 July 1998, in Rome Conference Official Records, *supra* note 25, at 103.

between two systems of responsibility did seem to garner some support in many countries.[28] So why was the separation of individual criminal responsibility from the question of state responsibility comprehensively accepted, especially when the ILC had set forth the idea of state criminality in its 1996 Draft Articles on State Responsibility? One explanation might simply relate to that of mandates of the drafting bodies. The ILC dealt with international criminal law as a separate topic and in a different format from state responsibility. Respectively, the task of the diplomatic conference as well as the preparatory bodies was to draw up a Statute to an international court dealing with individual criminal responsibility, nothing more and nothing less. The conference had no need or desire to take standings on matters of state responsibility when the ILC was simultaneously dealing with the issue. Thus, already the mandates steered away any discussion on more theoretical questions of responsibility.

Law-making with regard to state responsibility and individual criminal responsibility of international criminal law has thus proceeded both separately and in parallel. The relationship between the two responsibility regimes can be described as peaceful co-existence: no rules exist that would lay down an order of preference or the connection between the two regimes. Although the co-existence is generally endorsed, there is clear need to evaluate this interplay from a critical point of view; attention needs to be paid to the concurrence of state responsibility and individual criminal responsibility from the international legal perspective.

3 The tool-box view: Alleged complementarity between different responsibility regimes

The existence of two, and even several, responsibility regimes in international law has been described as a 'tool-box', of which the underlying implication is that the possibility of resorting to several mechanisms is beneficial for the overall assignment of responsibility. In other words, the more responsibility regimes, the more responsibility one ends up with. Since responsibility is considered an inherent ingredient of any legal system, its importance to the international legal system cannot be underestimated. The tool-box view thus builds on the assumption that it is beneficial for the international legal system as a whole.

The possibility of applying two responsibility systems to one and the same violation of international law has generally not been construed as a problem. On the contrary, views have been expressed about the complementary function the both regimes have in relation to each other. Antônio Augusto

---

28 Per Saland, 'International Criminal Law Principles', in Roy S. Lee (ed.), *The International Criminal Court: The Making of the Rome Statute – Issues, Negotiations, Results* (Kluwer, 1999) 189–216, at 199.

Cançado Trindade has described the relationship of the two systems in the following way:

> The international responsibility of the State and the international criminal responsibility of the individual are not mutually exclusive, but rather complement each other.[29]

In a similar vein, Andrea Bianchi has described the relationship between state and individual responsibility 'in terms of "complementarity"', and has further held that 'the duality of the regimes of state and individual responsibility should not be seen as a negative development'.[30] The multiplicity of systems has also, for example, been interpreted as beneficial for the victim; 'the tools for justice must be applied in combination, and the more flexible [sic] this is done the better it will serve the victims.'[31] Concerning legal responses to mass atrocities, Michael Reisman has noted that 'rather than a single institution, a *toolbox* of different institutions should be on hand. There is no general institution that can be applied as a paradigm for all circumstances.'[32] Similarly, André Nollkaemper and Harmen van der Wilt have urged for 'a synthesis of both individual and collective responsibility' in response to system criminality on the basis that 'the regimes of state responsibility and individual (criminal) responsibility are to a large extent each others [sic] mirror image and therefore complementary.'[33]

Most proponents of complementarity rely on the distinctive character of the two sets of responsibility: one system relates to *criminal* responsibility as opposed to the alleged *civil* nature of state responsibility.[34] To them, the domestic analogy brings legitimacy to the differentiation of responsibilities: since national legal systems separate between civil and criminal responsibility the duality of systems in international law is taken as a self-evident step in the progress of international law. Pierre-Marie Dupuy has described the separation of individual criminal responsibility from state responsibility as

---

29 Antônio Augusto Cançado Trindade, 'Complementarity between State Responsibility and Individual Responsibility for Grave Violations of Human Rights: The Crime of State Revisited', in Maurizio Ragazzi (ed.), *International Responsibility Today: Essays in Memory of Oscar Schachter* (Martinus Nijhoff, 2005) 253–69, at 258.

30 Andrea Bianchi, 'State Responsibility and Criminal Liability of Individuals', in Antonio Cassese (ed.), *The Oxford Companion to International Criminal Justice* (Oxford University Press, 2009) 16–24, at 16 and 24.

31 Volker Hüls, 'State Responsibility for Crimes under International Law: Filling the Justice gap in the Congo', <www.lawanddevelopment.org/docs/justicegapcongo.pdf> at 22.

32 W. Michael Reisman, 'Legal Responses to Genocide and Other Massive Violations of Human Rights', 59 *Law & Contemporary Problems* (1996) 75–80, at 79 (emphasis added).

33 André Nollkaemper and Harmen van der Wilt, 'Conclusions and Outlook', in Nollkaemper and Wilt, *System Criminality*, supra note 1, 338–353 at 347.

34 Whether or not state responsibility is a civil system has been questioned by, e.g., Antônio Augusto Cançado Trindade, who claims that it rather encompasses both civil and penal aspects. See Cançado Trindade, 'Complementarity', *supra* note 29, at 257.

'an evolution towards the individualisation of penal responsibility in the international order that closely parallels the one municipal legal systems underwent long ago.'[35]

The ICJ in the *Bosnian Genocide* case has confirmed the co-existence of the two responsibility regimes with respect to a number of wrongdoings,[36] which so far is the only international judicial decision that has elaborated on the relationship between state and individual responsibility. The concurrence of responsibilities came up when the respondent state in the case, Serbia-Montenegro, argued that the Court lacked jurisdiction to consider state responsibility concerning *acts* of genocide.[37] In addition, Serbia argued that state responsibility for acts of genocide could be established only after having found individual criminal responsibility for such acts, which in effect would make state responsibility subsidiary to individual criminal responsibility. Serbia argued that '[a]s genocide is a crime, it can only be established in accordance with the rules of criminal law, under which the first requirement to be met is that of individual responsibility.'[38] The ICJ discarded assertions about an order of precedence between the two responsibilities. Instead it upheld the position that state responsibility and individual criminal responsibility exist side-by-side by stating that 'the duality of responsibilities continues to be a constant feature of international law'.[39]

The co-existence of the two responsibilities is generally accepted uncritically. Only few scholars notice that the co-existence of two responsibility regimes creates political and legal challenges that will require the attention of the international community and need new formulas on how to move forward. Héctor Gros Espiell recognises that '[t]he political, intellectual, and legal challenge created by this mutual relationship and co-existence must be duly met in order to achieve the required progress.'[40] Another scholar exploring the duality of responsibility regimes is Gerry Simpson who holds that the 'two models now co-exist rather uncomfortably in the contemporary practice of international law.'[41] Thomas Franck also raised the question whether individual criminal liability and collective civil responsi-

---

35   Pierre-Marie Dupuy, 'International Criminal Responsibility of the Individual and International Responsibility of the State', in Antonio Cassese, Paolo Gaeta and John R. W. D. Jones (eds), *The Rome Statute of the International Criminal Court: A Commentary* (Oxford University Press, 2002), vol. ii, 1085–99, at 1098.
36   *Application of the Convention on the Prevention and Punishment of the Crime of Genocide (Bosnia and Herzegovina v. Serbia and Montenegro)*, ICJ Reports (2007) 43.
37   *Ibid.*, para. 156.
38   *Ibid.*, para. 157.
39   *Ibid.*, para. 172.
40   Héctor Gros Espiell, 'International Responsibility of the State and Individual Criminal Responsibility in the International Protection of Human Rights', in Maurizio Ragazzi (ed.), *International Responsibility Today: Essays in Memory of Oscar Schachter* (Martinus Nijhoff, 2005) 151–60, at 160.
41   Gerry Simpson, *Law, War & Crime: War Crimes Trials and the Reinvention of International Law* (Polity Press, 2007), at 58.

bility in fact reinforce or contradict one another.[42] In the following, the duality of regimes – focusing here on state responsibility and individual criminal responsibility – will be addressed from two concerns: first, the random application of the responsibilities and possible consequences thereof; and second, the fact that state responsibility and individual criminal responsibility are not as equal as generally portrayed.

4 Randomness in responsibilities and risk of dilution

The lack of international judicial bodies competent to decide on both state and individual responsibility leaves one studying the practice of states and international organisations (foremost the UN Security Council) concerning the election between the responsibilities when it comes to wrongdoings that fall within the ambit of both state responsibility and individual criminal responsibility.[43] Although, technically, the decisions of the Security Council do not amount to determinations of wrongfulness, and hence should be viewed as political decisions (with the exception of aggression) they do possess some legal weight.[44]

An examination of the UN Security Council practice discloses that both state responsibility and international criminal law have been resorted to regarding serious violations of international law. For example, when Iraq invaded Kuwait in August 1990, the Security Council held the Iraqi state responsible for aggression: 'Iraq is liable, under international law, for any

---

42 Thomas Franck, 'Individual Criminal Liability and Collective Civil Responsibility: Do They Reinforce or Contradict One Another?', 6 *Washington University Global Studies Law Review* (2007) 567–73.

43 The possibility to choose between two different legal remedies concerns a number of breaches of international law relating to gross violations upon the human dignity and life. These acts include according to André Nollkaemper: planning, preparing, or ordering wars of aggression, genocide, crimes against humanity, killings of protected persons in armed conflicts, terrorism, and torture. On the concurrence of the two responsibilities, see André Nollkaemper, 'Concurrence between Individual Responsibility and State Responsibility in International Law', 52 *International & Comparative Law Quarterly* (2003) 615–40, esp. at 618–19.

44 See, Vera Gowlland-Debbas, 'Security Council Enforcement Actions and Issues of State Responsibility', 43 *International & Comparative Law Quarterly* (1994) 55–98, at 61. According to Gowlland-Debbas, when 'there is a finding of a breach of an international obligation [by the Security Council], and one of a fundamental nature; there is a process of attribution; despite the evident political origin of this qualification, this finding forms the basis for the application of legal sanctions.' *Ibid.*, at 63. The rarity of judicial interpretations of responsibility further increases the relevance of Security Council acts. Additional importance to Security Council acts is brought about by the fact that states can collectively take legal countermeasures only through the UN system. The Security Council acts do also have a legal connection to international crimes by virtue of Article 39 in the UN Charter since they frequently are considered to be threats to international peace and security. The Rome Statute also recognises Security Council referrals and deferrals in the exercise of Chapter VII powers (Articles 13 and 16 in the Rome Statute).

direct loss, damage, including environmental damage or the depletion of natural resources, or injury to foreign Governments, nationals and corporations, as a result of Iraq's unlawful invasion and occupation of Kuwait.'[45] Shortly after dealing with the Iraqi aggression, the Security Council was faced with atrocities committed in the Balkans. Instead of focusing on state responsibility in this situation, individual perpetrators were now placed at the centre of the international community's approach to international crimes, most notably genocide, by the creation of the ICTY. The Security Council's reaction to the next genocide in the 1990s, the killing of approximately 800,000 mainly Tutsis by the Hutu community in 1994 to 1995 mirrored its approach to the Balkans. Thus, a second *ad hoc* international criminal tribunal, the ICTR, was created in Arusha, Tanzania, to deal with the individual criminal responsibility of perpetrators of the Rwandan genocide.

A more recent case illustrating the use of different responsibility regimes concerns the genocide in Darfur and the UN Darfur Commission, which was established in 2004 by the Security Council.[46] The Darfur Commission recommended resorting to both responsibility regimes: individual criminal responsibility for crimes committed by individuals, and state responsibility for direct and indirect responsibility of the Sudanese government.[47] According to the Darfur Commission:

> The importance of determining individual criminal responsibility for international crimes whether committed under the authority of the State or outside such authority stands in addition to State responsibility and is a critical aspect of the enforceability of rights and of protection against their violation.[48]

The Security Council, which was to consider and possibly implement the recommendations of the Darfur Commission, chose to enforce individual criminal responsibility through its referral of the situation in Darfur to the ICC despite the fact that Sudan is not a party to the Rome Statute.[49] Interestingly, the Prosecutor of the ICC noted the collective character of the crimes committed in Sudan by stating that '[t]he information gathered points to an ongoing pattern of crimes committed with the mobilisation of the whole state apparatus'.[50] In spite of this, the Security Council has not made reality of the aspect of state responsibility called for

---

45 SC Res. 687, 8 April 1991.
46 The International Commission of Inquiry on Darfur to the United Nations Secretary-General was established by SC Res. 1564, 18 September 2004.
47 Report of the International Commission of Inquiry on Darfur to the United Nations Secretary-General, 25 January 2005, at para. 593.
48 *Ibid.*, at para. 407.
49 SC Res. 1593, 31 March 2005.
50 Seventh Report of the Prosecutor of the ICC to the UN Security Council Pursuant to UNSC Res. 1593 (2005), 5 June 2008, at para. 98.

by the Darfur Commission, and commentators have deemed it unlikely that it will do so.[51]

The scarce practice of the Security Council with respect to wrongdoings for which two different responsibility regimes are available, shows that decisions are made on a case-by-case basis.[52] Instead of having consistent practice with regard to when to apply state responsibility and when to make use of individual criminal responsibility, the selection is guided by political considerations. This is naturally a consequence to the fact that the Security Council is a political organ which lacks judicial competence.[53] David Kennedy's statement that people have different ideas about how to attribute responsibility is true also in its international context:

> To unscramble the tangle of mixed administrative responsibility ... is a cultural and political project of interpretation, which will often turn on and be debated in legal language. Sometimes it will make sense – to us, to someone else – to focus responsibility on this or that person, agency, ally. Sometimes it will be more sensible to spread it around. And there is no one person responsible for deciding which is the best way to go. People will have different ideas about that and will push and pull the retrospective analysis in various directions.[54]

As a consequence, sometimes the individual perpetrators are in focus, other times the collective – the state. It seems awkward to be able to pick and choose between individual and collective understandings of responsibility, yet, uncertainty reigns. Who is ultimately to be punished: the collective or the individual?[55] Collective responsibility, that is state responsibility, will always be subjected to charges of over-inclusiveness, and similarly the under-

---

51 Christian Tomuschat, 'Darfur-Compensation for the Victims', 3 *Journal of International Criminal Justice* (2005) 579–89, at 588.
52 A certain settlement seems to exist on the choice between responsibility of international organisations and state responsibility. See, for example, Ralph Wilde, 'Enhancing Accountability at the International Level: The Tension between International Organization and Member State Responsibility and the Underlying Issues at Stake', 12 *ILSA Journal of International & Comparative Law* (2006) 395–415, at 401. Dual attribution of responsibility is acknowledge in principle in the Draft Articles on the Responsibility of International Organizations, which states in the Commentary: 'Although it may not frequently occur in practice, dual or even multiple attribution of conduct cannot be excluded.' *Supra* note 5, 56, para. 4.
53 It must be stressed here that judicial bodies are not free from non-legal considerations either. The indeterminacy of rules has been highlighted by critical legal scholars such as Martti Koskenniemi. See, for example, *From Apology to Utopia: The Structure of International Legal Argument* (Cambridge University Press, 2005), esp. at 590–6.
54 David Kennedy, *Of War and Law* (Princeton University Press, 2006), at 153–4.
55 Many authors dwell on this question. See, for example, Simpson, *Law, War & Crime*, *supra* note 41. George P. Fletcher calls this the 'classic dispute about the units of agency' which he describes in terms of 'do only individuals act or is it possible to take group action seriously as a basis for attributing collective guilt?' George P. Fletcher, *Romantics at War: Glory and Guilt in the Age of Terrorism* (Princeton University Press, 2002), at ix.

inclusive nature of individual responsibility for crimes that involve groups and collectives remains self-evident. It seems that responsibility remains trapped between collective and individuals notions of responsibility, both having its proponents in the international community, both having different visions in terms of the structure of international law and where it should be headed. State responsibility still represents the paradigm for a horizontal system with equal sovereign states, whereas individual criminal responsibility stands for an 'emerging cosmopolitic global order'.[56] As phrased by Gerry Simpson: 'punishing individuals through criminal sanction is important because it promises the renewal, perhaps completion, of international law.'[57]

The randomness by which the applicable responsibility is determined can, however, not only lead to uncertainty in which responsibility regime is resorted to; it can also be detrimental to the whole project of assigning responsibility. Ultimately it may lead to dilution of responsibility altogether. As the law stands today, there can never be certainty about which legal avenue that will be used – if any. Foreseeability suffers and disagreement about the appropriate unit to be punished or mechanisms to be used opens the door for politicisation, and ultimately for impunity. As it may be argued that predictability is an important part of rule of law, the fact that uncertainty prevails can actually in the long run undermine international rule of law.

The way in which the international community failed to address the systemic torture policy of the US, and in the particular case of Abu Ghraib, may serve as an example of dilution.[58] A systemic policy of torture would definitely fall under the scope of the crimes of the Rome Statute,[59] as well as both ordinary and aggravated state responsibility as codified into the ILC Articles on State responsibility.[60] Yet, the limits of both international criminal law and state responsibility are quickly revealed. No ICC investigation was launched; no unison acts by the international community against the US beyond mere rhetoric despite the violation of fundamental interests of the

---

56   Frédéric Mégret, 'Epilogue to An Endless Debate: The International Criminal Court's Third Party Jurisdiction and the looming Revolution of International Law', 12 *European Journal of International Law* (2001) 247–68, at 264.
57   Simpson, *Law, War & Crime, supra* note 41, at 55.
58   Although the US conducted an investigation into the Abu Ghraib abuses and eventually convicted 11 soldiers for the wrongdoings, no charges were brought against high-rank soldiers or the political leadership that approved of the torture policy. The existence of a policy of torture can hardly be denied, as it is established that torture was authorised by the US Government. The Abu Ghraib case could thus be seen as part of a systemic policy rather than an isolated incident of abuse. In any case, the US cannot be said to have investigated nor punished those responsible for the torture policy.
59   Torture is recognised as both potentially a war crime and crimes against humanity thus giving the ICC jurisdiction over the crime. See Articles 7(1)(f) and 8(2)(a)(ii) of the Rome Statute.
60   Some general legal wrongs, such as torture, fall 'in circumstances of extreme or systematic application' under the regime for serious breaches of peremptory norms of international law. See James Crawford, 'Third Report on State Responsibility: Addendum', UN Doc. A/CN.4/507/Add.4, 4 August 2000, at para. 407 and fn. 801.

international community. This hardly comes as a surprise; international practice reveals that in most cases of violations concerning collective obligations 'no reaction at all has been taken, apart from verbal condemnations.'[61] The tool-box hence failed to deliver its promise; many options of responsibility do not necessarily or automatically entail an increased likelihood of responsibility materialising.

The lack of rules and agreement regarding the choice between state responsibility and individual criminal responsibility not only involve a risk of dilution but has allowed tension to develop between the regimes. Instead of complementing each other, the two responsibilities are increasingly understood to stand against each other. The tool-box view has thus not managed to deter ideas of precedence, according to which one mechanism is more appropriate than the other.

5 Factual inequality of responsibility regimes

The tool-box view is built on the assumption that all responsibility regimes are equal yet different 'tools' on how to address violations of international law – there are no preferences or orders among the regimes. International practice and international legal opinion, however, proves the tool-box view wrong or at least problematic. First, there are international legal scholars and even international legal institutions that hold international criminal law to be superior to the law of state responsibility, and second, a factual preference for the former can be discerned.

The position adopted by the ICJ on the duality of responsibility regimes in the *Bosnian Genocide* case lacks unanimous support in international legal circles. Dissenting voices have argued that international criminal law is superior to state responsibility regarding wrongdoings that fall under both regimes. It has even been claimed that state responsibility is inappropriate altogether for certain wrongdoings. The prime example for the proponents of exclusive individual criminal responsibility is Judges Shi and Vereschetin of the ICJ who found in their joint declaration in the *Bosnian Genocide* case:

> The determination of the international community to bring *individual perpetrators* of genocidal acts to justice, irrespective of their ethnicity or the position they occupy, points to the most appropriate course of action … Therefore in our view, it might be argued that this Court is perhaps not the proper venue for the adjudication of the complaints which the applicant has raised.[62]

---

61 *Ibid.*, at para. 396.
62 *Application of the Convention on the Prevention and Punishment of the Crime of Genocide (Bosnia and Herzegovina v. Yugoslavia) (Preliminary Objections)*, ICJ Reports (1996) 595, Joint Declaration of Judges Shi and Vereschetin, at 632 (emphasis in original).

Indeed, the two judges of the ICJ expressed an overall sentiment among the international public as well as some contemporary international scholars that international justice is best being served through individual criminal responsibility. For example, when Radovan Karadzic, the former leader of Bosnian Serb troops, was caught in July 2008, 13 years after the Srebrenica genocide, largely nobody protested to the arrest except for some relic Serbian nationalist voices. The President of the European Commission called the arrest 'a very positive development that will contribute to bringing justice and lasting reconciliation in the Western Balkans'.[63] The Head Prosecutor of ICTY, Serge Brammertz, noted: 'it is also an important day for international justice because it clearly demonstrates that nobody is beyond the reach of law.'[64] No similar praise was presented when Bosnia-Herzegovina already in 1993 resorted to traditional state responsibility by bringing genocide charges before the ICJ. Yet, in international law this is precisely where inter-state disputes are supposed to be brought. Instead inter-state litigation and placing the blame on the collective is seen as prolonging hatred and a hindrance to reconciliation.

Interestingly, this appears also to be the view of the ICTY, which has pungently stated that unless,

> responsibility for these appalling crimes perpetrated in the Former Yugoslavia is not attributed to individuals, then whole ethnic and religious groups will be held accountable for these crimes and branded as criminal. In other words, 'collective responsibility' – a primitive and archaic concept – will gain the upper hand ...[65]

Such statements clearly go against the position taken by the ICJ regarding the equality of state responsibility and individual criminal responsibility.

The existence of a preference for individual criminal responsibility over state responsibility is recognised also by international legal experts on responsibility issues. According to André Nollkaemper a majority of states do not perceive state responsibility as the proper mechanism or vehicle to address international crimes.[66] The role of state responsibility has been described as ancillary since targeting the state seems to miss the point. James Crawford explained in his capacity as ILC Special Rapporteur on state responsibility that international practice in the 1990s demonstrated 'the

---

63 'Karadzic arrest: Reaction in quotes', BBC News, 22 July 2008, <news.bbc.co.uk/2/hi/asia-pacific/7518607.stm>.
64 *Ibid.*
65 First Annual Report of the ICTY, UN Doc. A/49/342-S/1994/1007, 29 August 1994, at para. 16.
66 André Nollkaemper, Lecture delivered at the 22nd Helsinki Summer Seminar on International Law: Linking State Responsibility and International Criminal Law, University of Helsinki, Finland, 17–28 August 2009.

limited results that can flow from the sanctioning of whole populations, and the dilemma of appearing to punish many in order to sanction a few controlling figures.'[67] Instead, states might opt for political responses through the UN, or from the legal avenues rather focus on international criminal law. Most scholars have indeed acknowledged the 'current fashionable focus'[68] on individual criminal responsibility. Mark Drumbl goes, however, even further when he explicates that criminal trials are put on a pedestal. According to him, individual criminal responsibility has become the '"first-best" practice' of justice and consequently this form of responsibility dominates globally when it comes to dealing with atrocities and massive human rights violations.[69]

The tendency to favour the principle of individual criminal responsibility of international criminal law in cases of serious violations of international law is visible also in the amount of human and financial resources invested in international criminal justice. During its first six years, the ICC employed nearly 600 persons and spent half a billion euros but conducted only one trial.[70] The same criticism has been raised against the *ad hoc* tribunals. The ICTY with a staff of 1,200 persons used over 100 million euros per year, and each conviction in the Rwanda Tribunal have cost approximately 30 million US dollars.[71] The rapid rise of international criminal law has also taken place within a relatively short period of time; no longer are the words of Gerhard O. W. Mueller from 1983 regarding international criminal law accurate: 'Its scope and jurisdictional claim are as broad as the universe, yet the number of scholars and practitioners is smaller than the smallest kinship group of the most remote Micronesian village.'[72]

The tension and competition between the two responsibility regimes has become noticeable also in the practice of the respective international institutions, *inter alia*, with regard to evidence in the *Bosnian Genocide* case. It has been alleged that the ICTY concealed evidence from the ICJ which would have proven direct Serbian guilt in the Bosnian genocide case with the purpose of keeping Serbia from being convicted before the World Court. Notwithstanding ICTY's firm denials of concealing evidence from the ICJ,

---

67   Crawford, 'Third Report', *supra* note 60, at para. 372.
68   André Nollkaemper and Harmen van der Wilt, 'Preface', in Nollkaemper and Wilt, *System Criminality, supra* note 1, vii–viii at vii.
69   Mark Drumbl, 'Collective Responsibility and Postconflict Justice', in Tracy Isaacs and Richard Vernon (eds), *Accountability for Collective Wrongdoing* (Cambridge University Press, 2011) 23–60, at 23.
70   Guénaël Mettraux, 'The Cost of Justice: Is the ICC Living Beyond Its Means?', International Criminal Law Bureau, 6 August 2009, <www.internationallawbureau.com/blog/?p=503>.
71   Mark Drumbl, 'International Criminal Law: Taking Stock of A Busy Decade', 10 *Melbourne Journal of International Law* (2009) 38–45, at 43.
72   Gerhard O. W. Mueller, 'International Criminal Law: *Civitas Maxima* – An Overview', 15 *Case Western Reserve Journal of International Law* (1983) 1–7, at 6.

the former Spokesperson Florence Hartmann of ICTY claim that the sole purpose of concealing parts of the Supreme Defence Council minute was to shield Serbia from the negative effect it would have on the proceedings before the ICJ. According to Hartmann the ICTY took into consideration 'that a genocide conviction would have had enormous political and economical [sic] consequences for Serbia.'[73] Arguably the politics of justice pursued by international institutions prioritised findings on individual criminal responsibility rather than determinations on collective responsibility. The World Court's reluctance to demand the notorious Supreme Defence Council document further supports such a conclusion.

6   Concluding remarks

This essay sought to raise the issue and to demonstrate that the ILC lawmaking in the field of international responsibility has generated problems. While the noticeable role of the ILC in codifying and developing different regimes of responsibility cannot be disregarded, the Commission's fragmented approach to responsibility deserves criticism. The relationship between state responsibility and individual criminal responsibility is left unregulated and unexplored, except for saving clauses laying down the independence of both regimes *vis-à-vis* each other.

International legal scholarship and practice has generally tended to hold the duality and even multiplicity of responsibility regimes as beneficial for the international legal order. According to the 'complementarity or toolbox view' a variety of legal avenues generates increased responsibility and justice. The purpose of this essay has nevertheless been to question the toolbox view; it has been argued here that duality or multiplicity of responsibility regimes can instead lead to lessened responsibility. The lack of rules regulating the relationship between the different responsibility regimes allows for political choice to enter the picture. Thus, predictability of which responsibility regime will be resorted to suffers, and there are no guarantees that any responsibility will be allocated at all. The perpetual play between collective and individual forms of responsibility may in fact result in dilution of responsibility. The tool-box view is further (at least implicitly) built on the assumption that the various responsibility regimes can and are equally resorted to. However, the proponents of complementarity seem to overlook the fact that individual criminal responsibility has if not completely set aside state responsibility with respect to heinous crimes, at least diverted attention and resources from the latter. Arguably, the two responsibility regimes coexist but to an increasing degree one can detect tension between these two forms of responsibility.

---

73   Florence Hartmann, 'Vital Genocide Documents Concealed', Bosnian Institute, <www.bosnia.org.uk/news/news_body.cfm?newsid=2341>.

A particular criticism of the manner in which the ILC dealt with different forms of responsibility thus concerns the normative vacuum it left state responsibility and individual criminal responsibility in. The aim here is not, however, to abandon responsibility as a social process and urge for strict rules on when to apply what regime. Rules are, after all, imperfect and cannot solve all situations that surface. One cannot but agree with Jan Klabbers who has stated that 'rules rarely, if ever, conclusively settle the debate'.[74] The creation of rules nevertheless requires discussion and debate as a starting-point; to date a comprehensive discussion on the forms, fundaments and functions of responsibilities has been lacking. In order to further develop international responsibility one needs to explore how to deal with current problems and how one wishes to move forward. After all, the law made by the ILC was neither meant to be static nor a straitjacket.

---

74 Jan Klabbers, 'The Meaning of Rules', 20 *International Relations* (2006) 295–301, at 300.

11 Law-making and international environmental law

The legal character of decisions of conferences of the parties

Malgosia Fitzmaurice

Introduction

The quick and seemingly unstoppable development of international environmental law has raised many questions relating to international law-making and legitimacy within the sphere of States' governance and their autonomy. One aspect of the development of international environmental law is of particular importance in this respect, namely certain institutional arrangements under Multilateral Environmental Agreements (MEAs), such as compliance procedures, and generally the powers of Conferences of the Parties (COPs)/Meetings of the Parties (MOPs) *vis-à-vis* the States parties to MEAs.[1] Wide functions of COPs raise several interesting legal problems relating to the extent of obligations of parties to MEAs and their consent to be bound by treaty provisions. Some authors consider these bodies to be of an autonomous character, which means that they have their own law-making powers and compliance mechanisms.[2]

This chapter will be devoted to functions of COPs, their legal character and the problems which may arise from the exercise of these functions.

1 Conferences of the parties: The general framework

There are over 500 international environmental agreements (bilateral and multilateral).[3] These agreements cover all areas of environmental protection: atmosphere (the protection of the ozone layer and climate change),

---

1 Duncan French and Malgosia Fitzmaurice, 'COP, Autonomy Soft Law and Ambiguity', background paper presented at a workshop held at Queen Mary, University of London, in March 2011 (manuscript of file with the author). Throughout the text the term COP will be used. It will cover both COPs and MOPs.
2 Robin Churchill and Geir Ulfstein, 'Autonomous Institutional Arrangements in Multilateral Environmental Agreements', 94 *American Journal of International Law* (2000) 623–59.
3 'Multilateral Environmental Agreements: Summary', Background paper presented by the Secretariat, UN Doc. UNEP/IGM/1/INF/1, 30 March 2001.

biodiversity, land, chemicals and hazardous substances, oceans and international watercourses. Many contemporary MEAs have established COPs, which, as plenary and supreme organs of the MEAs, have very varied and extensive functions. For example, the Convention on Biological Diversity defines the functions of its COP in the following manner:[4]

> The Conference of the Parties shall keep under review the implementation of this Convention, and, for this purpose, shall:
> (a) Establish the form and the intervals for transmitting the information to be submitted in accordance with Article 26 and consider such information as well as reports submitted by any subsidiary body;
> (b) Review scientific, technical and technological advice on biological diversity provided in accordance with Article 25;
> (c) Consider and adopt, as required, protocols in accordance with Article 28;
> (d) Consider and adopt, as required, in accordance with Articles 29 and 30, amendments to this Convention and its annexes;
> (e) Consider amendments to any protocol, as well as to any annexes thereto, and, if so decided, recommend their adoption to the parties to the protocol concerned;
> (f) Consider and adopt, as required, in accordance with Article 30, additional annexes to this Convention;
> (g) Establish such subsidiary bodies, particularly to provide scientific and technical advice, as are deemed necessary for the implementation of this Convention;
> (h) Contact, through the Secretariat, the executive bodies of conventions dealing with matters covered by this Convention with a view to establishing appropriate forms of cooperation with them; and
> (i) Consider and undertake any additional action that may be required for the achievement of the purposes of this Convention in the light of experience gained in its operation.[5]

The phenomenon of the COP is comparatively recent. They started to be established after the 1972 Stockholm Conference on Human Environment, a development that reflected the dissatisfaction with international

---

[4] Convention on Biological Diversity, 5 June 1992, in force 29 December 1993, 1760 UNTS 79, Article 23(4).

[5] Cf. United Nations Framework Convention on Climate Change (UNFCCC), 9 May 1992, in force 21 March 1994, 1771 UNTS 107, Article 7(2): 'The Conference of the Parties, as the supreme body of the Convention, shall keep under regular review the implementation of the Convention and any related legal instrument that the Conference of the Parties may adopt, and shall make, within its mandate, the decisions necessary to promote the effective implementation of the Convention'.

organisations and their very bureaucratic ways of operating.[6] The development of COPs was an alternative model.[7]

Historically, the prototype of what we now understand as COPs was established (with very limited powers) by the 1971 Ramsar Convention on Wetlands of International Importance.[8] According to the original Article 6 of the Convention, the Contracting Parties would, 'as the necessity arises, convene Conferences on the Conservation of Wetlands and Waterfowl' and that these Conferences should 'have an advisory character'. This Article was amended, effective 1986, to create the Conference of the Contracting Parties 'to review and promote the implementation of the Convention'; at the same time, the reference to the advisory character of the Conference was deleted.[9] The 1972 London Convention on the Prevention of Marine Pollution[10] created a body that enjoyed more powers than that of the Ramsar Convention, but it did not have any express authority to establish subsidiary bodies and it had more limited powers of supervision.[11] The term 'Conference of the Parties' was used was for the first time in the Convention on Trade in Endangered Species (CITES).[12]

Camenzuli conducted an extensive research into the powers and functions of various COPs and came to the conclusion that they vary a great deal, which enhances the flexibility of COPs. But she noted that their powers are expanding, including in law-making.[13] According to Camenzuli, in broad brush strokes a COP has the following powers: to set priorities and review the implementation of the relevant treaty based on reports submitted by governments; to consider new information from governments, NGOs and individuals; to make recommendations to the Parties on the implementation of the treaty; to make decisions necessary to promote effective implementation of the treaty; to revise the treaty if necessary; and to act as a forum for discussion on matters of importance.[14]

---

6   Churchill and Ulfstein, 'Autonomous Institutional Arrangements', *supra* note 2.
7   See the invaluable in-depth study of COPs and their history: Louise Kathleen Camenzuli, 'The Development of International Environmental Law at the Multilateral Environmental Agreements' Conference of the Parties and its Validity' (International Union for Conservation of Nature, 2007) <cmsdata.iucn.org/downloads/cel10_camenzuli.pdf>. The information in this section is based on this study.
8   Convention on Wetlands of International Importance, especially as Waterfowl Habitat, 2 February 1971, in force 21 December 1975, 996 UNTS 243.
9   Protocol to Amend the Convention on Wetlands of International Importance especially as Waterfowl Habitat (Paris Protocol), 3 December 1982, in force 1 October 1986, 22 ILM 698.
10 London Convention on the Prevention of Marine Pollution by Dumping of Wastes and Other Matter, 29 December 1972, in force 30 August 1975, 1046 UNTS 120 and the 1996 Protocol, 11 July 1996, in force 24 March 2006, 36 ILM 1.
11 Camenzuli, 'The Development of International Environmental Law', *supra* note 7, at 5.
12 Convention on International Trade in Endangered Species of Wild Fauna and Flora (CITES), 3 March 1973, in force 1 July 1975, 993 UNTS 243, Article XI.
13 Camenzuli, 'The Development of International Environmental Law', *supra* note 7, at 5–6
14 *Ibid.*, at 7.

As a rule, the powers of a COP are clearly set out in a treaty. However, some treaties would appear to grant rather unlimited powers to their respective COPs. For example, the London Convention provides that the COP is 'to consider any additional action that may be required'.[15] Similarly, the 1989 Convention on Long-range Transboundary Air Pollution provides that the COP can '[f]ulfil such other functions as may be appropriate under the provisions of the ... Convention'.[16] Finally the example of the United Nations Framework Convention on Climate Change may be given, which states that the COP is to '[e]xercise such other functions are required for the achievement of the objective of the Convention'.[17]

COPs fulfil functions relating to internal and external matters of the functioning of MEAs.[18] Camenzuli distinguishes the following areas in which, according to her, they play a role in the development of the international environmental law: (a) the power to decide on amendments to MEAs and the adoption of new protocols; (b) the decision-making and resolution powers; (c) supervisory powers; (d) interpretation; and (e) powers in respect of the creating of compliance mechanisms.[19] In the view of the present author, the treaty-amendment powers, certain decision-making processes and the interpretative functions of COPs are the examples of their lawmaking or perhaps quasi-law-making powers. The author of this chapter is of the view that, in general, the law-making powers of a COP are embodied in creating law for the parties to the treaty in absolute terms, without the possibility of opting-out from the decision. There are very few examples of such direct law-making powers.

2 Law-making by conferences of the parties

2.1 Amendments to multilateral environmental agreements

It may be said that MEAs constitute primary legislation and decisions of its COPs are secondary.

In general international law, the amendment of a treaty is a fairly classical procedure, requiring the consent of the parties. Only certain procedural aspects of MEAs are different: older treaties require adopting amendments by two-thirds majority,[20] while the most recent treaties have an amendment procedure based on consensus of the parties and, failing that, on two-thirds

---

15 London Convention, *supra* note 10, Article XIV(4)(f).
16 Convention on Long-range Transboundary Air Pollution, 13 November 1979, in force 16 March 1983, 1302 UNTS 217, Article 10(2)(c).
17 UNFCCC, *supra* note 5, Article 7(2)(m).
18 Camenzuli, 'The Development of International Environmental Law', *supra* note 7, at 7.
19 *Ibid.,* at 8.
20 London Convention, *supra* note 10; Convention on Migratory Species, *infra* note 54; and Ramsar Convention, *supra* note 8.

majority.[21] Within the framework of all MEAs, the procedure for adopting protocols is a combination of the requirement of consensus, two-thirds majority, and three-quarters majority. Consistently with the general rules of the law of treaties, amendments enter into force when a requisite number of ratifications has been achieved, and even then only have effect with respect to the States that ratified the amendment.

An example of direct law-making by the COP is the Montreal Protocol.[22] The Vienna Convention for the Protection of the Ozone Layer, to which the Montreal Protocol is attached, contains the classical provisions on the amendment of the Convention and its protocols. Amendments enter in force after a minimum number of ratifications and must be ratified by a party to enter into force with respect to that party.[23] However, 'adjustments' to the Montreal Protocol, which, for example, regulate the periods of phasing out of certain substances, can be adopted by majority, failing consensus.[24] Thus far no decision has been adopted on the basis of majority.[25] However, such a majority decision would be an example of a direct law-making, as it would be binding on all parties, including the minority.[26]

Mention also must be made of a procedure of amending annexes or appendices in certain MEAs, such as the International Convention for the Prevention of Pollution from Ships (MARPOL), which consists of an umbrella treaty and six annexes.[27] Amendments to the annexes are subject to the so-called 'tacit acceptance' procedure or opting-out. This procedure is based on a mechanism whereby a State is bound by a decision of an organ

---

21 Such a procedure can be found under the Montreal Protocol, *infra* note 22; the Biodiversity Convention, *supra* note 4; and United Nations Convention to Combat Desertification in Those Countries Experiencing Drought and/or Desertification, in particular in Africa, 17 June 1994, in force 26 December 1996, 1954 UNTS 3.

22 Montreal Protocol on Substances that Deplete the Ozone Layer, 16 September 1987, in force 1 January 1989, 1522 UNTS 3.

23 Vienna Convention on the Protection of Ozone Layer, 22 March 1985, in force 22 September 1988, 1513 UNTS 323, Article 9(5).

24 *Ibid.*, Article 2(9)(c): 'In taking such decisions, the Parties shall make every effort to reach agreement by consensus. If all efforts at consensus have been exhausted, and no agreement reached, such decisions shall, as a last resort, be adopted by a two-thirds majority vote of the Parties present and voting representing a majority of the Parties operating under Paragraph 1 of Article 5 [i.e. certain developing countries] present and voting and a majority of the Parties not so operating present and voting.'

25 Geir Ulfstein, 'Treaty Bodies and Regimes', in Duncan Hollis (ed.), *The Oxford Guide to Treaties* (Oxford University Press, 2012) 428–47, at 439.

26 Montreal Protocol, *supra* note 22, Article 2(9)(d): 'The decisions, which shall be binding on all Parties, shall forthwith be communicated to the Parties by the Depositary. Unless otherwise provided in the decisions, they shall enter into force on the expiry of six months from the date of the circulation of the communication by the Depositary'.

27 International Convention on the Protection from Pollution from Ships (MARPOL), 2 November 1973, in force 2 October 1983, 1340 UNTS 184; Protocol relating to the International Convention for the Prevention of Pollution from Ships, 17 February 1978, in force 2 October 1983, 1340 UNTS 61.

of the treaty unless it opts out within a prescribed period of time.[28] The opting-out procedure is traditionally evaluated in the doctrine of international law as characterised by a more pronounced role of the international organisation than the classical opting-in mechanism. Nevertheless, this procedure gives the opportunity to States to withdraw from the decision – thus it is not absolutely binding[29] and therefore cannot be classified as an example of direct law-making.

2.2 Decisions by COPs

Law-making by COPs through their decision-making processes has been the subject of many theories. According to one view, COPs can be seen as freestanding entities or structures, which are independent from the parties and have, at least to a certain extent, an autonomous character – they have their own law-making or rule-making power to formulate or operate mechanisms within the treaty regime, which may have binding effects on parties.[30] Churchill and Ulfstein call such institutions 'autonomous institutional arrangements' (AIAs).[31] On the other hand, some of the organs of MEAs, in particular COPs, can be seen as no more than a form of diplomatic conference, providing a continuous, or at least regular, context within which decisions can be more readily made than through the convening of *ad hoc* diplomatic conferences.

In fact, it is submitted that COPs may take on the character of either, depending on both the substantive nature of what they are discussing, and whether or not the decisions on a particular issue discussed will require subsequent validation to become binding on the parties. Their institutional character became more permanent when – as is the case now with several AIAs – they began to introduce new ways of amending the scope of treaty obligations, usually in relation to technical or administrative matters, in such a way as to have direct binding effect for the parties, including those who had not expressed their consent to the proposed amendment (at least in the traditional sense) and without resorting to a formal amendment of the treaty according to classical procedure as outlined above.[32]

The law-making activity of COPs leading to modifications of States' obligations may be found in so-called 'enabling clauses', which charge COPs with the elaboration of rules is some particular area without expressly providing

---

28 MARPOL Convention, *supra* note 27, Article 16(2)(g).
29 Malgosia Fitzmaurice, 'Expression of Consent to be Bound by a Treaty as Developed in Certain Environmental Agreements', in Jan Klabbers and René Lefebre (eds), *Essays on the Law of Treaties: Collection of Essays in Honour of Bert Vierdag* (Kluwer, 1998) 59–80, at 66.
30 Churchill and Ulfstein, 'Autonomous Institutional Arrangements', *supra* note 2, at 1.
31 *Ibid*.
32 Gerhard Loibl, 'Conference of the Parties and Modification of Treaty Obligations', in Mathew Craven, Malgosia Fitzmaurice and Maria Vogiatzi (eds), *Interrogating the Treaty: Essays in Contemporary Law of Treaties* (Nijmegen, 2006) 103–19, at 105.

for the actual amendment of the treaty. One example of the use of enabling clauses has been the establishment of non-compliance procedures. For example, the non-compliance procedure under the Montreal Protocol was created by virtue of Article 8, which states the following:

> The Parties, at its first meeting, shall consider and approve procedures and international mechanisms for determining non-compliance with provisions of this Protocol and for the treatment of Parties found in non-compliance.

Another example of such a clause can be found in Article 7(4) of the Cartagena Protocol[33] which states that the COP may adopt a decision identifying living modified organism (LMOs) to which the advance informed agreement procedure will not apply – as not being likely to have an adverse effect on the conservation and sustainable use of biodiversity – taking into account risks to human health. Similarly, Article 18(2)(a) provides that the COP shall take a decision within two years after the entry of the Cartagena Protocol on the detailed requirements for labelling of LMOs that are intended for direct use as food or food for processing.[34]

The most extensive use of enabling clauses was made in the Kyoto Protocol,[35] to the structure of which they are central. A series of highly controversial elements of the climate change regime were left to be decided at the COP. The most striking of the enabling clauses are Articles 6, 12 and 17, which authorise the COP to elaborate guidelines for, and set up the machinery to regulate, the so-called 'flexible mechanisms'. The provisions of Article 17, which charge the COP with the task of defining 'the relevant principles, modalities, rules and guidelines, in particular verification, reporting and accountability for emissions trading', are among the most fundamental of the whole Protocol. Due to the above, the Kyoto Protocol may be seen as a special case in relation to both the legal character of decisions taken under its enabling clauses, and the legal character of decisions of its non-compliance procedure.

These new 'new' functions of COPs gave rise to concerns about their legitimacy. Camenzuli is of the view that COP decision-making on the basis of majority is 'inconsistent with the traditional consent based structure of treaty law and, consequently, threatens its legitimacy and validity'.[36] Therefore she postulates that in order to avoid the risk of alienating powerful minorities, the law-making powers of a COP 'must be exercised

---

33 Cartagena Protocol on Biosafety to the Convention on Biological Diversity, 29 January 2000, in force 11 September 2003, 2226 UNTS 208.
34 Loibl, 'Conference of the Parties', *supra* note 32.
35 Kyoto Protocol to the United Nations Framework Convention on Climate Change, 11 December 1997, in force 16 February 2005, 2303 UNTS 148.
36 Camenzuli, 'The Development of International Environmental Law', *supra* note 7, at 26.

with caution'.[37] It may be noted, however, that the only example of such powers is the Montreal Protocol, under which terms a majority decision binds the minority in case of 'adjustments' where consensus by the Parties was not reached.[38] However, this rule was never implemented.

3 'Quasi legal' activities

3.1 Compliance procedures

Compliance procedures concern the measures that may be directed at the parties to MEAs in the case of non-compliance with the treaty provisions or the decisions of the COP. Compliance procedures are named 'quasi-legal' as they – with the possible exception of the compliance mechanism under the Kyoto Protocol – do not result in 'absolutely' binding decisions from which States cannot escape. However, through compliance procedures COPs exercise powers that shape the obligations of States parties to MEAs. The question that may be asked concerning compliance procedures in relation to law-making is whether they 'make' law for the parties to the MEAs.

Since the establishment of a Non-Compliance Committee under the Montreal Protocol in 1992, it has been a common practice of States parties to MEAs to create treaty bodies, called 'Compliance' or 'Implementation' Committees, which have the function of determining a State party's compliance with its international obligations and reporting non-compliance to the COP.[39] According to the UNEP Guidelines on Compliance, the term 'compliance' is defined as the 'fulfillment by contracting parties of their obligations under a [MEA] and any amendments to the [MEA]'.[40]

---

37   *Ibid.* at 26. See also Annecoos Wiersema, 'The New International Law-Makers? Conferences of the Parties to Multilateral Environmental Agreements', 1 *Michigan Journal of International Law* (2009) 231–87.
38   Camenzuli, 'The Development of International Environmental Law', *supra* note 7, at 26.
39   Montreal Protocol, *supra* note 22, Article 8 and Annex IV (Implementation Committee); Convention on Access to Information, Public Participation in Decision-making and Access to Justice in Environmental Matters (Aarhus Convention), 25 June 1998, in force 30 October 2001, 2161 UNTS 447, Article 15 (Compliance Committee); Decision VI/12, Conference of the Parties to the Basel Convention, 2002, UN Doc. UNEP/CWH.6/40, 6 February 2003, Annex (Committee); Kyoto Protocol, *supra* note 35, Article 18 (Compliance Committee). However, under the CITES the role of a compliance body is fulfilled by the Standing Committee. There is a vast literature on compliance regimes under MEAs, to wit: Olav Schram Stokke, Jon Hovi and Geir Ulfstein (eds), *Implementing the Climate Regime: International Compliance* (Earthscan, 2005); Jutta Brunnée, Meinhard Doelle and Lavanya Rajamani (eds), *Promoting Compliance in an Evolving Climate Regime* (Cambridge University Press, 2011); also generally see Tullio Treves, Laura Pineschi, Attila Tanzi, Cesare Pitea, Chiara Ragni and Francesca Romanin Jacur (eds), *Non-Compliance Procedures and Mechanisms and the Effectiveness of International Environmental Agreements* (T.M.C. Asser Institute, 2009).
40   Guidelines for Enhancing Compliance with Multilateral Environmental Agreements, UNEP Governing Council decision SSVII/4, 15 February 2002, in UNEP/GCSS.VII/6, 5 March 2002, Annex I, at para. 5.

It has to be stated at the outset that non-compliance mechanisms are not a part of dispute settlement procedures and that they form distinctive institutional arrangements. Their purpose is to be 'non-confrontational, non-judicial and [of] consultative nature'[41] or 'non-confrontational, transparent, cost-effective and preventive in nature, simple, flexible, non-binding and oriented in the direction of helping Parties [to implement the Convention]'.[42] As it was observed above, in most cases these mechanisms are established on the basis of 'enabling clauses' contained in MEAs. However, in certain cases there are ambiguities concerning the establishing of such systems, as the compliance system under the Kyoto Protocol illustrates. According to Article 18 of the Kyoto Protocol, a compliance mechanism was to be set up by means of an amendment to the Protocol. Due to political reasons, such an amendment was never made and the procedure was adopted on the basis of a decision of the COP. Therefore the decisions made under the procedure are, 'by definition non-binding, even though they bind, within the Kyoto system, States that want to obtain certain results'.[43]

Under all compliance procedures there are certain measures directed against a non-complying party. Most of the procedures follow more or less the same pattern but under the Kyoto Protocol regime consequences aimed at bringing a non-compliant party into compliance are more far-reaching.

Under the majority of non-compliance regimes the measures directed at assisting the party (such as financial and economic assistance) do not raise questions of law-making by the COP in relation to States parties of MEAs. However, the situation is different where the set of measures calls for

> [s]uspension, in accordance with the applicable rules of international law concerning the suspension of the operation of a treaty, of specific rights and privileges under the Protocol, whether or not subject to time limits, including those concerned with industrial rationalization, production, consumption, trade, transfer of technology, financial mechanism, and institutional arrangements.[44]

This is the example of the non-compliance procedure under the Montreal Protocol but copied in the regimes of other mechanisms (with the exception of the Kyoto Protocol). Such measures, enacted by the COP, in fact change the legal rights of a State party to MEAs from those originally contained in a treaty which the States parties had ratified into an altogether new regime,

---

41   Aarhus Convention, *supra* note 39, Article 15.
42   Basel Convention COP, Decision VI/12, *supra* note 39, at para. 2.
43   Tullio Treves, 'Introduction', in Treves *et al.*, *Non-Compliance Procedures, supra* note 39, at 4.
44   The fourth Meeting of the Parties in 1992, by Decision IV/18, finalised, in Annex V of its report, the 'Indicative list of measures that might be taken by a Meeting of the Parties in respect of non-compliance with the Protocol.'

to which parties subject to the measures are usually hostile. Measures involving the suspension of rights and privileges are especially contentious.

COP powers are even more far-reaching under the Kyoto Protocol regime, in which the Enforcement Branch may practically cut off the non-compliant party so as to prevent it from benefiting from the flexible mechanisms that are at the core of the whole system under the Kyoto Protocol. Flexibility mechanism under the Kyoto Protocol are the following: emissions trading; the clean development mechanism (CDM); and Joint Implementation (JI). JI and CDM are the two project-based mechanisms which feed the carbon market. JI enables industrialized countries to carry out joint implementation projects with other developed countries, while the CDM involves investment in sustainable development projects that reduce emissions in developing countries. The carbon market is a key tool for reducing emissions worldwide (it was worth 30 billion USD in 2006 and is still expanding).[45]

3.2 Interpretive functions

COPs can also engage in other law-making or quasi-law-making activities such as interpretation of relevant MEAs. Such interpretations provide essential guidance to the parties beyond the bare text of a treaty and thereby facilitate compliance.

As Peter Davis shows in his excellent article, there are numerous examples of such interpretive functions of COPs leading to a change in the scope of States parties' obligations.[46] For example, CITES COP has provided interpretation and detailed guidance on various issues pertaining to the primary rules of CITES.[47] The issue as to which species can be regarded as captive stock is a case in point. CITES makes special provision for specimens that are captive bred or artificially propagated. The treaty stipulates that specimens of Appendix I animals 'bred in captivity for commercial purposes' and specimens of Appendix I plants 'artificially propagated for commercial purposes' shall be treated as Appendix II specimens.[48] Appendix I species mostly may not be commercially traded. Being treated as Appendix II specimens, however, allows trade in captive bred animals or artificially propagated plants, subject to certain conditions. The 1997 Harare COP adopted a

---

45 <unfccc.int/kyoto_protocol/mechanisms/items/1673.php>.
46 Peter Davis, 'Non-Compliance: A Pivotal or Secondary Function of CoP Governance?', 15 *International Community Law Review* (2013) 77-101, at 79-82.
47 Cited *ibid.*, e.g. interpretation of 'readily recognizable parts or derivative' (Article 1(b); CITES Resolution Conf. 9.6 (Rev.)); 'specimens ... acquired before the provisions of [CITES] applied' (Article VII(2); CITES Resolution Conf. 13.6); 'personal and household effects' (Article VII(3); CITES Resolution Conf. 13.7); reservations (Article XXIII(2); CITES Resolution Conf. 4.25 (Rev CoP14)); as to the listing criteria for the inclusion of species in the Appendices (CITES Resolution Conf. 9.24 (Rev. CoP14)); and on the issue of ranching (CITES Resolution Conf. 11.16 (Rev. CoP14)).
48 CITES, *supra* note 12, Article VII(4).

resolution, which notes that an animal specimen 'bred in captivity' must be 'born or otherwise produced in a controlled environment', and the parents must have either mated in a controlled environment (if reproduction is sexual) or were in a controlled environment when offspring development commenced (in case of asexual reproduction).[49] The 2000 CITES Gigiri COP established criteria to be satisfied before plants can be considered 'artificially propagated'.[50]

Another instance of a COP authorised to provide interpretations of ambiguous wording in a primary agreement is the Executive Body of the Long Range Transboundary Air Pollution Convention. For example, the 1985 Sulphur Dioxide Protocol stipulated that parties 'shall reduce their national annual sulphur emissions or their transboundary fluxes by at least 30% as soon as possible and at the latest by 1993, using 1980 levels as the basis of calculation of reductions'.[51] Four years after the Protocol's adoption, the parties in the Executive Body reached a 'common understanding' in interpreting this obligation:

> The obligation for the Parties to reduce their national annual sulphur emissions or their transboundary fluxes by at least 30% ... at the latest by 1993 ... means that reduction to that extent should be reached in that time frame *and the levels maintained or further reduced after being reached.*[52]

The final example that Davis[53] provides is the 1979 Convention on Migratory Species (CMS Convention).[54] The question arose as to the interpretation of Article II(1)(e), which indicates that a migratory species is 'endangered' where 'it is in danger of extinction throughout all or a significant portion of its range'. The CMS COP in 1997 adopted a resolution to clarify the term 'endangered' which is to be interpreted as meaning a species 'facing a very

---

49   Resolution Conf. 10.16 (Rev.).
50   CITES Resolution Conf. 11.11 (Rev. CoP15). All these examples are from Davis, 'Non-Compliance', *supra* note 46.
51   Protocol to the 1979 Convention on Long-Range Transboundary Air Pollution on the Reduction of Sulphur Emissions or their Transboundary Fluxes by at least 30 per cent, 8 July 1985, in force 2 September 1987, 1480 UNTS 215, Article 1.
52   See Report of the 7th session of the Executive Body, doc. ECE/EB.AIR/20, para. 22 (emphasis added). Davis, 'Non-Compliance', *supra* note 46.
53   Davis, 'Non-Compliance', *supra* note 46. This approach has led to the listing of various species in Appendix I. For example, the 17th meeting of the CMS Convention's Scientific Council held in November 2011 endorsed proposals to list both the Far Eastern Curlew and the Bristle-thighed Curlew on Appendix I. Having noted such endorsements, the 10th meeting of the CMS COP held after the said Scientific Council's meeting duly approved Appendix I status for both species.
54   Convention on the Conservation of Migratory Species of Wild Animals, 26 June 1979, in force 1 November 1983, 1651 UNTS 333.

high risk of extinction in the wild' and that the Parties would be guided in this regard by findings of the IUCN Council or by an assessment by the CMS Convention's Scientific Council.[55]

There has been an extensive discussion on the powers of interpretation of international agreements by international courts and tribunals, in particular regarding human rights treaties, a comprehensive analysis of which exceeds the scope of this Chapter. Suffice it to say that there are several explanations on such an interpretation of treaty provisions: it can be regarded as 'subsequent practice', or so-called 'evolutive' or 'dynamic' interpretation, but it is often very difficult to make fast and clear division between these two methods.

Davis is of the view that COP interpretive decisions can be viewed under the Vienna Convention on the Law of Treaties (VCLT) as 'any subsequent agreement between the parties regarding the interpretation of the treaty or the application of its provisions' and as 'any subsequent practice in the application of the treaty which establishes the agreement of the parties regarding its interpretation'.[56] He states:

> An authentic interpretation by a given treaty regime's CoP should legitimately be regarded as such an agreement or evidence of such a practice particularly bearing in mind the CoP's role as the plenary and political body in which all State Parties are represented and can actively participate.[57]

On the other a view, such interpretations by COPs constitute a form of 'dynamic' or 'evolutive' interpretation, which is based on the concept of a treaty as 'a living instrument' and is meant to introduce changes in social conditions during the existence of a treaty through an interpretive process.[58] This type of interpretation, used especially by human rights courts and tribunals, is often challenged by States parties to the relevant treaty and even by some of judges sitting on such courts and tribunals. Similar activities of COP also cause controversy and States do not always support far-reaching 'interpretations' of a treaty, which result in some instances in widening of the scope of the States parties' obligations and narrowing of their rights.

---

55 Resolution 5.3, 16 April 1997.
56 Vienna Convention on the Law of Treaties, 23 May 1969, in force 27 January 1980, 1155 UNTS 331, Article 31(3)(a) and (b).
57 Davis, 'Non-Compliance', *supra* note 46, at 84.
58 On dynamic or evolutive interpretation, see Malgosia Fitzmaurice, 'Dynamic (Evolutive) Interpretation of Treaties, Part I', 21 *Hague Yearbook of International Law* (2008) 101–57, and 'Dynamic (Evolutive) Interpretation of Treaties, Part II', 22 *Hague Yearbook of International Law* (2009) 3–31.

4 Theories on the legal nature of COP decisions

The legal issue under consideration in this Chapter is the situation where COPs are charged with making decisions which purport to modify or extend the obligations of the parties, or which set up procedures or consequences regarding non-compliance, but the treaty provisions do not either set out a clear procedure for adopting such decisions and/or do not specify their legal nature (whether the parties are bound by them or not). There are several examples of such uncertain, ambiguous provisions, for example Article 18 of the Kyoto Protocol. Likewise there is uncertainty regarding the legal character of measures adopted against Russia under the Montreal Protocol non-compliance procedure). As a result, a number of theories concerning the legal nature of COP decisions have been suggested. They broadly fall in three categories:

1. Theories deriving the binding force of COP decisions from the intentions of the parties. These theories, of which there are several varieties, are in their broadest sense treaty-based;
2. Theories which, assuming that the decisions do not have formally binding legal force, nevertheless attempt to find some interminable ('soft law' or '*de facto*') status for them; and
3. Theories grounding the decisions' formally binding force on a basis outside of the law of treaties.

4.1 Theories based on the law of treaties: General issues

Treaty-based theories look at two possibilities. Firstly, emphasis has been placed on the wording of enabling clauses mandating the decisions of COPs – such as wording in the Kyoto Protocol, in particular the use of the word 'rules' in Article 17.[59] But it has been doubted whether this in itself would constitute a sufficient basis for the binding force of a decision of a COP.[60] An alternative approach looks beyond the treaty text for an expression of the parties' intention that the decision should be binding. In effect, this theory treats COP decisions, if taken by consensus, as agreements in a simplified form, which are binding on the parties.[61] In this case the wording of the decision is important. For instance Brunnée noted that many of the

---

[59] 'The Conference of the Parties shall define the relevant principles, modalities, rules and guidelines, in particular for verification, reporting and accountability for emissions trading. ...'
[60] Jutta Brunnée, 'Reweaving the Fabric of International Law? Patterns of Consent in Environmental Framework Agreements', in Rüdiger Wofrum and Völker Röben (eds), *Developments in International Law-Making* (Springer, 2005) 101–27, at 112.
[61] Churchill and Ulfstein, 'Autonomous Institutional Arrangements', *supra* note 2, at 640.

decisions use the word 'shall', normally employed for legally binding commitments.[62] An instance of this may be seen in the creation of the non-compliance procedure under the Basel Convention,[63] which was effected by a decision of the COP, made on its own motion in the absence of any enabling clause but, apparently, without subsequent objection from the parties.

In fact, the process of construing the parties' intention will always have to take into account not only all the written sources which may be said to comprise the agreement – such as the enabling clause and the actual decision of the COP – but also surrounding circumstances, including both prior and subsequent practice of the parties, in accordance with the rules of interpretation of treaties of the VCLT.

Whatever the particular factors to be taken into account in interpreting the intentions of the parties, it is submitted that, from a theoretical point of view, either of the above bases would be capable of creating binding obligations on the parties arising from COP decisions. The effectiveness of the first basis, involving a clear mandate of the COP, has to been referred to above. Regarding the second basis, though it may appear contradictory, on the face of it, an informal decision of the COP could in effect cause the modification of the provisions of the treaty in a manner not provided for in it due to the great flexibility and permissiveness of the law of treaties. Such an agreement would not, of course, actually amend the terms of the treaty, but it could provide that (i) the parties would not enforce certain of its provisions, (ii) the parties would interpret certain provisions in a particular way, or (iii) the terms of the subsequent informal agreement would take priority if in conflict with the original treaty according to Article 30 of the VCLT.

4.2 Theories based on the law of treaties: Specific issues

There are several theories which support the validity (including any legally binding consequences) of the decisions of COP based on particular provisions of the VCLT. Camenzuli is of the view[64] that the validity of COP acts and decisions is derived from Article 31 of the VCLT, in particular

---

62   Brunnée, 'Reweaving the Fabric of International Law?', *supra* note 60, at 111.
63   Basel Convention on the Control of Transboundary Movements of Hazardous Wastes and Their Disposal, 22 March 1989, in force 5 May 1992, 1673 UNTS 126; Basel Convention COP, Decision VI/12, *supra* note 39.
64   Camenzuli, 'The Development of International Environmental Law', *supra* note 7, at 18–20.

paragraphs 2 and 3.[65] She gives some examples of such decisions: the resolution concerning the meaning of the term 'pre-Convention specimen' for the purposes of CITES[66] and the indicative list of categories of incremental cost to be used by the Financial Mechanisms under the Montreal Protocol.[67] Other examples include the 1985 Resolution of the Consultative Meeting to the London Convention adopting the moratorium on the dumping of radioactive waste at sea[68] and the 1989 decision of the CITES COP on the ban of international trade in African elephant products.[69]

While these decisions are very important, States nevertheless retain their right not to accept them. Consider the following example. Dumping of high-level radioactive wastes has never been allowed under the London Convention. In 1983 a moratorium was put on the dumping of low-level radioactive wastes while studies were carried out regarding economic and social aspects of radioactive waste dumping. Following the completion of these studies, the parties agreed in 1993 to amend Annexes I and II to the London Convention to ban the dumping of all radioactive wastes.[70] This legally binding amendment entered into force on 20 February 1994.[71] Initially, Russia did not accept this amendment, but in 2005 it decided to adopt it. Thus, COP law-making powers follow classical international law based on consent of States.

Camenzuli is of the view that some of the interpretative powers of COPs amount to the exercise of the international legislation. An example would be the expansion of the definition of dumping in the London Convention

---

65   VCLT, *supra* note 56, Article 31(2)–(3):
   2. The context for the purpose of the interpretation of a treaty shall comprise, in addition to the text, including its preamble and annexes:
      (a) any agreement relating to the treaty which was made between all the parties in connection with the conclusion of the treaty;
      (b) any instrument which was made by one or more parties in connection with the conclusion of the treaty and accepted by the other parties as an instrument related to the treaty.
   3. There shall be taken into account, together with the context:
      (a) any subsequent agreement between the parties regarding the interpretation of the treaty or the application of its provisions;
      (b) any subsequent practice in the application of the treaty which establishes the agreement of the parties regarding its interpretation;
      (c) any relevant rules of international law applicable in the relations between the parties.
66   Resolution Conf. 5.11.
67   Decision II/8, Appendix I, June 1990, in UN Doc. UNEP/OzL.Pro.2/3, 29 June 1990.
68   Res. LDC.21(9), 1985.
69   Amendments to Appendices I and II of the Convention, adopted by the Conference of the Parties at its seventh meeting in Lausanne, Switzerland, from 9 to 20 October 1989. See Camenzuli, 'The Development of International Environmental Law', *supra* note 7, at 10–20.
70   Resolution LC.51(16), 12 November 1993.
71   <www.imo.org/blast/mainframe.asp?topic_id=1508#Radioactive>.

by the Consultative Meeting deciding that this term covers the disposal of wastes into or under the sea bed but not from land by tunnelling.[72] Camenzuli opines that in such cases the action of COP might better regarded as an agreement *inter partes* modifying or supplementing the MEA, constituting a form of an agreement within the treaty, in line with Articles 39 and 41(1)(b) VCLT, rather than subsequent agreement or practice of States, within the meaning of Articles 31(3)(a) and (b) VCLT.[73]

The second specific issue relating to the law of treaties is the relationship of general international law to certain measures provided for in cases of non-compliance under these procedures.[74] The 'classical' non-compliance procedure was adopted under the Montreal Protocol by the COP.[75] At the same meeting, the COP adopted so-called 'indicative list of measures' in case of non-compliance, which included the suspension of specific rights and privileges.[76]

A number of other non-compliance procedures have the same or similar provisions. For instance the procedure under the Aarhus Convention provides that one of the measures that can be adopted by the COP is to 'suspend, in accordance with the applicable rules of international law concerning the suspension of the operation of a treaty, the special rights and privileges accorded to the Party concerned under the Convention'.[77] Another example is provided by the CITES: one of the measures to achieve compliance that can be taken by the Standing Committee (this procedure does not have a special body dealing with non-compliance) is to '[r]ecommend the suspension of commercial or all trade in specimens of one or more CITES-listed species'.[78] In this procedure the express reference to 'the applicable rules of international law' is omitted.

There are, however, procedures which do not provide for the suspension, such as those under the Basel[79] and the Espoo Conventions.[80] The Kyoto

---

72   Res. LDC.41(13), 1990.
73   Camenzuli, 'The Development of International Environmental Law', *supra* note 7, at 20.
74   See generally on this subject, e.g., Martti Koskenniemi, 'Breach of Treaty or Non-Compliance? Reflections on the Enforcement of the Montreal Protocol', 3 *Yearbook of International Environmental Law* (1992) 121-161; Malgosia Fitzmaurice and Catherine Redgwell, 'Environmental Non-Compliance Procedure and International Law', 31 *Netherlands Yearbook of International Law* (2000) 35-65.
75   Decision IV/5, November 1992, in UN Doc. UNEP/Ozl.Pro4/5, 25 November 1992.
76   See *supra* note 44 and accompanying text.
77   Decision I/7, 2002, UN Doc. ECE/MP.PP/2/Add.8, 2 April 2004, as amended by Decision II/5, 2005, UN Doc. ECE/MP.PP/2005/2/Add.6, 13 June 2005.
78   CITES Resolution Conf. 14.3 (2007), Annex, para. 30.
79   Basel Convention COP, Decision VI/12, *supra* note 39.
80   Convention on Environmental Impact Assessment in a Transboundary Context, 25 February 1991, in force 10 September 1997, 1989 UNTS 309; Decision II/4, Meeting of the Parties to the Convention, February 2001, in UN Doc. ECE/MP.EIA/4, 7 August 2001, Annex IV, revised by Decision III/2, Meeting of the Parties to the Convention, June 2004, in UN Doc. ECE/MP.EIA/6, 13 September 2004, Annex II.

Protocol's non-compliance procedure does not contain a general provision on suspension of rights but it does contain provisions relating to suspension of non-complying party from participation in flexibility mechanisms.[81] Being so specific in their application, these provisions do not give rise to quite the same problems in terms of their relationship with other fields of international law, though they give rise to problems in relation to 'bindingness', legality and legitimacy of such a decision.

There are several problems with the expression 'in accordance with the applicable rules of international law concerning suspension of the operation of the treaty' used, *inter alia*, in the compliance procedures under the Montreal Protocol and the Aarhus Convention. The first problem is identifying what rules actually are being referred to. The rules of the law of treaties expressly referring to suspension are found in Article 60 of the VCLT, paragraph 2 of which provides a gradation of the available measures, depending on the position of parties in relation to the breach:

1   A specially affected party is entitled to invoke breach of a treaty as a ground for suspending the operation of a treaty in whole or to terminate it either in their relations with the defaulting States or as between all parties;
2   The other parties, with the exclusion of the defaulting States, by unanimous agreement, are entitled to suspend the treaty or to terminate it either in their relations with the defaulting States or as between all parties;
3   Any party, other than the defaulting party, may invoke the breach as grounds for the partial or total suspension of the treaty between it and the defaulting party if the breach is such as to radically change the position of every party with respect to the further performance of its obligations under the treaty.

However, Article 60 only refers to the 'material breach of a treaty'. Suspension under non-compliance procedures may concern non-material breaches, which is a different issue altogether. Mention also must be made of the procedural rules contained in Articles 65–6 regarding several safeguards, which would have to be incorporated in suspension procedure of non-compliance, if it were to follow Article 60. But the critical question is whether a basically non-confrontational non-compliance procedure would fall into the remit of the 'materiality' of the breach as required under the VCLT.

4.3 Theories based on 'soft law' or 'de facto' status

Considering in particular the Kyoto Protocol COP decisions regarding the flexible mechanisms, it has been postulated that, even if the decisions do

---

81   Decision 27/CMP.1, 2005, in UN Doc. FCCC/KP/CMP/2005/8/Add.3, 30 March 2006.

not have binding force in full sense, they nevertheless may affect the parties' rights and obligations in that failure to comply with them may have consequences. This has been described as '*de facto* law making'.[82] This notion is arguably subject to the same criticism as the term 'soft law', as it attempts to blur what should be a clear distinction between what is legally binding and what is not.

4.4 Theories assuming binding force outside the law of treaties

Finally, it has been suggested that international institutional law has been applicable to COPs, which are considered autonomous institutional arrangements or AIAs. The consequence of such an approach would be the applicability of the concept of 'implied powers' – another possible basis for regarding the decisions of COPs as legally binding.[83] There are, however, some inherent difficulties with this approach. Strictly speaking, COPs are not international organisations and therefore applying by analogy the theory of implied powers to them may be too far reaching an interpretation of the treaties which establish them.

There are views, however, which presuppose that COPs are in fact international organisations and therefore enjoy implied powers. This view is based on a presumption that there is no internationally accepted definition of what constitutes an international organisation. Consequently, the substantive, especially law-making decisions of COPs would be subject to the doctrine of *ultra vires*.[84]

4.5 Conclusions to this section

As it can be seen from the above analysis, none of these theories solves fully or satisfactorily the question of the sources of powers of COPs. In the view of the present author, any reliance on theories underlying functioning of international organisations is attractive but perhaps not quite appropriate to be applied in the context of COPs, which – despite their degree of independence – are not separate international law entities in the way international organisations are. They do not have a separate existence, which could be isolated from treaties constituting them; they are organically linked to such a treaty. Also the term *de facto* law-making does not really answer why States tend to comply with the resulting *de facto* law. The law of treaties, which is the most viable option generally speaking, does not in fact give binding force to the decisions of COPs as they are not hard law (with perhaps an exception

---

82   Brunnée, 'Reweaving the Fabric of International Law?', *supra* note 60, at 111.
83   Churchill and Ulfstein, 'Autonomous Institutional Arrangements', *supra* note 2, at 633–4.
84   Camenzuli, 'The Development of International Environmental Law', *supra* note 7, at 20 and 24.

of the Enforcement Branch decisions under the Kyoto Protocol compliance regime, but even the binding power of these decisions can be disputed).

It may be argued that the so-called enabling clauses included in MEAs can give, to certain degree, a power deriving from a treaty to make binding decisions. This explanation seems to be very far-fetched, as these clauses are in fact already very vague and it can be argued that at times fleshing them out by COP may be too extensive and may go too far.

5 Compliance with COP decisions

A different question is the legitimacy of COP law-making activities, the extensive consideration of which exceeds the framework of this Chapter and also partly belongs to the sphere of international relations. The question may be posed differently: why do States parties to MEAs comply (mostly) with decisions of COPs, which are not fully authorised by international law? There are several theories in international law and international relations, which attempt to explain why States abide by the rules of international law. In short, the main theories are as follows:

In their book *The New Sovereignty*, Chayes and Handler Chayes present a model based on a so-called managerial, process-oriented approach.[85] They are of the view that legal norms alone are not sufficient to evoke compliance, but rather must form the part of the nexus of interactions between parties and play an important role within interactions aimed at promoting compliance. The adherence to legal norms is not a result of a coercive action but is linked to the legitimacy of norms that result from a correct process. Chayes and Handler Chayes present the view that the lack of compliance is not wilful but rather a result of other factors such as the lack of relevant information or the lack of capacity. Managerial strategy is 'verbal, interactive, and consensual'. It means that this approach is non-adversarial and cooperative. Instances of apparent non-compliance should be seen as problems to be solved rather than wrongs to be punished. The normative framework is provided by a treaty and the managerial approach builds on the parties' sense of obligation 'to comply with legally binding prescriptions'.[86] Chayes and Handler Chayes express views similar to institutionalists (Keohane and Nye[87]) who base compliance on interdependence of a diversified nature between States resulting in institutional co-operation, enhancing compliance through various methods such as reporting, monitoring and verification.

---

85 Abram Chayes and Antonia Handler Chayes, *The New Sovereignty: Compliance with International Regulatory Agreements* (Harvard University Press, 1998). See also Abram Chayes, 'Compliance without Enforcement', 91 *American Society of International Law Proceedings* (1997) 53–56; Abram Chayes and Antonia Handler Chayes, 'On Compliance', 47 *International Organization* (1993) 175–205.

86 Chayes and Chayes, New Sovereignty, *supra* note 85, at 110, see also at 109.

The theory of compliance by Koh is based on close vertical interactions between various actors, both private and public, through discursive interpretations of international norms, mainly by domestic institutions, as the key policy-makers.[88]

Brunnée and Toope represent a so-called 'interactional theory', which is also based on interactions by States, which rest on 'stable patterns of expectations' and 'is first and foremost the theory of obligation'.[89] The basis of his theory is the premise is that 'power of international law rests in a felt sense of obligation, 'rooted in a specific form of legal legitimacy'.[90] These authors analyse the climate change regime from the point of view of its success. They are of the view that a long-term agreement to control climate change has the chance of success only if it is based on 'strong shared understandings, respects the requirements of legality and is embedded in vibrant practice of legality'.[91]

Transformationalists (Downs Rocke and Barstoon) are of the view that compliance appears to be high in regimes requiring slightly more from States than they are expected to do in the absence of a regime. For regimes which are based on 'in-depth cooperation', such as in cases of arms control, trade and the environmental treaties, eliciting compliance from States is highly problematic and, according to these authors, non-compliance is wilful. In instances of such cooperation, relying on enforcement is perhaps more effective as than the soft approach adopted by managerial theory.[92]

Jacobson and Brown Weiss adhere to yet a different approach. According to these authors there is a nexus of factors that influence the compliance of States, such as the character of the problem, the characteristics of the treaty and most importantly, national factors, which include, *inter alia*, economic status, administrative capacity, the links between national, provincial and local governments. These authors argue that according to empirical research, if countries are to comply, engaging them in the agreement is of fundamental importance. Jacobson and Brown Weiss distinguish three alternative compliance strategies: sunshine; incentives; and sanctions. The selection of strategies depends upon individual States' intent and capacity,

---

87 Robert O. Keohane and Joseph S. Nye, Jr., 'Power and Interdependence Revisited', 41 *International Organization* (1987) 725–53; Robert O. Keohane and Joseph S. Nye, Jr., *Power and Interdependence: World Politics in Transition* (Little, Brown & Co., 1977).
88 Harold Hongju Koh, 'The 1998 Frankel Lecture: Bringing International Law Home', 35 *Houston Law Review* (1998) 623–681, Harold Hongju Koh, 'Why Do Nations Obey International Law', 106 *Yale Law Journal* (1997) 2599–659.
89 Jutta Brunnée and Stephan J. Toope, *Legitimacy and Legality in International Law: An Interactional Account* (Cambridge University Press, 2010), at 124.
90 *Ibid.*, at 124.
91 *Ibid.*, at 217.
92 George W. Downs, David M. Rocke and Peter N. Barsoom, 'Is the Good News about Compliance Good News about Cooperation?', 50 *International Organization* (1996) 379–406.

as well as upon the type of international agreement, e.g. trade, labour, human rights, the environment.[93]

Mention also must be made of Thomas Franck's theory of legitimacy, which is based on a presumption that States comply with international law even in instances when it does not further their own interests. Therefore, he argues international law has a 'compliance pull' which is underscored by the perception by its addresses as being legitimate.[94]

The theory which in the most apposite manner explains the compliance by States with rule of international law – in this case the decision of COPs – is a matter of a personal choice. All these theories have a certain application to COPs. The approach of Chayes and Handler Chayes – the 'cooperative problem-solving approach', which is based on transparency – is, in the view of the present author, particularly befitting compliance procedures and also the law-making activities of COPs.[95]

6   Conclusions

This Chapter deals with the expansion of powers of COPs established on the basis of MEAs. These powers are used to fill gaps in vague provisions in treaties and set up compliance regimes. These functions (not provided for in primary treaties) may be based on so-called enabling clauses but equally may not have any legal grounds, not even a very general one (example of which can be setting up of the compliance regime under the 1989 Basel Convention). This Chapter endeavoured to present all current theories concerning the new functions of COPs deriving both form the law of treaties and outside it. None of the provided theories appear to be satisfactory in explaining the legal issues concerning the functions of COP. It is incontrovertible, however, that their decisions influence the behaviour and the scope of obligations of parties to MEAs. It is a new way of international law-making and a new way of expressing consent to be bound, which modifies traditional ways enumerated in Article 11 of the VCLT. Finally it must be mentioned that, in the view of author of this Chapter, one of the most important questions is the legitimacy of such activities by COP, which also remains unresolved.

---

92   George W. Downs, David M. Rocke and Peter N. Barsoom, 'Is the Good News about Compliance Good News about Cooperation?', 50 *International Organization* (1996) 379–406.
93   Edith Brown Weiss and Harold Karan Jacobson, 'A Framework for Analysis', in Edith Brown Weiss and Harold Karan Jacobson (eds), *Engaging Countries: Strengthening Compliance with International Environmental Accords* (MIT Press, 1998) 1–18.
94   Thomas M. Franck, *The Power of Legitimacy among Nations* (Oxford University Press, 1990); Thomas M. Franck, 'Legitimacy in the International System', 82 *American Journal of International Law* (1988) 705–59.
95   Chayes and Handler Chayes, *The New Sovereignty, supra* note 85, at 10–15.

12 In search of a voice

EU law constraints on Member States in international law-making

Panos Koutrakos

Introduction

The international role of the EU has been at the very centre of the existential crisis, which shaped its constitutional voyage in the 2000s. The process of the drafting, negotiation and ratification of the Treaty Establishing a Constitution for Europe,[1] the metamorphosis of the latter into the Treaty of Lisbon[2] and its negotiation following the adjustments necessitated by the Irish referendum, all were marked by a distinct focus on the international posture of the Union. The tone was set in December 2001, when the Laeken Declaration, which kick-started the process that led to the entry into force of the Lisbon Treaty eight years later, posed the following question:[3]

> Does Europe not, now that [it] is finally unified, have a leading role to play in a new world order, that of a power able both to play a stabilising role worldwide and to point the way ahead for many countries and peoples?

The ambition illustrated by the above statement is accompanied by a sense of responsibility, which the Union appears to assume. The European Security Strategy, adopted in December 2003, states that 'Europe should be ready to share in the responsibility for global security and in building a better world'.[4] The Laeken Declaration also referred to the Union's 'responsibilities in the governance of globalisation' and pointed out that 'Europe needs to shoulder [them]'.[5]

---

1 Treaty Establishing a Constitution for Europe, 29 October 2004, not in force, OJ 2004 C 310/1.
2 Treaty of Lisbon amending the TEU and the Treaty establishing the European Community, 13 December 2007, OJ 2007 C 306/1.
3 Laeken Declaration: The Future of the European Union, European Council, SN 273/01, 15 December 2001, at 2.
4 A Secure Europe in a Better World: European Security Strategy, European Council, 12 December 2003, at 1.
5 Laeken Declaration, *supra* note 3, at 2.

This focus on the EU's international role is borne out by the provisions of the Lisbon Treaty.[6] In substantive terms, the Union has assumed various roles on the international scene over the years,[7] and exporting its norms and standards has been paramount among them.[8] However, the prominence of the international role of the EU has had an impact on the Member States and the manner in which they exercise their powers as sovereign subjects of international law both in terms of their interactions with third countries and their participation in international organisations.

This chapter will focus on a specific aspect of the impact of EU law on the international role of Member States, namely the role of the Court of Justice.[9] Over the years, Jan Klabbers has criticised the Court in a cogent and spirited manner for its preoccupation with strengthening the application of EU law and the scope of its own jurisdiction, often to the detriment of the effectiveness of international law.[10] While the Court has been central to the shaping and development of EU external relations, this chapter will examine its case law of the last few years, which, in addition to causing controversy, has shed new light on the limits imposed by EU law on the international role of Member States.

1 The starting point: The duty of cooperation

The starting point for the study of the role of the Member States within the Union's constitutional order is governed by the duty of cooperation. Set out in Article 4(3) of the Treaty on European Union (TEU),[11] this has been an important tool in the Court's armoury, which has contributed to the constitutionalisation of the Union legal order over the years. In the international legal order, the relationship between the Member States and the Union is also governed by the duty of cooperation which the Court set out in the early

---

6   See, among others, Panos Koutrakos, 'Primary Law and Policy in EU External Relations: Moving Away from the Big Picture?', 33 *European Law Review* (2008) 666–86.
7   Cremona refers to the EU as a market player, a rule generator, a stabiliser and a magnet and neighbour: Marise Cremona, 'The Union as a Global Actor: Roles, Models and Identity', 41 *Common Market Law Review* (2004) 553–573.
8   Marise Cremona, 'Values in EU Foreign Policy', in Malcolm Evans and Panos Koutrakos (eds), *Beyond the Established Legal Orders: Policy Interconnections Between the EU and the Rest of the World* (Hart, 2011) 275–317.
9   For the impact on the international role of Member States by procedural frameworks laid down in secondary legislation, see Geert de Baere and Panos Koutrakos, 'The Interactions between the European Court of Justice and the Legislature in the European Union's External Relations', in Philip Syrpis (ed.), *The Relationship between the Judiciary and the Legislature in the Internal Market* (Cambridge University Press, 2012) 243 at 257 *et seq.*
10 See Jan Klabbers, *Treaty Conflict and the European Union* (Cambridge University Press, 2009), ch. 6, and Jan Klabbers, '*Völkerrechtsfreundlich*? International Law and the Union Legal Order', in Panos Koutrakos (ed), *European Foreign Policy: Legal and Political Perspectives* (Edward Elgar, 2011) 95–114.
11 Treaty on European Union, 7 February 1992, in force 1 November 1993, OJ 2010 C 83/1.

1990s. The foundation of this duty is the requirement of unity in the international representation of the Union and the Member States.[12] Over the years, the duty of cooperation has been applied in different contexts and in various ways.

In cases where there appears a concerted EU position, the Court has held that the Member States are under 'special duties of action and abstention'.[13] This raises two questions: how is an EU position construed, and what types of 'special duties' does it entail for Member States. In relation to the latter, it is clear that a Member State may not negotiate and conclude an agreement with a third country. In relation to the former, the limited case-law so far suggests a rather broad approach to the scope of what constitutes an EU position. The first case where this arose was decided in the mid-1970s and it became one of the classic authorities on EU external competence. In *Kramer*,[14] the Court held that Member States were prevented from assuming obligations in the context of the North-East Atlantic Fisheries Convention[15] in which certain Member States participated. This was because the subject-matter of these measures fell within the exclusive competence of the Community in the light of Article 102 of the 1973 Act of Accession that set out a timetable pursuant to which the Community would adopt secondary measures on the matter under dispute, namely the conservation of the biological resources of the sea.[16] In addition to being prevented from assuming any obligations in this area, the Member States were also required 'to use all the political and legal means at their disposal in order to ensure the participation of the Community in the Convention and in other similar agreements'.[17]

Therefore, the provision of a timetable for the adoption of internal measures by the Union imposed on Member States both negative duties (not to assume any international obligations) and positive duties (to facilitate the Union's participation in an international agreement in which they are already parties).

Similar duties are also imposed where the Union institutions have adopted a decision to initiate negotiations of an international agreement. This was

---

12 See Marise Cremona, 'Defending the Community Interest: the Duties of Cooperation and Compliance', in Marise Cremona and Bruno de Witte (eds), *EU Foreign Relations Law: Constitutional Fundamentals* (Hart, 2008) 125–69, and Christophe Hillion, 'Mixity and Coherence: The Significance of the Duty of Cooperation', in Christophe Hillion and Panos Koutrakos (eds), *Mixed Agreements Revisited: The EU and its Member States in the World* (Hart, 2010) 87–115.
13 Case C-266/03 *Commission v. Luxembourg* [2005] ECR I-4805, para. 59, Case C-433/03 *Commission v. Germany* [2005] ECR I-6985, para. 65, Case C-246/07 *Commission v. Sweden* [2010] ECR I-3317, para. 74.
14 Joined Cases 3, 4 and 6/76 *Kramer* [1976] ECR 1279.
15 24 January 1959, in force 27 June 1963, 486 UNTS 157.
16 22 January 1972, in force 1 January 1973, OJ 1972 L 73/14.
17 *Kramer, supra* note 14, para. 40.

the case in the two *Inland Waterways* judgements,[18] where Luxembourg had signed, ratified, and implemented, and Germany had ratified and implemented, inland waterway transport agreements with Romania, Poland and Ukraine without consulting or cooperating with the Commission.

The genesis of this formulation ('special duties of action and abstention') is to be found in a ruling about the Common Fisheries Policy, which was rendered in 1981.[19] The Council had been trying to discuss common rules on the conservation of fishery resources in the waters under the jurisdiction of the Member States since the beginning of 1979. Having failed to do so, it adopted a series of interim measures, anticipating agreement on common rules by late 1979. The UK government decided to adopt a set of specific measures about fishery conservation that the Commission deemed to violate the duty of cooperation. The Court accepted its argument, and pointed out a number of factors: the existence of exclusive Community competence since 1 January 1979, following the expiration of the transitional period;[20] the Member States should be free to act in order to meet the needs raised by the development of the relevant biological and technological facts in the area by amending the existing conservation measures in a limited way and by no means creating a new conservation policy; the Council had already adopted a set of rules that were applicable on an interim basis; these had been adopted in anticipation of the adoption of a permanent set of common rules by the Council, which was only a matter of time.

What we see here is a principle, introduced in the internal market sphere and spelled out in this specific context of Community competence, extended to apply in the context of the negotiation of international agreements.

2 The role of Member States in cases where there is no EU action

The Union legal order imposes duties on Member States even in cases where the EU has not acted on the international plane. In Case C-45/07 *Commission v. Greece*, the Court elaborated on the specific implications of this arrangement.[21] Greece had submitted a proposal to the International Maritime Organisation (IMO) Maritime Safety Committee in which it asked it to examine the creation of check lists or other appropriate tools for assisting the contracting States of the International Convention for the Safety of Life at Sea (SOLAS)[22] in monitoring whether ships and port facilities complied with the requirements of an Annex to that Convention, as well as the

---

18   *Commission v. Luxembourg, supra* note 13; *Commission v. Germany, supra* note 13.
19   Case 804/79 *Commission v. UK* [1981] ECR 1045, para. 28.
20   See Case 32/79 *Commission v. UK* [1980] ECR 2403.
21   Case C-45/07 *Commission v. Greece* [2009] ECR I-701.
22   1 November 1974, in force 25 May 1980, 1184 UNTS 3.

International Ship and Port Facility Security Code (ISPS Code).[23] The Commission objected to the submission of this proposal as its subject matter fell within the Union's exclusive competence following the adoption of Regulation 725/2004 on enhancing ship and port facility security.[24] This measure was intended to incorporate in substance both the SOLAS Convention and the ISPS Code in EU law.

The starting point for, and the foundation of, the judgement is the duty of cooperation as set out in primary law, as well as the setting of a common transport policy as one of the Union's objectives. The Court concludes that the submission of the Greek proposal set in motion a process that could have led to the adoption of new rules that would then have forced the Union to act in order to incorporate them in its legal order.

This judgement is interesting on a number of grounds. First, it confirms the wide construction of the duty of cooperation. The Greek government had argued that, in fact, it had been the Commission that had violated the duty of cooperation. Greece had sought to raise the matter at the Maritime Safety Committee (an EU body set up under Regulation 725/2004), but the Commission, responsible for the discussion at the Committee, had failed to submit its proposal. The Court rejected this argument, and, in a thinly disguised slap on the Commission's wrist, pointed out that:

> [a]ny breach by the Commission of Article 10 EC cannot entitle a Member State to take initiatives likely to affect Community rules promulgated for the attainment of the objectives of the Treaty, in breach of that State's obligations.[25]

This conclusion is hardly surprising, given the specific legal context of the procedure pursuant to which the Court rendered its ruling. It is recalled that enforcement actions brought under Article 258 of the Treaty on the Functioning of the European Union (TFEU)[26] have been consistently viewed by the Court to be of an objective nature: it is the existence of a violation by a Member State that determines the outcome of the case irrespective of other considerations that might have a bearing on the Commission's decision to bring the action under Article 258 TFEU.

Second, this judgement raises the issue of a Member State acting as a medium for the Union in an international context. The Court accepted early on that a Member State may act as the medium through which the Union exercises its competence in the context of an international organisation. It

---

23 12 December 2002, UN Doc. SOLAS/CONF.5/34, Annex 1.
24 Regulation (EC) No 725/2004 of the European Parliament and of the Council of 31 March 2004 on enhancing ship and port facility security, OJ 2004 L 129/6.
25 *Commission v. Greece, supra* note 21, para. 26.
26 25 March 1957, in force 1 January 1958, OJ 2010/C 83/47. See, for instance, Case 416/85 *Commission v. UK* [1988] ECR 3127.

held so expressly in the *ILO* Opinion[27] and confirmed it in the *IMO* case.[28] However, the question is raised whether, when the Member States are in such a position, they are under even more onerous duties than those imposed normally by the duty of cooperation.[29] This judgement may not provide a definitive answer, as the subject-matter of the dispute fell within the exclusive competence of the Union, a fact that was not disputed by either of the parties. However, suffice it to point out that the ruling itself is couched in quite broad terms. In particular, it does not only apply to cases where a Member State is instrumentalised in order to achieve the Union's objectives in circumstances where the Union itself may not do so for objective reasons. Instead, it applies to whatever it is a Member State does in the context of an international set of rules and procedures:

> [t]he mere fact that the Community is not a member of an international organisation in no way authorises a Member State, acting individually in the context of its participation in an international organisation, to assume obligations likely to affect Community rules promulgated for the attainment of the objectives of the Treaty.[30]

3 The Member States in cases where they coexist with the EU in international organisations

In the context of mixed agreements, the relationship between the EU and the Member States is shaped by a tension over competence: how far can the EU go in exercising and enforcing its competence and to what extent are the Member States free to act independently? This tension is considerable and constant. It is also translated within the internal structure of the EU, where inter-institutional disputes are frequent, and in the context of which the Council, the Commission and the Parliament spend considerable energy and time.[31]

And yet, while permeating almost everything the Union does on the international scene, this tension is often concealed, as it is being addressed on the basis of practical arrangements reached between the EU and the Member States. This is illustrated by the well-known PROBA 20 agreement, which is an arrangement applicable to commodity agreements negotiated within the context of the 1970 Integrated Commodity Programme of the

---

27 Opinion 2/91 *Convention No 170 ILO on Safety in the Use of Chemicals at Work* [1993] ECR I-1061.
28 *Commission v. Greece, supra* note 21.
29 See Marise Cremona, 'Extending the Reach of the AETR Principle: Comment on *Commission v. Greece* (C-45/07)', 34 *European Law Review* (2009) 754–68, at 764.
30 *Commission v. Greece, supra* note 21, para. 30.
31 See Panos Koutrakos, 'Legal Basis and Delimitation of Competence in EU External Relations' in Cremona and de Witte (eds), *EU Foreign Relations Law, supra* note 12, 171–98.
32 See Panos Koutrakos, *EU International Relations Law* (Hart, 2006) 161–4.

United Nations Conference on Trade and Development.[32] Another example is the arrangement on voting reached between the Commission and the Council in the context of the Food and Agriculture Organization (FAO) and which the Court sanctioned and enforced in 1996.[33] In practical terms, once the EU institutions and the Member States agree to bypass the matter of principle about the existence and nature of Union competence in a given context, they have proved capable of setting out procedural arrangements on an *ad hoc* basis, which would enable them to coexist as a matter of practice.

An interesting aspect of the relationship between the EU and Member States in the context of international agreements concluded by both is about the freedom of Member States to act on their own: to what extent does their coexistence with the Union limit the scope for autonomous initiatives as sovereign subjects of international law?

In the last few years, this question has been addressed in two important cases. The first is the *Mox Plant* case.[34] As this judgement has been analysed exhaustively,[35] suffice it to recall that the Court held that Ireland acted against the duty of cooperation by initiating proceedings against another Member State before an international tribunal for the violations of provisions of UNCLOS[36] in areas covered by EU law.

The legal and policy context of this case was so specific as to caution against any general conclusions about the restrictions on the legal position of Member States. It is recalled that in Article 282, UNCLOS enables Member States to rely upon the judicial system set up under the EU Treaties in order to resolve disputes between them in the context of UNCLOS. This justifies the conclusion reached in the judgement as to the appropriate forum for resolving the dispute between Ireland and the UK.

Furthermore, the line of reasoning followed by the Court is convoluted and somewhat unhelpful. A considerable part of the judgement is about seeking to ascertain whether, 'by becoming a party to the Convention, [the Union had] elected to exercise its external competence in matters of environmental protection'.[37] This process is fraught with problems, heavily dependent upon general criteria and factors difficult to establish. It is also of

---

33 Case C-25/94 *Commission v. Council* [1996] ECR I-1469.
34 Case C-459/03 *Commission v. Ireland* [2006] ECR I-4635.
35 See, for instance, Cremona, 'Defending the Community Interest', *supra* note 12, at 149–52; Nikolaos Lavranos, 'The Scope of the Exclusive Jurisdiction of the Court of Justice', (2007) 32 *European Law Review* 83–94; Eleftheria Neframi, 'La mixité éclairée dans l'arrêt Commission contre Irlande du 30 mai 2006 (affaire Mox): une double infraction, un triple apport', *Revue du Droit de l'Union europeenne* (2007) 687–713.
36 United Nations Convention on the Law of the Sea, 10 December 1982, in force 16 November 1994, 1833 UNTS 3.
37 *Commission v. Ireland*, *supra* note 34, para. 96.

questionable usefulness. Instead, it is the existence of Union legislation in the area of the dispute, the submission of this legislation by Ireland to the international tribunal and the right of Ireland under UNCLOS to bring the action before the Court of Justice that should determine the outcome of the dispute.

Another layer in the study of the international role of Member States is added by the more recent *PFOS* judgement.[38] It is recalled that Sweden was found to have acted contrary to EU law by having proposed the listing of a substance known as perfluorooctanesulfonic acid (PFOS) in an Annex to the Stockholm Convention on Persistent Organic Pollutants.[39] What is interesting about this case is that Sweden had sought to get EU agreement on the matter; it had sought to convince the Union to make the proposal the subject-matter of a concerted action. The Union institutions had not adopted a decision refusing to propose the listing of the specific substance. Instead, they proposed the listing of two other substances.

This judgement has attracted criticism.[40] In effect, does the Court not expect the Member States to remain silent? Is there anything differentiating the duty imposed on Sweden in the context of this agreement to which it participates from another agreement to which it would not participate because its rules would fall within the Union's exclusive competence? Has the Court not viewed the Stockholm Convention as if its rules fall within the Union's exclusive competence?

The judgement has a distinct policy focus. This has two dimensions. On the one hand, any proposal to list substances under the Stockholm Convention has financial implications. This is because Article 13 of the Convention provides for financial aid to developing countries or countries with economies in transition. The Court mentions these time and again, as it points out that they had been raised by the Presidency at a meeting of the Council Working Party on International Environmental Issues.[41] On the other hand, there appears to be a choice made by the Union institutions to bring the EU rules on organic pollutants closer to the Stockholm Convention. This is achieved by prioritising the listing in the latter of those covered by the former. The substance that Sweden proposed to be listed was not among these. And therein lay the problem: what Sweden deemed to be 'a decision-making vacuum', the Court characterised as 'a Community strategy'[42] and 'a concerted common strategy'.[43]

A unilateral proposal is viewed as a deviation from this concerted common strategy, and is ruled out because it would have 'consequences' for

---

38 Case C-246/07 *Commission v. Sweden* [2010] ECR I-3317.
39 22 May 2001, in force 17 May 2004, 2256 UNTS 119.
40 See Andres Delgado Casteleiro and Joris Larik, 'The Duty to Remain Silent: Limitless Loyalty in EU External Relations?', 36 *European Law Review* (2011) 524–41.
41 Case C-246/07 *Commission v. Sweden*, para. 39.
42 *Ibid.*, para. 76.
43 *Ibid.*, para. 91.

the Union. This conclusion is substantiated on the basis of three alternative arguments. The first is based on voting: under the Convention, either the Union would vote or the Member States. If the Member States voted, given that Sweden had made the proposal, then the effect of the proposal would have been to deprive the Union from its voting rights. If the Union had voted, it would not have had the votes to prevent the adoption of the proposal. Therefore, either way, the Union would have been bound by the listing of PFOS. The second argument is based on the Convention's provisions on opt-out. While these enable a party to opt out, provided that it does so within a year from the date on which the depositary communicated the amended Annex,[44] the Court felt that that was not possible. This was because the Convention did not allow it to exercise voting rights concurrently with its Member States.

While intervening States argued that opting out was possible, the Court did not examine their arguments. Instead, it responded by relying on a third argument related to legal uncertainty: the Court held that to opt out from an amendment proposed and voted for by several Member States could give rise to legal uncertainty for the Member States, the Secretariat of the Convention as well as other parties to the Convention. Legal certainty, like effectiveness, appears to be the last refuge of a weak line of reasoning. In this context, the argument is not convincing because there is no explanation as to how the exercise by the Union of a right which is bestowed upon it by the Convention would give rise to legal uncertainty: would it be the apparent disagreement between its position and that of some of its Member States? Would it be the emergence of questions as to the application of the Convention rules to the product in relation to Sweden and other States which might have voted for it? These are valid questions, and they are far from straightforward to address. And yet, they are being ignored by depriving Member States from a freedom that mixity is purported to protect.

There is another question that the reliance upon 'legal certainty' by the Court in *PFOS* raises. This has to do with the very wide scope of actors, which the Court views as affected by it. In addition to the Member States, it refers to the Secretariat of the Convention and to third parties, which are parties to the Convention. This is not easy to follow. The whole question here is what the Union's deeply idiosyncratic legal order requires a Member State to do in the context of a mixed agreement. It has been a constant in EU external relations law that this question is internal to the Union, and of no interest to third parties,[45] whose interests to know with whom they are dealing are intended to be addressed on the basis of the declarations of

---

44 See Stockholm Convention, *supra* note 38, Articles 25(4), 22(3)(b) and (4).
45 Ruling 1/78 *Draft Convention of International Atomic Energy Agency* [1978] ECR 2151.

competence.[46] And yet, the Court appears prepared to protect the interests of third parties by reducing the scope of what Member States may do when they act along with the Union as sovereign subjects of international law without substantiating its conclusion sufficiently.[47]

4 The Member States and their pre-existing agreements

An area where the Member States have seen their activities as fully sovereign subjects of international law being curtailed by the Court of Justice is where they have concluded agreements prior to their accession to the EU. This is covered by Article 351 TFEU, which reads as follows:

> The rights and obligations arising from agreements concluded before 1 January 1958 or, for acceding States, before the date of their accession, between one or more Member States on the one hand, and one or more third countries on the other, shall not be affected by the provisions of the Treaties.
>
> To the extent that such agreements are not compatible with the Treaties, the Member State or States concerned shall take all appropriate steps to eliminate the incompatibilities established. Member States shall, where necessary, assist each other to this end and shall, where appropriate, adopt a common attitude.
>
> In applying the agreements referred to in the first paragraph, Member States shall take into account the fact that the advantages accorded under the Treaties by each Member State form an integral part of the establishment of the Union and are thereby inseparably linked with the creation of common institutions, the conferring of powers upon them and the granting of the same advantages by all the other Member States.

Therefore, a balance ought to be struck between the obligations that Member States have assumed pursuant to such agreements, and their duty to comply with EU law. How is the balance to be struck in practice? Over the years, the Court of Justice has rendered a number of rulings that appear to restrict the room for manoeuvre which Member States have in their effort

---

46   See Joni Heliskoski, 'EU Declarations of Competence and International Responsibility', in Malcolm Evans and Panos Koutrakos (eds), *The International Responsibility of the European Union: European and International Perspectives* (Hart, 2013) 189–212.

47   The conclusion reached by the Court is viewed by Heliskoski in the light of the mixed nature of the Stockholm Convention, and is, therefore, interpreted as confined to mixed agreements: Joni Heliskoski, 'The Obligation of Member States to Foresee, in the Conclusion and Application of their International Agreements, Eventual Future Measures of the European Union', in Anthony Arnull, Catherine Barnard, Michael Dougan and Eleanor Spaventa (eds), *A Constitutional Order of States? Essays in EU Law in Honour of Alan Dashwood* (Hart, 2011) 545–64, at 561–3. However, it is not entirely clear how this argument is affected by the *IMO* judgement.

to eliminate incompatibilities. For instance, they are required as a matter of EU law to renounce pre-existing agreements if any political or practical difficulties make their renegotiation impossible.[48]

The story of the interpretation and application of Article 351 TFEU has been told often[49] and well, not least by Jan Klabbers,[50] who criticises it for its consistent effort to by-pass international law in favour of EU law. In fact, he suggests that there is no longer any point for a Member State to try and squeeze the application of a pre-existing treaty within the scope of application of the first paragraph of Article 351 TFEU – the Court is likely to interpret the second paragraph in such a way as not to allow the Member State to apply the agreement in question.

The criticism against the Court has been levelled more recently following the three *BITs* judgements, which the Court rendered in 2009.[51] In three cases against Sweden, Austria and Finland, the Court ruled that certain pre-existing bilateral investment treaties (BITs) were incompatible with EU law. It was the transfer clause of these Agreements, guaranteeing to the investors of each party the free transfer, without undue delay, of payments connected with an investment, which was problematic. The Court held that it was contrary to the freedom of the Union to impose restrictions on the movement of capital from a third country in relation to direct investment, as a safeguard measure, or in order to implement economic sanctions decided within the context of Common Foreign and Security Policy.[52]

What differentiates these cases from the other Article 351 TFEU cases is that the incompatibilities in question had not, in fact, arisen. They were all possible and would arise as and when the Union decided to exercise the right laid down in the above TFEU provisions. However, the Court held that the effectiveness of any restrictive measures that the Union may be required to impose under the above provisions would depend on whether they would be capable of being applied immediately. The transfer clause in the contested BITs would undermine such an objective. The Court also noted that the Agreements provided no other clause that would enable the Member States to apply EU restrictive measures immediately.[53] It also concluded, albeit without further elaboration, that no international law mechanism would allow the Member States to fulfil their EU obligations and deviate from the BITs.

---

48 See, for instance, Case C-170/98 *Commission v. Belgium* [1999] ECR I-5493 and Case C-62/98 *Commission v. Portugal* [2000] ECR I-5171.
49 See, for instance, Koutrakos, *EU International Relations Law*, supra note 32, ch. 8.
50 See Klabbers, *Treaty Conflict and the European Union*, supra note 10, ch. 6 and Jan Klabbers, 'Moribund on the Fourth of July? The Court of Justice on Prior Agreements of the Member States', 26 *European Law Review* (2001) 187–197.
51 Case C-249/06, *Commission v. Sweden* [2009] ECR I-1335; Case C-205/06, *Commission v. Austria* [2009] ECR I-1301; Case C-118/07 *Commission v Finland*, [2009] ECR I-10889.
52 See TFEU Articles 64(2), 66 and 75.
53 The insertion of a regional economic integration organisation clause, while mentioned by Austria, had not actually been followed up.

The *BITs* judgements may be viewed as an unwarranted restriction on the ability of the Member States to act as sovereign subjects of international law: the mere possibility of future EU law action prevents them from maintaining an international agreement that is not inconsistent with current EU law and which was concluded prior to their accession to the Union. However, the temptation to adopt this perspective should be resisted. Two points are worth making. First, the judgements should be understood as being confined to the very specific legal context within which they were rendered: it is the specific nature of the restrictive measures which the Council may be called upon to adopt under the specific TFEU Treaty legal bases which renders the transfer clause problematic. Any transfer of capital could be carried out with a click of a button – literally. Therefore, any time required by a Member State in order to adjust its policy and render it compatible with the EU restrictions would undermine the latter, and deprive them of their purpose.

Second, the notion of effectiveness in the EU law vocabulary is charged. One hardly needs to be reminded of the central role that it played in the formative years of the Union, when the Court introduced the principles that gradually constitutionalised the EU legal order. This principle of *effet utile* marked the development of a legal order that the Court shaped out of the bare provisions of the Treaties. This is a different notion to the one that emerges in the *BITs* judgements. The latter is construed more narrowly, and emerges from the very specific practical implications of measures designed to restrict the movement of capital.[54] Rather than a general policy imperative that shapes the nature of the Union legal order, effectiveness in the latter case is inextricably linked to the very specific characteristics of the transactions to which the TFEU provisions apply.

5 Conclusion

To argue that the impact of EU law on the contribution of Member States to international law-making has been profound is to state the obvious. The constraints imposed by EU membership emerge in different contexts: in areas where there is Union action (*Inland Waterways*), or in areas where there is no definitive Union movement (*IMO*), in areas where Member States coexist with the Union in the context of a specific organisation (*PFOS*) or where they participate on their own (*IMO*), and in areas where they cannot possibly predict what the Union may do (*BITs*).

---

[54] See Panos Koutrakos, 'Annotation of Case C-205/06 *Commission v Austria* and Case C-249/06 *Commission v Sweden (re: Bilateral Investment Treaties)*', 46 *Common Market Law Review* (2009) 2059–76. See also Eileen Denza, 'Bilateral Investment Treaties and EU Rules on Free Transfer: Comment on *Commission v Austria, Commission v Sweden,* and *Commission v Finland*', 35 *European Law Review* (2010) 263–74.

And yet, the Union has become an international player in the absence of a well-ordered legal framework governing its coexistence with the Member States, a firm set of rules of procedures which would determine who is to do what under what circumstances. As the EU is positively middle-aged, it is remarkable how both the Union and its Member States should still be struggling to find their way around each other on the international scene. Even though its external relations law has been developing for about 40 years, fundamental questions about the practicalities of the relationship between the Union and its Member States are still addressed incrementally. While its role is still pivotal, the Court of Justice is loathe to make general pronouncements about the state of the law and its evolution. Instead, its judgements are about adjudicating upon specific disputes and addressing specific questions. Therefore, one underestimates the specific legal and policy context of a dispute brought before Europe's judges at one's peril. Be that as it may, it is a testament to the flexibility of the Union's system, the willingness of the main actors to compromise and the ingenuity of the practical arrangements to which they have recourse, often on an *ad hoc* legal basis, that the Union's complex external relations system has been managed as a matter of course without major crises.

As for the role of the Court of Justice, two implications are worth pointing out. The first is about its position in the wider constellation of power within the Union's architecture: while the role of any judge is inherently political, the position of the Union's judges at the very centre of the management of EU external relations renders it even more political. This runs the risk of upsetting the balance between the Union's legislature and judiciary, and also rendering the Court's role more sensitive and controversial. On the other hand, one ought not to lose sight of the fact that judgements are not abstract pronouncements about the state of the law, or the desirability of certain approaches to legal questions. Therefore, the temptation to read them as if they were legislative rules should be resisted firmly.

The central role, which it has been called upon to occupy in the area of external relations, raises the expectation that the Court of Justice should substantiate its judgements with greater clarity. Put differently, the opaque reasoning that characterises a number of the judgements discussed in this chapter and the paucity of arguments upon which broad conclusions are reached are not conducive to the effective conduct of both the EU and its Member States on the international scene. This point should not underestimate the objective constraints, which are inherent in the function of the Court of Justice within the Union's constitutional architecture. The need for consensus among the Judges, the inevitable compromises which their deliberation must entail, the absence of dissenting opinions, the reluctance of the Court to bind itself in the future – all these are bound to have an impact on the line of reasoning of the judgements. These objective factors notwithstanding, there is considerable scope for the clarity of the line of reasoning followed by the Court to be improved. This is a concern that is by no means confined to the areas discussed in this chapter, the case-law on the interpretation of mixed agreements being a case in point.[55] In fact, it may be argued that the opaque reasoning of the Court's case-law is hardly confined to the area of external relations, and that it has also been a recent feature of the law of the internal market.[56] While this may well be true, it is worth pointing out that, in the area discussed in this chapter, there is a layer that adds yet another dimension to this discussion, namely the nature of the Member States as sovereign subjects of international law, as well as the interests of third parties which interact with them. The Court's case-law has profound implications for both and, therefore, the clarity of its reasoning is of paramount importance.

Against this background of incremental development, the increasingly active role of the Court of Justice, the increasingly politicised nature of its function and the opaque reasoning of its judgements, it is high time the Union institutions and the Member States reduced their appetite for disputes. Instead, they should focus on the management of their relationship on the international scene by promoting pragmatic procedural mechanisms. There can be no device that could rule out conflicts, neither can there be any formula that would provide hard and fast rules as to who is to do what in what way in each and every international context. However, the only viable alternative is a pragmatic approach that would accept the international role of the Member States whilst addressing the peculiarities of individual cases in which this is carried out under the umbrella of the duty of cooperation.

---

55 It is interesting that, in the recent Case C-240/09 *Lesoochranárske zoskupenie VLK* [2011] ECR I-1255, Advocate General Sharpston first pointed out the lack of clarity of the case-law, then she viewed the judgement in Case C-431/05 *Merck Genéricos v. Merck* [2007] ECR I-7001 as a clarification, only to proceed to articulate a line of reasoning not entirely easy to follow and reach a conclusion with which the Court subsequently disagreed. On the interpretation of mixed agreements, see Panos Koutrakos, 'The Interpretation of Mixed Agreements', in Hillion and Koutrakos (eds), *Mixed Agreements Revisited, supra* note 12, 116–137.

56 See Nic Shuibhne, 'Editorial: Seven Questions for Seven Paragraphs', 36 *European Law Review* (2011) 161–2.

13 'In principle the full review'
What justice for Mr Kadi?

Päivi Leino

1 Introduction

On 11 September 2001, I was the freshly appointed acting assistant professor of international law at the University of Helsinki, and preparing for my final international law exam for the LLM degree at the London School of Economics to be held the following morning. That was the day when, in the middle of my exam preparations, I could witness 'LIVE' the Twin Towers falling in New York, and the world changed, once again, with a heavy influence on how many an international law exam question would be formulated during the years to come.

About a month later, on 17 October 2001, the UN Al-Qaida Sanctions Committee published an addendum to its list of terrorism suspects, including, in particular, Mr Kadi, an international businessman and a national of Saudi Arabia, with substantial financial interests in the EU, identified as being an individual associated with Al-Qaida and Usama bin Laden, the culprit behind the September 11 events. In the EU, this addendum was promptly implemented through a Commission Regulation.[1] The funds and other financial resources of Mr Kadi were frozen throughout the EU as of 20 October 2001. Since then, Mr Kadi has attempted to get his name removed from the list both through the available means within the UN and through the EU system of available remedies. In fact, few individuals – given the stringent rules on access to Union courts – have been able to claim a 'direct concern' with EU law and thus have an opportunity to address

---

1 Commission Regulation (EC) No 2062/2001 of 19 October 2001 amending, for the third time, Regulation No 467/2001 prohibiting the export of certain goods and services to Afghanistan, strengthening the flight ban and extending the freeze of funds and other financial resources in respect of the Taliban of Afghanistan and repealing Regulation (EC) No 337/2000, OJ 2001 L 277/ 25. Kadi's name was added, together with others, to Annex I to that regulation, and subsequently included in Annex I to Council Regulation (EC) No 881/2002 of 27 May 2002 imposing certain specific restrictive measures directed against certain persons and entities associated with Usama bin Laden, the Al-Qaida network and the Taliban, and repealing Council Regulation (EC) No 467/2001 prohibiting the export of certain goods and services to Afghanistan, strengthening the flight ban and extending the freeze of funds and other financial resources in respect of the Taliban of Afghanistan, OJ 2002 L 139/9, upon its adoption.

the EU Courts this many times,[2] assisting international and EU lawyers in increasing their knowledge of the relationship between international law, EU law and human rights law. In his troubles, Mr Kadi is not alone. For example, the appeal by Mr Othman, who 'finds himself in a factual and legal situation in every way comparable' to that of Mr Kadi,[3] was effectively pending before the General Court between 2001 and 2009, while the ruling of the Court of Justice (CJEU) in the case of Mr Kadi was expected.[4]

Mr Kadi's dilemma is that he claims to be innocent, but has no access to a forum where he could prove his listing to be without foundation. Instead, his available means of redress have been practically limited to the EU Courts where he has been able to challenge the EU implementing measure. In 2008, the CJEU, in an appeal case from the General Court (*Kadi I*),[5] decided to annul the relevant regulation to the extent it applies to Mr Kadi due to failures to observe his procedural rights (*Kadi II*).[6] Soon afterwards, another Regulation was adopted to give effect to the Al-Qaida sanctions listing while giving somewhat more attention to the procedural criticisms raised by the CJEU. On 30 September 2010, the General Court created yet another chapter in the *Kadi* story when it delivered a ruling (*Kadi III*).[7] In the latest ruling, the General Court had been specifically asked by Mr Kadi to address the procedural guarantees that the EU member states are required to respect when implementing an UN Security Council resolution imposing restrictive measures on an individual. This ruling has also been appealed (*Kadi IV*),[8] making sure that the matter will remain on the EU judicial agenda for another couple of years.

---

2   See *infra* notes 5–8.
3   Mr Othman is a Jordanian citizen who has lived since 1993 in the UK, where he was granted temporary political asylum in 1994. He was arrested in February 2001 and held for questioning in an investigation under the Prevention of Terrorism (Temporary Provisions) Act 1989. During a search of his home, the police found and seized a substantial amount of money in cash in a number of different currencies. His two bank accounts were furthermore frozen in implementation of measures determined by the Sanctions Committee. In December 2001, Mr Othman went into hiding fearing arrest and indefinite detention. He was arrested by the police and held in prison in the UK from October 2002 to March 2005, when he was released, under strict surveillance, following a judgement by the House of Lords holding that the UK scheme of 'detention without trial', to which he was subject, was unlawful. He was once more arrested on 11 August 2005 and held in prison under the new UK anti-terrorist measures. Mr Othman unsuccessfully appealed the decision to deport him to Jordan and to hold him pending deportation, but the decision has not been given effect pending the outcome of the action before the ECtHR.
4   See Case T-318/01 *Othman v. Council and Commission* [2009] ECR II-1627, at para. 82. See also Cases C-399/06 P and C-403/06 P *Hassan v. Council and Commission, and Ayadi v. Council* [2009] ECR I-11393.
5   T-315/01 *Kadi v. Council and Commission* [2005] ECR II-3649 ('*Kadi I*').
6   Joined Cases C-402/05 P and C-415/05 P *Kadi and Al Barakaat International Foundation v. Council and Commission* [2008] ECR I-6351 ('*Kadi II*').
7   Case T-85/09 *Kadi v. Commission* [2010] ECR II-5177 ('*Kadi III*').
8   Joined Cases C-584/10 P, C-593/10 P, and C-595/10 P *Commission v. Kadi*, Judgment of 18 July 2013 (not yet reported) ('*Kadi IV*').

An excessive amount has been written on the *Kadi* saga so far.[9] Many of these comments concentrate on how EU law is bad, insufficient or immature[10] when it does not deliver the justice that Mr Kadi has been calling for. Instead of engaging in a passionate defence of the EU regime, I wish to argue that the problem for Mr Kadi in receiving justice in the EU Courts is rather one of 'field constitution', the language used to structure the relevant social field so as to attain particular normative conclusions,[11] in this case the way in which the CJEU sees itself limited to 'safeguard what it perceives to be the integrity and the values of the EU legal order'[12] or a 'defence of the realm' of the autonomy of the EU legal order. Such a choice of language forms a prior political decision, which finally leads to a choice of which authority should have the competence to deal with the matter.[13] If the 'field constitution' determining the possible outcomes of Mr Kadi's case is so stringent that only certain outcomes are possible, then there is little hope for Mr Kadi in the new steps in the EU judicial saga: they will simply reinforce earlier evaluations and institutional choices.[14] Instead, the situation has called for 'Kadi justice', as Jan Klabbers has called it:

> a shorthand for the idea that meaningful and just judgments need not always be based on the application of legal rules, but that justice

---

9   For a critical summary of the comments by international and European law scholars until *Kadi II*, see Sara Poli and Maria Tzanou, 'The *Kadi* Rulings: A Survey of the Literature', 28 *Yearbook of European Law* (2009) 533–58.

10 From the point of view of the role of international law in the EU legal order, see, for example, Jan Klabbers, '*Völkerrechtsfreundlich*? International Law and the Union Legal Order' in Panos Koutrakos (ed.), *European Foreign Policy: Legal and Political Aspects* (Edward Elgar, 2011) 95–114, at 97–9, 114. On the other hand, similar claims are often made of international law, see Martti Koskenniemi, 'The Fate of Public International Law: Between Technique and Politics', 70 *Modern Law Review* (2007) 1–30, at 1–2.

11 See Martti Koskenniemi, 'The Effect of Rights on Political Culture', in Philip Alston *et al.* (eds), *The EU and Human Rights* (Oxford University Press, 1999) 99–116, at 106.

12 Takis Tridimas, 'The Principle of Legality, Human Rights and the Management of Risks', in Malcolm Evans and Panos Koutrakos (eds), *Beyond the Established Legal Orders: Policy Interconnections between the EU and the Rest of the World* (Hart, 2011) 179–202, at 182.

13 See Koskenniemi, 'The Effect of Rights', *supra* note 11, at 106. Focusing on the choice of language as the key moment at which both procedural and substantive political priorities are set, this is a method resembles that developed by Foucault (from whom in fact, it has been received), for whom, too, 'discourse' is prior to politics. Michel Foucault, *The Order of Things: An Archaeology of the Human Sciences* (Tavistock/Routledge, 1970/2004), at xiv.

14 This is not to say that a discussion of competence and legal basis might not occasionally contribute to getting people off the sanctions lists, as was recently the case for Mr Pye Phyo Tay Za. See Case C-376/10 P *Tay Za v. Council*, Judgement of 13 March 2012 (not yet reported), in which the Court's Grand Chamber found that ex-Articles 60 and 301 TEC could not be used as a legal basis for restrictive measures against Myanmar to the extent that these were directed at 'natural persons on the sole ground of their family connection with persons associated with the leaders of the third country concerned, irrespective of the personal conduct of such natural persons' (para. 66).

may sometimes be equally well served by decisions based on the individual senses of right and wrong of those making the decisions, and that such a system may usefully complement the Rule of Law.[15]

Mr Kadi's agony is related to nothing less than the United Nations Charter, which provides that the decisions of the Security Council for the maintenance of international peace and security are to be carried out by the UN Member States directly and through their action in the appropriate international agencies.[16] The obligations prevail over the UN members' other obligations under any other international agreement. As is evident from a study of *Kadi I* and *Kadi II*, and even some of the previous case law,[17] much of the focus of the EU Courts has been on the choice of legal basis and the existence of competence to adopt the EU act. As Klabbers has found, the EU Courts have tended to pay less attention to the Security Council measure and instead focus on the EU implementing act.[18] The EU Court cases have dwelled at length on the question of 'primacy of which system over the other'[19] and the relationship between international law and EU law, even if it has been long acknowledged that the Union 'must respect international law in the exercise of its powers.'[20] Advocate General (AG) Maduro emphasised in his *Kadi* Opinion the main function of the CJEU as evidenced by case law:

> although the Court takes great care to respect the obligations that are incumbent on the Community by virtue of international law, it seeks, first and foremost, to preserve the constitutional framework created by the Treaty.[21]

This vision and constitutional function determines the field constitution of the *Kadi* discourse in the EU – even if a certain amount of constitutional imagination has never been entirely unknown to the CJEU either, would it feel the urge to use it. The field constitution needs to be examined from the

---

15 Jan Klabbers, 'Kadi Justice at the Security Council?', 4 *International Organizations Law Review* (2007) 293–304 at 294.
16 Article 48(2) of the UN Charter. In the legal order of the EU, the implementation of the said Charter provisions is guaranteed by the current Article 351 TFEU and Article 347 TFEU.
17 Case C-84/95 *Bosphorus Hava Yollari Turizm ve Ticaret AS* [1996] ECR I-3953.
18 Klabbers, '*Völkerrechtsfreundlich?*', *supra* note 10, at 107.
19 For one analysis of the 2005 rulings, see Christian Tomuschat, 'Case T-306/01, *Ahmed Ali Yusuf and Al Barakaat International Foundation v. Council and Commission*; Case T-315/01, *Yassin Abdullah Kadi v. Council and Commission*', 43 *Common Market Law Review* (2006) 537–51.
20 Case C-162/96 *A. Racke GmbH & Co. v. Hauptzollamt Mainz* [1998] ECR I-3655, at para. 45. For an analysis, see Jan Klabbers, 'Annotation to case C-162/96, *Racke v. Hauptzollamt Mainz*', 36 *Common Market Law Review* (1999) 179–89.
21 *Kadi II*, *supra* note 6, Opinion of Advocate General Poiares Maduro, at para. 24.

point of view of Mr Kadi; his interest in getting off the sanctions list. The *Kadi III* ruling strikes as somewhat different compared with the previous lot: since the CJEU had already previously interpreted the same legal framework, the General Court now had no need to analyse the same spectrum of questions for a second time, but could concentrate on the procedural dimension; thus, the premises of *Kadi III* differ from the earlier case law on the matter.

The *Kadi* saga also represents one of the dilemmas of fragmentation and the anxiety of 'losing control'[22] in a world governed by specialised regimes. From this perspective, the question is whether there is another field constitution that might be more responsive to the wishes of Mr Kadi. In the UN, despite the lack of a comprehensive and balanced approach taking account of both the security concerns and the rights of the terrorism suspects at the same time, some additional procedural guarantees have been put in place and could in the best case scenario help Mr Kadi. The problem is, even in the UN the fight against terrorism has been largely focused on security, and the modest human rights guarantees are a result of the need to reply to concerns before they actually challenge the regime more fundamentally. The human rights organs might be Mr Kadi's best chance – but will they deliver justice?

2 The 'field constitution' in *Kadi I* and *Kadi II*

What exactly does the 'field constitution' defined by the EU Courts' jurisprudence look like? In *Kadi I*, Mr Kadi put forward three grounds of annulment alleging breaches of his fundamental rights: the right to a fair hearing, respect for property and the principle of proportionality and, finally, breach of the right to effective judicial review. All of these are essentially 'human rights grounds' – but this is not the language that has traditionally been the most helpful basis for arguments in the EU Courts.[23] Later, and perhaps for this reason, Mr Kadi put forward a fourth ground, alleging lack of competence and that the relevant acts had been adopted *ultra vires*. The way that the General Court and the CJEU have analysed Mr Kadi's case has, however, followed a different pattern entirely, focusing on four factors: the questions of legal basis and competence; the relationship between EU law and international law; and the scope of judicial review. Only then, finally, have the Courts felt prepared to examine some of Mr Kadi's human rights arguments, but largely limiting to a study of his procedural rights, which is closely linked the Courts' own role in securing judicial review. For example, Mr Kadi's arguments relating to his right of property have only been briefly touched upon.

---

22 See Martti Koskenniemi and Päivi Leino, 'Fragmentation of International Law? Postmodern Anxieties', 15 *Leiden Journal of International Law* (2002) 553–79.
23 Cf. *Tay Za v. Council, supra* note 14.

First, as regards the choice of legal basis and competence, the General Court decided, in *Kadi I*, to consider whether the Council had been competent to adopt the contested regulation and used the correct legal bases. With this decision, the Court turned the matter to a large extent to a rather traditional case of competence, where a substantive part[24] of its considerations concerned competence and the choice of legal basis instead of a human rights examination, which the applicant had asked for. Ultimately, the Court confirmed the choice of legal basis by the Council. In the appeal stage, AG Maduro also speculated thoroughly at the Council's choice of legal basis, disagreeing with the conclusion of the General Court. He, none the less, believed that

> where pleas are raised concerning alleged breaches of fundamental rights, it is preferable for the Court to make use of the possibility of reviewing those pleas as well, both for reasons of legal certainty and in order to prevent a possible breach of fundamental rights from subsisting in the Community legal order, albeit by virtue of a measure that merely has a different form or legal basis.[25]

The CJEU was not fully convinced of the need to engage in such an analysis. Instead, in *Kadi II*, the CJEU discussed the choice of legal basis thoroughly, finally confirming that the Council's choice had been correct. This is clearly one element of the field constitution.

A second precondition for a substantive examination has, in the Courts' view, been a thorough examination of the relationship between the international legal order of the United Nations and the domestic or Community legal order: a consideration that effectively determines the scope of review of lawfulness undertaken by the Courts themselves. The General Court found in *Kadi I* that EU law 'must be interpreted, and its scope limited, in the light of the relevant rules of international law'.[26] Since the provisions of the UN Charter have the effect of binding the Union, the latter must adopt all the measures necessary to enable its Member States to fulfil their UN obligations.[27] Even AG Maduro reflected in depth on the relationship between the two legal orders, arguing that the Community's municipal legal order and the international legal order in no way 'pass each other like ships in the night'.[28] The CJEU continued the discussion concerning the relationship between the two legal regimes and ultimately rejected the claimed 'immunity from jurisdiction'[29] – a precondition for an analysis of the scope of judicial review, which has seemed to form the third core issue in many ways.

---

24 *Kadi I, supra* note 5, paras 64–135.
25 *Kadi II, supra* note 6, Opinion of Advocate General Poiares Maduro, at para. 16.
26 *Kadi I, supra* note 5, at paras 190 and 199, respectively.
27 *Ibid.*, at para. 204.
28 See *Kadi II, supra* note 6, Opinion of Advocate General Poiares Maduro, at para. 22.
29 See *Kadi II, supra* note 6, paras 300, 305.

A crucial question all along has been what kind of judicial review is on offer in the EU: whether the Security Council resolutions at issue fall outside the ambit of the Court's judicial review and, if not, what level of scrutiny is required. In principle, of course, the regulation implementing the relevant Security Council resolution is a Union measure of 'direct and individual concern to an individual', and as such this fact alone should suffice to guarantee that the Union judicial machinery stands to provide the necessary judicial safeguards to protect the individual from the institutions acting in bad faith, or in breach of their Treaty obligations.[30] But what happens when the Union institutions are only acting to give effect to a previous UN measure, and in doing so have no discretion and, in fact, no idea as to whether proper evidence supports the necessary conclusion?

The Court General seemed clearly aware of such complexities when it confirmed, in *Kadi I*, that it had no authority to question the lawfulness of Security Council resolutions as such but would instead rely on a method of interpretation and thus apply EU law in a manner compatible with the Member States' UN obligations.[31] There was some room for review: the Court could check the lawfulness of the Security Council resolutions with regard to *jus cogens*,[32] and carry out a complete review of lawfulness with regard to the institutions' rules of jurisdiction, external lawfulness and essential procedural requirements. In this context, the Court would also review the procedural and substantive appropriateness of the regulation; its internal consistency and proportionality in relation to the relevant Security Council resolutions.[33] However, there were clear limits to the EU Court's review function: it would not assess even indirectly the compatibility of the Security Council's resolutions with Union fundamental rights, or examine whether there had been an error of assessment of facts and evidence or whether the relevant measures were appropriate and proportionate, since such a review would be impossible to carry out without trespassing on the Security Council's prerogatives.[34]

The CJEU's line of interpretation, in *Kadi II*, was more extensive and required the Union judicature to 'ensure the review, in principle the full review, of the lawfulness of all Community acts in the light of the fundamental rights forming an integral part of the general principles of Community law'.[35] Such a review also applied to measures now at stake, i.e. a Union measure designed to give effect to a Security Council resolution.

---

30 See Article 263 TFEU.
31 *Kadi I, supra* note 5, at para. 225.
32 The Court defined *jus cogens* as a 'body of higher rules of public international law binding on all subjects of international law, including the bodies of the United Nations, and from which no derogation is possible'. *Ibid.*, at para. 226.
33 See *ibid.*, at paras 279–80.
34 *Ibid.*, at paras 283–4.
35 *Kadi II, supra* note 6, at para. 326.

And not surprisingly, it is the words 'in principle the full review', which have since then formed the main question of interpretation: does this require a 'principle of full review', this is, 'full review without any exceptions', or 'in principle, the full review' – but in practice a bit less? The Court's reasoning circled strongly around its own role in securing judicial review: a task it could not undertake because the contested regulation had been so poorly reasoned. Communication of the grounds is, the Court argued, necessary for the rights of defence and to enable the applicant to consider the usefulness of an appeal, on the one hand, and to enable the judicature to review the lawfulness of the Union measure, on the other.[36] The CJEU was not convinced of the arguments claiming that review could not take place without risking the element of unpredictability required for sanctions to work: judicial review could take into account this objective through techniques that accommodate legitimate security concerns and 'the need to accord the individual a sufficient measure of procedural justice'.[37]

But discussion of competence, system talk concerning the intriguing interrelationships between the different legal regimes or even thorough exploration of the scope of review of each Court are no guarantee of a quick delivery justice. Only then – after having established the appropriate standard of review – have the Courts considered it appropriate to consider the substantive claims of Mr Kadi. The General Court found, in *Kadi I*, that ultimately the sanctions directed at Mr Kadi could be upheld: the challenged measures did pursue an objective of fundamental public interest for the international community, and underlined that the freezing of funds affecting Mr Kadi was only a 'temporary precautionary measure'. As a consequence, the freezing of funds could not be considered 'an arbitrary, inappropriate or disproportionate interference with the fundamental rights of the persons concerned'.[38] The limited discretion of the EU institutions in giving effect to the Security Council resolutions made it not worthwhile to hear Mr Kadi, since no hearing could alter the outcome. While this undoubtedly constituted a limitation of Mr Kadi's right of access to a court it was a justified one; thus there was no reason to annul the regulation.

Mr Kadi was not satisfied with this conclusion and appealed. He found support in AG Maduro, who was dissatisfied with *Kadi I* in terms of the right to be heard and the right to effective judicial review: 'it is unacceptable in a democratic society to impair the very essence of that right'.[39] Many of the

---

36 *Ibid.*, at para. 337.
37 *Ibid.*, at para. 344. In the security context, the ECJ has previously accepted that transparency can be more limited as it argued in *Sison* that 'The Community Court's review of the legality of such a decision must therefore be limited to verifying whether the procedural rules and the duty to state reasons have been complied with, whether the facts have been accurately stated, and whether there has been a manifest error of assessment or a misuse of powers'. Case C-266/05 P *Sison v. Council* [2007] ECR I-1233, at para. 34.
38 *Kadi I*, *supra* note 5, at paras 248–51.
39 *Kadi II*, *supra* note 6, Opinion of Advocate General Poiares Maduro, at paras 51–2.

facts gave him cause to worry. There was a real possibility that the EU sanctions against Mr Kadi were disproportionate or even misdirected, and could remain in place indefinitely. Maduro encouraged the CJEU to annul the regulation due to infringements of the right to be heard, the right to judicial review and the right to property. So far, in fact, AG Maduro's Opinion strikes as the most original contribution since he speaks, at least for a part of the time, a different language from that of the EU Courts; the language of human rights instead of the language of competence.

The CJEU spent, in *Kadi II*, much less time discussing the human rights related elements, but agreed with AG Maduro's conclusion as regards the procedural shortcomings and established a breach of Mr Kadi's rights of defence, since he had not been able to defend his rights properly before the EU Courts. Moreover, the CJEU found that the imposition of the restrictive measures in respect of Mr Kadi constituted an unjustified restriction of his right to property. As a result, the CJEU annulled the regulation as regards Mr Kadi.

In terms of the field constitution, it is important to note that so far, the CJEU has not engaged in any sort of a balancing act between the need for public security and the prevention of terrorism, on the one hand, and the protection of the rights of the individual, on the other.[40] There has perhaps been no need since the procedural shortcomings have been so pathetically obvious: no statement of reasons has had the joyful company of a complete absence of the rights of defence. Therefore, while *Kadi II* confirms that the executive enjoys no immunity, it is silent on the standards by which it will be held accountable.[41] The question thus is: whether the EU judicature will ever be prepared to engage in such an analysis, or whether this falls outside its field constitution.

3 The 2010 ruling: 'In principle the full review' – and finally, the Sanctions Committee speaks

In *Kadi II*, the CJEU maintained the effects of the annulled act for a period of not more than three months in order to provide an opportunity to remedy the infringements. The ruling had, of course, no direct bearing on the UN Sanctions Committee or its listing procedures, but the Committee did provide a summary of reasons for Mr Kadi's inclusion on the sanctions list, which was transmitted to him and published on the internet. The Commission informed Mr Kadi of its plan to adopt a legal act maintaining his listing and gave him the opportunity to comment on the grounds and to provide any additional information. A month later, Mr Kadi requested the Commission to disclose the relevant evidence and to provide him an

---

40 See Takis Tridimas, 'The Principle of Legality, Human Rights and the Management of Risks', in Malcolm Evans and Panos Koutrakos (eds), *Beyond the Established Legal Orders: Policy Interconnections between the EU and the Rest of the World* (Hart, 2011) 179–202, at 182–3.
41 *Ibid.*

opportunity to comment on such evidence, and attempted to refute the allegations made in the summary by providing evidence supporting his claims. But instead of engaging in a discussion, the Commission, under pressure from the Court's three months deadline and the listing made by the UN that required implementing in the EU, simply adopted a new Regulation, where it justified the further inclusion of Mr Kadi in the Annex. Later, the Commission sent him a letter arguing that the summary of reasons was enough to comply with the Court's judgement and that it had been entitled to disregard the evidence put forward by Mr Kadi. In *Kadi III*, where the sufficiency of these measures came to be scrutinised, the General Court could embark more directly on a human rights analysis, since the CJEU had already taken a position on many of the core parameters (legal basis,[42] competence, relationship between EU and international law and the scope of judicial review). As a consequence, the ruling had a different emphasis.

As regards the field constitution, a question of interest is whether the reforms in the Treaty of Lisbon, which came into force in December 2009, between *Kadi II* and *Kadi III*, would have any effect on the outcome, since they do have the general objective of improving the legal protection of terrorism suspects. In addition to a legally binding Charter of Fundamental Rights, now applicable in all areas of EU action, the Treaty provisions relating to restrictive measures were specifically developed to establish that when the Council adopts such measures against natural or legal persons and groups or non-State entities, these acts would include necessary provisions on legal safeguards.[43] Similarly, the provisions regarding the EU Courts' jurisdiction were widened to specify that while the Courts, in general, have no jurisdiction in the area of common foreign and security policy, they do have jurisdiction to review the legality of decisions providing for restrictive measures against natural or legal persons.[44] Thus, one wonders: what kind of 'legal safeguards' did the Treaty-makers have in mind and what could they deliver for Mr Kadi? Surely a 'review of legality' should be wider than the previous Court review, which had been restricted to procedural matters?

In *Kadi III*, the General Court first stressed, following *Kadi II*, its task to now ensure 'in principle the full review' of the lawfulness of the contested regulation in the light of fundamental rights, without affording any immunity from jurisdiction. The need of such review was linked to the lack of effective judicial protection through the UN Sanctions Committee or the Office of the Ombudsperson, which did not, in its view, constitute an independent and impartial body that could be responsible for hearing and

---

42 This is of course not to say that the questions concerning the legal basis for sanctions would now have been settled for all eternity. For a recent ruling concerning the relationship between Article 75 TFEU and Article 215 TFEU, see C-130/10 *Parliament v. Council*, Judgment of 19 July 2012 (not yet reported).
43 Article 24 TEU and Article 215(2) and (3) TFEU.
44 Article 275 TFEU.

determining actions against individual Sanctions Committee decisions. The Court was concerned about the requirement of consensus among the Sanctions Committee members for removal from the list, and the fact that evidence was not shared between the Members; consequently, there was no mechanism to ensure that the persons concerned were given sufficient information for their effective defence. CJEU criticism in *Kadi II* thus remained fundamentally valid.

As regards the scope of judicial review, the Court referred to its case law concerning the People's Mojahedin Organisation of Iran (the so-called *PMOI* jurisprudence):

> The Community judicature must not only establish whether the evidence relied on is factually accurate, reliable and consistent, but must also ascertain whether that evidence contains all the relevant information to be taken into account in order to assess the situation and whether it is capable of substantiating the conclusions drawn from it.[45]

It underlined the effect of fund-freezing measures on those being subject to them, pointing out to how all Mr Kadi's funds and other assets had been 'indefinitely frozen for nearly 10 years' and without any chance of gaining access to them without an exemption from the UN Sanctions Committee.[46] With this argument, it is perhaps useful to point out, the General Court took a clear distance from its own argumentation in *Kadi I* relating to the temporary nature of the measures: the measures had in practice proved to be nothing but temporary.

The Court was not convinced by the sufficiency of the measures undertaken by the Commission to comply with the CJEU ruling: providing a summary of reasons containing a 'number of general, unsubstantiated, vague and unparticularised allegations' and supported by no evidence did little to satisfy the requirements of a fair hearing and effective judicial protection – instead Mr Kadi should have been able to rebut the

---

45 *Kadi III*, supra note 7, at para. 142. The General Court refers in paras 137–147 to the jurisprudence concerning Council Regulation (EC) No 2580/2001 of 27 December 2001 on specific restrictive measures directed against certain persons and entities with a view to combating terrorism, OJ 2001 L 344/70 – Case T-228/02 *Organisation des Modjahedines du peuple d'Iran v. Council* [2006] ECR II-4665, Case T-256/07 *People's Mojahedin Organization of Iran v. Council* [2008] ECR II-3019 and Case T-284/08 *People's Mojahedin Organization of Iran v. Council* [2008] ECR II-3487 – and points out that the CJEU has used some of these justifications in the *Kadi* ruling. It is, however, unclear to what extent the same criteria are applicable. While both are based on Security Council resolutions, in SC Res. 1373 of 28 September 2001 the Council does not, in fact, identify individuals but this is left to UN Member States. The Council takes these decisions itself based on available documentation and internal preparation.

46 *Kadi III*, supra note 7, at para. 149.

allegations.[47] Mr Kadi's rights of defence had been observed only in the most formal and superficial sense without any perspective of questioning the outcome.[48] The fact that the General Court itself had been unable to undertake a review of the lawfulness of the contested regulation was yet another reason to conclude that Mr Kadi's fundamental right to effective judicial review had been breached.[49] Consequently, the contested regulation, so far as it concerns Mr Kadi, was annulled again.

The General Court was rather clear in establishing that there must be a review, but again, focused merely on the procedural requirements set in *Kadi II*. And unfortunately for Mr Kadi, the ruling, even if largely confirming Mr Kadi's arguments, provided him with no quick relief, since it was immediately appealed by both the Commission, the Council and the UK, a high number of Member States[50] have intervened in support of their arguments, basically stating that the Court got it wrong, and that its analysis of the CJEU's 'in principle the full review' was mistaken. Therefore, the story will continue, and Mr Kadi's agony will continue as far as the EU remedies are concerned, since the annulled regulation will stand as long as the appeal is pending.[51]

Rescue arrived at a point in time when few believed that the UN Sanctions Committee would ever engage itself in Mr Kadi's matter – after all, the strengthening of the UN mechanisms had taken place after his case became pending. A couple of days before the oral hearing in *Kadi IV* was to take place in Luxembourg, the Al-Qaida Sanctions Committee announced it had decided, following review of a delisting request submitted through the office of the Ombudsperson and based an extensive report by the latter, to remove Mr Kadi from its sanctions list.[52] Subsequently, the assets freeze, travel ban and arms embargo ceased to apply to Mr Kadi without further ado or public justification. This decision was implemented by the European Commission on 11 October 2012, and entered into force in all EU Member States two days later.[53] Even if Mr Kadi's agony therefore has now come to an sudden

---

47 *Ibid.*, at para. 157.
48 *Ibid.*, at para. 171.
49 *Ibid.*, at para. 183.
50 According to the Order of the President of the Court of 23 May 2011, in addition to the Council and the Commission, the UK and France, the Czech Republic, Spain, Austria, Ireland and Denmark have intervened in support of the Council, and the Netherlands, Luxembourg, the Slovak Republic, Bulgaria, Italy and Finland have intervened in support of the Council, the Commission and the UK.
51 See Protocol (No 3) on the Statute of the Court of Justice of the EU, OJ 2012 C 326/210, Article 60.
52 Press Release: Security Council Al-Qaida Sanctions Committee Deletes Entry of Yasin Abdullah Ezzedine Qadi from Its List, UN Doc. SC/10785, 5 October 2012.
53 Commission Implementing Regulation (EU) No 933/2012 of 11 October 2012 amending for the one hundred and eightieth time Council Regulation (EC) No 881/2002 imposing certain specific restrictive measures directed against certain persons and entities associated with the Al Qaida network, OJ 2012 L 278/11.

end, 11 years after it began, his case remains pending before the CJEU at least for the time being, and it is to be wished that the CJEU pronounces itself on the points of law before it, not least because the same considerations remain relevant for others in Mr Kadi's previous position.

It would seem unlikely that the CJEU would now be satisfied with the formal procedural safeguards that were quickly put in place after *Kadi II*, especially noting its clear annoyance with the Council more recently in other similar cases.[54] In March and April 2012 the General Court delivered two further judgements relating to restrictive measures where the Court annulled the contested measures since, in its view, the Council had not managed to adduce proof of some of its allegations.[55] The reforms brought by the Treaty of Lisbon – which the General Court did not find necessary to resort to in support of its conclusion in *Kadi III*[56] – would also support such a finding. But at the same time, the CJEU is likely to remain true to the constraints of its mission: preserving the constitutional framework created by the Treaty. So far, the EU Courts have not needed to step outside their own comfort zone, and there has been little need to do so.

But the position of the EU legislature is also uncomfortable, even if it – or at least some heavyweight members of the Council – has some limited say in how the UN sanctions procedures operate. The Lisbon Treaty reforms relating to sanctions have so far merely symbolised an acknowledgement that certain safeguards are necessary, but these are easier to realise for some sanctions than for others.[57] When the role of the EU legislature is limited to simply giving effect to a previous UN decision, as is the case in the Al-Qaida regime, then these safeguards will be difficult to guarantee. From Mr Kadi's perspective, the function of judicial review has made itself known: courts can annul individual measures, and even establish certain criteria for future consideration by the legislature. But it is only this far that a Court – even one with a clear bias to protect its own institutional prerogatives – will stretch. In particular, EU Courts cannot engage in full-scale international law-making, the responsibility for which remains on the agenda of the United Nations, where the relevant bodies have so far had only a limited interest in addressing some of the most fundamental deficits of the sanction procedures.

---

54 See *Othman v. Council and Commission, supra* note 4, at para. 97, where the CJEU refused to maintain the effects of the contested acts; after all, due to *Kadi II*, the Council should have been aware of the relevant requirements
55 See Joined Cases T-439/10 and T-440/10 *Fulmen and Fereydoun Mahmoudian v. Council*, Judgment of 21 March 2012 (not yet reported), at paras 103–104, and Case T-509/10 *Manufacturing Support & Procurement Kala Naft v. Council*, Judgment of 25 April 2012 (not yet reported), at para. 125.
56 See, however, *Fulmen and Fereydoun Mahmoudian v. Council, supra* note 55, at para 87.
57 Cf. in relation to the regime based on SC Res. 1373, 28 September 2001, where the Security Council does not, in fact, identify individuals but this is left to UN Member States. In the EU, the Council takes these decisions itself based on available documentation and internal preparation.

4 The security constitution: What role for human rights?

While the EU judicature has in the context of anti-terrorism measures so far been mainly concerned about questions of its own competence and considerations relating to procedure, globally, the discussion evolving around the fight against terrorism has tended to circle around the objective of security. Even though the claims presented by Mr Kadi before the EU Courts constitute rather traditional rights talk, he has had difficulties in finding a forum that would address his claims in the same language. Globally, the confusion between 'security talk' and 'rights talk' has led to security being presented as a collective good. An example of this is the United Nations Global Counter-Terrorism Strategy from 2006, where the UN Member States resolve

> To consistently, unequivocally and strongly condemn terrorism in all its forms and manifestations, committed by whomever, wherever and for whatever purposes, as it constitutes one of the most serious threats to international peace and security;
>
> To take urgent action to prevent and combat terrorism in all its forms and manifestations ... .[58]

The UN Global Counter-Terrorism Strategy is an excellent example of a security-based constitution, where the individual is not primarily conceived of as a bearer of rights but, instead, as a potential security risk. As Tuori has demonstrated, unlike in 'traditional' rule-of-law and *Rechtstaat* constitutionalism, 'security talk is not rights talk; rights are neither the aim nor the means of constitutionalisation but rather its putative limit.'[59] Individuals, in their turn, are treated as a potential risk exactly because they are subjects of rights. Tuori continues,

> According to traditional rule-of-law and *Rechtstaat* constitutionalism, individual rights were supposed to impose constraints on the measures that could be taken in order to promote general security. If security is re-conceptualised as a constitutional right, it is absorbed within the constitution and assigned (at least) equal weight as individual and political rights. Constitutionalisation of the security system entails the danger of a reversal of the relationship between security as a collective good or public interest and individual liberty rights: the danger of according default primacy to the former instead of the latter.[60]

---

58 GA Res. 60/288, 20 September 2006, at paras 1–2.
59 Kaarlo Tuori, 'European Security Constitution', in Martin Scheinin *et al.*, 'Law and Security: Facing the Dilemmas', *EUI Working Papers* LAW 2009/11, 1–6, at 5. Tuori uses the Presidency Conclusions of the Tampere European Council of 15 and 16 October 1999, Doc. no. 200/1/99, as his example.
60 Tuori, 'European Security Constitution', *supra* note 59, at 5.

In such a 'field constitution', there is an obvious risk that the rights of terrorism suspects might not get the attention they merit, or that the right of the general public to security is treated as absolute with little attention given to how such security is actually secured. In terrorism-related debates in general, human rights – and in particular those of terrorism suspects – at most figure as an afterthought. In the UN action plan quoted above, for example, it is only the final part of the plan that relates to the need to respect human rights.[61] The same pattern applies to the EU's own Counter-Terrorism Strategy,[62] which states the Union's strategic commitment to combat terrorism globally while respecting human rights. However, human rights-related concerns are effectively only discussed in the context of a 'range of conditions which may create an environment in which individuals can become more easily radicalised'; a reason for the Union to 'promote even more rigorously good governance, human rights, democracy as well as education and economic prosperity, and engage in conflict resolution'.[63] No mention is made of the potential effect of counter-terrorism measures themselves on the realisation of human rights. For such a vocal proponent of international human rights, which the EU wishes to be seen as,[64] surely this is a rather fundamental omission?

This is not to claim that no one would have realised that, occasionally, human rights of terrorism suspects might be at stake when anti-terrorism measures are adopted.[65] Even the UN Sanctions Committee procedures have experienced some slow progress since the adoption of the first post-September 11 measures. First, the Security Council adopted a de-listing procedure and requested the Secretary General to establish a focal point for such requests;[66] a regime that proved less than helpful, since the requirement of consensus in the Sanctions Committee practically hindered any de-listing, and because the powers of the focal point were extremely limited. Second, the Security Council subsequently strengthened the regime by

---

61 GA Res. 60/288, 20 September 2006, Annex, pt. IV: 'Recognizing that effective counter-terrorism measures and the protection of human rights are not conflicting goals, but complementary and mutually reinforcing, and stressing the need to promote and protect the rights of victims of terrorism.'
62 The European Union Counter-Terrorism Strategy, EU Doc. 14469/4/05 REV 4, 30 November 2005, forwarded to the Justice and Home Affairs Council of 1 December 2005 for agreement and subsequently adopted by the European Council. For a discussion, see Jan Klabbers, 'Europe's Counter-terrorism Law(s): Outlines of a Critical Approach', in Malcolm Evans and Panos Koutrakos (eds), *Beyond the Established Legal Orders: Policy Interconnections between the EU and the Rest of the World* (Hart, 2011) 205–24, at 212.
63 See EU Counter-Terrorism Strategy, *supra* note 62, at para. 1.
64 For a discussion of the EU's role as the messenger of good values, see Päivi Leino, 'Journey towards All That is Good and Beautiful: Fundamental Rights and "Common Values" as Guiding Principles of EU Foreign Relations Law' in Marise Cremona and Bruno de Witte (eds), *EU Foreign Relations Law: Constitutional Fundamentals* (Hart, 2008), ch. 9.
65 For perhaps the most eloquent presentation of the core arguments, see Philippe Sands, *Lawless World: America and the Making and Breaking of Global Rules* (Allen Lane, 2005).
66 SC Res. 1730, 19 December 2006.

establishing the Office of the Ombudsperson to assist the Sanctions Committee in the consideration of delisting requests and with a strengthened role in entering a dialogue with the designating States and to gather information through a particular Monitoring Team.[67] Following these reforms, some previously listed persons and entities have, in fact, been delisted,[68] including, more recently, a Mr Kadi of Saudi Arabia.

But these improvements have failed to satisfy the critics. The UN's own Special Rapporteur on the promotion and protection of human rights and fundamental freedoms while countering terrorism[69] has consistently held that the role of the Security Council has transformed into a judicial or quasi-judicial one, at the same time as 'its procedures continue to fall short of the fundamental principles of due process as reflected in international human rights treaties and customary international law'.[70] Even after the improvements mentioned above, the main problem with the mechanism from the targets' point of view remains largely the same: those who are

> dissatisfied with the freeze of their assets or the restriction of their movement can only hope that their state of residence or citizenship will negotiate with whatever country had recommended their listing (designating state) to reach a mutual agreement to recommend the delisting of the individual.[71]

Keeping in mind the fundamental nature of these concerns, one could expect that some serious questioning of the global security constitution would flow from diverse human rights bodies, which have various mandates to evaluate the relevant measures, either following appeals or at their own initiative, against their own constitution formed by various human rights instruments. But even these bodies have proved sensitive to the rules of the security constitution. The ECtHR has, for example, had the opportunity to address various anti-terrorism measures several times, both before and after 11 September 2001. In *Chahal v. UK* the Human Rights Court accepted that Article 13 of the European Convention on Human Rights 'only required a

---

67 SC Res. 1904, 17 December 2009. Following a period of two months, the Ombudsperson presents to the Committee the principal arguments concerning the delisting request. After the Committee consideration, it decides whether to approve the delisting request through its normal decision-making procedures. The Ombudsman Office was further strengthened by SC Res. 1989, 17 June 2011.
68 For an updated list, see <www.un.org/sc/committees/1267/latest.shtml>
69 GA Res. 64/168, 18 December 2009, and HRC Res. 13/26, 26 March 2010.
70 Report of the Special Rapporteur on the Promotion and Protection of Human Rights and Fundamental Freedoms while Countering Terrorism, UN Doc. A/65/258, 6 August 2010, at para. 70.
71 Jared Genser and Kate Barth, 'When Due Process Concerns Become Dangerous: The Security Council's 1267 Regime and the Need for Reform', 33 *Boston College International & Comparative Law Review* (2010) 1–42, at 3.

remedy that was "as effective as can be" in circumstances where national security considerations did not permit the divulging of certain sensitive information'.[72] In its 2011 Grand Chamber ruling in *Al-Jedda v. the UK*, the Human Rights Court had much understanding to the needs of security and ultimately relied on tools of interpretation. After a thorough explanation of the functions of the United Nations and the Security Council, the Court argued, it must be presumed that the latter

> does not intend to impose any obligation on Member States to breach fundamental principles of human rights. In the event of any ambiguity in the terms of a Security Council Resolution, the Court must therefore choose the interpretation which is most in harmony with the requirements of the Convention and which avoids any conflict of obligations. In the light of the United Nations' important role in promoting and encouraging respect for human rights, it is to be expected that clear and explicit language would be used were the Security Council to intend States to take particular measures which would conflict with their obligations under international human rights law.[73]

Possible conflict was thus to be resolved through interpretation. But in the situation of Mr Kadi or his fellow-suspects, tools of interpretation might not just deliver the outcome he has persistently been asking for: either your name is on the list, or it is not on the list, there is no middle way. The case of *Al-Jedda* also illustrates how the choice of field constitution is determinative of the outcome. Even if the matter could have been equally well examined from the perspective of 'security' as well as from that of 'human rights', the Court's reasoning demonstrated a clear bias towards security; and this 'choice of the frame determined the decision'.[74]

In the human rights bodies one could, however, expect a different bias towards human rights. The UN Human Rights Committee has, in fact, in a case concerning the existence of a possible duty for Belgium to initiate a delisting procedure with the United Nations Sanctions Committee, examined the matter from a human rights point of view, but needed to give in to certain realities of competence relating to its own function and the competence of the Member States as limited by the procedures of the UN Sanctions Committee. The Human Rights Committee underlined that

> the State party is bound to provide the authors with an effective remedy. Although the State party is itself not competent to remove

---

72   *Chahal v. UK*, Application no. 22414/93, ECtHR Grand Chamber, Judgment of 15 November 1996, at para. 150.
73   *Al-Jedda v. UK*, Application no. 27021/08, ECtHR Grand Chamber, Judgement of 7 July 2011, at para. 102.
74   For the latter point, see Koskenniemi, 'The Fate of Public International Law', *supra* note 10, at 6.

the authors' names from the Sanctions Committee's list, the Committee is nevertheless of the view that the State party has the duty to do all it can to have their names removed from the list as soon as possible, to provide the authors with some form of compensation and to make public the requests for removal. The State party is also obliged to ensure that similar violations do not occur in the future.[75]

Therefore, the limitations of competence by the Member State concerned and the Human Rights Committee itself resulted in a challenge to international law-making: Belgium – and other State parties – were to make sure that similar violations would not take place in the future. Again, the capacity of the Human Rights Committee to deliver justice was not enough, even if it did try to stretch it as far as it could without actually engaging in law-making.

The Belgian case also underlines the simplicity of arguing that 'international law is good, EU law is bad'. This is not just an EU problem – none or next to none – of the other UN Member States have any more information than the EU bodies have when implementing the Security Council resolution. In essence, the situation of Mr Kadi evidences of a large-scale system failure. Most UN Member States, even Sanctions Committee members, could not nationally provide for any better procedural guarantees during the implementing phase through a genuine hearing and presentation of evidence, or subsequently, a higher standard of judicial review than that provided by the EU Courts for the EU implementation measures. And when implementing measures are annulled, the relevant legislatures are placed under an obligation to adopt yet another implementing measure to give effect to the Member States' obligations under the UN Charter. And since the relevant members of the UN Sanctions Committee are unlikely to be much more generous in providing evidence to those giving effect to the sanctions in different parts of the world, the legislatures adopt yet another implementing act based on equally limited information than they had in their use the last time around.

The case law at large also underlines how the disclosure of evidence is the blind spot of the procedures: listings are made as political decisions by Member State diplomats, based on classified information that is not necessarily evenly shared, even between the deciding States. The Sanctions Committee itself does not have access to the evidence it is basing its decisions on, and is listing individuals based on undisclosed intelligence.[76] These procedural shortcomings are to a large extent a consequence of the deficiencies in the UN system and, as such, prevail in all national systems in

---

75 *Sayadi and Vinck v. Belgium*, Communication no. 1472/2006, HRC, Views of 22 October 2008, UN Doc. CCPR/C/94/D/1472/2006, at para. 12.
76 Lisa Ginsborg and Martin Scheinin, 'Judicial Powers, Due Process and Evidence in the Security Council 1267 Terrorist Sanctions Regime: The *Kadi II* Conundrum', *EUI Working Papers* RSCAS 2011/44, at 9.

which UN sanctions are implemented. Any minor changes in the EU decision-making procedures used to implement the Al-Qaida regime thus constitute mere window dressing:

> Unfortunately, the EU Commission or Council cannot share with the EU Courts evidence that they do not possess, and the 1267 Committee of the Security Council cannot share with the EU evidence it does not possess.[77]

In the UN sanctions regime political decision-makers are forced to trust, some more and others less blindly, on secret intelligence. Consequently, political responsibility suffers at the same time as politics is replaced by technical expertise.[78] It is clear that the evidence in question is no popular science that could or even should be freely distributed among anyone interested in studying it. But it is a problem that those with political responsibility are denied access to the evidence, and are thus not in any position to reason their decisions, other than with reference to the overarching objective of fighting terrorism; an objective that very few would dare to disagree with. Professional knowledge is not necessarily politically dispassionate but should be understood as politics of policy expertise, which stresses the need to subject its results to critical examination.[79] The outcome of Mr Kadi's s case is yet another reminder of the need to maintain some element of genuine political control over these choices.

Finally, and as Mr Kadi's ultimate victory can be taken to prove, it is not evident that security and human rights are entirely separate discussions even if they have often pursued parallel avenues. Instead, human rights and security are closely linked. Genser and Barth have demonstrated how judicial discontent at international and national level

> has reached the level of invalidating national and regional implementation of a binding Security Council resolution, the failure to address these due process concerns has created a security crisis.[80]

The existence of such case law – both from the EU Courts and others – witnesses to the difficulties involved in sustaining the fund-freezing measures without some reforms going to the basics of the way in which the Sanctions Committee functions. While the individual cases only concern the possible annulment of a measure in relation to one particular applicant, if and when these rulings are repeated enough of times, then they just might provide the

---

77 *Ibid.*, at 10.
78 For a general discussion of such regimes, see Koskenniemi, 'The Fate of Public International Law', *supra* note 10, at 10.
79 For a discussion on this, see David Kennedy, *The Dark Sides of Virtue: Reassessing International Humanitarianism* (Princeton University Press, 2004), at 125.
80 Genser and Barth, 'When Due Process Concerns Become Dangerous', *supra* note 71, at 7.

impetus to international law-making that satisfies the core criteria established by the Courts. While Mr Kadi might now be off the hook, some of his companions in misfortune have a way to go still if their primary means of getting justice is limited to creating pressure in the Courts in order to convince the relevant UN Member States of the necessity to reform the relevant UN decision-making structures. If the judicature is prepared to intervene, the security dimension of annulled sanction measures might ultimately force the law-maker to have a second look at the procedural deficits involved, where mere human rights talk earlier failed to do the trick. In that case, it might be that the 'globalization of security' would be followed by a 'globalization in rights protection'.[81] What ultimately tempted the Sanctions Committee to reverse its course in relation to Mr Kadi is anyone's guess. 'Whoops, a mistake' might just not be enough for an excuse.

5 Conclusions

Since 2001, human rights activists have persistently called for a proper balancing of human rights and security concerns in the context of anti-terrorism measures. While the international society has managed to develop draconian sanctions for those suspected of crimes, they argue, it has not managed to protect the rights of the innocent. Human Rights Watch, among others, has underlined how

> these post-September 11 laws, when viewed as a whole, represent a broad and dangerous expansion of government powers to investigate, arrest, detain, and prosecute individuals at the expense of due process, judicial oversight, and public transparency.[82]

In his Opinion in *Kadi II*, AG Maduro provided a number of thoughtful insights into Mr Kadi's situation, underlining how it is never an easy task for a court or the political institutions to apply wisdom in matters relating to the threat of terrorism: the political process often becomes 'overly responsive to immediate popular concerns, leading the authorities to allay the anxieties of the many at the expense of the rights of a few'. For Maduro,

> This is precisely when courts ought to get involved, in order to ensure that the political necessities of today do not become the legal realities of tomorrow. Their responsibility is to guarantee that what may be

---

[81] Hayley J. Hooper, 'Liberty before Security: Case T-85/09 *Yassin Abdullah Kadi v. Commission (No. 2)* [2010] ECR 00000 (30 September 2010)', 18 *European Public Law* (2012) 457–70, at 470.

[82] Human Rights Watch, 'In the Name of Security: Counterterrorism Laws Worldwide since September 11' (June 2012), at 4.

politically expedient at a particular moment also complies with the rule of law without which, in the long run, no democratic society can truly prosper.[83]

It is specifically when the scope of discretion as to the choice of measures and how to implement them is wide that procedural considerations become particularly important, since the correct procedure is the only guarantee for the affected individual that his case has been thoroughly examined and that the reasons for the decisions are right and proper. One of the core explanations for the deficits in the global protection of terrorism suspects has been that international rules are inadequate, and that existing international rules are not up to the task of meeting current challenges as regards global terrorism and the protection of human rights.[84] However, complaining about the inadequacies of the international legal order is a distraction from the more pressing concerns: to reassure the public that the 'process of assessment is sound and is motivated by the application of the proper criteria'.[85] The question is less about there being no standard to implement, than it is about an unwillingness to implement that standard. In a system that is already coming to a certain age, the procedural hiccups are no longer an infant disease. There has certainly been both time and opportunities to reconsider the procedures that were put in place as a quick reaction to the sudden events of September 11. The permanent nature of temporary sanctions evidences how temporary 'crisis' arrangements often tend to become more permanent than intended: absolute necessity and temporariness contradict the fact that the state of exception has become the rule.[86]

Since 2001, Mr Kadi has consistently held that 'he is the victim of a serious miscarriage of justice and affirmed that he has never been involved in terrorism or in any form of financial support for such activity, whether connected with Usama bin Laden or Al-Qaeda or otherwise'. Moreover, he argues, his inclusion in the list has damaged his personal and professional reputation.[87] It would be difficult to disagree. The system, despite its reforms, allowed for an individual who has consistently held that he is innocent to stay on the list for more than 11 years. If he is innocent – which we are never likely to know for certain – then this is all the more a scandal. After 11 years and three subsequent court appeals, it is doubtful whether there is anyone in Europe who has had the opportunity to consider the evidence and the grounds for the inclusion of Mr Kadi on the sanctions list, the lawfulness of the EU institutions have faithfully and persistently

---

83 *Kadi II*, *supra* note 6, Opinion of Advocate General Poiares Maduro, at paras 44–45.
84 See Sands, *Lawless World*, *supra* note 65, at 234.
85 *Ibid.*, at 235.
86 Giorgio Agamben, *State of Exception* (Kevin Attell, trans., The University of Chicago Press, 2005), at 9.
87 See *Kadi I*, *supra* note 5, para. 136.

defended even without any knowledge of whether their loyalty is factually justified. The EU institutions certainly cannot be blamed for disrespect of their UN obligations – but at some point one should begin to wonder whether the regime is indeed worthy of such loyalty.

6 Epilogue

On 18 July 2013, the CJEU delivered its ruling in *Kadi IV*.[88] It dismissed the appeals and confirmed once again that the EU measures implementing UN sanctions enjoy no immunity from jurisdiction. It embarked on an examination of whether the EU Charter of Fundamental Rights, in particular respect for the rights of defence and the right to effective judicial protection, had been infringed in relation to the specific circumstances of Mr Kadi. The institutional politics of the Court were ever present: so the Court established an infringement of the said rights based on the fact that not only Mr Kadi himself, but also the Court, had been denied access to the information and evidence relied on when adopting the measures. For the Court, the procedure followed in Mr Kadi's case did not live up to satisfactory fundamental rights standards: while the European Commission had disclosed the evidence available to it, namely the summary provided by the Sanctions Committee, the Commission had not sought the assistance of the Sanctions Committee to obtain the disclosure of further information or evidence and it had not examined carefully and impartially the comments made by Mr Kadi. In addition, the Commission had failed to provide a statement of reasons that was 'individual, specific and concrete'.[89] Of interest here is the Court's rejection of the pragmatic excuse offered by the Council and the Commission that they had indeed provided all the evidence they had in their possession. The Court was not satisfied with this and seemed to have faith in the possibilities of acquiring further information, if needed, by cooperating with the UN.

If an EU measure implementing restrictive measures is challenged, the CJEU argued, the Court must examine not only the above-mentioned safeguards but also compliance with procedural and competence rules. Again, the Court found the disclosure of evidence to be of paramount importance: while security considerations may preclude the disclosure of some of the evidence to the person concerned, such limitations do not apply to the Court; should the Court find that the secrecy argumentation does not preclude the disclosure of information to the person concerned, it should give the EU authority (in this instance, the Commission) the opportunity to disclose the relevant information. If the authority refused, then the Court could only examine the lawfulness of the contested measure on the basis of

---

88 *Kadi IV, supra* note 8.
89 *Ibid.*, para. 116.

the disclosed material.[90] If none of the reasons provided by the authority for listing a person were not sufficiently detailed and specific, the EU Courts would annul the contested decision.[91] Such a review was 'indispensable to ensure a fair balance between the maintenance of international peace and security and the protection of fundamental rights and freedoms of the person concerned, those being shared values of the UN and the European Union'.[92]

The Court also underlined the substantial negative impact of restrictive measures on the person concerned, and that the improvements introduced on the UN side still did not guarantee effective judicial protection. With this finding, the CJEU concurred with the recent findings of the ECtHR.[93] The Court thus sent a clear message to the UN Sanctions Committee that the requirements of judicial protection had not yet been satisfied, using the same language of institutional politics that is familiar from its old *Solange* jurisprudence.[94] For the person concerned, the essence of effective judicial protection would necessarily imply the possibility of a finding by a court that the listing of his name was unlawful, so as to restore his reputation and to receive a form of reparation for suffered non-material harm.[95] While the CJEU found a part of the statement of reasons for including Mr Kadi on the list to be insufficiently detailed, some of the other reasons were indeed sufficiently detailed and specific. Despite the errors of law by the General Court, the CJEU upheld the operative part of its ruling, since none of the allegations presented against Mr Kadi in the summary provided by the Sanctions Committee justified the adoption of EU restrictive measures against him. The 'full review' therefore did not imply a need to satisfy a procedural requirement, but a requirement to examine also the substance of evidence.

There is nothing particularly striking in the recent judgement. After all, the CJEU not only buttressed its own institutional politics by interpreting its previous rulings on the actions of some of the other EU institutions, which rather clearly failed to live up to standards. It also considered the relevance of the recent case law from Strasbourg in times when EU has perhaps moved a step closer to acceding to the ECtHR, and the relationship between the two Courts and their jurisprudence provokes more than merely an academic interest. As for Mr Kadi, one can only wonder whether this ruling lived up

---

90   *Ibid.*, para. 127.
91   *Ibid.*, para. 130.
92   *Ibid.*, para. 131.
93   On this, see also *Nada v. Switzerland*, Application no. 10593/08, ECtHR Grand Chamber, Judgment of 12 September 2012, para. 211.
94   For a discussion of the said jurisprudence, see e.g. Päivi Leino, 'When Every Picture Tells a Story: The European Court of Justice and the Jigsaw Puzzle of External Human Rights Competence' in Jarna Petman and Jan Klabbers (eds), *Nordic Cosmopolitanism: Essays in International Law for Martti Koskenniemi* (Martinus Nijhoff, 2003) 261–90.
95   *Kadi IV, supra* note 8, para. 134.

to the Court's standards and established that his listing almost 12 years earlier had been unlawful, thus restoring his reputation, or whether it is lost forever. As for the UN sanctions regime, it is evident that the pressure coming from national, regional and international human rights bodies keeps building up. This ruling certainly articulated a number of requirements that have to be satisfied by the sanctions regime. It is, of course, possible that this jurisprudence contributes to a further reform of the Sanctions Committee procedures. However, it might also further blur the sanctions regime by provoking the Sanctions Committee to avoid the identification of those who are targeted. This might enable to the Committee to ignore some of the criticism raised in *Kadi*, and open up a new discussion of what kind of judicial review might be necessary. In this respect, Mr Kadi's case is only a partial victory – but a victory nonetheless.

14 Law-making by human rights treaty bodies

Geir Ulfstein

1 Introduction

Treaty bodies are used in different parts of international law: international arms control, international environmental law and international human rights. What they have in common is that they are established by treaties but they are neither formal international organisations nor international courts. They may exercise different kinds of functions, including law-making, supervision and dispute settlement.

International human rights are special in the sense that, rather than being of a reciprocal interstate character, they apply to the relationship between individuals and the state while being a common global concern. This special character is reflected in a combination of an individual and a collective approach to their supervision. First, both regional human rights courts and treaty bodies deal with individual complaints, i.e. an individual approach. Second, the treaty bodies examine reports from states, i.e. a collective approach. The treaty bodies also adopt General Comments based on their case law.[1]

All of these activities may be seen as law-making in a wider sense: the treaty bodies determine the precise scope of the vague obligations in the relevant conventions – including through their dynamic ('evolutive') interpretation. This is performed on an individual basis in cases of individual complaints – similar to the functions of courts. The examination of state reports assesses the implementation of international obligations and thus also has legal – and possibly law-making – elements, albeit of a more administrative character. The adoption of General Comments resembles legislation, i.e.

---

1   I will not deal with the power to conduct special investigations. Only two human rights bodies have such a power, see Convention against Torture and Other Cruel, Inhuman or Degrading Treatment or Punishment, GA Res. 39/46, 10 December 1984, in force 26 June 1987, 1465 UNTS 85, Article 20; Convention on the Elimination of All Forms of Discrimination against Women, GA Res. 34/180, 18 December 1979, in force 3 September 1981, 1249 UNTS 13, Article 8. The power to receive interstate complaints has never been used in practice.

law-making in the proper sense, by setting out general guidelines for the interpretation of the treaty obligations.

In this chapter I will examine the legal basis for the different functions of the treaty bodies. I will also address to what extent the treaty bodies should act as legal organs or policy organs. With respect to their legal function, it is also relevant to discuss how far the treaty bodies should go in their lawmaking – given that they their formal role is that of dispute settlement and supervision of implementation.

The treaty bodies must ensure that human rights are effectively protected through their interpretation. But, given that their findings have a 'soft law' character, they should also have an eye on methods of interpretation that will persuade national constitutional organs, including domestic courts. Finally, in the current treaty body strengthening process,[2] they may need the political support of states. I will focus on law-making by the UN human rights treaty bodies, especially the Human Rights Committee (HRC).[3]

2 Examination of state reports

While the ICCPR entered into force in 1976,[4] it was not until the end of the Cold War that its supervisory body, the HRC, could exercise its general functions in examining state reports and adopting General Comments. The reasons are partly political and partly legal. In terms of the legal matters, Article 40 of the Covenant establishes:

> 1. The States Parties to the present Covenant undertake to submit reports on the measures they have adopted which give effect to the rights recognized herein and on the progress made in the enjoyment of those rights …
>
> 4. The Committee shall study the reports submitted by the States Parties to the present Covenant. It shall transmit its reports, and such general comments as it may consider appropriate, to the States Parties. The Committee may also transmit to the Economic and Social Council these comments along with the copies of the reports it has received form States Parties to the present Covenant.

---

[2] See Office of the United Nations High Commissioner for Human Rights, 'The Treaty Body Strengthening Process', <www2.ohchr.org/english/bodies/HRTD/index.htm>.

[3] In preparing this chapter I have benefited from the work on the book Helen Keller and Geir Ulfstein (eds), *UN Human Rights Treaty Bodies: Law and Legitimacy* (Cambridge University Press, 2012).

[4] International Covenant on Civil and Political Rights, UNGA Res 2200A (XXI), 16 December 1966, in force 23 March 1976, 999 UNTS 171.

As will be seen, this article does neither make it clear that the Committee's reports and its General Comments are two different supervisory functions nor what the content of its reports and its General Comments may be.

During the Cold War, the Committee members from the communist countries emphasised the need for a 'constructive dialogue' and the Committee did not adopt any Concluding Observations about the relevant state's implementation of its human rights obligations. It was only after the end of the Cold War, in 1992, that the Committee commenced its adoption of Concluding Observations on the basis of examination of state reports and its oral examination.[5]

It would seem beyond doubt that the HRC – and the other treaty bodies entrusted with examination of state reports – has the competence to adopt Concluding Observations on states' implementation of their international obligations on the basis of state reports. The question is how this function should be exercised and, in our context, whether the treaty bodies' recommendations should have a legal or a policy character.[6]

The treaty bodies should clearly comment on the legal aspects of the relevant state's implementation of its obligations. This requires that the treaty body has a composition with sufficient legal credibility. It is also wise to phrase the findings as 'concerns' – as is the practice of the HRC – rather than to determine whether the international obligations have been violated. Such determinations are generally more appropriate in dealing with individual cases.

However, the treaty bodies have not shied away from giving policy recommendations. This would also seem to be acceptable and advisable. But their activity in providing policy advice should reflect their composition: lawyers are not necessarily policy experts. Furthermore, the concreteness of the treaty bodies' advice should depend on their knowledge both about the factual situation in the relevant country and its political and cultural traditions. The treaty bodies should leave enough room for the national policymaking organs and not impose specific solutions on a country if the international obligations leave room for policy choices, bearing in mind that international human rights obligations generally give directions concerning result, not the means to be applied. Finally, the advice should be sufficiently connected to the obligations contained in the relevant convention.

3   General comments

The functions of the General Comments have also developed in the last decades. Although such Comments were adopted by the HRC already

---

5   Walter Kälin, 'Examination of State Reports' in Keller and Ulfstein (eds), *UN Human Rights Treaty Bodies, supra* note 3, 16–73 at 36–7.
6   See the discussion *ibid.*, at 41–71.

during the Cold War, they were short and mainly of a technical or procedural character. It was only after the end of the Cold War that the Committee started to adopt Comments that contained 'significant normative guidance'.[7]

It is interesting to note that the legal basis for General Comments is not necessarily only the explicit wording of Article 40 of the Covenant. It has also been claimed that their legality may be supported by subsequent state practice since no state has ever protested against the fact that the Committee adopts such Comments – states have even engaged in their drafting. Furthermore, reference is made to the possible 'implied powers' of the Committee, a concept that was accepted by the ICJ with respect to the United Nations in the *Reparations* case.[8]

The competence to adopt General Comments is now firmly established. As with the Concluding Observations it is a question about how this competence should be exercised.

First of all, it should be made clear when the treaty body pronounces on international obligations and when it gives policy advice. Moreover, statements about international obligations should generally be based on the case law of the treaty body, primarily the case law developed on the basis of individual complaints. The reason is that the treaty bodies are hardly mandated nor equipped to adopt general obligations for states, i.e. law-making in its proper sense, without a basis in case law – even if the Comments have a soft law character. In its General Comments, the treaty bodies should furthermore apply a balance between a dynamic interpretation and respect for state consent to the relevant conventions (see section 5 below). As with Concluding Observations, policy advice should be sufficiently connected to the legal obligations. Finally, transparency and involvement of relevant stakeholders should be applied in the adoption of General Comments.[9]

4 Individual complaints

The HRC's competence to adopt Views in determining individual complaints has a clear legal basis in the (First) Optional Protocol to the ICCPR.[10] However, there have been divergent opinions in terms of the legal status of the Views; the competence to adopt interim measures; as well as the powers to take action to follow up the implementation of its Views. These concerns will be examined in the following. The applicable methods of interpretation will be discussed in section 5 below.

---

7 Helen Keller and Leena Grover, 'General Comments of the Human Rights Committee and their Legitimacy' in Keller and Ulfstein (eds), *UN Human Rights Treaty Bodies, supra* note 3, 116–99, at 124.
8 *Reparation for Injuries Suffered in the Service of the United Nations (Advisory Opinion)*, ICJ Reports (1949) 174; Keller and Grover, 'General Comments', *supra* note 7, at 127–8.
9 See the discussion *ibid.*, at 142–99.
10 Optional Protocol to the International Covenant on Civil and Political Rights, 16 December 1966, entry into force 23 March 1976, 999 UNTS 171, Article 5(4).

4.1 Views

Human rights scholarship has accepted that the HRC's Views are not legally binding, but, on the other hand, it is held that states are not free to choose a different interpretation than that of the HRC.[11] There is a presumption that the HRC's interpretation is correct, and the relevant state must present its counter-arguments if it prefers a different interpretation.

HRC stated in its General Comment No. 33 that the Committee's function is not 'as such, that of a judicial body'.[12] But the Committee said that its Views have 'some important characteristics of a judicial decision'.[13] The Views have been adopted 'in a judicial spirit', including 'the impartiality and independence of Committee members, the considered interpretation of the language of the Covenant, and the determinative character of the decisions'.[14] Furthermore, the Committee held that its Views represents 'an authoritative determination' and that states 'must use whatever means lie within their power in order to give effect to the views of the Committee'.[15] This gives an impression of the Views as tantamount to being legally binding. The draft of the General Comment attracted strong criticism from some states and the General Assembly applied the unusual approach of voting in favour of not 'taking note' of the Comment.[16]

The ICJ expressed its opinion about the legal status of the HRC's decisions in the *Diallo* case.[17] The Court held that it was 'in no way obliged, in the exercise of its judicial functions, to model its own interpretation of the Covenant on that of the Committee'.[18] Furthermore, the ICJ only applied the HRC's practice as support for its own interpretation, which it deemed to be 'fully corroborated by the jurisprudence of the Human Rights Committee'.[19] But the Court stated that the HRC's practice should be given 'great weight' since the HRC 'was established specifically to supervise the application of that treaty'.[20] The ICJ also referred to the need for promoting 'the

---

11 See generally about the legal status of Views: Geir Ulfstein, 'Individual Complaints' in Keller and Ulfstein (eds), *UN Human Rights Treaty Bodies*, *supra* note 3, 73–116, at 94–100.
12 General Comment No. 33: The Obligations of States Parties under the Optional Protocol to the International Covenant on Civil and Political Rights, UN Doc. CCPR/C/GC/33 (5 November 2008) para. 11.
13 *Ibid.*
14 *Ibid.*
15 *Ibid.*, paras 13 and 20.
16 See promotion and protection of human rights: implementation of human rights instruments, Report of the Third Committee, UN Doc. A/64/439/Add.1, 7 December 2009, paras 11–13.
17 *Ahmadou Sadio Diallo (Republic of Guinea v. Democratic Republic of Congo)*, ICJ Reports (2010–II) 692.
18 *Ibid.*, para. 66.
19 *Ibid.*
20 *Ibid.*

necessary clarity', the 'essential consistency' and 'legal security' for both individuals and states.[21]

The HRC has sought – without explicitly saying so – to give the impression that its Views are legally binding. On the one hand, it is not difficult to understand that the Committee may want to strengthen the effects of its Views through an expansive interpretation. This may also increase the political pressure on states parties to implement such Views. On the other hand, the approach of the Committee may be criticised from a strictly legal perspective. Moreover, the Committee may have weakened its own legitimacy, and that of other human rights treaty bodies, by indirectly giving support to sentiments that such organs disregard the requirement of state consent as a basis for international obligations. This may also generate reluctance among states concerning ratification of new human rights conventions and protocols with individual complaints procedures.

It is therefore submitted that, rather than giving the impression that its Views are legally binding, the HRC should concentrate on the scope of the states' obligation to, according to the ICJ, attach 'great weight' to such Views. This may establish a common legal ground for the Committee and states parties, which may also promote the possibilities for actual implementation of the Committee's Views at the national level. Such an approach does not only make good legal sense, but it lays the basis for further refinements of the good faith obligations of states parties. According 'great weight' to the findings of treaty bodies in cases of individual complaints should, as has been referred to above, entail a presumption of the correctness of such findings, and require states parties, including national courts, to present good reasons for any conflicting opinion.

4.2 Interim measures

Two questions arise with respect to interim measures: the first is to what extent treaty bodies have the power to adopt such measures and the second is which legal status to be accorded to them.[22]

Neither the Covenant nor the Optional Protocol provides an explicit basis for the adoption of interim measures. There were earlier different opinions about the 'implied powers' of the HRC to adopt interim measures.[23] But there is an obvious need to prevent execution of a death penalty or expulsion of a person to a country where she or he might be in danger, before the relevant committee has made its final determination. This should in itself suffice to demonstrate the competence of these committees to adopt interim measures. Subsequent human rights treaties, such as the Optional Protocol

---

21   Ibid.
22   See generally on interim measures: Ulfstein, 'Individual Complaints', *supra* note 11, at 100–3.
23   Dominic McGoldrick, *The Human Rights Committee: Its Role in the Development of the International Covenant on Civil and Political Rights* (Clarendon Press, 1991) at 131.

to the Convention on the Elimination of All Forms of Discrimination against Women (CEDAW), have included an express basis for adopting interim measures.[24]

However, implied powers would not necessarily determine the legal status of such measures. There have been different opinions in legal scholarship on whether such measures are legally binding. In recent years, several international courts and treaty bodies have clarified their position as to the legal status of interim measures, and they have all concluded that such measures are legally binding. For example, the HRC established in its General Comment No. 33 that its interim or provisional measures are legally binding: 'Failure to implement such interim or provisional measures is incompatible with the obligation to respect in good faith the procedure of individual communication established under the Optional Protocol.'[25]

In relation to international courts it may be argued that, since they can issue binding final judgments, they should also have the competence to adopt binding interim measures. States parties have accepted that these courts should be delegated powers to adopt judgements in order to fulfil the objectives of the treaty, and they have a composition and procedures to exercise such powers in a way states find trustworthy. It can be argued that, when international courts can make final binding decisions, they should *a fortiori* have the competence to impose the temporary restrictions on states represented through binding interim measures.

No such inference from the binding status of the final decisions may be drawn in the case of treaty bodies. It is, however, equally relevant for treaty bodies, in their function of receiving individual Communications, that they were established in order to protect individual human rights. If states were free to disregard interim measures in cases where it would result in irreparable harm, such as execution of a death penalty or expulsion to torture in another state, the objective of the treaty bodies would not be fulfilled, since the subsequent finding of the treaty body in the relevant case would have no possibility of influencing the decision of the state, much less of being accorded 'great weight'. Furthermore, interim measures are by nature of a temporary and not final character.

While acknowledging the absence of an explicit basis in the treaties for binding interim measures, it should be sufficient for accepting their binding character that such a legal status is necessary in order to fulfil what was intended by the individual complaints procedures, i.e. the protection of the individual through findings by the relevant treaty body. Thus, as argued by Christian Tomuschat, an effective interpretation (*effet utile*) should be applied.[26]

---

24 Optional Protocol to the Convention on the Elimination of All Forms of Discrimination against Women, GA Res 54/4, 6 October 1999, entry into force 22 December 2000, 2131 UNTS 83, Article 5(1).
25 General Comment No 33, *supra* note 12, para 19.
26 Christian Tomuschat, *Human Rights: Between Idealism and Realism* (2nd edn, Oxford University Press, 2008) at 218.

4.3 Follow-up measures

The legal power of the treaty bodies to address non-compliance by states parties has also been a matter of controversy. In their submissions to the ongoing treaty body strengthening process, China has, for example, stated that '[f]ollow-up procedures should not burden the States parties with extraneous obligations', while Russia has said that '[f]ollow-up procedures have been developed by treaty bodies and are not covered by international treaties. Thus, States parties are under no obligation to work with committees on follow-up procedures'.[27]

The decision to publish the Views of the HRC was taken without any express basis in the First Optional Protocol.[28] A consensus was gradually developed that follow-up procedures could be based on the HRC's implied powers.[29] This is plausible, given the need for effective implementation of the treaty obligations. The Optional Protocol to CEDAW is an example of a more recent treaty explicitly providing for an obligation for states parties to report on their follow up on findings by the CEDAW Committee.[30] However, the treaty bodies have no powers to put pressure on non-complying states – except for 'naming and shaming'.

5 Methods of interpretation

The treaty bodies are bound to interpret the obligations of states parties as set out in the human rights conventions, but the ambit of these obligations may be extended through effective and dynamic interpretation. Such interpretation techniques are commonly used by the treaty bodies.

The treaty bodies have been criticised for an excessively expansive interpretation.[31] It is difficult to see that the treaty bodies generally apply interpretation methods deviating from the methods used in other parts of international law.[32] But writers have pointed to examples where the treaty bodies allegedly may have gone too far in their interpretation. Kerstin

---

27 See 'The Treaty Body Strengthening Process: Individual Submissions by States Parties', <www2.ohchr.org/english/bodies/HRTD/StakeholdersContextConsultations.htm>.
28 Torkel Opsahl, 'The Human Rights Committee' in Philip Alston (ed), *The United Nations and Human Rights: A Critical Appraisal* (2nd edn, Clarendon Press, 2002) 369–444 at 421.
29 Alfred de Zayas, 'Petitions before the United Nations Treaty Bodies: Focus on the Human Right Committee's Optional Protocol Procedure' in Gudmundur Alfredsson et al. (eds), *International Human Rights Monitoring Mechanisms: Essays in Honour of Jacob Th. Möller* (Martinus Nijhoff, 2009) 35–77 at 75. See also Markus Schmidt, 'Follow-up Activities by UN Human Rights Treaty Bodies and Special Procedures Mechanisms of the Human Rights Council: Recent Developments', *ibid.*, 25–35 at 26.
30 Optional Protocol to CEDAW, *supra* note 24, Article 7(4).
31 Kerstin Mechlem, 'Treaty Bodies and the Interpretation of Human Rights', 42 *Vanderbilt Journal of Transnational Law* (2009) 905–47 at 908.
32 Birgit Schlütter, 'Aspects of Human Rights Interpretation by the UN Treaty Bodies' in Keller and Ulfstein (eds), *UN Human Rights Treaty Bodies, supra* note 3, 261–320 at 317.

Mechlem refers to General Comments adopted by the Committee on Economic, Social and Cultural Rights (CESCR) on the obligations of international organisations, states' extra-territorial obligations and the concept of 'core obligations'.[33] Urfan Khaliq and Robin Churchill speak of the CESCR's 'quasi-legislative approach to certain issues, notably the rights to adequate housing and water' and that the HRC with regard to the right to life has adopted 'an extremely expansive approach, one that encompasses, inter alia, housing, health and nutrition'.[34]

The expansion of treaty obligations through an effective or dynamic interpretation is a double-edged sword to the extent that states may argue that the treaty bodies do not respect traditional canons of treaty interpretation, and thus engages in law-making beyond their mandate as supervisory bodies. Such opinions may prevent implementation of the treaty bodies' findings in domestic law. But they may also prevent the necessary political and financial support by states in the current treaty body strengthening process. It is therefore of importance that the treaty bodies balance the need for effective human rights protection through their interpretation while respecting accepted methods of treaty interpretation.

6 Conclusions

The treaty bodies have been very successful in clarifying and developing their role as supervisory organs, especially after the end of the Cold War. But this expansion has led to two difficulties: criticism of going too far in both their legal and policy functions, and reaching – and over-reaching – their capacity to dealing with state reports and individual complaints, resulting in increasing backlogs.

It would seem advisable that the treaty bodies took note of both these restraints. They should ensure effective human rights protection, but only as far as their mandate allows. Hence, they should engage in law-making only to the extent allowed by accepted principles of treaty interpretation. Furthermore, the policy advice should not be at the expense of the treaty bodies' core legal functions. The shortage of resources in the UN system may also have the effect of requiring more prioritising in exercising the treaty bodies' different functions. But that is another story.

---

33 Mechlem, 'Treaty Bodies', *supra* note 31, at 931, 935 and 940.
34 Urfan Khaliq and Robin Churchill, 'The Protection of Economic and Social Rights: A Particular Challenge?' in Keller and Ulfstein (eds), *UN Human Rights Treaty Bodies, supra* note 3, 199–260 at 260.

Part IV
Uncertainties and gaps

15 Peremptory law-making

Enzo Cannizzaro

The term *jus cogens* is gradually spilling over the limits of scholarly works and is more and more employed in judicial and diplomatic practice. The notion of peremptory law is not used univocally. Quite the contrary, a wide variety of opinion has been expressed as to its nature, its effects and its role in the international legal dynamics. The present chapter does not intend to engage in an in-depth discussion of these different conceptions. It has a more limited scope. It intends to explore *jus cogens* from a methodological angle by analysing the ways in which *jus cogens* has been determined in the judicial practice and in particular in the case law of the ICJ. The hope is that such analysis might shed some light, however pale, on the study of one of the most impenetrable mysteries surrounding the notion of *jus cogens* – namely, how a hierarchically superior norm can assert itself in a legal order deprived of institutionalised law-making procedures.

1 *Jus cogens* in naturalist law-making: Verdross

The doctrine of *jus cogens* has developed primarily as part of the tradition of *ius naturae*.[1] That natural law is the most obvious ancestry of *jus cogens* can hardly be doubted. In the international law of the early-20th century, this notion was evoked in opposition to the triumphing voluntarist conceptions, and as a limit to the unfettered freedom of states to pursue whatever interests they deemed fit.[2]

---

1 For a recent conceptualisation of *jus cogens* according to the natural law theory, see Mary Ellen O'Connell, '*Jus Cogens*: International Law's Higher Ethical Norms', in Donald Earl Childress, III (ed.), *The Role of Ethics in International Law* (Cambridge University Press, 2012) 78–98. See also Vaughan Lowe, *International Law* (Oxford University Press, 2007) at 58.
2 For a positivist conception of *jus cogens*, see, e.g. André de Hoog, *Obligations Erga Omnes and International Crimes: A Theoretical Inquiry into the Implementation and Enforcement of the International Responsibility of States* (Kluwer Law International, 1996) at 44–8. For a few international scholars there is no such notion as *jus cogens*; see in particular Prosper Weil, 'Towards Relative Normativity in International Law', 77 *American Journal of International Law* (1983) 413–442; Michael Glennon, 'De l'absurdité du droit impératif (*jus cogens*)', 100 *Revue générale de droit international public* (2006) 529–36.

The work of Alfred Verdross is usually considered as an appropriate yardstick for testing the natural law conception of *jus cogens*. It will thus be interesting to see what this test can offer in terms of methodology.

Writing in 1937, Alfred Verdross observed that 'the existence of such norms in general international law is particularly contested by those authors who base the whole international law on the wills of the States; consequently, they know no other international law but treaty law'.[3] What Verdross had presumably in mind was to demonstrate that there are certain rules rooted in international ethics, which not only prohibit certain conduct to be performed, but furthermore prohibit any engagement to perform them. So, Verdross pioneered the idea that international law had already evolved to the point of establishing a normative limit to the will of states by virtue of which the mere existence of an engagement to behave in an unethical manner would be deemed invalid. In his view, 'no juridical order can admit treaties between juridical subjects, which are obviously in contradiction to the ethics of a certain community'.[4]

Verdross went well beyond the mere assertion that such peremptory rules exist. He also made an effort to determine them on the basis of a purely logical deductive method. For our purposes, this is undoubtedly the most interesting – and yet least persuasive – part of his work.

Verdross did not determine *jus cogens* on the basis of a process of deduction from universal principles of ethics, albeit that such procedure might have seemed the most logical application of a natural law approach. Instead, Verdross started from the opposite end: 'in order to advance the solution of our problem, it is necessary to see what treaties are regarded to be *contra bonos mores*'. By so doing, the methodology for determining *jus cogens* was inadvertently reversed. Rather than being deduced *in abstracto* from the principles of universal ethics, *jus cogens* would be deduced from the observations of its effects on and within the international legal order. This, then, led Verdross to conclude that such treaties are regarded 'as being *contra bonos mores*, which *restrict the liberty of one contracting party in an excessive or unworthy manner or which endanger its most important rights*'.[5] That is to say, a treaty is invalid, if it prevents a state 'from fulfilling the universally recognized tasks of a civilized State'.

Thus, paradoxically, and quite contrary to its naturalist premise, this methodology ended up defining *jus cogens* not in absolute and immutable terms as the earthly transposition of transcendent ethical virtues, but rather in historical and contingent terms.[6] *Jus cogens* was identified with the rules

---

3   Alfred Verdross, 'Forbidden Treaties in International Law', 31 *American Journal of International Law* (1937) 571–7, at 571.
4   *Ibid.*, at 572.
5   *Ibid.*, at 574 (italics in the original).
6   For a similar view, see Paul Tavernier, 'L'identification des règles fondamentales – un problème résolu?', in Christian Tomuschat and Jean-Marc Thouvenin (eds), *The Fundamental Rules of the International Legal Order:* Jus Cogens *and Obligations* Erga Omnes (Martinus Nijhoff Publishers, 2006) 1–20, at 15.

necessary and proper to allow or oblige a state to discharge its basic tasks, namely, the maintenance of the public order, the defence against external attacks, the care for the bodily and the spiritual welfare of its citizens at home and the protection of its nationals abroad. Seen through contemporary lenses, this result cannot appear but paradoxical: a treaty imposing limitations on the military ability of a state to defend its citizens would be invalid while a treaty of aggression would not. Such an end result can hardly be considered consistent with the idea of *jus cogens* as an immutable set of rules reflecting universal principles – rather, in this, *jus cogens* is but the consequence of the legal sensitivities of the given era. For a disenchanted observer this sorry conclusion reveals the way in which the notion of international ethics is dependent on the historical and social realities of the time in which it is developed.

2   *Jus cogens* as positive law: Article 53 of the Vienna Convention

Possibly in reaction to the inherent subjectivity of the notion of *jus cogens*, the Vienna Conference on the Law of Treaties, while accepting the notion as such, decided to adopt a radically different methodology in terms of determining its content.

Jus cogens is defined by Article 53 of the Vienna Convention as follows: '[a] peremptory norm of general international law is a norm accepted and recognized by the international community of States as a whole as a norm from which no derogation is permitted and which can be modified only by a subsequent norm of general international law having the same character'. Many an author has contended that this definition is tautological.[7] Admittedly, Article 53 is drafted in an unusually circular manner, defining the notion of *jus cogens* through reference to the effect it is designed to produce. But is there anything beyond this seemingly hopeless bootstrapping exercise that Article 53 could tell us more about the nature of *jus cogens*?

An analytical inquiry into the provision reveals a number of indications about the process of formation of *jus cogens*. First, Article 53 indicates that a norm of *jus cogens* can only be found within the larger realm of general international law. The brief reference to general international law points to *jus cogens* norms being, in principle, customary norms.[8]

Second, Article 53 specifies that the process through which a customary rule acquires peremptory nature is based on the acceptance and recognition – by the international community as whole[9] – of the idiosyncratic quality of the said rule; it is unlike any 'ordinary rule' in that no derogation is

---

7   See, among others, Bruno Simma, 'From Bilateralism to Community Interest in International Law', 250/VI *Recueil des Cours* (1994) 217–384, at 286–287.
8   Michel Virally, 'Réflexions sur le "jus cogens"', 12 *Annuaire français du droit international* (1966) 5–29, at 8.
9   Pierre-Marie Dupuy, 'L'unité de l'ordre juridique international', 297 *Recueil des Cours* (2002) 9–490, at 276.

permitted from it and it can be modified only by a subsequent norm of general international law having the same idiosyncratic character.

This complex process is aimed at establishing a hierarchical relationship between *jus cogens* and 'ordinary' rules. *Jus cogens* does not merely require states to comply with it even at the cost of disregarding inconsistent law, but it also affects the validity of inferior law. If Article 53 conceives of *jus cogens* as higher law, it seems logical to assume that it should prevail not only upon treaties, but also upon every other international law rule not having peremptory nature. This is an obvious inference from the fact that it is not Article 53 that determines the hierarchical nature of peremptory rules but such determination is a consequence of the acceptance and recognition by the international community as a whole.

Accordingly, in spite of its seemingly tautological character, Article 53 sheds considerable light on how to determine *jus cogens* norms. It describes a purely positivistic procedure that is articulated in two logical steps.

As the first step, peremptory nature requires generality. This appears perfectly natural, for the very notion of *jus cogens* is inextricably linked with the existence of collective interests. There would be no reason to limit the contractual freedom of states, if the realisation of the interests pursued through certain treaties would not be inconsistent with the common interests of the community. Generality, in turn, is normally connected with consistent practice accompanied by *opinio juris*.

As the second step, a general rule acquires peremptory nature through a process of recognition and acceptance by the international community as a whole as a rule from which no derogation is permitted. Here, recognition and acceptance seem again to mirror the twin elements of practice and *opinio juris* that are necessary to produce a customary rule – quite like in the first step. However, whereas in the first phase practice and opinion refer to the material conduct required by the rule, in the second phase they refer to the invalidating or terminating effect of *jus cogens*.

Summing up, the procedure laid down by Article 53 is based on the presumption that the material conduct and the peremptory effect correspond to distinct customary rules. One can hardly expect such an overcomplicated procedure to apply in practice.

3 *Jus cogens* in judicial practice prior to the Vienna Convention

The existence of a sphere of rules protecting fundamental values of the international community has long been recognised in judicial practice, even if such rules have not necessarily connected to the effect of invalidating or terminating conflicting treaties.

In the *Corfu Channel* case of 1949, the ICJ found that respect for territorial integrity is one of the 'fundamental basis of international relations'. The Court regarded the doctrine of intervention 'as a manifestation of a policy of force, such as has, in the past, given rise to most serious abuses and such as cannot, whatever be the present defects in international organisation, find a place in international law'.[10] Although the settlement of the dispute did not require the Court to pronounce on the validity or the termination of a treaty as such, this dictum is unequivocal in many respects.

For one, the Court's finding underlines that neither a previous wrong committed by Albania, nor a pressing need to collect evidence of the alleged wrongdoing, could have justified the forcible reaction by the UK. Such a finding is wholly based on a difference in value between the interests that the respective rules seek to protect. In other words, the prohibition of forcible intervention is deemed to override other competing interests by virtue of its 'fundamental' value.

Second, and even more interestingly, the Court's argument also conveys the idea that the superiority of a higher rule is not so much based on the formal level of the source from which it emanates, but rather on the fundamental character of the interests protected.[11] This is hardly surprising, if one takes into account the fact that the *Corfu Channel* case was decided well prior to the drafting of the Vienna Convention, at a time in which no special procedure for the production of higher law rule was still devised.

Third, and in a sense connected with the preceding observation, the Court's finding does not refer to any methodology for determining the fundamental nature of the prohibition to forcible intervention. This observation is not entirely irrelevant, if one considers that the prohibition of forcible intervention had probably acquired legal force only a few years earlier, with the entry into force of the United Nations Charter.[12]

Around the same time as the *Corfu Channel* case, the Court made in its 1948 Advisory Opinion on the *Reservations to the Convention on the Prevention and Punishment of the Crime of Genocide*, a brief but meaningful reference to the importance of the Genocide Convention, whose provisions it found to 'endorse the most elementary principles of morality'.[13] In the same passage, the Court also noted that the principles underlying the Convention are 'principles which are recognized by civilized nations as binding on States,

---

10 *Corfu Channel Case (United Kingdom v. Albania)*, ICJ Reports (1949) 4, at 35.
11 The notion of *jus cogens* rests on the fundamental importance of the underlying obligation for the international community as a whole according, among others, to Roberto Ago, 'Fifth Report on State Responsibility', UN Doc. A/CN.4/291, 22 March 1976, at paras 99 and 101; Alexander Orakhelashvili, *Peremptory Norms in International Law* (Oxford University Press, 2006); and Simma, 'From Bilateralism to Community Interest', *supra* note 7. For a different conception, see Robert Kolb, *Théorie du jus cogens international: Essai de relecture du concept* (Presses Universitaires de France, 2001).
12 See Stefan Talmon, 'The Duty Not to "Recognize as Lawful" a Situation Created by the Illegal Use of Force or Other Serious Breaches of a *Jus Cogens* Obligation: An Obligation Without Real Substance?', in Tomuschat and Thouvenin, *The Fundamental Rules*, *supra* note 6, 99–126, at 99.
13 *Reservations to the Convention on the Preservation and Punishment of the Crime of Genocide (Advisory Opinion)*, ICJ Reports (1951) 15, at 23.

even without any conventional obligation' and that a consequence of such recognition is 'the universal character both of the condemnation of genocide and of the co-operation required "in order to liberate mankind from such an odious scourge"'. The Court may have alluded to a resolution adopted by the General Assembly in 1946, in which the Assembly had declared that genocide 'shocks the conscience of mankind ... and is contrary to moral law and to the spirit and aims of the United Nations'.[14]

When considering international judicial practice prior to the entry into force of the Vienna Convention, a third case to be taken into account is the *Barcelona Traction* case.[15] True, the case did not concern the notion of peremptory rules at all; instead, the Court chose to address in *obiter dicta* the different, albeit interrelated, notion of *erga omnes* obligations. The Court famously drew a distinction between obligations 'arising vis-à-vis another State' and obligations incumbent upon a state that are owed to the international community as a whole, expressly labelled as 'obligations *erga omnes*'. Whereas reciprocal obligations protect individual interests, *erga omnes* obligations by nature protect collective interests.[16]

Thus, quite surprisingly, the Court, in order to distinguish between these two categories of obligations, referred to the importance of the protected interests. Let us see how the argument of the Court unfolds along three major passages.

First, the Court distinguished between different categories of obligations in the by-now famous sentence: 'an essential distinction should be drawn between the obligations of a State towards the international community as a whole, and those arising vis-à-vis another State in the field of diplomatic protection'.

---

14   The Crime of Genocide, GA Res. 96 (I), 11 December 1946, at para. 1.
15   *Barcelona Traction, Light and Power Company, Limited (Belgium v. Spain) (Second Phase)*, ICJ Reports (1970) 3, at para. 33.
16   According to the ILC:

> [W]hether or not peremptory norms of general international law and obligations to the international community as a whole are aspects of a single basic idea, there is at the very least substantial overlap between them. The examples which the International Court has given of obligations towards the international community as a whole all concern obligations which, it is generally accepted, arise under peremptory norms of general international law. Likewise the examples of peremptory norms given by the Commission in its commentary to what became article 53 of the Vienna Convention involve obligations to the international community as a whole. But there is at least a difference in emphasis. While peremptory norms of general international law focus on the scope and priority to be given to a certain number of fundamental obligations, the focus of obligations to the international community as a whole is essentially on the legal interest of all States in compliance – i.e. in terms of the present Articles, in being entitled to invoke the responsibility of any State in breach.

ILC, 'Report on the Work of its 53rd Session', *Yearbook of the International Law Commission* (2001) Vol. II (2) at 111–12, para. 7.

It then, as the second step, referred to the collective nature of the interests protected by *erga omnes* obligations in that 'by their very nature the former are the concern of all States'.

And finally it simply underlined the importance of such interests: 'in view of the importance of the rights involved, all States can be held to have a legal interest in their protection'.

The sequence of the above sentences conveys a certain sense of confusion. In all evidence, the Court seems to have conflated two conceptually different notions: on the one hand, the notion of *erga omnes* obligations based on the *structure* of a certain rule; and, on the other, the notion of peremptory law based on the higher *rank* of a particular rule. Nonetheless, when perusing the *Barcelona Traction* judgement, one can find no reference to – let alone clarification of – a special procedure by which such higher-ranking rules might be formed.

4 *Jus cogens* in judicial practice after the Vienna Convention

For many years after the entry into force of the Vienna Convention, the ICJ abstained from referring expressly to the notion of *jus cogens*. Occasionally, however, the Court has referred to the special *status* of certain rules by virtue of the fundamental character of the interests protected.

For example, in the 1980 case of the *US Diplomatic and Consular Staff in Tehran*, the Court alluded to the fundamental character of the principle of diplomatic inviolability and excluded that this principle could be breached in response to a breach of other international rules.[17] A few years later, in the 1986 decision on the merits of the *Nicaragua* case, the Court came very close to finding that the prohibition of use of force enshrined in Article 2(4) of the United Nations Charter is a principle of *jus cogens*. The Court observed that the customary nature of the prohibition to use force is confirmed by the fact that States frequently refer to that principle in their statements released before international fora not only as a 'principle of customary international law but also (as) a fundamental or cardinal principle of such law'. The Court went on to note that the two parties to the proceedings, Nicaragua and the

---

17 *United States Diplomatic and Consular Staff in Tehran (US v. Iran)*, ICJ Reports (1980) 3, at para. 84 ('the principle of the inviolability of the persons of diplomatic agents and the premises of diplomatic missions is one of the very foundations of this long-established regime, to the evolution of which the traditions of Islam made a substantial contribution. The fundamental character of the principle of inviolability is, moreover, strongly underlined by the provisions of Articles 44 and 45 of the Convention of 1961'). However, the prohibition to breach the principle of inviolability of diplomatic agents is not based on its hierarchical superiority over other rules but rather, as the Court implicitly recognised, on the particular instrumental function discharged by these rules.

US had themselves recognised the *jus cogens* nature of that rule – Nicaragua had done so explicitly, the US had done so in a more nuanced manner.[18]

Possibly inspired by the wording of Article 53(2) of the Vienna Convention, the *Nicaragua* judgement suggests that recognition is the main element for bestowing peremptory nature to a rule of customary law. There is a difference, however, between the logic of the *Nicaragua* judgement and the logic of the Vienna Convention. Article 53 of the Vienna Convention indicates that a customary rule is part of *jus cogens*, if it is recognised as one from which no derogation is permitted. In *Nicaragua*, the Court rather seems to have inverted the argument by indicating that a rule is part of *jus cogens*, if it is recognised as a fundamental rule of the international legal order. In the latter conception, the impermissibility of a derogation is a consequence of the higher status of *jus cogens*, and not one of its constitutive elements.

In an analogous vein, the Court found, in its Advisory Opinion of 1996 on the *Legality of the Threat or Use of Nuclear Weapons*, that 'great many rules of humanitarian law applicable in armed conflict are so fundamental to the respect of the human person and "elementary considerations of humanity"' that they are 'to be observed by all States whether or not they have ratified the conventions that contain them, because they constitute intransgressible principles of international customary law'.[19] Similarly, in its Advisory Opinion of 2004 on the *Legal Consequences of the Construction of a Wall in the Occupied Palestinian Territory*, the Court found that a breach of the right to self-determination as well as grave breaches of humanitarian law entail the legal consequences envisaged by the ILC's draft articles on state responsibility for serious breaches of obligations arising from peremptory norms of general international law, '[g]iven the character and the importance of the rights and obligations involved'.[20]

18   *Military and Paramilitary Activities in and against Nicaragua (Nicaragua v. US)*, ICJ Reports (1986) 14, at para. 190:

> A further confirmation of the validity as customary international law of the principle of the prohibition of the use of force expressed in Article 2, paragraph 4, of the Charter of the United Nations may be found in the fact that it is frequently referred to in statements by State representatives as being not only a principle of customary international law but also a fundamental or cardinal principle of such law. The ILC, in the course of its work on the codification of the law of treaties, expressed the view that 'the law of the Charter concerning the prohibition of the use of force in itself constitutes a conspicuous example of a rule in international law having the character of *jus cogens*'. Nicaragua in its Memorial on the Merits submitted in the present case states that the principle prohibiting the use of force embodied in Article 2, paragraph 4, of the Charter of the United Nations 'has come to be recognized as *jus cogens*'. The US, in its Counter-Memorial on the questions of jurisdiction and admissibility, found it material to quote the views of scholars that this principle is a 'universal norm', a 'universal international law', a 'universally recognized principle of international law' and a 'principle of jus *cogens*'.

19   *Legality of the Threat or Use of Nuclear Weapons (Advisory Opinion)*, ICJ Reports (1996) 226, at para. 79.
20   *Legal Consequences of the Construction of a Wall in the Occupied Palestinian Territory (Advisory Opinion)*, ICJ Reports (2004) 131, at para. 159.

Paradoxically, the cases in which the Court has expressly referred to *jus cogens*, thereby explicitly admitting its existence, do not provide much information about the procedure for its coming into being. In the 2006 judgement on the *Armed Activities on the Territory of the Congo*, the Court merely found the prohibition to commit genocide to 'assuredly' have this status, without bothering to explain why this should be so.[21] A similarly succinct assertion is contained in the 2006 judgement on *Jurisdictional Immunities*, in which the Court referred to its previous decision in the *Arrest Warrant* case,[22] and clarified that this case concerned rules 'which undoubtedly possess the character of *jus cogens*'.[23]

The *Jurisdictional Immunities* case contains an interesting, yet ambiguous, statement on the role of practice, as the Court notes:

> [a]gainst the background of a century of practice in which almost every peace treaty or post-war settlement has involved either a decision not to require the payment of reparations or the use of lump sum settlements and set-offs, it is difficult to see that international law contains a rule requiring the payment of full compensation to each and every individual victim as a rule accepted by the international community of States as a whole as one from which no derogation is permitted.[24]

A plausible reading of this passage is that the Court did not exclude the existence of an individual right to reparation. The existing practice of derogation should, however, indicate that even if such a rule did exist, it would not have peremptory character.[25] In other words, the very practice of

---

21   *Armed Activities on the Territory of the Congo (New Application 2002) (Democratic Republic of the Congo v. Rwanda)*, ICJ Reports (2006) 6, at para. 64.
22   See *Arrest Warrant of 11 April 2000 (Democratic Republic of the Congo v. Belgium)*, ICJ Reports (2002) 3.
23   *Jurisdictional Immunities of the State (Germany v. Italy; Greece Intervening)*, ICJ, Judgment of 3 February 2012, at para. 95. In its decision in the case of *Questions Relating to the Obligation to Prosecute or Extradite (Belgium v. Senegal)*, ICJ, Judgment of 20 July 2012, at para. 99, the Court said:

> In the Court's opinion, the prohibition of torture is part of customary international law and it has become a peremptory norm (*jus cogens*). That prohibition is grounded in a widespread international practice and on the *opinio juris* of States. It appears in numerous international instruments of universal application (in particular the Universal Declaration of Human Rights of 1948, the 1949 Geneva Conventions for the protection of war victims; the International Covenant on Civil and Political Rights of 1966; General Assembly resolution 3452/30 of 9 December 1975 on the Protection of All Persons from Being Subjected to Torture and Other Cruel, Inhuman or Degrading Treatment or Punishment), and it has been introduced into the domestic law of almost all States; finally, acts of torture are regularly denounced within national and international fora.

24   *Jurisdictional Immunities*, *supra* note 23, at para. 94.

derogation should entail that no peremptory rules exists to grant a right to reparation 'to each and every individual victim'.

In *Jurisdictional Immunities*, the Court seems to go along the road indicated by Article 53 of the Vienna Convention – but in the reverse direction. Rather than seeking to demonstrate the existence of a *jus cogens* rule through the practice of invalidating or terminating inconsistent treaties, it refers to the practice of concluding and managing agreements so as to demonstrate that even if a rule establishing an individual right to reparation did exist, it would have no *jus cogens* character. One can hardly resort to the Court's statement to demonstrate that the existence of *jus cogens* requires a practice of invalidation or termination of inconsistent treaties.

5 Concluding remarks

In spite of the many attempts of legal scholarship at precise determinations, the process of peremptory law-making still appears mysterious. The vicissitudes of *jus cogens* in the history of the legal thought highlight how difficult it can be to demonstrate the existence of a sphere of higher law, beyond the sphere of the individual state interests. The existence of different conceptions of *jus cogens* – ranging from those firmly anchored in natural law to those inspired by radical positivismus – certainly makes the search for a common ground even more difficult. From the confines of the terrain of philosophy, the diverging views may well seem an insurmountable problem. The divergence may however come to appear less insurmountable the more readily one abandons the strict confines of the theoretical plane and opens up to the methodological and effectual ones.

The preceding analysis suggests that, beyond paralysing theoretical divergences, the different determinations of *jus cogens* norms exhibit a certain convergence in the effectual methodology, based on the ascertainment that a rule has acquired a fundamental role in the international legal system. The search for 'fundamentality' requires one to analyse the respective importance of interests and rules in the light of the overall legal balance on which the international society rests in a given historical era. In a sense, this can be seen to constitute a 'third way' between the conceptions of *jus cogens* as transcendental law, on the one hand, and those, on the other, that require each effect of a higher law to be grounded in formal law-making procedures.

25　See Enzo Cannizzaro, 'Is there an Individual Right to Reparation? Some thoughts on the ICJ judgment in the jurisdictional immunities case', in Denis Alland, Vincent Chetail, Olivier de Frouville and Jorge E. Viñuales (eds), *Unity and Diversity of International Law: Essays in Honour of Professor Pierre-Marie Dupuy/Unité Et Diversité Du Droit International: Mélanges En L'Honneur Du Professeur Pierre-Marie Dupuy* (Martinus Nijhoff, forthcoming).

16 Law-making and the law of the sea

The BP *Deepwater Horizon* oil spill in the Gulf of Mexico

James E. Hickey, Jr.

'The Technology laws and regulations, and practices for containing, responding to and cleaning up spills lag behind the real risks associated with deepwater drilling into large, high pressure reservoirs of oil and gas located far offshore and thousands of feet below the ocean's surface'.
National Commission on the BP *Deepwater Horizon* oil spill and offshore drilling.[1]

1 Introduction

One obvious reason to 'make' international law is to reduce uncertainty in planning future human enterprise. This is no less true for the international law of the sea than it is for other substantive areas of international law. The 2010 BP *Deepwater Horizon* explosion and oil spill in the Gulf of Mexico underscores how the emerging new reliance on deepwater and ultra-deepwater ocean drilling and production of vast new oils reserves below the deep ocean floor raises legal uncertainties about the effective application of the existing law of the sea to address this sort of activity now and in the future. The question is an important one for several reasons. First, over a half of new discoveries of oil and gas reserves are found in deepwater zones.[2] Second, increasingly oil and gas development is moving away from land-based sources. Third, the indisputable link between gross domestic product (GDP) and the availability of affordable and reliable sources of energy continues to be an economic reality.

Recently, a series of laws have been applied after the *Deepwater Horizon* accident to assign responsibility and exact penalties. BP has agreed to pay fines and penalties under US domestic law of about USD 4.5 billion, to plead guilty to 14 criminal charges and to settle civil charges under US securities

---

1 *Deep Water: The Gulf Disaster and the Future of Offshore Drilling – Report to the President* (US Government Printing Office, 2011).
2 'Oil's Future is in Deepwater Drilling', *CNN Money*, 11 January 2011, <money.cnn.com/2011/01/11/news/economy/oil_drilling_deepwater/index.htm>.

laws.[3] It also faces additional penalties under the US Oil Pollution Act of 1990 and the Clean Water Act. And two BP supervisors have been indicted for criminal manslaughter. Going forward, a larger fundamental question looms about jurisdiction to act to prevent spills and accidents involving deepwater and ultra-deepwater oil and gas drilling and production. One area of uncertainty involves the current law of the sea.

This chapter lays out the essential relevant facts of deepwater and ultra-deepwater drilling and production in the context of the BP *Deepwater Horizon* oil spill in the Gulf of Mexico and it raises some of the potential legal uncertainties surrounding the applicable international law of the sea that may need to be addressed now and in the future. Those law of the sea legal uncertainties include the legal status of deepwater oil rigs and production facilities, the jurisdiction of coastal states that are exposed to potentially catastrophic harm from deepwater and ultra-deepwater drilling and production accidents such as the BP spill and the harm to the marine environment, especially to unique and discrete deepwater marine ecosystems.

2 Deepwater and ultra-deepwater drilling in the context of the BP Deepwater Horizon oil spill[4]

On the 20 April 2010 the BP *Deepwater Horizon* oil drilling rig exploded causing a 'blowout' (discharge of oil) in the Gulf of Mexico over 40 nautical miles (74 kilometres) off the coast of the US state of Louisiana. By any measure, this was the largest offshore oil drilling and production accident in US history. It has also produced wide-ranging effects of catastrophic proportions. The rig was owned and operated by Transocean and leased to BP and it flew the flag of the Marshall Islands.

2.1 The effects of the spill

The drilling rig floated in 4,992 feet (1,522 metres) of water and the oil reservoir being drilled was located another two and one half miles (about four kilometres) below the seabed. Over the three months following the explosion, an estimated total of 4.9 million barrels of oil (some 206 million gallons or 780 million litres) was discharged into the ocean waters of the Gulf until it was stopped in July of 2010. By way of contrast, the 1989 crash of the oil tanker, *Exxon Valdez*, in Prince William Sound Alaska discharged nine million gallons (34 million litres) of oil.

The current estimate of the combined spill costs including clean up, natural resource damages, economic losses, domestic law penalties, etc. is about USD 41 billion and counting. Additional fines and penalties could

---

3   Clifford Kraus and John Schwartz, 'BP Will Plead Guilty and Pay Over $4Billion', *The New York Times*, 16 November 2012, A1.
4   Unless indicated otherwise, this section draws heavily from *Deep Water, supra* note 1.

drive the costs several tens of billions of dollars higher.[5] At one point, 47,000 people and 7,000 vessels were involved to respond to the spill. A year and a half later, there were still about 1,000 personnel involved in the Gulf region. In addition to state government claims – the US Gulf Coast states are Alabama, Florida, Louisiana, Mississippi and Texas – and federal government claims, over 100,000 private claims have been made for property and economic losses.

The immediate natural resources effects from the oil discharged included harm to shell and finfish – including to crabs, shrimp, oysters, jellyfish, sea turtles, tuna, sharks, snapper, grouper and marlin. Ocean mammals such as whales and dolphin were also affected. Birds (sea and land) like pelicans, osprey, bald eagles, peregrine falcons, northern gannets and laughing gulls suffered harm from oiled feathers and oil ingestion. The spill also affected floating seaweed beds and phytoplankton. Some 1,100 miles (1,769 kilometres) of coast was affected, including impacts felt by beaches, salt marshes and mangrove swamps.

Unique to an oil spill at depths of deepwater (over 1,000 feet or 300 metres deep) and ultra-deepwater (over 10,000 feet or three kilometres deep) are the effects experienced by the discrete deepwater marine ecosystem. The Macondo well, at which the *Deepwater Horizon* operated, occurred in the deep ocean bathpelagic zone (3,300–13,000 feet or one to four kilometres deep). It is only relatively recently that deepwater and deep seabed areas have been discovered to have unique (intense pressure, cold temperatures and little or no light), rich and diverse marine habitats that include cold water corrals, fish, light-producing worms and giant squid. The deepwater ecosystem of the Gulf was exposed to massive amounts of discharged oil from the BP spill. Oil on the seabed in very cold deepwater habitats dissipates slowly. The nature and severity of the impacts to the deepwater ecosystem around wellhead site, short- and long-term, are not yet known or quantifiable.

Economic losses were suffered by all aspects of tourism and fishing (commercial and sport) as well as by disruptions to other oil and gas operations in the Gulf, all of which are critical activities to the Gulf coast communities. The indirect long-term economic (and environmental) effects on consumer confidence (tourists, fishers and fish eaters, etc.) and to the Gulf coast marketing 'brand' are unknown but no less real. In a larger economic market context, the fishing resources of the Southern coastal US (including the Gulf) produce more than a third of the total US seafood supply and the Gulf of Mexico, in particular, produces a third of the US domestic oil supply, an increasing amount of which is from deepwater reservoirs.

The BP *Deepwater Horizon* oil spill also affected human physical and mental health. Immediately, 11 people died and the explosion of the rig injured 17 people. The larger human community suffered from fear, anxiety, stress and

---

5 Kraus and Schwartz, 'BP Will Plead Guilty' *supra* note 3.

depression with the direct and indirect consequences that this produces on families, friends and colleagues. Such effects almost certainly will never be reduced to accurate financial calculation much less be the object of monetary compensation.

2.2 *The growing phenomenon of deepwater and ultra-deepwater oil and gas drilling and production*

The ability to drill for oil and gas at deepwater and ultra-deepwater is a technology that has rapidly emerged only since the late 1990s. Prior to the 1990s, offshore oil exploitation was at relatively shallow depths close to shore and used more or less a traditional, decades-old, platform technology fixed structurally in some manner to the seabed.

This new deepwater and ultra-deepwater exploitation technology opens a potentially dominant new frontier of ocean exploitation of oil and gas far offshore at unprecedented water depths. It also presents new challenges and risks not encountered before in several respects.

First, there is a huge potential for significant oil recovery from deepwater zones. It is plausible that deepwater and ultra-deepwater drilling will become ubiquitous in the decades ahead. Some of the deepwater fields found to date have over a billion barrels of oil potential. They are so large that they are often described as 'elephants'. In 1990 in the Gulf of Mexico, most oil and gas recovered came from shallow water reservoirs at less than 250 feet (about 75 metres) below the surface of the ocean and relatively near the coast. However, by 1998, less than a decade later, the weighted average of oil production came, not from shallow water reservoirs, but from deepwater wells.

The new phenomenon of deepwater oil and gas exploitation is not confined to the Gulf. Deepwater reservoirs, zones and basins are now for the first time being exploited all around the world: in the Northeast Atlantic west of the Shetland islands; off the coast of Brazil (the Compos Basin); off the deepwater coast of West Africa (Guinea and Angola); and off the Northeast coast of Australia, to name a few locations. From 2001 to 2004, 11 new, major oil fields have been found at ocean depths of 7,000 feet (some two kilometres) or more.

Second, these emerging new deepwater oil and gas resources require new and unique exploitation technology. Generally, deepwater and ultra-deepwater drilling and production requires a balance between drilling to the 'pay zone' below the seabed and at the same time doing so in a way that keeps under control the tremendous pressure at the wellhead and that does not result in a blowout like the *Deepwater Horizon* and does not fracture the pipe or the geological formation holding the reservoir.

Traditional, shallow water drilling and production facilities anchored and fixed to seabed close to shore are not useful because at deepwater and ultra-deepwater the depths are too great to use fixed facilities. At deepwater depths, mobility and size are the keys to drilling and production facilities. A new mobile oil drilling unit (MODU) has been developed for deployment at deepwater reservoir sites.[6] MODUs for deepwater and ultra-deepwater drilling and production generally are of two types – semisubmersibles (such as the *Deepwater Horizon*) and drillships. Semisubmersibles are either towed to a drilling location or use their own propulsion systems to navigate to deepwater oil and gas sites. A drillship is a massive vessel that is modified to drill oil and gas wells. Both semisubmersibles and drillships are mobile at the well site during drilling and are manoeuvred by propellers and thrusters using dynamic positioning technology to stay positioned over the well site during drilling and production. These facilities are huge by comparison to small, shallow water, facilities fixed structurally to the ocean floor. For example, the *Deepwater Horizon* had 123 people 'on board', weighed some 33,000 tons and had four supporting decks of workspace on top of which an oil derrick reached 20 stories above the drilling platform.

Third, the great horizontal distances from shore and the great vertical distances from the ocean surface to the deepwater wellhead of deepwater and ultra-deepwater drilling and production facilities pose, special, extremely difficult challenges to deal with accidents at the wellhead on the seabed surface or below. Equipment and operations are accessible at the ocean floor only by remotely operated vehicles controlled by operators thousands of feet above the well.[7] In addition, the conditions of low temperature and high pressure at the seabed add substantially to the complexity of facilities control. The BP blowout took three months to bring under control and to stop oil discharges after the explosion, in large part because of the wellhead's distance from shore and depth below the ocean surface. Accidents at offshore, shallow water, fixed facilities are far more accessible for responders to accidents and are a different order of magnitude: lower in risk and potentially catastrophic harm.

3 Legal uncertainties in the law of the sea applied to deepwater and ultra-deepwater drilling and production

In its essential respects, the current international law of the sea addressed here predated the discovery of vast deepwater and ultra-deepwater oil and gas resources and the development of the technology to exploit those resources. The current law of the sea was mostly codified in 1958 in the four

---

6 For a description, see 'How Does a Drillship Work?', *Rigzone*, <www.rigzone.com/training/insight.asp?i_id=306>.
7 Curry Hagerty and Jonathan Ramseur, 'Deepwater Horizon Oil Spill: Selected Issues for Congress', Congressional Research Service Report no. 7–5700, 30 July 2010.

Geneva conventions on the law of sea[8] and in 1982 in the Law of the Sea Convention.[9]

That codification confirms the historical evolution of systematic, creeping, coastal state jurisdiction over the oceans and ocean activities – for example, extension of the territorial sea of coastal states from three to twelve miles, the recognition of coastal resource jurisdiction over the continental shelf and the establishment of the 200-mile exclusive economic zone (EEZ) extending coastal state resource jurisdiction over seabed and superjacent water column.

The phenomenon of deepwater and ultra-deepwater oil and gas exploitation using MODUs reveals uncertainties in the law of the sea, which ought to be resolved in some definite manner. Those uncertainties in the law of the sea as presently codified include uncertainty about the legal status of MODUs, the jurisdiction of coastal states and the special peril posed to unique and diverse deepwater marine ecosystems.

3.1 Uncertainty in the legal status of deepwater and ultra-deepwater mobile oil drilling units

One legal uncertainty about MODUs used for deepwater and ultra-deepwater oil and gas exploitation is whether under the law of the sea they have the legal status of ships (vessels) or of offshore installations or both?[10] This is not a new question. However, it is one that remains unresolved with clarity in the context of spills and that continues to create uncertainties in the legal status of MODUs used for deepwater and ultra-deepwater oil and gas drilling and exploitation.

Both the 1958 Geneva Conventions on the law of the sea and the 1982 Law of the Sea Convention refer to ships and vessels, and to offshore installations, devices and structures. However, nowhere are these terms defined.

MODUs are considered to be ships or vessels because they navigate by self-propulsion from deepwater site to deepwater site and also move by self-propulsion with propellers, thrusters and GPS positioning technology while on-site drilling and even during production. As ships, they have the right of freedom of navigation that other ships have not only on the high seas

---

8   Convention on the High Seas, 29 April 1958, in force 30 September 1962, 450 UNTS 11; Convention on the Continental Shelf, 29 April 1958, in force 10 June 1964, 499 UNTS 311; Convention on the Territorial Sea and the Contiguous Zone, 29 April 1958, in force 10 September 1964, 516 UNTS 205; Convention on Fishing Conservation of the Living Resources of the High Seas, 29 April 1958, in force 20 March 1966, 559 UNTS 285.
9   UNCLOS, 10 December 1982, in force 16 November 1994, 1833 UNTS 3.
10 See Hossein Esmaeili, *The Legal Regime of Offshore Oil Rigs in International Law* (Ashgate, 2001), at 20–68. Another remote possibility is that MODUs because of their sheer size might be considered 'artificial islands'. However, artificial islands are more akin to permanent attachment to the seabed with 'landfill' (rocks and soil) than to free-floating oil and gas facilities not fixed to the seabed.

but also in the waters of the EEZ. MODUs as ships or vessels also have the right of innocent passage in the territorial sea and straits used for international navigation and they would have the nationality of the state whose flag they fly.

As ships or vessels, deepwater MODUs typically are registered with an open-registry, flag of convenience state. The *Deepwater Horizon* was registered in the Marshall Islands and flew its flag. MODUs as ships or vessels may be subject to non-binding, 'soft law', maritime industry codes[11] addressing construction standards, vessel design and equipment requirements. As ships or vessels, MODUs may be subject to certification inspections (for mortgage, insurance and marketing purposes) by so-called shipping industry 'classification societies', such as the American Bureau of Shipping and Det Norske Veritas, which are concerned with physical characteristics of ships. In the BP spill, the US Coast Guard concluded that the Marshall Islands as flag state of the *Deepwater Horizon* 'entrusted all flag state duties' to classification societies 'without sufficient oversight which may have been [a] factor' in the accident.[12]

For MODUs that are foreign flagged ships or vessels, this may limit coastal state authority in the territorial sea or EEZ. For example, the US Coast Guard exercised only limited inspection authority over the *Deepwater Horizon* in terms of vessel 'seaworthiness' concerns and 'not the drilling aspects' of the rig.[13] This included Coast Guard oversight limited to such matters as hull structure, navigation equipment, lifesaving equipment, fire protection and worker health and safety. The US Government Accounting Office (GAO) found the 'Coast Guard's scheme for overseeing the safety of foreign-flagged MODUs [to be] insufficient because it defers heavily to the flag to ensure safety'.[14] Oddly, Coast Guard authority was limited to areas of the *Deepwater Horizon* above the water line and not to 'the sub platform' (i.e. underwater or seafloor) drilling systems.[15]

Alternatively, MODUs also have the status of an offshore installation, device or structure used to explore and exploit deepwater oil and gas reserves. The 1958 Continental Shelf Convention in Article 5(2) refers to 'installations and other devices necessary for ... [continental shelf]

---

11   Such as the Code for the Construction and Equipment of Mobile Offshore Drilling Units, IMO Res. A.1023(26), 2 December 2009.
12   'Explosion, Fire Sinking and Loss of Eleven Crew Members Aboard the Mobile Offshore Drilling Unit Deepwater Horizon in the Gulf of Mexico', 20–2 April 2010, Comments of the Commandant, United Sates Coast Guard, September 2011 at 3.
13   Hagerty and Ramseur, 'Selected Issues', *supra* note 7, at 38.
14   Stephen L. Caldwell and Frank Rusco 'Deepwater Horizon: Coast Guard and Interior could Improve their Offshore Energy Inspection Programs', Testimony before the Subcommittee on Coast Guard and Maritime Transportation, Committee on Transportation and Infrastructure, House of Representatives, US Government Accountability Office Doc. no. GAO-12-203T, 2 November 2011, at 10.
15   Curran Hagerty and Jonathan Ramseur, 'Deepwater Horizon Oil Spill: Highlighted Actions and Issues', Congressional Research Service, 13 September 2010, at 2–3.

exploration and exploitation of ... natural resources'. The 1982 Law of the Sea Convention in Articles 60 and 80 refers to 'installations and structures' in the EEZ and continental shelf, respectively. Under both treaties, the coastal state has authority over permissions, construction and operation of deepwater oil and gas drilling and production facilities in those maritime zones.

As an installation, device or structure engaged in oil and gas exploitation of the US EEZ seabed, the *Deepwater Horizon* fell under the authority, not of the US Coast Guard, but of the US Minerals Management Service (now the Bureau of Ocean Energy Management, Regulation and Enforcement [BOEMRE]) of the Department of Interior, which regulates leasing of drill sites, exploration and exploitation operations and deals with environmental issues.

This split in status of deepwater MODUs such as the *Deepwater Horizon* as both ship and installation also contributes to operational uncertainty. US practice apparently is treat MODUs as ships until the rig is connected to the wellhead ('latched') and to treat it as an installation until it is 'unlatched' from the wellhead (even though it continues to move and manoeuvre by propellers and thrusters while latched).[16] In the *Deepwater Horizon* explosion and blowout, there was uncertainty on the part of those involved including the crew as to who was in charge – the MODU operator, Transocean or the captain of the MODU.[17]

3.2 Uncertainty in coastal state jurisdiction

When the law of the sea was mostly codified in the late 1950s and early 1980s, the jurisdiction of coastal states over oil and gas drilling and production was certain. Offshore oil and gas facilities were in shallow waters close to shore and the facilities were installations fixed firmly to the seabed. Those facilities located variously in the territorial sea, in the continental shelf and/or in the EEZ were, and are, subject to coastal state exclusive jurisdiction, which assures that the coastal has complete jurisdiction over leasing, exploration and exploitation over oil gas resources in the seabed of those maritime zones and over the authorisation, establishment, use and operations of oil and gas installations and structures.[18]

---

16 Rebecca K. Richards, 'Deepwater Mobile Oil Rigs in the Exclusive Economic Zone and the Uncertainty of Coastal State Jurisdiction', 10 *Journal of International Business & Law* (2011) 387–411, at 423.
17 *Ibid.* at 423. The Republic of The Marshall Islands acknowledged that there 'were instances of confusion regarding decision making authority during the casualty' that posed 'challenges for maintaining a clear command structure, especially in emergency situations'. However, it did not accept that the confusion 'was a causal factor in the causality'. Deepwater Horizon Marine Causality Investigation Report, Republic of the Marshall Islands, IMO Doc. 8764597, 17 August 2011, at ii.
18 Convention on the Territorial Sea and the Contiguous Zone, *supra* note 8, Article 2; Continental Shelf Convention, *supra* note 8, Article 2(1); UNCLOS, *supra* note 9, Articles 2(2), 56, 57, 60, 77 and 80.

With the emergence of deepwater and ultra-deepwater oil and gas resource exploration and exploitation and use of MODUs in the late 1990s, coastal state jurisdiction is far less certain. Churchill and Lowe aptly summarised (without explanation) the uncertainty with regard to coastal state jurisdiction and deepwater MODUs:

> Coastal state jurisdiction [under the law of the sea] is plainly an inadequate basis for the regulation of such mobile units [i.e. MODUs] and activities upon them. Yet neither the 1958 [Continental Shelf] Convention nor the 1982 Convention deals specifically with the issue.[19]

That inadequacy may produce uncertainty in coastal state jurisdiction over deepwater and ultra-deepwater MODUs in several respects. First, as mentioned above, the status of MODUs as, at the same time (or alternatively), foreign vessels and ships subject to flag state jurisdiction and also oil and gas installations, devices and structures subject to exclusive coastal state jurisdiction makes determining the extent of coastal state control at a particular stage of exploitation or moment sometimes difficult to ascertain. Second, with respect to the outer limits of continental shelf where deepwater and ultra-deepwater oil reservoir zones are located, coastal state jurisdiction may be limited in ways not experienced with shallow water reservoirs closer to shore. For example, with regard to coastal state authority in the outer continental shelf beyond 200 miles, the superjacent waters in which MODUs operate are high seas and not part of the EEZ of a coastal state. In addition, if oil and gas resources are exploited by deepwater and ultra-deepwater MODUs in this part of the ocean floor, the coastal state (although it has exclusive exploitation rights) must pay a portion of the site value to the International Seabed Authority after the first five years of production.[20] In any event, the legal questions surrounding the actual determination of precise outer limits of coastal state jurisdiction over oil and gas reservoirs, are sufficiently unwieldy that the 1982 Law of the Sea Convention in Annex II establishes a 21-person Commission on the Limits of the Continental Shelf to sort them on a case by case basis where claims extend beyond 200 nautical miles from the baselines from which the breadth of the territorial seas is measured.[21] Those outer limits at deepwater depths are also difficult to determine because the ocean floor's configuration is constantly changing

---

19 R. R. Churchill and A. V. Lowe, *The Law of the Sea* (3rd edn, Manchester University Press, 1999), at 154.
20 UNCLOS, *supra* note 9, Article 82.
21 'Despite its detail, the formula [for continental shelf delimitation] in the 1982 Convention leaves room for considerable uncertainty'. Churchill and Lowe, *Law of the Sea, supra* note 16 at 149. See Donald Rothwell, 'Issues and Strategies for Outer Continental Shelf Claims', 23 *International Journal of Marine & Coastal Law* (2008) 185–211.

and some areas have not been charted or are in need of re-charting. The isobaths (used in some delimitations) are not easy to determine, and at deepwater and ultra-deepwater sites, the nature, composition and thickness of sedentary rock may simply not be known with any confident degree of certainty.[22] That information is important to separate coastal state jurisdiction over continental shelf, continental shelf beyond 200 miles and from the geological deep seabed beyond the limits of coastal state jurisdiction subject to the International Seabed Authority.

3.3 The unique peril posed by deepwater and ultra-deepwater operations to deepwater marine ecosystems

Not addressed specifically by the current codified law of the sea is the impact of deepwater and ultra-deepwater oil and gas drilling and production on unique deepwater marine ecosystems in the event of a spill like the *Deepwater Horizon*. As mentioned above, these ecosystems operate at high pressure, low light and cold temperatures not experienced by other marine ecosystems. In addition, these marine ecosystems are not directly accessible by humans. Reliance must be had on remotely operated vehicles from the ocean surface. The blowout of the *Deepwater Horizon* exposed 'deepwater ecosystems ... to large volumes of oil for an extended period'.[23] The *Deepwater Horizon* oil spill raised:

> Public and scientific concern ... on the impacts ... of a deepwater plume of highly dispersed oil droplets and dissolved gases at between 3,200 and 4,200 feet deep and extending many miles ... [from] the wellhead.[24]

Those concerns included 'depletion of the oxygen supply on which aquatic species depend', 'potential impacts of deepwater oil and dispersant concentrations on individual species' and 'acute toxicity to exposed organisms' and 'reports of dead and dying deepwater corals'.[25] It has been estimated that over 1,700 species live in the marine ecosystem near the Macondo wellhead of the *Deepwater Horizon*.[26]

Unfortunately, 'scientific understanding of the deepwater ecosystem has not advanced with the industrial development of deepwater drilling and production':[27] 'Scientists simply do not yet know how to predict the ecolo-

---

22 Churchill and Lowe, *Law of the Sea, supra* note 19, at 148–9.
23 *Deep Water, supra* note 1, at 182.
24 *Ibid.*
25 *Ibid.*
26 Mark Schrope, 'Deep Wounds', 472 *Nature* (2011) 152–4, at 154.
27 *Deep Water, supra* note 1, at 182.

gical consequences and effects on key species that might result from oil exposure in the water column ... far below ... the surface.'[28]

This means that the required baseline information to assess and measure natural resources damages and to assign responsibility and to identify and impose restoration efforts are presently missing with regard to deepwater marine ecosystems affected by deepwater and ultra-deepwater oil and gas accidents like the *Deepwater Horizon*. Marine natural resources preservation and pollution prevention efforts 'presume sufficient prior knowledge to determine what is different after the spill' and such prior knowledge is 'generally lacking for deepwater ecosystems'.[29]

The current international law of the sea does not address this significant problem (nor do industry, national or regional efforts for that matter). The law of the sea as codified in the late 1950s and early 1980s has only general obligations and encouragements for states individually and cooperatively to protect and preserve the marine environment. For example, Article 24 of the 1958 High Seas Convention requires states to 'draw up' regulations 'to prevent pollution of the sea by discharge of oil' from 'the exploitation and exploration of the seabed and its subsoil'. Article 5(7) of the 1958 Continental Shelf Convention only obliges states to take 'all appropriate measures' to protect 'living resources of the sea from harmful agents'. The 1982 Law of the Sea Convention in Article 208(1) requires states in seabed under their jurisdiction 'to prevent, reduce and control pollution of the marine environment arising from' 'seabed activities' and 'installations and structures under their jurisdiction'. And Article 145 requires the International Seabed Authority to make rules for, *inter alia*, pollution prevention from deep seabed 'drilling' and the 'construction and operation or maintenance of installations' on the deep seabed.

4 Conclusion

The recent and continuing phenomenon of the exploration and exploitation of oil and gas in deepwater and ultra-deepwater reservoirs around the globe is growing at a significant rate. The 2010 BP *Deepwater Horizon* oil spill in the Gulf of Mexico underscores the uncertainty in the currently codified international law of the sea to deal with this phenomenon. Those uncertainties exist about the legal status under the law of the sea of deepwater and ultra-deepwater facilities for drilling and production of oil and gas. In addition, coastal states, which bear the potentially catastrophic harm from blowouts like the *Deepwater Horizon*, have uncertain jurisdiction to deal with the deepwater and ultra-deepwater oil and gas drilling and production.

---

28 *Ibid.*, at 174.
29 Robin Craig, 'Legal Remedies for Deep Marine Oil Spills and Long-Term Ecological Resilience: A Match Made in Hell', 6 *Brigham Young Law Review* (2011) 1863–98, at 1885.

Finally, there is legal uncertainty about how to deal with the harm to unique deepwater marine ecosystems affected by deepwater and ultra-deepwater accidents.

Those uncertainties and gaps in the law of the sea need to be filled. Some have called for a discrete comprehensive international legal treaty regime to deal with all aspects of all offshore oil rigs including deepwater and ultra-deepwater facilities.[30] Others have called for complete and certain coastal state regulatory jurisdiction over all deepwater and ultra-deepwater exploration and exploitation, reflecting a further extension of the historical creeping coastal state jurisdiction in the law of the sea.[31]

Perhaps what is needed is something 'in between' in the form of a discrete agreement aimed at resolving those legal uncertainties. There is precedent for such an approach. Uncertainties and gaps relating to fisheries conservation and management in the law of the sea were resolved by a special agreement. There, the 1982 Law of the Sea Convention acknowledges, but does not directly address, transboundary fishing cooperation among states and regional fishing organisations. That gap was partially filled in 1995 by the UN Fish Stocks Agreement (FSA) that addresses discretely the problems of straddling stocks (fish in both the high seas and EEZ) and highly migratory fish stocks.[32]

A similar agreement could be reached to remove the legal uncertainties associated with deepwater and ultra-deepwater oil and gas drilling. Such an agreement could serve several purposes. It could help to ensure protection and preservation of deepwater unique marine ecosystems, to clarify jurisdiction over MODUs, to help the efficient and relatively safe exploration and exploitation of oil and gas, to protect coastal communities and to make certain that coastal states have needed jurisdiction in recognition that overwhelmingly it is coastal states that suffer the potentially catastrophic consequences of an oil spill from deepwater and ultra-deepwater as shown by the BP *Deepwater Horizon* accident. At the end of the day, perhaps, it is not so important which pathway towards certainty in the law of sea is taken to address the problem, as it is that some law certain be made, and be made in the near future.

---

30   Esmaeili, *Legal Regime, supra* note 10, at 263.
31   Richards, 'Deepwater Mobile Oil Rigs', *supra* note 16, at 410–11.
32   Agreement for the Implementation of the UNCLOS of 10 December 1982 Relating to the Conservation and Management of Straddling Stocks and Highly Migratory Fish Stocks, 4 August 1995, in force 11 December 2001, 2167 UNTS 3.

17 Slowly but surely?

The challenge of the responsibility to protect

Marja Lehto[*]

The responsibility to protect (RtoP) may have been alluded to as a norm,[1] an emerging norm,[2] an emerging principle[3] and a standard,[4] its normative character is far from settled. The concept was formulated by the International Commission for Intervention and State Sovereignty (ICISS) in 2001 and endorsed, with a brief definition, by the UN Summit in 2005. While the World Summit Outcome Document (WSOD) reflected the agreement of more than 150 heads of state or government, it did not introduce new legal commitments.[5] At the same time, there is no doubt that the ICISS, which launched the concept as a response to the call of the UN Secretary-General Kofi Annan to enhance humanitarian protection in face of mass atrocities, had the ambition to trigger a normative change. The Commission's report presented the new concept as a principle supported by existing legal instruments. Depending on further developments, in particular action taken by the UN Security Council, the Commission expected RtoP to be recognised

---

[*] The views expressed in the article are those of the author and do not necessarily reflect the views of the Finnish Ministry for Foreign Affairs.

1 The International Coalition for the RtoP calls it 'a new international security and human rights norm', see <www.responsibilitytoprotect.org>.
2 *A More Secure World: Our Shared Responsibility*, Report of the High-Level Panel on Threats, Challenges and Change, UN Doc. A/59/565, 2 December 2004 (hereinafter High-Level Panel's report), para 202.
3 *The Responsibility to Protect*, Report of the International Commission on Intervention and State Sovereignty (International Development Resource Centre, Ottawa, 2001) (hereinafter ICISS report), para. 2.25 at 16.
4 Edward C. Luck, 'The Responsibility to Protect: The First Decade', 3 *Global Responsibility to Protect* (2011), 387–99, at 389.
5 ICISS report. For the definition, see the WSOD, GA Res. 60/1, 24 October 2005, paras 138 and 139. According to this definition, each state has the responsibility to protect its population from genocide, war crimes, ethnic cleansing and crimes against humanity, while the international community also has a responsibility to use appropriate peaceful means, in accordance with the UN Charter, to help to ensure such protection. In this context, collective action could be taken by the UN Security Council in accordance with Chapter VII of the Charter, should peaceful means prove inadequate and national authorities manifestly fail their responsibility to protect populations.

as a new rule of customary international law.[6] The report refrained from proposing a specific codification project but mentioned in passing an international convention, and even an amendment to the UN Charter, as possible outcomes in the future.[7]

The development of the concept during the first ten years, with considerable resources being invested in its mainstreaming and consolidation by the UN Secretary General and by the International Coalition for the RtoP, as well as in a growing number of academic contributions, is nevertheless impressive. Judging from the popular support of the concept, it would be a good candidate to be added to the list of recent law-making projects in which NGOs have played an instrumental role. Such projects have notably also touched on the sensitive areas where security considerations and human rights intersect. The Convention against Anti-Personnel Mines,[8] the Statute of the International Criminal Court,[9] and the Convention on Cluster Munitions,[10] to name the most prominent ones, extend their reach to core areas of state sovereignty, such as criminal jurisdiction and national defence, in order to ban indiscriminate weapons or to fight impunity. Even if the objective of the RtoP – safeguarding vulnerable populations from genocide and other similar crimes – is equally compelling, no serious negotiations have been opened to date to elaborate a legal instrument on the topic,[11] and even many of its advocates deny that it could be enshrined in legal terms.[12]

Should it be concluded that the RtoP is rather devoid of legal content? A failed project of international law-making? Or is it too early to assess its impact on legal thinking? Could the promise of protection, prevention and timely action, even if by now broadly mainstreamed and tamed, still challenge the prevalent understanding of state sovereignty, territorial integrity and non-interference in internal affairs of states? This article focuses on the question whether the RtoP should be seen as a normative breakthrough. It will discuss the origins of the concept in the debates on the 'right to intervene' and humanitarian intervention in the 1990s, its formulation in 2001 and 2005 as well as further developments. It is argued that the confusion about the legal nature of the RtoP is largely due to the existence of two successive and partly

6   ICISS report, para. 6.17, at 50.
7   *Ibid.*, para. 8.26, at 74.
8   Convention on the Prohibition of the Use, Stockpiling, Production and Transfer of Anti-Personnel Mines and on their Destruction, 18 September 1997, in force 1 March 1999, 2056 UNTS 211.
9   Rome Statute of the International Criminal Court, 17 July 1998, in force 1 July 2000, 2187 UNTS 3.
10 Convention on Cluster Munitions, 30 May 2008, in force 1 August 2010, 48 ILM 357
11 See, however, Constitutive Act of the African Union, 11 July 2000, in force 26 May 2001, 2158 UNTS 3, which has influenced the formulation of the relevant paragraphs of the WSOD.
12 Ekkehard Strauss, *The Emperor's New Clothes? The United Nations and the Implementation of the Responsibility to Protect* (Nomos 2009); Carsten Stahn, 'Responsibility to Protect: Political Rhetoric or Emerging Legal Norm?', *101 American Journal of International Law* (2007); Luck, 'The First Decade', *supra* note 4, at 393.

overlapping normative projects that have left their mark on the understanding of the concept. The first project aimed at filling a lacuna in existing legal regulation and creating a new exception to the UN Charter's prohibition of the use of force. The second project, while hardly less ambitious, views the concept as 'firmly anchored in well-established principles of international law'[13] and seeks to influence the interpretation, implementation and enforcement of the relevant rules. Whereas the focus of the first project was on humanitarian intervention, that of the second one covers two much broader topics: how to make the Security Council's action more consistent and effective, and how to mobilise resources and expertise across the UN system to the prevention of the kind of humanitarian disasters that could require intervention.

1 Right to intervene

Humanitarian intervention is by no means a new concept, and the origins of the RtoP can be traced to very early times in the history of international law.[14] It is nevertheless convenient to begin this brief account from the late 1980s when a related term, that of right/obligation to intervene (*le droit/devoir d'ingérence*) was coined by Mario Bettati, professor in international law, and Bernard Kouchner, one of the founders of the NGO *Médecins sans Frontières* and later Foreign Minister of France.[15] The way the two concepts relate to each other is intriguing. The Report of the ICISS as well as practically all the subsequent documents that have alimented the discussion on the RtoP have deemed it necessary to take distance from the 'right to intervene' and to underline the groundbreaking nature of their own undertaking.[16] At the same time, the RtoP can be seen as a follow up to the *droit d'ingérence*.[17] The emergence of the French concept in the late 1980s has been said to amount to a conceptual leap that eventually made possible the development of the notion of the RtoP.[18] Professor Bettati himself has confirmed this interpretation in a recent comment characterising the latter concept as the right to intervene that has just changed the name.[19] Without denying the

---

13 *Implementing the Responsibility to Protect*, Report of the Secretary-General, UN Doc. A/63/677, 12 January 2009 (hereinafter Implementing report), para. 10 a, at 9.
14 As discussed by Stahn, 'Rhetoric', *supra* note 12, at 111–13.
15 Mario Bettati and Bernard Kouchner, *Le devoir d'ingérence – ou peut-on les laisser mourir?* (Denoël, 1987).
16 ICISS report, para. 2.4, at 11; High-Level Panel's report, para. 201; *In Larger Freedom: Towards Development, Security and Human Rights for All*, Report of the Secretary-General, UN Doc. A/59/2005, 21 March 2005 (hereinafter Larger Freedom report), para. 125; Implementing report, para. 10(a), at 7.
17 *La responsabilité de protéger*, présentation, <www.franceonu.org/spip.php?article3978>.
18 *La responsabilité de protéger*, intervention of France at the UN General Assembly, 23 July 2009, <www.franceonu.org/spip.php?article4071>.
19 Jean Bernard Cadier, 'Et l'ONU ressuscita le droit d'ingérence ...', *France24*, 18 March 2011, <www-france24.com>.

new elements and approaches introduced by the ICISS, the case for continuity from the right to intervene to the RtoP can be defended. The pertinent elements include the moral argument for intervention, questioning of the nature and limits of state sovereignty and law-making ambition.

Le devoir d'ingérence – ou peut-on les laisser mourir? (The obligation to intervene – or should we let them die?) was the provocative title of Bettati's and Kouchner's book published in 1987. Referring to the experience of civil wars in Africa, the authors argued for free access to humanitarian aid and suggested that there were situations in which territorial borders would have to be transgressed without an authorisation by the sovereign. In a true spirit of non-governmental *sans-frontièrisme*,[20] they called for action that could extend from military interventions to private clandestine operations conducted without passport or visa.[21] The contribution of the book to the development of a coherent theory of humanitarian intervention was limited but it contained a forceful moral call to take action to respond to humanitarian emergencies. This call was to resonate with many later initiatives taken in the 1990s, from the multinational military operations in crisis areas to the establishment of international criminal tribunals, not to speak of the ICISS report itself, which were all prompted by civil society activism and justified by a moral and political necessity, or, to use Kouchner's term, by 'the logic of extreme urgency'.[22]

In raising the matter of sovereignty, Bettati and Kouchner brought the debate into the legal sphere. Their main criticism was a general one concerning the alleged bias of the international legal system, which in their view gave priority to state interests over humanitarian values and allowed for sovereignty – 'a legal iron curtain'[23] – to be used as a shield for injustice and inhumanity.[24] According to a phrase later attributed to Kouchner, it would be lawful even if inelegant for a state to massacre its own population.[25] Both authors used the concept of sovereignty mainly in the way of a political argument, and faced criticism for the lack of a proper legal analysis,[26] but

---

20   Mario Bettati, *Droit d'ingérence. Mutation de l'ordre international* (Editions Odile Jacob, 1996), at 78–88.
21   Bernard Kouchner, 'La Morale de l'extrême urgence', in Bettati and Kouchner, *Devoir d'ingérence*, supra note 15, 271–7, at 272–3.
22   Ibid.
23   Bettati, *Droit d'ingérence*, supra note 20, at 22.
24   Mario Bettati, 'Un droit d'ingérence humanitaire?', in Bettati and Kouchner, *Devoir d'ingérence*, supra note 15, at 26.
25   Olivier Corten, 'Les ambiguïtés du droit d'ingérence humanitaire', *Le courrier de l'UNESCO*, August 1999, <www.operationspaix.net/spip.php?page=references&id_mot=347&date=2004>.
26   Yves Sandoz, 'Droit ou devoir d'ingérence, droit à l'assistance: de quoi parle-t-on?', 74 *Revue Internationale de la Croix-Rouge* (1992), No. 795, 225–37; Anne Ryniker, 'The ICRC's position on "humanitarian intervention"', 83 *International Review of the Red Cross* (2001), No. 842, 527–32, at 528.

their argumentation set a precedent by describing the essential problem of humanitarian protection in terms of a conflict between state sovereignty and human rights. When UN Secretary-General Kofi Annan, in his Millennium Report of 2000, spoke of 'a real dilemma' asking which of the fundamental principles of humanity or sovereignty should prevail when they are in conflict, he subscribed to views that were widely shared at the time.[27]

Bettati's and Kouchner's book was instrumental in triggering a new normative development in order to facilitate humanitarian action in emergency situations. What it advocated in the first place was the international recognition of the right to humanitarian assistance as a new human right,[28] a matter that was introduced by France to the UN General Assembly with the result of two resolutions being adopted concerning humanitarian assistance to victims of natural disasters and similar emergencies.[29] The authors had nevertheless been prepared to extend the application of the concept of the *devoir d'ingérence* to all situations of inhumanity and barbarism.[30] Reflecting this broader ambition, the concept of the right to intervene continued its life and later became a catchword for humanitarian intervention. In 1996, Bettati welcomed a legal change that seemed to him to be underway,[31] evidenced by different kinds of normative intervention against 'the territorial opacity of states',[32] such as strengthening of human rights, enhanced accountability for atrocities and multinational peace operations. All this would in his view lead to a gradual acceptance of the right of intervene. Appropriate legal instruments would be drafted in due course.[33]

Greater legal precision was not required before the spring of 1999 when NATO launched the 'Operation Allied Force' against the Federal Republic of Yugoslavia (FRY), with the stated objective of protecting the population of Kosovo and without having obtained an authorisation of the UN Security Council. The Kosovo intervention generated considerable sympathy as well as many genuine attempts to square the humanitarian imperative with the requirements of legality. When a resolution to condemn the NATO action was presented to the UN Security Council, it was defeated by a great majority of member states, with some of them arguing that humanitarian concerns

---

27 *We the Peoples: The Role of the United Nations in the 21st Century*, Report of the Secretary-General, UN Doc. A/54/2000, 27 March 2000 (hereinafter Millennium report) at 47–8.
28 Bernard Kouchner, 'La loi de l'oppression minimale', in Bettati and Kouchner, *Devoir d'ingérence, supra* note 15, 17–22.
29 GA Res. 43/131, 8 December 1988; GA Res. 45/100, 14 December 1990. These resolutions were later recalled in the UN International Law Commission's work on the Protection of Persons in the Event of Disasters as well as in the guidelines of the International Federation of the Red Cross on International Disaster Response Law.
30 Kouchner, 'La Morale', *supra* note 21, at 277.
31 Bettati, *Droit d'ingérence, supra* note 20, at 324.
32 *Ibid.*, at 44.
33 *Ibid.*, at 324.

could take precedence over territorial integrity.[34] The first scholarly assessments, written while the operation was still underway, saw that the recourse to armed force could be justified[35] and might even augur the emergence of a new norm making unauthorised armed interventions lawful under certain conditions.[36] An intense legal debate followed, and a year later, the Independent International Commission on Kosovo famously concluded that the NATO intervention had been illegal but legitimate, suggesting that the moral imperative of protecting vulnerable people might override 'legalistic' considerations in case of humanitarian catastrophes.[37]

These reactions could have told about a new normative understanding, for which some support was to be found from earlier developments at the UN. The NATO action had been preceded by repeated warnings by the alliance to Belgrade, without much protest from other UN members. In other contexts, member states had overlooked rather expansive interpretations of the Security Council's use of force mandates.[38] The contours of a possible law-making project were nevertheless articulated mainly in scholarly contributions, as well as in the report of the International Commission on Kosovo. If there was an aura of legality on the NATO action, it remained unsubstantiated. While the participating NATO member states had first claimed to be acting 'out of overwhelming humanitarian necessity' in a situation in which a UN authorisation was not within reach,[39] this argument was not pursued further. When ten NATO states had to defend the legality of their action before the ICJ, only one of them referred to the concept of necessity and to that of an obligation to intervene while others were content to raise procedural arguments.[40] The ICISS, which set out to solve the problem of humanitarian intervention,[41] encountered considerable reluctance

---

34 'Security Council rejects demand for cessation of use of force against Federal Republic of Yugoslavia', UN Press Release SC/6659, 26 March 1999. See also UN Doc. A/54/33 and Corr.1. on a similar episode at a UNGA sub-committee.
35 Bruno Simma, 'NATO, the UN and the Use of Force: Legal Aspects', 10 *European Journal of International Law* (1999), 1–22.
36 Antonio Cassese, '*Ex inuria ius oritur*: Are We Moving towards International Legitimation of Forcible Humanitarian Countermeasures in the World Community?', 10 *European Journal of International Law* (1999), 25–30, at 25. See also Cassese, 'A Follow-Up: Forcible Humanitarian Countermeasures and Opinio Necessitatis', 10 *European Journal of International Law* (1999), 791–9.
37 Independent International Commission on Kosovo, *The Kosovo Report* (2000), <reliefweb.int> (hereinafter Kosovo report), at 61.
38 Most notably related to the no-fly zones in Iraq. For more details, see Scott L. Silliman, 'The Iraqi Quagmire: Enforcing the No-Fly Zones', 36 *New England Law Review* (2002), 767–73.
39 UN Doc. S/PV.3988 and S/PV.3989, 24 March and 26 March 1999. See especially the statements of Mr Eldon and Sir Jeremy Greenstock on behalf of the UK.
40 *Legality of the Use of Force (Serbia and Montenegro v. Belgium)*, CR 1999/15, Oral Proceedings of 10 May 1999, at 15–18.
41 'This report is about the so-called right to humanitarian intervention', ICISS report, at VII.

towards reviewing the legal rules on the use of force and formulated its report accordingly.[42]

2 Responsibility to protect

The ICISS report pledged allegiance to the UN Security Council as the legitimate representative of the international community and the appropriate source for authority. The question of unauthorised interventions was raised with regard to situations of 'extreme urgency' where the Security Council is unable to act but left with little elaboration.[43] At the same time, the Commission seemed to share the basic presumption of the earlier debate that legal restraints were at the heart of the problem. As if echoing those who had defended a new right to intervene, the ICISS framed the debate as being about a new or emerging norm of international law. The most concrete of the Commission's proposals in this respect, and the one that comes closest to the earlier discussion, was the list of threshold criteria that any armed intervention for humanitarian purposes should fulfil.[44] These criteria were presented to the Security Council and member states in the hope that they would be applied to situations of a threatening mass killing or ethnic cleansing. Moreover, it was suggested that the United Nations General Assembly adopt a declaratory resolution 'giving weight to those principles and to the whole idea of the "responsibility to protect" as an emerging international norm'.[45]

The idea of formulating substantive criteria for humanitarian intervention had been a central part of the short-lived but intensive legal debate that followed the 1999 Kosovo war.[46] The Kosovo Commission, too, had concluded that the time had come to present a 'framework for humanitarian intervention' to be adopted by the UN General Assembly and introduced to the Charter either by way of a formal amendment or by the Security Council's actions case by case.[47] The proposals concerning guidelines or criteria for intervention were generally made with the aim that they would fill in a lacuna in existing law and serve as a basis on which the lawfulness of future interventions could be tested. It may be assumed that the ICISS, too, saw the threshold criteria as an element that could bridge the gap between

---

42 *Ibid.*, paras 1.9 and 6.14.
43 *Ibid.*, para. 6.37.
44 *Ibid.*, at XII and paras 4.18–4.43 (just cause, right intention, military force as the last resort, proportional means, reasonable prospects of success).
45 *Ibid.*, at 110.
46 For support to the idea, see Cassese, '*Ex inuria*' and 'Follow-up', *supra* note 36; Frederik Harhoff, 'Unauthorised Humanitarian interventions – Armed Violence in the Name of Humanity?', 70 *Nordic Journal of International Law* (2001) 65–119; for arguments against, see Martti Koskenniemi, ' "The Lady Doth Protest Too Much": Kosovo and the Turn to Ethics in International Law', 65 *The Modern Law Review* (2002), No. 2, 159–75, at 167–9.
47 Kosovo report, at 4–5.

legitimacy and legality in case of Kosovo-type unauthorised interventions, but if this was the case, the proposal was not well received. The High-Level Panel reiterated it while reserving the criteria for the exclusive use of the Security Council.[48] The Summit Outcome Document effectively closed the door for any attempt to legally frame a 'right to intervene' by putting full stop at the end of the paragraph dealing with the collective response by the international community after having cited the existing prerogatives of the Security Council in accordance with Chapter VII of the UN Charter.

Further development of the RtoP after the Summit has been undertaken mainly by Secretary-General Ban Ki-moon and his special representative,[49] on the one hand, and by the NGO coalition and academic writers, on the other. While the former have chosen a cautious course in order to preserve the fragile consensus in the UN General Assembly, the latter have known no such limitation and have been able to rely on a growing interest in and support for the concept among transnational civil society networks. Ban Ki-moon's agenda in defence of the RtoP has been essentially non-legal,[50] taking distance from the initial normative discussion that was closely related to the thematic of intervention. Meanwhile, the view of the RtoP as a legal norm has also prevailed, and the legal aspects and implications of the doctrine have received considerable academic attention. The Security Council, on its part, had made little use of the concept before the spring of 2011 when it adopted Resolution 1973 (2011) authorising the establishment of a no-fly zone in Libya and citing the responsibility to protect civilian population.[51] While the resolution was hailed as the first concrete implementation of the doctrine of RtoP,[52] and 'a watershed in the emerging doctrine of the responsibility to protect',[53] the Libya operation invited mixed reactions and has so far not given rise to clear conclusions.

Trying to avoid a divisive debate, the successive reports of the Secretary-General focused on making the new concept operative while not departing

---

48 High-Level Panel's report, paras 207, 208, 209. See also Larger Freedom report, para. 126.
49 In addition to the Implementation report, see also 'Early warning, assessment and the Responsibility to Protect', UN Doc. A/64/864, 14 July 2010; 'The Role of Regional and Sub-regional arrangements in Implementing the Responsibility to Protect', UN Doc. A/65/877–S/2011/393 28 June 2011 and 'Responsibility to Protect: Timely and Decisive Response', UN Doc. A/66/874, 25 July 2012. In 2007, the Secretary-General appointed a Special Adviser, Mr Edward C. Luck, to develop the conceptual, institutional and political dimensions of the RtoP.
50 The Implementation report, para. 10 a, denied that any new obligations could be derived 'just from the relatively recent enunciation and acceptance of the Responsibility to protect'.
51 SC Res. 1973, 17 March 2011. See also SC Res. 1970, 26 February 2011, preamble, para. 9.
52 Ramesh Thakur, 'UN breathes life into "responsibility to protect"', 21 March 2011, <www.thestar.com/prinarticle/957664>.
53 UN Secretary-General Ban Ki-moon's address to the Sofia Forum, UN Doc. SG/SM/13548, 6 May 2011.

from the Summit Outcome Document. This meant restricting the scope of application of the concept to genocide, crimes against humanity, war crimes and ethnic cleansing ('RtoP crimes') as triggers of collective responsibility. As the WSOD had stressed the need for the international community to support and assist states in their efforts to prevent atrocities, assistance and capacity-building became a separate file of the RtoP, implying a long-term involvement on the part of the international community. According to the 2009 Implementation report, which was widely endorsed by the subsequent UN General Assembly debates,[54] the concept of the RtoP rests on three pillars: obligations of states, assistance, and response as the last resort. Instead of trying to ensure an early recourse to coercive measures,[55] Secretary-General Ban Ki-moon stressed that protection of populations was not primarily a military matter, and defined the protection mandate in terms of a long continuum of measures.[56] Later, prevention has been understood to address not only imminent atrocities but also their 'root causes' by way of sustainable economic development, good governance and the rule of law.[57] Described in the report as 'narrow but deep', the notion of the RtoP was put forward as an umbrella concept for a wide range of UN activities, few of which were new. The division of the concept into three pillars made it possible to separate the different issues from each other, with much of the debate concentrating on the inherently broad subjects of prevention and assistance. This method facilitated consensus on the RtoP as states could indicate their reservations towards 'pillar three', or coercive measures, while embracing other elements of the concept.[58] On the basis of this carefully balanced reinterpretation of the RtoP, the concept can appropriately be described as a policy agenda,[59] or as 'a continuum of steps to implement existing legal obligations'.[60] As was pointed out in the UN General Assembly debate in 2009, the challenge seemed to be to create UN-wide 'culture of the responsibility to protect' with prevention as a priority.[61]

54 UN Doc. A/63/PV.97; UN Doc. A/63/PV.98; UN Doc. A/63/PV.99; UN Doc. A/63/PV.100 and UN Doc. A/63/PV.101 of 23–28 July 2009.
55 As his predecessor had done, see Kofi Annan, Speech to the General Assembly, UN Doc. A/58/PV.7, 3 September 2003, at 3–4.
56 Implementation report, para. 14.
57 Christoph Mikulaschek, 'The United Nations Security Council and the Responsibility to Protect: Policy, Process, and Practice', in *Report from the 39th International Peace Institute Vienna Seminar on Peacemaking and Peacekeeping*, 20–49, at 27.
58 Kai Michael Kenkel, 'Brazil and R2P: Does Taking Responsibility Mean Using Force?', 4 *Global Responsibility to Protect* (2012), 5–32.
59 Alex J. Bellamy, 'The Responsibility to Protect – Five Years On', 24 *Ethics & International Affairs* (2010), 143–69, at 144.
60 Strauss, *New Clothes, supra* note 12, at 115.
61 UN Doc. A/63/PV.97, at 7.

3 An emerging norm?

The broad acceptance of the RtoP, attested by the recent debates at the United Nations General Assembly,[62] does not imply that states regard it as a legal norm. Academic writers and NGOs, however, frequently refer to RtoP as a norm, or an 'emerging norm', although different meanings are endowed to the term. From a clear law-creating ambition in 1999, when proposals were made of creating a limited exception to the Charter-based prohibition of the use of force, the interpretation of the RtoP as a norm has grown more nuanced. Among the many contributions to the debate, Orford's historical analysis of the exercise of international authority by the UN is particularly interesting.[63] The lack of a coherent conceptual framework that would render the Security Council's action more consistent and predictable has been one of the sources for recurrent criticism.[64] Orford points out that the expansion of the Security Council's executive action over decades took place without 'Charter amendments, new treaties or doctrinal elaboration' relying on the systematisation of the practice through piecemeal operational steps.[65] While no doctrinal development was deemed necessary, or possible, during the Cold War, the legitimacy deficit of the UN Security Council action was becoming increasingly obvious towards the end of the 1990s. The great contribution of the ICISS, in Orford's view, was to answer to this pressing need and to provide the necessary justification for the Security Council's executive action by linking it to the factual capacity to protect.[66] Already this is for her a clear proof of the normative nature of the principle, irrespective of whether or not the WSOD can be interpreted to impose new obligations on states.[67]

Orford thus subscribes to the view put forward by the High-Level Panel in 2004 that RtoP amounts to a complement to the Security Council's Chapter VII powers.[68] By providing a justification for military action within states in situations of mass atrocity, it is seen as an enabling norm that adds to the authority of the UN Security Council.[69] The High-Level Panel retained the attribute 'emerging' when speaking of such a norm, as the Security

---

62 Luck, 'The First decade', *supra* note 4, at 389.
63 Anne Orford, *International Authority and the Responsibility to Protect* (Cambridge University Press, 2011).
64 Andrea Bianchi, 'Ad-hocism and the Rule of Law', 13 *European Journal of International Law* (2002), No.1, 263–72.
65 Orford, *International Authority*, supra note 63, at 5–6.
66 Anne Orford, 'From Promise to Practice? The Legal Significance of the Responsibility to Protect Concept', 3 *Global Responsibility to Protect* (2011), 400–424, at 418–419.
67 *Ibid.*, at 421.
68 High-Level Panel's report, paras 199 and 203.
69 Orford, 'Promise to Practice', *supra* note 66; see also Ramesh Thakur, Book review (Orford, *International Authority and the Responsibility to Protect*), 23 *European Journal of International Law* (2012), 284–289, at 288.

Council had not yet embraced the concept, but the Libya operation authorised by the Security Council in March 2011, with an express reference to the responsibility of states to protect their populations, supports this interpretation and was welcomed as 'a textbook case of how the principle of the RtoP should be applied'.[70] In this scenario, the Summit Outcome Document is seen to provide the Security Council an additional trigger for military action in the sense that intervention can be authorised for humanitarian reasons without the consent of the territorial state, and even where there is no threat or breach of international peace and security.[71] Some authors go further claiming that the new trigger could replace the old one so that the Security Council could no longer employ the trigger of threat or breach of peace in case of 'RtoP situations'.[72]

In this context, a particular problem has been raised with regard to the wording of the WSOD concerning the requirement that the territorial state should 'manifestly fail' to protect its population before the international community could step in.[73] It is feared that this requirement (a 'complementarity trap') could bar the Security Council from taking preventative coercive action.[74] Other scholars have been concerned about the narrowing down of the generic concept of humanitarian crises in the ICISS report to the four specified crimes, noting that this could introduce a new threshold for intervention, unduly limiting the freedom of margin within which the UN Security Council acts.[75] Brunnée and Toope point out that some of the situations in which the Security Council has previously authorised military action, such as in Somalia in 1992, have been far too chaotic to allow for the identification of specific crimes.[76] Still others hold a positive view of the link to 'RtoP crimes' maintaining that clear legal benchmarks based on international standards and jurisprudence bring to the debate on the RtoP much-needed clarity, providing a useful tool for the Security Council.[77]

Some of these assessments seem to overload the Summit Outcome Document with legal implications that contrast with its nature as a political

---

[70] Gareth Evans, Interview with Nayan Chanda, 15 April 2011, <yaleglobal.yale.edu/print/7095>.
[71] Jutta Brunnée and Stephen J. Toope, *Legitimacy and Legality in International Law* (Cambridge University Press, 2010).
[72] *Ibid.*, at 336.
[73] WSOD, para. 139.
[74] Stahn, 'Rhetoric', *supra* note 12, at 116–17.
[75] Brunnée and Toope, *Legitimacy*, *supra* note 71, at 331.
[76] *Ibid.*
[77] Don Hubert and Ariela Blätter, 'The Responsibility to Protect as International Crimes Prevention', 4 *Global Responsibility to Protect* (2012), 33–66, at 34–36. Similarly, Anne Peters, 'The Responsibility to Protect: Spelling Out the Hard Legal Consequences for the UN Security Council and Its members', in Ulrich Fastenrath *et al.* (eds), *From Bilateralism to Community Interest. Essays in Honour of Bruno Simma* (Oxford University Press, 2011), 297–325, at 299.

declaration. While the Security Council can benefit from relying on the WSOD as a consensus document that reflects the will of the large membership of the UN, it may be doubted how much the language on the RtoP adds in legal terms. The Security Council's practice in interpreting the Charter has been evolving, with humanitarian considerations gradually growing in importance since the early 1990s. In particular, the concept of a threat to peace has proved remarkably resilient. Had the Security Council authorised the Kosovo intervention, it would hardly have faced accusations of acting *ultra vires*. The dilemma in the spring of 1999 was not that the Security Council was conceived to be *legally* barred from authorising action for humanitarian reasons and once the NATO proceeded with the air campaign, there were less objections against the operation as such than against it being carried out without proper authorisation. In the same way, it may be asked whether the Security Council would have been unable to adopt Resolution 1973 (2011) on Libya without a reference to the responsibility of the Libyan authorities to protect the population.[78] As for the 'complementarity trap', it was obviously added to the text deliberately so as to raise the threshold for intervention. In any event, it will be up to the Security Council to give a concrete interpretation to the term 'manifest failure'.

The narrowing down of the concept of the RtoP to the 'RtoP crimes' has undoubtedly provided clarity in terms of political debate and consensus-building at the General Assembly, given that there has been a pre-existing agreement on the condemnation of these crimes, three of which have been made subject to international prosecution. It is less clear, what contribution the exact definitions of the crimes as based on the ICC Rome Statute and relevant case law can give to the implementation of the RtoP. It does not seem sensible that the UN Security Council, in order to be able to take 'timely and decisive' action, should wait until the commission of specific crimes has been established. Moreover, it may not always be possible to make a distinction from the outset between situations that fall into the 'RtoP' category, and those that do not.[79] Rather, the mention of the four crimes in the Summit Outcome Document should be seen as a threshold of gravity in a more general sense, in addition to limiting the option of forcible intervention to situations that are related to mass atrocities while excluding other man-made or natural emergencies.[80]

A further question concerns the capacity of the RtoP to become mandatory for the Security Council. Even if the High-Level Panel had spoken somewhat vaguely about 'a collective responsibility of the international community',[81] interpreted by some authors as referring not only to the right

---

78 Resolutions 1970 (2011) and 1973 (2011), *supra* note 51, notably made no mention of the residual responsibility of the international community.
79 Strauss, *New Clothes*, *supra* note 12, at 134–5.
80 According to Strauss, *ibid.*, at 129, the drafting history of the WSOD supports this interpretation.
81 High-Level Panel's report, para 201.

but also to an obligation to intervene,[82] the WSOD made it clear that any action depended on consideration case by case by the Security Council.[83] Discussion continues, though, on how to render the implementation of the RtoP more automatic,[84] an 'international reflex action',[85] so that more states would recognise protection of vulnerable populations as a moral duty.[86] It has also been posited that the adoption of the WSOD, as well as the subsequent consolidation of the RtoP, would impose on the Security Council 'a duty to authorise',[87] or at least a procedural obligation on permanent members to give explanations for veto in case of humanitarian catastrophes.[88] Close to this discussion comes the argument about the responsibility not to veto,[89] following a proposal in the ICISS report that the permanent members of the Security Council should agree on a 'code of conduct' for the use of veto with respect to actions that are needed to stop or avert a significant humanitarian crisis. A permanent member, in other words, should not use its veto to obstruct the adoption of a majority resolution, provided that its vital national interests were not claimed to be involved.[90] Unlike the proposal on the 'duty to authorise', which would run counter to the political nature and logic of the Security Council's action, the proposals to increase automaticity in authorisations aim only at streamlining its working methods. At the same time, they are vulnerable to the criticism of tending to lower the bar for the use of force, and intuitively preferring forcible measures to other means.[91]

The most far-reaching assessments of the legal implications of the RtoP are related to the re-characterisation of the concept of sovereignty by the ICISS report. For Orford, the alternative theory of authority inherent in the

---

82 Anne-Marie Slaughter, 'Security, Solidarity, and Sovereignty: The Grand Themes of UN Reform', 99 *American Journal of International Law* (2005), 619–31, at 621.
83 WSOD, para. 139.
84 Jonas Claes, 'Protecting Civilians from Atrocities: Meeting the Challenge of R2P Rejectionism', 4 *Global Responsibility to Protect* (2012), 67–97, at 69.
85 Orford, *International Authority*, supra note 63, at 3.
86 Kofi A. Annan, 'Foreword', 3 *Global Responsibility to Protect* (2011), 381–2, at 382. See also Millennium report, at 47–8.
87 Anne Peters, 'Humanity as the A and Ω of Sovereignty', 20 *European Journal of International Law* (2009), 513–44.
88 Peters, 'Hard Consequences', *supra* note 77.
89 Ariela Blätter and Paul D. Williams, 'The Responsibility Not to Veto', 3 *Global Responsibility to Protect* (2011), 301–322; Daniel H. Levine, 'Some Concerns About "The Responsibility Not to Veto"', 3 *Global Responsibility to Protect* (2011), 323–45; Blätter and Williams, 'A Reply to Levine', 3 *Global Responsibility to Protect* (2011), 346–51.
90 ICISS report, para. 6.21.
91 Levine, 'Some Concerns', *supra* note 89; Peter Hilpold, 'From Humanitarian Intervention to Responsibility to Protect: Making Utopia True?', in Ulrich Fastenrath *et al.* (eds), *From Bilateralism to Community Interest. Essays in Honour of Bruno Simma* (Oxford University Press, 2011), 462–76, at 473. See also Barry Buzan, 'A Reductionist, Idealistic Notion that Adds Little Analytical Value', Comments by 21 Authors, Special Issue 1 *Security Dialogue* (2004), 396–7.

concept of the RtoP amounts to 'one of the most significant normative shifts in international relations since the creation of the UN in 1945'.[92] According to Brunnée and Toope, the idea of responsible sovereignty 'signals a fundamental shift in international law'[93] and a great 'potential for transformative change in the deep structures of sovereignty'.[94] Slaughter speaks of 'a tectonic shift in the very definition of sovereignty'.[95] Building on Orford's theory of international authority, Peters presents a tentative theory of state sovereignty defined in terms of capacity to provide protection.[96] In claiming that the principle of the RtoP implies a concept of state sovereignty that is subordinate to human security and has value only in so far as it can protect human life, she can rely on some of the core documents of the RtoP.[97] On a more daring basis, she holds that the endorsement of the RtoP at the UN signifies acceptance of a concept of conditional sovereignty.[98] Other writers have gone as far as referring to RtoP as 'a duty to ensure the security and well-being of the citizens'.[99] It should be recalled in this context that the promise of humanitarian concerns overriding state consent, even in the ICISS report, was limited to grave humanitarian catastrophes where the state refuses to cooperate. The Summit Outcome Document limits the protection mandate of the international community even further.

4   Concluding remarks

There is a striking discrepancy between the political process at the UN, on the one hand, and the high expectations raised by the RtoP in civil society, on the other. The clearest articulation of the concept so far in the Summit Outcome Document amounts to little more than a reinstatement of the provisions of the UN Charter. The subsequent UN process has modified the concept of the RtoP considerably and come up with a vast policy agenda that remains equally far from the original ambition of amending the Charter as from the burgeoning expectations of a normative breakthrough. It is obvious that the ideas put forward by the ICISS in 2001 continue to have appeal, influencing perceptions of legitimacy and creating expectations as to how

---

92   Orford, 'Promise to Practice', *supra* note 66, at 424.
93   Brunnée and Toope, *Legitimacy*, *supra* note 71, at 326.
94   *Ibid.*, at 337.
95   Slaughter, 'Security, Solidarity', *supra* note 82, at 627.
96   Peters, 'The A and Ω', *supra* note 87.
97   ICISS report, paras 1.32–1.36; Larger Freedom report, para. 135. See also Annan, 'Foreword', *supra* note 85, at 381.
98   For cogent criticism of this argument, see Emily Kidd White, Catherine E. Sweetser, Emma Dunlop and Amrita Kapur, 'Humanity as the A and Ω of Sovereignty: Four Replies to Anne Peters, 20 *European Journal of International Law* (2009), 545–67.
99   Hanspeter Neuhold, Legal Crisis Management: Lawfulness and Legitimacy of the Use of Force', in Ulrich Fastenrath *et al.* (eds), *From Bilateralism to Community Interest: Essays in Honour of Bruno Simma* (Oxford University Press, 2011), 278–96, at 285.

states and the UN Security Council should act. Could it mean, as Kofi Annan stated at the time of the Kosovo war, that an international humanitarian norm taking precedence over concerns of state sovereignty would be 'slowly but surely emerging'?[100] States are still masters of international law-making[101] but transnational civil society networks increasingly often get their views known and listened to. In this sense, the RtoP remains a challenge. At the same time, there is no obvious law-making project to be promoted. As an echo from the earlier debate, the search for a new norm continues, while the concept as formulated at the UN best lends itself to serving as a framework for reinforcing existing legal obligations.

---

100 Kofi Annan, Speech at the University of Michigan, 30 April 1999.
101 Andrea Bianchi, 'The Fight for Inclusion: Non-State Actors and International Law', in Ulrich Fastenrath *et al.* (eds), *From Bilateralism to Community Interest. Essays in Honour of Bruno Simma* (Oxford University Press, 2011), 39–57, at 49. See also Jan Klabbers, 'The Undesirability of Soft Law', 67 *Nordic Journal of International Law* (1998), 381–91, at 391.

18 Treaties, custom and universal jurisdiction

*Rain Liivoja**

The principle of universal criminal jurisdiction constitutes one of the pillars in the edifice of international criminal justice. By and large, universal jurisdiction refers to the (purported) authority of every state to make its law applicable to, and to empower its courts to try, certain offences solely on grounds that they are of universal concern, i.e. even where that state has no substantive connection to the offence.[1]

The obvious conceptual and practical significance of this principle is closely matched by the amount of controversy surrounding it. For one, there is uncertainty as to which offences – other than piracy, if any[2] – could be regarded as being of universal concern for criminal law purposes. This problem is compounded by the fact that the rationale for placing piracy under a special jurisdictional regime – the lack of territorial jurisdiction over the high seas – does not apply to offences such as genocide, crimes against humanity and war crimes, which are often seen as being subject to universal jurisdiction.[3] But even if one accepts that universal jurisdiction applies

---

* I am grateful to Monique Cormier and Anna Hood for their perceptive comments on an earlier draft of this chapter. The usual disclaimer applies.

1 For definitions of universal jurisdiction along these lines, see *Restatement, Third, Foreign Relations Law of the United States* (2 vols, 1987), § 404; Kenneth C. Randall, 'Universal Jurisdiction under International Law', 66 *Texas Law Review* (1988) 785–841, at 788; *Polyukhovich v. Commonwealth*, [1991] HCA 32, (1991) 172 CLR 501, at 659 (Toohey J); *The Princeton Principles on Universal Jurisdiction* (Program in Law and Public Affairs, Princeton University, 2001), principle 1(1); *Universal Criminal Jurisdiction with regard to the Crime of Genocide, Crimes against Humanity and War Crimes*, Resolution of the Institut de droit international (26 August 2005), para. 1; Report of the AU-EU Technical *Ad hoc* Expert Group on the Principle of Universal Jurisdiction, EU Doc. 8672/1/09 REV 1 (April 2009), para. 8.

2 See, for example, *Arrest Warrant of 11 April 2000 (Democratic Republic of the Congo v. Belgium)*, ICJ Reports (2002) 3, Separate Opinion of President Guillaume, para. 12: 'international law knows only one true case of universal jurisdiction: piracy'; Sienho Yee, 'Universal Jurisdiction: Concept, Logic, and Reality', 10 *Chinese Journal of International Law* (2011) 503–30, at 511: 'The experience and reality of international relations are such that universal jurisdiction over crimes other than piracy has not been established as a matter of international law.'

beyond piracy, there are uncertainties as to the possible procedural preconditions for its exercise: Is the presence of the accused necessary for any proceedings to commence or could an extradition request be made on the basis of universal jurisdiction? Should priority be given to proceedings in states that have some connection with the offence, as a result of the application of the principle of *forum non conveniens*?

More generally, there is much disagreement about whether universal jurisdiction is a good idea to begin with.[4] Perhaps the principal problem is that the use of universal jurisdiction to prosecute foreign dignitaries has the clear potential for inflaming international relations. Also, prosecuting cases far away from the scene of the crime involves serious practical problems, in particular, the availability of evidence and witnesses. In stark contrast to the enthusiasm of the 1990s, these considerations have in the past decade had a chilling effect on universal jurisdiction, leading at least one commentator to perform a '*post mortem*' on the principle.[5] That said, the discussion over the nature and scope of universal jurisdiction has recently been reinvigorated as a result of it being placed on the agenda of the UN General Assembly at the request of the Group of African States.[6]

Much ink has been spilt in attempts to clarify the circumstances under which universal jurisdiction operates and to reflect upon the wisdom of having and using it. This chapter, however, considers the preliminary and largely methodological question of how the principle can be grounded in the sources of international law. I argue that universal jurisdiction does not derive – indeed, it cannot derive as a matter of principle – from treaty provisions (section 1). Rather, it is based exclusively on customary international law. With respect to custom, I argue that the comparatively scant case law is not necessarily an insurmountable obstacle in establishing universal jurisdiction (section 2). Indeed, the adoption by a large number of states of legislation purporting to attach universal jurisdiction to certain offences is sufficient for a customary law rule to emerge.

---

3   See, for example, Eugene Kontorovich, 'The Piracy Analogy: Modern Universal Jurisdiction's Hollow Foundation', 45 *Harvard International Law Journal* (2004) 183–237; Luis Benavides, 'Universal Jurisdiction over War Crimes', in Rain Liivoja and Tim McCormack (eds), *Routledge Handbook of the Law of Armed Conflict* (Routledge, forthcoming).
4   The exchange between former US Secretary of State Henry Kissinger and Human Rights Watch Executive Director Kenneth Roth has become a classic on this point. See Henry A. Kissinger, 'The Pitfalls of Universal Jurisdiction', 80 *Foreign Affairs* (2001) no. 4, 86–96, and Kenneth Roth, 'The Case for Universal Jurisdiction', 80 *Foreign Affairs* (2001) no. 5, 150–4.
5   See Luc Reydams, 'The Rise and Fall of Universal Jurisdiction', in William A. Schabas and Nadia Bernaz (eds), *Routledge Handbook of International Criminal Law* (Routledge, 2010) 337–54, at 349–50.
6   See GA Res. 64/117, 16 December 2009; GA Res. 65/33, 6 December 2010; GA Res. 66/103, 9 December 2011; GA Res. 67/98, 14 December 2012; and the documents referred to therein.

1 Treaties

The idea of treaty-based universal jurisdiction emanates from certain multilateral conventions dealing with transnational offences. Such treaties generally (i) define an offence, (ii) oblige states parties to criminalise the offence under national law, (iii) establish which states have jurisdiction to prosecute the offence and (iv) oblige states to either prosecute any suspects caught in their territory or to hand them over to another state prepared to do so (the so-called *aut dedere aut iudicare* principle).[7] One example of such a treaty is the 1984 Torture Convention.[8] Article 1 of this Convention defines 'torture' and Article 4 requires parties to ensure that all acts of torture are offences under domestic law. Article 7(1) contains the principle of *aut dedere aut iudicare*:

> The State Party in the territory under whose jurisdiction a person alleged to have committed any offence referred to in article 4 is found shall in the cases contemplated in article 5, if it does not extradite him, submit the case to its competent authorities for the purpose of prosecution.

It is important to note that this is a purely procedural obligation that is not itself a basis for exercising jurisdiction.[9] The question of jurisdiction is addressed separately in Article 5. Paragraph 1 on this Article provides that each state party 'shall take such measures as may be necessary to establish its jurisdiction' over the offences defined in the Convention:

> (a) When the offences are committed in any territory under its jurisdiction or on board a ship or aircraft registered in that State;
> (b) When the alleged offender is a national of that State;
> (c) When the victim is a national of that State if that State considers it appropriate.

These paragraphs essentially reiterate several 'traditional' bases of criminal jurisdiction: territoriality and flag principles in sub-paragraph (a), active personality principle in sub-paragraph (b) and passive personality principle in sub-paragraph (c).

---

7 The prototype appears to be the Convention for the Suppression of Unlawful Seizure of Aircraft, 16 December 1970, in force 14 October 1971, 860 UNTS 105. The jurisdictional arrangements of the Convention are, however, very particular given that the Convention offences can only take place on an aircraft.
8 Convention against Torture and Other Cruel, Inhuman or Degrading Treatment or Punishment, GA Res. 39/46, 10 December 1984, in force 26 June 1987, 1465 UNTS 85.
9 Yee, 'Universal Jurisdiction', *supra* note 2, at 513: ' "Extradite or prosecute" is a means of exercising jurisdiction; it is not jurisdiction itself'; Report of the AU-EU Expert Group, *supra* note 1, para. 11.

Paragraph 2 of Article 5 goes on to address the situation where none of the traditional bases of criminal jurisdiction apply:

> Each State Party shall likewise take such measures as may be necessary to establish its jurisdiction over such offences in cases where the alleged offender is present in any territory under its jurisdiction and it does not extradite him pursuant to article 8 to any of the States mentioned in paragraph 1 of this article.

There are two common ways of interpreting and conceptualising this type of provision. For one, as has already been mentioned, a number of commentators take the view that this is in fact universal jurisdiction or at least some sub-species thereof.[10] In the alternative, these types of provisions have been regarded as creating a distinct basis of jurisdiction, which is based on the mere presence of the suspect in the territory. As three judges on the International Court of Justice (ICJ) put it in *Arrest Warrant*, treaties can establish 'an *obligatory territorial jurisdiction* over persons, albeit in relation to acts committed elsewhere'.[11]

Both of these approaches suffer from serious defects. To address the second one first, the problem is that the presence of the suspect in the prosecuting state is something that occurs only after the offence has taken place. Roger O'Keefe has correctly noted that 'the nexus relied on to ground prescriptive jurisdiction over given conduct must exist at the time at which the conduct is performed' because otherwise a form of retroactive criminalisation would occur.[12] Thus, as Judge Loder put it in *Lotus*, 'the subsequent presence of a guilty person cannot have the effect of extending the jurisdiction of the State'.[13]

The problem with the first approach – the idea that treaties create a form of universal jurisdiction – is that treaties by their very nature are not universal; they only bind states parties thereto.[14] A number of commentators

---

10 See, for example, Michael P. Scharf, 'Application of Treaty-Based Universal Jurisdiction to Nationals of Non-Party States', 35 *New England Law Review* (2001) 363–382; Roger O'Keefe, 'Universal Jurisdiction: Clarifying the Basic Concept', 2 *Journal of International Criminal Justice* (2004) 735–60, especially at 747.
11 *Arrest Warrant*, *supra* note 2, Joint Separate Opinion of Judges Higgins, Kooijmans and Buergenthal, para. 41 (emphasis added).
12 O'Keefe, 'Clarifying the Basic Concept', *supra* note 10, at 742.
13 *The SS "Lotus" (France/Turkey)*, PCIJ Publications Ser. A, No. 10 (1927), Separate Opinion of Judge Loder, at 35 (emphasis removed).
14 Vienna Convention on the Law of Treaties, 23 May 1969, in force 27 January 1980, 1155 UNTS 331, Article 26: 'Every treaty in force is binding upon the parties to it and must be performed by them in good faith.'

have drawn attention to this problem.[15] Also, the US Court of Appeals for the Second Circuit has held, with respect to the Montreal Convention for the Suppression of Unlawful Acts against the Safety of Civil Aviation,[16] that

> [t]he ... Convention, unlike the customary international law principles of criminal jurisdiction (including universal jurisdiction), creates a basis for the assertion of jurisdiction that is moored in a process of formal lawmaking and that is binding only on the States that accede to it. The jurisdiction thus created is not a species of universal jurisdiction, but a jurisdictional agreement among contracting States to extradite or prosecute offenders who commit the acts proscribed by the treaty – that is, the agreements between contracting States create *aut dedere aut punire* ('extradite or prosecute') jurisdiction.[17]

An attempt can be made to dispel the concern about the constraints of treaties as a source of law by pointing out that while indeed '[a] treaty does not create either obligations or rights for a third State without its consent'[18] – *pacta tertiis nec nocent nec prosunt* – no actual *obligations* are created for third states by allowing their nationals to be prosecuted by states parties to the treaty. Nonetheless, it is difficult to see how states could endow themselves by treaty with a right to exercise, *vis-à-vis* non-party nationals, jurisdiction that none of them had as a matter of customary law. So perhaps more than the *pacta tertiis* rule, the idea of treaty-based universal jurisdiction runs counter to the general principle of law that one cannot give what one does not have – *nemo dat quod non habet*.

In view of these considerations the two approaches to treaty-based jurisdictional arrangements are indefensible. Yet there exists a third possibility, which has perhaps not been paid sufficient attention. This approach would regard the jurisdictional provision under consideration as a treaty-based

---

15   Rosalyn Higgins, *Problems and Process: International Law and How We Use It* (Clarendon, 1994), at 63–65; Iain Cameron, *The Protective Principle of International Criminal Jurisdiction* (Dartmouth, 1994), at 80; Antonio Cassese, 'Is the Bell Tolling for Universality? A Plea for a Sensible Notion of Universal Jurisdiction', 1 *Journal of International Criminal Justice* (2003) 589–95, at 591, 594; Claus Kreß, 'Universal Jurisdiction over International Crimes and the Institut de Droit International', 4 *Journal of International Criminal Justice* (2006) 561–85, at 566. See also Institute of International Law, 'Universal Criminal Jurisdiction', para. 2: 'Universal jurisdiction is primarily based on customary international law. It can also be established under a multilateral treaty *in the relations between the contracting parties*, in particular by virtue of clauses which provide that a State party in the territory of which an alleged offender is found shall either extradite or try that person' (emphasis added).
16   23 September 1971, in force 26 January 1973, 974 UNTS 177.
17   *US v. Yousef*, 327 F3d 56 (US Court of Appeals, 2nd Circuit, 2003), at 96, citing Higgins, *Problems and Process, supra* note 15, at 64.
18   Vienna Convention on the Law of Treaties, *supra* note 14, Article 34.

form of what is known in many national legal systems as the principle of vicarious administration of justice or the principle of representative jurisdiction (*stellvertretende Strafrechtspflege, principe de la compétence par représentation*). This is a subsidiary basis for criminal jurisdiction, a typical example of which can be found in the German Penal Code:

> German criminal law shall apply to other offences committed abroad if the act is a criminal offence at the locality of its commission or if that locality is not subject to any criminal law jurisdiction, and if the offender ... was a foreigner at the time of the offence, is discovered in Germany and, although the Extradition Act would permit extradition for such an offence, is not extradited because a request for extradition within a reasonable period of time is not made, is rejected, or the extradition is not feasible.[19]

A provision of a similar nature can be found in a number of other Continental legal systems[20] and in South American criminal law,[21] but is not particularly well-known elsewhere.[22] In cases contemplated by this type of provision, the prosecuting state lacks original jurisdiction. The only reason to exercise jurisdiction is the desire to fill a void that would emerge otherwise. Thus, the *forum deprehensionis* effectively steps into the shoes of a state that has original jurisdiction. While doubts can be expressed about this arrangement being recognised in customary law – except, perhaps, as regional or special custom – there is no obvious reason why states could not enter into such arrangements by treaty.

Under this approach, the state where the suspect is captured and prosecuted would neither exercise its own quasi-territorial jurisdiction nor universal jurisdiction belonging to all states. Rather, it would apply jurisdiction delegated to it by other parties to the treaty. The jurisdiction over a national of a non-party would thus be conditional on at least one of the parties having jurisdiction over that person by virtue of one of the traditional jurisdictional principles. According to Sienho Yee, in such a situation 'at least one party to the regime can legitimately exercise jurisdiction based on a traditional criterion, and the prosecuting State party is

---

19 Strafgesetzbuch [Penal Code], 15 May 1871 (Germany), Section 7(2)(2).
20 See, e.g., Strafgesetzbuch [Penal Code], 15 May 1974 (Austria), section 65(1)(2); Karistusseadustik [Penal Code], 6 June 2001 (Estonia), Riigi Teataja I 2001, 61, 364 ... RT I 04.04.2012, 1, section 7(3); Rikoslaki [Penal Code], 19 December 1889 (Finland), 39/1889, Chapter 1, section 3(1); Code pénal [Penal Code], 22 July 1992 (France), Article 113-8-1; Schweizerisches Strafgesetzbuch [Penal Code], 21 December 1937 (Switzerland), SR 311.0, Article 7.
21 See, e.g., Código Penal [Penal Code], 24 July 2000 (Colombia), Ley N° 599, Article 16(6).
22 See Jürgen Meyer, 'The Vicarious Administration of Justice: An Overlooked Basis of Jurisdiction', 31 *Harvard International Law Journal* (1990) 108–16.

simply performing the function of that other party in its stead, for whatever reason (such as its inability or unwillingness to do so)'.[23]

One of the distinct advantages of this approach is that it avoids the thorny question about how to identify treaties that generate universal jurisdiction. After all, there is no principled way of telling how widely a treaty has to be ratified in order to be seriously considered as giving rise to jurisdiction that is in any way universal. Construing such treaties instead as creating representative jurisdiction, their impact would be directly proportionate to the number of ratifications – the more states parties, the more likely it is for one of the parties to have original jurisdiction over the offence, which would bring the perpetrator within the reach of the treaty regime.

Some commentators support the idea of treaty-based universal jurisdiction partly in order to bolster the jurisdiction of the International Criminal Court (ICC) over non-party nationals.[24] However, the legality of the jurisdiction of the ICC is in no way premised on the possibility of creating universal jurisdiction by treaty. The possibility of delegating criminal jurisdiction by treaty seems to be one fairly convincing way of explaining the competence of the Court: by becoming parties to the Rome Statute, states have given to the Court a part of their own territorial and active personality jurisdiction with respect to certain offences.[25]

2 Custom

When it comes to establishing universal jurisdiction as a matter of customary international law, there are admittedly some difficulties relating to the density of the state practice and clarity of the *opinio juris*. Commentators who are sceptical about the notion of universal jurisdiction in general – or doubt whether it extends to offences other than piracy – have drawn attention to two factors. First, cases where a conviction has been obtained on the basis of the universality principle are few and far between.[26] Second, in a number of

---

[23] Yee, 'Universal Jurisdiction', *supra* note 2, at 515. See also Cassese, 'Is the Bell Tolling for Universality? A Plea for a Sensible Notion of Universal Jurisdiction', at 591, 594: 'it may be contended that [treaty-based] jurisdiction does not extend to offences committed by nationals of states not parties, unless the crime (1) is indisputably prohibited by customary international law ...; or (2) the national of a non-contracting state engages in prohibited conduct in the territory of a state party, or against nationals of that state.'

[24] See Michael P. Scharf, 'The ICC's Jurisdiction over the Nationals of Non-Party States: A Critique of the U.S. Position', 64 *Law & Contemporary Problems* (2001) 67–117; Scharf, 'Application of Treaty-Based Universal Jurisdiction', *supra* note 10.

[25] See generally Dapo Akande, 'The Jurisdiction of the International Criminal Court over Nationals of Non-Parties: Legal Basis and Limits', 1 *Journal of International Criminal Justice* (2003) 618–50.

[26] John B. Bellinger, III, and William J. Haynes, II, 'A US Government Response to the International Committee of the Red Cross's Customary International Humanitarian Law Study', 89 *International Review of the Red Cross* (2007) no. 866, 443–471.

these cases – perhaps the majority – other bases of jurisdiction have been operational as well; in other words, only very few cases have been decided solely on the basis of universal jurisdiction. But neither of these points is necessarily fatal to the argument that certain offences other than piracy are subject to universal jurisdiction as a matter of customary international law.

It is convenient to address the second point – the lack of pure universal jurisdiction cases – first. It is indeed true that cases purporting to apply universal jurisdiction have most often been brought by states that also have some substantive connection to the offence, the victims or the perpetrator. The prosecution of Adolf Eichmann in Israel is a case in point. Eichmann's crimes were directed against the Jewish people, leading the District Court of Jerusalem to place some reliance on the passive personality and protective principles,[27] notwithstanding the difficulty that the State of Israel did not exist at the time the offences were committed.[28]

In more recent cases, the defendants have mostly become resident in the state where they were prosecuted,[29] and a number of legal systems regard residency as a sufficient basis for the exercise of jurisdiction (as an extension of sorts of the active personality principle). For example, in the recent Finnish trial of Francoise Bazaramba for his involvement in the Rwandan genocide, the defendant had been a resident of Finland for over three years by the time an investigation was commenced,[30] and under Finnish law, residency, even if obtained after the alleged offence took place, appears to be a sufficient basis for jurisdiction.[31]

However, in cases with a potentially 'mixed' jurisdictional basis, courts have often either emphasised the particular significance of universal jurisdiction or failed to explore seriously the alternative bases of jurisdiction. In *Eichmann*, for instance, even though the Supreme Court subscribed to the District Court's views as to the applicability of the protective and passive personality principles, it most emphatically stated that the 'State of Israel ... was entitled, pursuant to the principle of universal jurisdiction and in the capacity of a guardian of international law and an agent for its enforcement, to try the appellant.'[32] In *Bazaramba*, the District Court of Itä-Uusimaa based

---

27 See *Attorney General v. Eichmann*, (1961) 36 ILR 5 (District Court of Jerusalem, Israel), paras 30–38.
28 See James E. S. Fawcett, 'The *Eichmann* Case', 38 *British Year Book of International Law* (1962) 181–215, at 190–2.
29 Reydams, 'The Rise and Fall of Universal Jurisdiction', *supra* note 5, at 348.
30 *Prosecutor v. Bazaramba*, District Court of Itä-Uusimaa, Finland, 11 June 2010, at part IV, section 4.5.
31 See Penal Code (Finland), Chapter 1, section 6(1): 'Finnish law applies to an offence committed outside of Finland by a Finnish citizen. ....'; and section (3)(1), equating to a Finnish citizen 'a person who was permanently resident in Finland at the time of the offence or is permanently resident in Finland at the beginning of the court proceedings'.
32 CrimA 336/61 *Attorney General v. Eichmann*, (1962) 16(3) PD 2033, (1962) 36 ILR 277 (Supreme Court, Israel), at 304.

Finnish jurisdiction with respect to the crime of genocide squarely on the universality principle.[33] The Court invoked residency only to support the alternative charges of murder.[34] This approach to jurisdiction was not altered on appeal.[35]

To return to the more general problem of the scarcity of case law, it is indeed true that the total number of cases relying on universal jurisdiction has not been all that great nor has it been geographically overly representative. While precise figures are difficult to come by, there have probably been just over 30 prosecutions under the universality principle in fewer than 20 countries – Australia, Canada, Israel, the US and a handful of European states.[36]

Yet the small number of cases should not be decisive as to the existence of a rule of customary international law. While the offences that arguably fall under universal jurisdiction are certainly far too common from the perspective of the victims, they are not common enough to result in extensive case law in a large number of states. The arrival of a suspected war criminal in, say, the Cook Islands, is not exactly a daily occurrence. Furthermore, the evidentiary and other practical difficulties in successfully mounting prosecutions under universal jurisdiction also contribute to the small number of cases.

Accordingly, while actual cases and the reactions of other states to them are a significant source of state practice, they do not accurately reflect the attitude of the international community towards universal jurisdiction. Potentially the greatest source of evidence for the purposes of establishing customary law on this point comes from national legislation – states enacting the principle in national criminal law.

Admittedly, the role of domestic legislation in constituting practice for the purpose of customary international law has been downplayed by eminent commentators. Some of them have argued that only the conduct of organs capable of representing the state in inter-state affairs counts as state

---

33 *Bazaramba (District Court), supra* note 30, at part III. Penal Code (Finland), Chapter 1, section 7(1): 'Finnish law applies to an offence committed outside of Finland where the punishability of the act, regardless of the law of the place of commission, is based on an international agreement binding on Finland or on another statute or regulation internationally binding on Finland (*international offence*). Further provisions on the application of this section shall be issued by Decree.' See also Asetus rikoslain 1 luvun 7§:n soveltamisesta [Decree on the Application of Section 7 of Chapter 1 of the Penal Code], 16 August 1996, 627/1996, section 1(3) (listing the crime of genocide as an international offence).
34 *Bazaramba (District Court), supra* note 30, at part III.
35 *Prosecutor v. Bazaramba,* Court of Appeal of Helsinki, Finland, 30 March 2012.
36 Máximo Langer, 'The Diplomacy of Universal Jurisdiction: The Political Branches and the Transnational Prosecution of International Crimes', 105 *American Journal of International Law* (2011) 1–49, at 42, reports the total number of cases as 32, and mentions 13 States (Australia, Austria, Belgium, Canada, Denmark, France, Germany, Israel, The Netherlands, Norway, Spain, Switzerland, UK). *Prosecutor v. Bemba Gombo,* ICC Pre-Trial Chamber II, *Amicus Curiae* Observations on Superior Responsibility Submitted by Amnesty International (20 April 2009), at footnote 71, adds three States to the list (Finland, Sweden and the US).

practice[37] – legislatures clearly are not such organs. Inasmuch as this objection is based on the extreme voluntarist approach of construing customary law as some sort of a tacit treaty, it has gone decidedly out of fashion. Reflecting a different reality, the Principles on the Formation of International Law adopted by the International Law Association in 2000 (the ILA Principles) confidently note that '[t]he practice of the executive, legislative and judicial organs of the State is to be considered, according to the circumstances, as State practice'.[38]

Other commentators have held that only real, physical acts constitute state practice.[39] Another version of this theory holds that claims or statements are relevant only when made in terms of a specific dispute.[40] The notion that actions speak louder than words certainly holds true in international law. However, as the commentary to the ILA Principles points out, 'there seems to be no inherent qualitative difference' between physical and verbal acts.[41] Moreover, making statements is a rather common form of state practice and indeed the only form on some topics (for example, the recognition of other states).[42] Thus, the Principles stipulate that '[v]erbal acts, and not only physical acts, of States count as State practice'.[43] As regards the ostensible requirement that verbal acts relate to a particular dispute in order to be considered state practice and not be merely abstract, Michael Akehurst has accurately observed 'there is no clear dividing line between the two classes of assertions; they merge into one another', especially as 'assertions about a particular dispute are [sometimes] dressed up as assertions *in abstracto*, and vice versa'.[44]

In practice, states and courts often turn to national legislation in search of evidence of customary rules of international law.[45] For example, in the landmark case of *Paquete Habana*, the US Supreme Court relied extensively

---

37 See, in particular, Karl Strupp, 'Les règles générales du droit de la paix', 47 *Recueil des Cours* (1934) 259–595, at 313–14.
38 International Law Association, *Statement of Principles Applicable to the Formation of General Customary International Law: Final Report of the Committee on Formation of Customary (General) International Law*, London Conference (2000), section 9.
39 Notably, Anthony A. D'Amato, *The Concept of Custom in International Law* (Cornell University Press, 1971), at 88; *Fisheries (UK v. Norway)*, ICJ Reports (1951) 116, Dissenting Opinion of Judge Read, at 116 and 191.
40 See Hugh Thirlway, *International Customary Law and Codification: An Examination of the Continuing Role of Custom in the Present Period of Codification of International Law* (Sijthoff, 1972), at 58.
41 ILA Principles, *supra* note 38, commentary to section 4, at para. (a).
42 See Michael Akehurst, 'Custom as a Source of International Law', 47 *British Year Book of International Law* (1974–1975) 1–53, at 2–3.
43 ILA Principles, *supra* note 38, section 4. See also Jean-Marie Henckaerts and Louise Doswald-Beck, *Customary International Humanitarian Law* (reprinted, corrected edn, 2 vols, Cambridge University Press, 2009) vol. i, at xxxviii–xl.
44 Akehurst, 'Custom as a Source of International Law', *supra* note 42, at 4.
45 *Ibid.*, at 8–10.

on historic pieces of domestic law of various states to determine the existence of a customary law rule that fishing vessels were exempt from capture as prizes in armed conflict.[46]

Customary law relating to universal jurisdiction can and should be deduced from the legislation of various states making certain crimes of international concern subject to their legal systems without any substantive link to the offence. For example, while the Cook Islands have not had the occasion to rely on universal jurisdiction for the purposes of a prosecution, it is significant that their law makes grave breaches of the 1949 Geneva Conventions and the 1977 Additional Protocol I offences under national law whether committed 'in the Cook Islands or elsewhere' and 'regardless of [the] nationality or citizenship' of the perpetrator.[47]

A tally of domestic legal systems recognising the principle of universality goes beyond the scope of this contribution. However, the few studies that have been compiled on this point show the situation in much better light than the comparatively meagre supply of jurisprudence.[48] That said, something of a difficulty is presented by the failure of domestic law to distinguish between a customary law-based *right* to exercise jurisdiction and a treaty-based *obligation* to exercise jurisdiction.

With that in mind, the jurisdiction applicable as a matter of national law to genocide and crimes against humanity – rather than the grave breaches of the Geneva Conventions – would be a better indicator of the existence of universal jurisdiction in customary international law. While the crime of genocide is defined in a dedicated treaty, the Genocide Convention only makes reference to territorial jurisdiction and the jurisdiction of international tribunals[49] – it does not create a treaty-based jurisdictional regime. Crimes against humanity, while codified in the Rome Statute,[50] do not have an independent treaty basis at all – there is no international agreement placing an obligation on states to make crimes against humanity part of national criminal law, or to prosecute or extradite persons suspected of having committed such offences. Thus, any state that, by virtue of domestic law, is willing to prosecute genocide or crimes against humanity without any substantive link to the offence is effectively endorsing a customary law-based universal jurisdiction with respect to those offences.

---

46 *The Paquete Habana*, 175 US 677 (1900), at 686 *et seq.*
47 Geneva Conventions and Additional Protocols Act 2002 (Cook Islands), section 5(1) and (3).
48 See, in particular, Amnesty International, *The Pinochet Case: Universal Jurisdiction and Absence of Immunity for Crimes against Humanity*, AI Index EUR 45/01/99 (January 1999); Amnesty International, *Universal Jurisdiction: The Duty of States to Enact and Implement Legislation*, AI Index IOR 53/002/2001–53/018/2001 (1 September 2001); Report of the AU-EU Expert Group, *supra* note 1.
49 Convention on the Prevention and Punishment of the Crime of Genocide, GA Res. 260 A (III), 9 December 1948, in force 12 January 1951, 78 UNTS 277, Article 6.
50 Rome Statute of the International Criminal Court, 17 July 1998, in force 1 July 2000, 2187 UNTS 90, Article 7.

Having said all this, when assessing the existence of a rule of customary international law where practice is contested, it is critical to take into account negative or contradictory practice. The most vocal protests against the use of universal jurisdiction have come from the US and Israel over the attempts to have their officials prosecuted in different European countries. US Secretary of Defence Donald Rumsfeld memorably threatened to have NATO headquarters removed from Brussels if Belgium did not tone down its legislation on international crimes, which made extensive use of universal jurisdiction.[51] Israel engaged in political countermeasures against the UK, including cancelling a 'strategic dialogue' meeting in 2010, because of the real possibility of Israeli politicians being arrested when visiting Britain.[52] In 2003, Belgium reduced the scope of its universal jurisdiction legislation and, in 2011, the UK made it more difficult for ordinary citizens to obtain arrest warrants for suspected war criminals present in Britain. But based on the material that is in the public record, it does not appear that the US or Israel would have objected to the principle of universal jurisdiction as such. Their objections were of a political character. Both States basically claimed that criminal law was being used imprudently and in a manner likely to inflame international relations.

Given that a significant proportion of the defendants in proceedings premised on universal jurisdiction have come from African states, the African Union (AU) has also taken umbrage with the principle. Starting in 2008, the AU Assembly has adopted a series of decisions on what it calls the 'abuse of the principle of universal jurisdiction'. In the first of these decisions, the Assembly took the view that '[t]he political nature and abuse of the principle of universal jurisdiction by judges from some non-African States against African leaders, particularly Rwanda, is a clear violation of the sovereignty and territorial integrity' of these States'.[53] It resolved that the relevant warrants of arrest 'shall not be executed in African Union Member States' and requested 'all UN Member States, in particular the EU States, to impose a moratorium on the execution of those warrants' pending discussions between the AU, the EU and the UN.[54] In a more recent decision, the Assembly went as far as to urge '[AU] Member States to use the principle of reciprocity to defend themselves against the abuse of the principle of Universal Jurisdiction'.[55]

---

51 Craig S. Smith, 'Rumsfeld Says Belgian Law Could Prompt NATO to Leave', *The New York Times*, 12 June 2003.
52 Adrian Blomfield, 'Israel suspends Britain security meeting', *The Telegraph*, 3 November 2010.
53 Assembly/AU/Dec.199(XI), 1 July 2008, para. 5(ii).
54 *Ibid.*, paras 5(iv) and 8.
55 Assembly/AU/Dec.420(XIX), 16 July 2012, para. 5.

But in this very string of decisions, the AU Assembly explicitly recognised that

> universal jurisdiction is a principle of International Law whose purpose is to ensure that individuals who commit grave offences such as war crimes and crimes against humanity do not do so with impunity and are brought to justice, which is in line with Article 4(h) of the Constitutive Act of the African Union.[56]

Moreover, in a recent decision, the Assembly welcomed 'the elaboration [by the AU Commission] of a Model National Law on Universal Jurisdiction over International Crimes' and encouraged 'Member States to fully take advantage of this Model National Law in order to expeditiously enact or strengthen their National Laws in this area'.[57] The Model Law in question stipulates that the highest court of original jurisdiction in a state

> shall have jurisdiction to try any person charged with committing any crime prohibited under this law, regardless of whether such a crime is alleged to have been committed in the territory of the State or abroad and irrespective of the nationality of the victim, provided that such a person shall be within the territory of the State at the time of the commencement of the trial.[58]

The offences mentioned by the Model Law are genocide, crimes against humanity, war crimes, piracy, trafficking in narcotics and terrorism.[59] Accordingly, AU member states clearly recognise the principle of universality. Moreover, they recognise it as applicable to a fairly broad range of offences – indeed, 'pushing ... the boundaries of the crimes covered by that principle'[60] – and without the need for the defendant to be present in the prosecuting state for proceedings to be initiated. Only *in absentia* trials are excluded[61] and extradition on the basis of universal jurisdiction seems perfectly compatible with the Model Law. As Dapo Akande rightly notes,

---

56 Assembly/AU/Dec.199(XI), *supra* note 53, para. 3.
57 Assembly/AU/Dec.419(XIX), 16 July 2012, para. 11.
58 African Union (Draft) Model National Law on Universal Jurisdiction over International Crimes, Meeting of Government Experts and Ministers of Justice/Attorneys General on Legal Matters (2012), section 4(1). Subsection (2) adds that the court '[shall] accord priority to the court of the State in whose territory the crime is alleged to have been committed, provided that the State is willing and able to prosecute'.
59 *Ibid.*, section 8.
60 Dapo Akande, 'The African Union, the ICC and Universal Jurisdiction: Some Recent Developments', *EJIL:Talk!*, 29 August 2012 <www.ejiltalk.org/the-african-union-the-icc-and-universal-jurisdiction-some-recent-developments>.
61 *Ibid.*

> [t]he Model Law and its endorsement by AU leaders contributes to the State practice regarding the principle of universal jurisdiction. Even if the Model Law is not used by States, acceptance of the Model Law by the AU Assembly is also evidence of the *opinio juris* of African States regarding the application of the principle.[62]

It should also be noted that some African states have not only refrained from objecting to particular uses of universal jurisdiction by European states, but actively assisted these states in carrying out proceedings. One commentator has observed that, when Belgium carried out proceedings with respect to individuals suspected of having taken part in the Rwandan genocide, 'local authorities offered the most extensive judicial cooperation, despite the absence of a treaty between Belgium and Rwanda'.[63] More recently, Finnish courts were able to hold public hearings in Rwanda and Tanzania for weeks on end.[64]

In sum, far from collectively objecting to the principle of universality, many African states seem to wholeheartedly endorse the principle. What does this mean? The contentious legal issue emerges from the very same AU Assembly decisions on the 'abuse of universal jurisdiction' that I mentioned above. The Assembly has repeatedly called upon 'all concerned States to respect International Law and particularly the immunity of state officials when applying the Principle of Universal Jurisdiction'.[65] The concerns are about immunities and these concerns are entirely legitimate. The judgement of the ICJ in *Arrest Warrant* made it quite clear that, whatever the rule for international tribunals, certain high-ranking state officials enjoy immunity before national courts of other states while in office, even for international crimes.[66]

There is, moreover, admitted difficulty in determining the range of officials entitled to such immunity. In *Arrest Warrant*, the ICJ noted somewhat ambiguously that 'in international law it is firmly established that ... certain holders of high-ranking office in a State, *such as* the Head of State, Head of Government and Minister for Foreign Affairs, enjoy immunities from jurisdiction in other States'.[67] The open-endedness of this view, compounded by the limited ratification and uncertain customary law status of the 1969 Special Missions Convention,[68] means that it is not at all clear which high

---

62 *Ibid.*
63 Damien Vandermeersch, 'Prosecuting International Crimes in Belgium', 3 *Journal of International Criminal Justice* (2005) 400–421, at 412.
64 See Rain Liivoja, 'Dish of the Day: *Justice sans frontiers à la finlandaise*', 1 *Helsinki Review of Global Governance* (2010) 20–22; Minna Kimpimäki, 'Genocide in Rwanda: Is It Really Finland's Concern?', 11 *International Criminal Law Review* (2011) 155–76.
65 Assembly/AU/Dec.243(XIII) Rev.1, 3 July 2009, para. 6; similarly, Assembly/AU/Dec.271(XIV), 2 February 2010, para. 7.
66 *Arrest Warrant, supra* note 2, at paras 58–61.
67 *Ibid.*, at para. 51 (emphasis added).
68 Convention on Special Missions, GA Res. 2530 (XXIV), 8 December 1969, in force 21 June 1985, 1400 UNTS 231.

state officials, other than the 'big three', are entitled to immunity under international law. This has been a source of dispute between European and African states, resulting in several contentious cases before the ICJ.[69] Also, the AU Assembly recently requested the AU Commission to study the advisability of obtaining, through the UN General Assembly, an advisory opinion of the ICJ on the question of immunities of Heads of State and senior state officials from states that are not parties to the Rome Statute.[70]

All of the above suggests that protests by African states against the use of universal jurisdiction with regard to prosecutions of their state officials relate more properly to the scope of immunities under international law than universal jurisdiction. Hence these objections do not have a negative impact on the existence of universal jurisdiction in customary law.

3 Concluding remarks

This chapter made two related arguments about the sources of international law as a basis for universal jurisdiction. First, I suggested that universal jurisdiction cannot be based on a treaty as a treaty only creates a legal regime as between its states parties. I also suggested that treaty provisions that ostensibly create universal jurisdiction should rather be seen as devices for allowing a state that captures a suspect to prosecute him/her on behalf of another party to the treaty that has jurisdiction deriving from customary law.

Second, I argued that, when it comes to the purported rules of customary international law that deal with universal jurisdiction, a singular focus on case law is not justified. The legislation of various states should also be taken into account as state practice. Finally, I also argued that, on closer examination, protests made by states with respect to the exercise of universal jurisdiction are often not really directed against universal jurisdiction as such but relate to a separate legal matter (in particular, immunity).

---

69 Djibouti brought a case against France in the ICJ, arguing that its Director of Public Prosecutions and Head of National Security would be entitled to such immunity. The Court disagreed: *Certain Questions of Mutual Assistance in Criminal Matters (Djibouti v. France)*, ICJ Reports (2008) 177, at para. 194. Congo also instituted proceedings against France, claiming that its Minister of the Interior was entitled to immunity. However, Congo later had the case removed from the General List: *Certain Criminal Proceedings in France (Republic of the Congo v. France) (Order)*, ICJ Reports (2010) 635. Most recently, Rwanda has sought to bring a claim against France, alleging that the Chief of General Staff of its Defence Forces and the Chief of Protocol attached to the Presidency are entitled to immunity. So far, France has not expressed its acceptance of the Court's jurisdiction in this matter: International Court of Justice, 'The Republic of Rwanda applies to the International Court of Justice in a dispute with France', Press Release No. 2007/11 (18 April 2007). For a discussion of the dispute underlying Congo's application, see Charles Chernor Jalloh, 'Universal Jurisdiction, Universal Prescription? A Preliminary Assessment of the African Union Perspective on Universal Jurisdiction', 21 *Criminal Law Forum* (2010) 1–65.

70 Assembly/AU/Dec. 419(XIX), *supra* note 57, at para. 3.

19 Making the right choice

Constructing rules for anti-terrorist operations

Jarna Petman

When *Operation Infinite Justice* was launched in Afghanistan in October 2001 as a response to the terrorist attacks of 11 September 2001, it was a start of a military campaign that is not finished yet. While military involvement as such was not a novelty to the counter-terrorist strategy, what did mark a significant shift in the strategy was the conceptualisation of the response to the attacks as an all-out, open-ended 'war'.[1] The fight against terrorism was rhetorically and conceptually pushed from the paradigm of crime control to that of just war, in which the enemies were depicted 'as wrong as they are evil'.[2] This would soon be reflected in the newly draconian anti-terrorism measures.

Immediately after September 2001, a security-orientated discourse was so pervasive that most states hurriedly introduced far-reaching legislative changes with very little public debate or analysis. Some of them did so out of national sense of imminent threat; many of them did so in response to international mandates, the UN and the various regional bodies pushing binding resolutions, legal frameworks and plans of action down to the national level.[3] As the subsequent terrorist attacks – the 2002 Moscow theatre siege, the 2004 Beslan school hostage-taking, the 2004 Madrid train bombing and the 2005 suicide bombings on the London transport system – raised the stakes, the legislative shift was irrevocably toward prevention and surveillance.[4] Originally, not only legislatures, but also courts were so taken by the amplified need to promote maximum security that they too opted for

---

1   For an analysis, see Frédéric Mégret, ' "War"? Legal Semantics and the Move to Violence', 13 *European Journal of International Law* (2002) 361–400.
2   George W. Bush, 'State of the Union Address', 29 January 2002, *Archives*, <georgewbush-whitehouse.archives.gov/news> (also in *ibid.*, '[E]vil is real, and it must be opposed ... God is near'). Cf. Jarna Petman, 'The Problem of Evil and International Law' in Jarna Petman and Jan Klabbers (eds), *Nordic Cosmopolitanism: Essays in International Law for Martti Koskenniemi* (Martinus Nijhoff, 2003) 111–40.
3   See Kim Lane Scheppele, 'The International Standardization of National Security Law', 4 *Journal of National Security Law & Policy* (2010) 437–53.
4   See, e.g., Stella Burch Elias, 'Rethinking "Preventive Detention" from A Comparative Perspective: Three Frameworks for Detaining Terrorist Suspects', 41 *Columbia Human Rights Law Review* (2009) 99–234.

acquiescence in the face of the executive's claims to wider, if not absolute, discretion.[5] It was not long, however, before the ill-considered laws and the overreaches of power and authority began to generate constitutional challenges around the world.[6]

It was in the language of legal rules – especially human rights – that the critique against the excesses of the war on terror has been expressed.[7] Nevertheless, as I hope the following pages will show, legal rules are not trumps. While rules such as human rights are fundamental, they are also contestable. That is to say, there is considerable indeterminacy in the scope of every rule.[8] A rule – a right – would be determinate, if it were to tell the practitioner what to do, how to decide between competing claims, for example. Thus, to claim that a rule is indeterminate is merely to claim that the rule allows choice rather than constraining or compelling it.[9] This does not mean arbitrariness, however. Even in the conditions of indeterminacy, it is entirely possible for there to be predictable patterns and regularities in interpretation and application alike. Indeed, much of legal professionalism consists in making predictions on the basis of such patterns and regularities. The claim of indeterminacy is quite simply that none of these patterns and regularities is a necessary consequence of rules.

And so, decisions on human rights, for example, are both indeterminate and non-arbitrary in that they can be explained only by reference to criteria outside the scope of their formal justifications.[10] Decisions are non-arbitrary because the legal culture 'encompasses shared understandings of proper institutional roles and the extent to which the status quo should be maintained or altered. This culture includes "common sense" understandings of what rules mean'.[11] Importantly, any given regime of rules in the legal order can, upon a shift in the direction of political winds or with a more

---

5   See John Ip, 'The Supreme Court and the House of Lords in The War on Terror: *inter arma silent leges?*', 19 *Michigan State Journal of International Law* (2011) 1–61, and Helen Fenwick and Gavin Phillipson, 'Covert Derogations and Judicial Deference: Redefining Liberty and Due Process Rights in Counterterrorism Law and Beyond', 56 *McGill Law Journal* (2011) 863–918.

6   See Kim Lane Scheppele, 'The Constitutional Role of Transnational Courts: Principled Legal Ideas in Three–Dimensional Political Space', 28 *Penn State International Law Review* (2010) 451–461; and Eyal Benvenisti, 'Reclaiming Democracy: the Strategic Uses of Foreign and International Law by National Courts', 102 *American Journal of International Law* (2008) 241–74.

7   See Joan Fitzpatrick, 'Speaking Law to Power: The War against Terrorism and Human Rights', 14 *European Journal of International Law* (2003) 241–64.

8   See Frederick Schauer, *Playing by the Rules: A Philosophical Examination of Rule-Based Decision-Making in Law and in Life* (Clarendon, 1991) at 31–4.

9   See Mark Kelman, *A Guide to Critical Legal Studies* (Harvard University Press, 1987) 245–6 and 257–62; and Joseph Singer, 'The Player and the Cards: Nihilism and Legal Theory', 94 *Yale Law Journal* (1984) 1–70 at 9–26.

10 See Jarna Petman, *Human Rights and Violence: The Hope and the Fear of the Liberal World* (Hart, forthcoming).

11 Singer, 'Player and the Cards', *supra* note 9, at 22.

gradual societal change, generate a different kind of culture with a different kind of understanding of what rules and rights might mean, and thus lead to opposite decisions.[12]

Accordingly – and as I seek to demonstrate in what follows – the recognition (or introduction) of pertinent rules will not be enough to constrain the excesses in the ongoing war on terror; what will also be needed is the power and the willingness to interpret and implement those rules in a certain way. Now, let me look into some of the attempts to restrain the overreaches of power in the antiterrorist operations so as to demonstrate the indeterminate nature of rules and to highlight the importance of the moment of application.

1 A War without rights?

In the 'war against terror', definitions have certainly mattered, as euphemisms such as 'unlawful enemy combatant', 'military commission', 'extraordinary rendition flight', 'torture light' and 'enhanced interrogation' have played a significant role in distorting the legal field. Many of the critics of the war have argued that the conceptual confusion has brought into being a 'legal vacuum', a 'legal black hole', or, indeed, a 'lawless world'.[13] They have called for the application of human rights to fill the void and remedy the scandal. However, such legal mystification of the situation has overlooked the fact that the various phenomena and procedures adopted in the war against terror have been deeply legal creations, stipulated by constitutional law, special regulations and extradition arrangements. Instrumentalised, law has in concrete ways been complicit in the war effort. In this, violence has become legalised in new and creative ways. It may well be that the question of how to bring in the rules is the wrong one, and we should instead be asking how to apply the rules that already exist.[14]

At the heart of the question of what legal rules, if any, govern the various actors in the war on terror, there lie the confusion and the tension between the paradigms of armed conflict and criminal law enforcement.[15] Is the 'war' against terrorism a state of war or peace? If the former is the case, and the rules of the law of armed conflict are applicable even to the counter-terrorist operations that blur the legal boundaries between police and military

---

12 Robert W. Gordon, 'Critical Legal Histories', 36 *Stanford Law Review* (1984) 57–125 at 125.

13 Cf. Johan Steyn, 'Guantánamo Bay: the Legal Black Hole', 53 *International & Comparative Law Quarterly* (2004) 1–15 at 14; Philippe Sands, *Lawless World: The Whistle-Blowing Account of How Bush and Blair Are Taking the Law into Their Own Hands* (Penguin, 2006).

14 Cf. Ralph Wilde, 'Legal "Black Hole"? Extraterritorial State Action and International Treaty Law on Civil and Political Rights', 26 *Michigan Journal of International Law* (2005) 739–806 at 785–806.

15 See David Turns, 'The "War on Terror" through British and International Humanitarian Law Eyes: Comparative Perspectives on Selected Legal Issues', 10 *New York City Law Review* (2006) 435–77 at 439–45.

operations, then is this conflict to be regarded an international or a non-international one? That is to say, is this a war between dissident armed groups within the territory of a single state, or between a government and insurgent forces in its own territory? The normative difference between the two categories is notable in that the law of international armed conflicts is highly regulated, with numerous treaties – such as the four Geneva Conventions of 1949 – covering the field in great detail, whereas the law of non-international conflicts is remarkably vague and general, providing very few safeguards for the insurgents.[16] The privilege of prisoner-of-war status, for example, exists only in international armed conflict. The rules applicable in international armed conflict specify that everyone is either a combatant or a civilian, and that enemy combatants are entitled to a prisoner-of-war status provided that they satisfy the requirements of lawful belligerency.[17]

While a captured insurgent will not be regarded a prisoner-of-war, she will still have to have *some* legal status. But what status might that be? This question has gained urgency in the anti-terrorism campaign in which the actual distinction between civilians and combatants has been put to the test. Because of the prevailing uncertainty as to the distinction between the paradigms of war and crime, the criminality of the terrorist is regarded *neither* military nor civilian. Instead, considered *both* an enemy and a criminal, the terrorist has been labelled an 'unlawful enemy combatant'. What rights might such unlawful belligerents have in the field of operations?

---

16 The legal regime governing international armed conflicts is codified primarily in the four Geneva Conventions of 1949: Geneva Convention (I) for the Amelioration of the Condition of the Wounded and Sick in Armed Forces in the Field, 12 August 1949, in force 21 October 1950, 75 UNTS 31; Geneva Convention (II) for the Amelioration of the Condition of the Wounded, Sick, and Shipwrecked Members of Armed Forces at Sea, 12 August 1949, in force 21 October 1950, 75 UNTS 85; Geneva Convention (III) Relative to the Treatment of Prisoners of War, 12 August 1949, in force 21 October 1950, 75 UNTS 135; Geneva Convention (IV) Relative to the Protection of Civilian Persons in Time of War, 12 August 1949, in force 21 October 1950, 75 UNTS 287. The Geneva Conventions were supplemented by the Protocol (I) Additional to the Geneva Conventions of 12 August 1949, and Relating to the Protection of Victims of International Armed Conflicts, 8 June 1977, in force 7 December 1978, 1125 UNTS 3.

The legal regime governing non-international (intra-state) armed conflicts is codified primarily in Article 3 common to all four Geneva Conventions, providing for minimal obligations. Common Article 3 was supplemented by the Protocol (II) Additional to the Geneva Conventions of 12 August 1949, and relating to the Protection of Victims of Non-International Armed Conflicts, Geneva, 8 June 1977, in force 7 December 1978, 1125 UNTS 609.

For an analysis of the ways in which the gap between the two regimes seems to have begun to close, see Sandesh Sivakumaran, 'Re-envisaging the International Law of Internal Armed Conflict', 22 *European Journal of International Law* (2011) 219–64.

17 See Geneva Convention III, *supra* note 16, Article 4.

1.1 'War on terror' as a non-international armed conflict

In June 2006, the US Supreme Court came to address the question of how to classify and regulate the ongoing campaign against global terrorism. In *Hamdan v. Rumsfeld*, a Yemeni national who had been captured during the US invasion of Afghanistan as an alleged al-Qaeda affiliate and was now held as an 'alien unlawful enemy combatant' at Guantánamo Bay, was challenging the legality of his detention and his eligibility for trial by a 'military commission'.[18] Such commissions had been established through presidential order to expressly deny the novel category of 'alien unlawful enemy combatants' the rights that the Geneva Conventions guaranteed to lawful combatants.[19]

It was the Administration's position that the conflict in Afghanistan was in fact composed of two separate armed conflicts: one between the US and the Taliban (fighting on behalf of Afghanistan), and another between the US and al-Qaeda.[20] The Third Geneva Convention relative to the Treatment of Prisoners of War applied to Taliban by virtue of Afghanistan being a state party to the Conventions. It did not apply to al-Qaeda, however, because it was a non-state actor and it was not a High Contracting Party to the Convention; as specified by Common Article 2, the Geneva Conventions apply to all cases of international (inter-state) armed conflict when at least one of the warring states has ratified the Conventions.[21] On the other hand, since the conflict with al-Qaeda was not confined to the territory of a single state but was 'international in scope',[22] it was also excluded from even the minimum baseline protections of Common Article 3, which has traditionally been interpreted to apply only to non-international (intra-state) armed conflicts given its reference to 'armed conflict not of an international character occurring in the territory of one of the High Contracting Parties'.[23] In other words, the argument was that as Hamdan had been

---

18 *Hamdan v. Rumsfeld*, 548 US 557 (2006).
19 See 'Military Order, Detention, Treatment, and Trial of Certain Non-Citizens in the War Against Terrorism', 66 *Federal Register* 57,833 (13 November 2001).
20 See the arguments presented before the Court of Appeals for the District of Columbia in *Hamdan v. Rumsfeld*, 415 F 3d 33 (DC Cir., 2005) at 41–2.
21 According to Article 2, common to all four Geneva Conventions, *supra* note 16, the Conventions 'shall apply to all cases of ... armed conflict which may arise between two or more of the High Contracting Parties ... Although one of the Powers in conflict may not be a party to the present Convention, the Powers who are parties thereto shall remain bound by it in their mutual relations'.
22 See *Hamdan v. Rumsfeld (Supreme Court)*, *supra* note 18, at 2795–6.
23 Under Article 3, common to all four Geneva Conventions, *supra* note 16, certain minimum rules of war apply to armed conflicts 'not of an international character' to ensure that persons 'taking no active part in the hostilities, including members of armed forces who have laid down their arms and those placed *hors de combat* by sickness, wounds, detention, or any other cause, shall in all circumstances be treated humanely', thus prohibiting acts such as 'cruel treatment and torture', 'humiliating and degrading treatment' and 'the passing of sentences and the carrying out of executions without previous judgement pronounced by a regularly constituted court affording all the judicial guarantees which are recognized as indispensable by civilized peoples'.

captured in the context of the conflict with al-Qaeda – an armed conflict which the Administration considered neither international nor non-international in character – he was not entitled to any of the protections afforded to detainees by the Geneva Conventions.

The Supreme Court was of a different opinion, holding that the military commission prosecuting Hamdan lacked power to proceed because President Bush did not have authority to set up military commissions that violated the procedural requirements of both military justice law and the Geneva Conventions.[24] To invalidate the claim that the armed conflict in which Hamdan had been captured could be classified as neither an interstate nor an intra-state one, the Court chose to apply a strictly literal reading of the letter of the Geneva Conventions, particularly that of Common Article 3. Because much depended on the phrase 'armed conflict not of an international character', the Court interpreted it in 'its literal meaning' to stand 'in contradistinction to a conflict between nations', thereby bringing within its ambit any and all armed conflicts that do not fit within the inter-state armed conflict paradigm of Common Article 2.[25] By interpreting the scope of Common Article 3 so broadly, the Court consciously moved away from the traditional interpretation of the Article, which was to regulate intra-state armed conflicts only. Indeed, while the Court acknowledged that 'an important purpose' of Common Article 3 was to furnish minimal protection to rebels in civil wars, it concluded that the intention behind the provision was for its scope of application to be 'as wide as possible'.[26] And so the Court found that there was 'at least one provision of the Geneva Conventions that applies ... even if the relevant conflict is not one between signatories':[27] Common Article 3 was thus interpreted to apply as a 'minimum yardstick' of protection in all conflicts,[28] even against terrorists.

1.2 *'War on terror' as an international armed conflict*

While the US Supreme Court identified the totality of the global war on terror in June 2006 as an 'armed conflict not of an international character'

---

24 In response to the Supreme Court's *Hamdan* decision, President Bush signed in October 2006 an Act of Congress, Military Commissions Act of 2006 (Pub. L. No. 109–366, 120 Stat. 2600 [17 October 2006]), the stated purpose of which was to give a Congressional authorisation to the trial of 'alien unlawful enemy combatants' by 'military commission' for 'violations of the law of war, and for other purposes'. This was, in turn, amended by a bill passed by the US House of Representatives and signed by President Obama in 2009, namely Military Commissions Act of 2009; see National Defense Authorization Act for Fiscal Year 2010, H.R. 2647, Pub. L. No. 111–84, 123 Stat. 2190 (28 October 2009), Title XVIII.
25 See *Hamdan v. Rumsfeld (Supreme Court), supra* note 18, at 2796.
26 See *ibid.*, at 2796.
27 See *ibid.*, at 2756–7.
28 Cf. *Military and Paramilitary Activities in and against Nicaragua (Nicaragua v. US)*, ICJ Reports (1986) 14, at 113 and 218; cf. also *Prosecutor v. Tadić*, Case No. IT-94-I-A, ICTY Appeals Chamber, Judgment, 15 July 1999, para. 102.

in order to apply the protections of Common Article 3 to the treatment of detained terrorist suspects, the Supreme Court of Israel would six months later reach a diametrically opposite conclusion when seeking to explicate the legal framework underpinning – and limiting – the methods and means of warfare used by the Israeli Defence Forces against Palestinian militants in the West Bank and Gaza Strip.

In *Public Committee against Torture in Israel v. Government of Israel* (*Targeted Killings*) of 2006,[29] the Supreme Court of Israel, sitting as the High Court of Justice,[30] examined the legality of the policy of 'targeted frustration of terrorism', whereby Israel has since the beginning of the second or al-Aqsa *intifada* in 2000 been killing in targeted strikes individual members of militant Palestinian organisations suspected of terrorism.[31] The starting point in *Targeted Killings* was that a continuous situation of armed conflict has existed between Israel and 'various terrorist organizations' since September 2000. According to the Court, the applicable law in this conflict was that governing international armed conflicts on two separate grounds. For one, the Court considered that the 'considerable military capabilities' of modern terrorist organisations posed such dangers that the struggle against them could not be 'restricted within the state and its penal law' but constituted 'a part of the international law dealing with armed conflicts of international character' instead'.[32] Moreover, in the view of the Court, the fact that the conflict crossed the borders of the state and took place within a context of belligerent occupation situated it firmly within the normative framework of international armed conflict.[33]

By placing so much emphasis on the military capabilities of terrorist organisations, that 'at times ... exceed those of the state', the Court was highlighting the fact that although they 'do not act in the name of the state', terrorist organisations can inflict harm equivalent to that inflicted by a state

---

29   Supreme Court of Israel, HCJ 769/02 *Public Committee against Torture in Israel et al. v. Government of Israel et al.* (2006) 53(4) PD 817, 46 ILM 375 [hereinafter *Targeted Killings*].
30   The Supreme Court of Israel may function both as a Court of Appeals (hearing civil and criminal appeals from the district courts) and a High Court of Justice (sitting as a court of first instance in constitutional and administrative cases); see Basic Law: Judicature, 5744 (1984), 83 *Laws of the State of Israel* (1983–84) 101 at 104.
31   The policy's controversial nature is underscored by the fact that, as of the date of *Targeted Killings*, '338 Palestinians had been killed as a result of this policy, 128 of whom, including 29 children, were innocent bystanders', as noted by Orna Ben–Naftali and Keren Michaeli, 'Case Note: *The Public Committee against Torture in Israel v. The Government of Israel*', 101 *American Journal of International Law* (2007) 459–65 at 460.
32   *Targeted Killings, supra* note 29, at para. 21.
33   *Ibid.*, at para. 18.

and thus act *as if* they were states.[34] Perhaps it felt such emphasis was needed to strengthen the weak argument that relied on the border-crossing character of the armed conflict – in international law, it is not the border that determines the nature of the dispute, but the identity of the parties. In the Geneva Conventions, Common Article 2 defines an international armed conflict as 'arising between two or more states'.[35] All other conflicts are rendered non-international. The Palestinians are not a state in international law, however, and thus the armed conflict between Israel and the Palestinians cannot be regarded international in nature. Moreover, since some parts of the Palestinian Territories are under belligerent occupation by Israel and others are under the jurisdiction of the Palestinian Authority, in neither of the cases could those parts be considered legally part of the state of Israel, and therefore the armed conflict between Israel and the Palestinians could not be regarded non-international either. And yet, one could hardly conclude that the conflict was subject to no rules of humanitarian law at all. As much was noted by the Supreme Court in *Targeted Killings*:

> Every struggle of the State – against terrorism or any other enemy – is conducted according to rules and law ... There are no 'black holes' ... [T]he State's struggle against terrorism is not conducted 'outside' the law. It is conducted 'inside' the law, with tools that the law places at the disposal of democratic states.[36]

Having defined the applicable normative framework, it remained for the Court to explain how to qualify 'unlawful combatants' under the rules governing international armed conflicts. Reiterating its refusal to consider terrorists as outlaws, the Court concluded, 'God created them as well in his image; their human dignity as well is to be honoured; they as well enjoy and are entitled to protection, even if most minimal, by customary international law'.[37] Invoking Additional Protocol I to the Geneva Conventions,[38] the Court held that terrorists are civilians and therefore may be attacked – by targeted killings, if

---

34   Cf. *Nicaragua*, *supra* note 28, para. 195 (including the acts of armed force by irregular forces within the meaning of 'armed attack', if such acts are 'of such gravity as to amount to an actual armed attack [by a state]'); cf. also SC Res. 1368, 12 September 2001 (an implicit acceptance by the Security Council that the terrorist attacks on the US were armed attacks). But cf. *Armed Activities on the Territory of the Congo (Democratic Republic of the Congo v. Uganda)*, ICJ Reports (2005) 168 at para. 147 (deliberately avoiding pronouncing on the nature of terrorist attacks).
35   See Common Article 2, *supra* note 21.
36   *Targeted Killings*, *supra* note 29, at para. 61.
37   *Ibid.*, at para. 25.
38   See Additional Protocol I, *supra* note 16, Article 51(3) (providing that civilians enjoy immunity from deliberate attack 'unless and *for such time* as they take *a direct part* in hostilities').

need be – only 'for such time' as they take a 'direct part' in hostilities, subject to the customary international requirement of 'proportionality'.[39]

The Supreme Court of Israel thus reaffirmed that there were legal guarantees governing any anti-terrorist operation conducted by the state. To reach this conclusion, the Court built on both national and international law to construct a paradigm that differed from both national criminal law and the law of war. That this was a politically savvy construction was highlighted by the fact that, although the Court seemed to conclude that ends do not justify the means, it still left room for *some* ends to justify otherwise illegal means,[40] for everything about this novel paradigm hinged on the notion of proportionality – that is to say, on discretionary evaluation of the context.[41]

1.3 'War on terror' as an internal armed conflict

As was noted by Judge Barak, the President of the Supreme Court in *Targeted Killings*, the war on terror is not waged in a legal vacuum, but is conducted with 'tools that the law places at the disposal of democratic states'.[42] Whether to use the existing legal tools in relation to military counter-terrorist operations, however, remains a matter of choice. One such choice deals with the applicability of human rights law alongside the traditional legal framework of international humanitarian law to a state's own agents during anti-terrorist operations. Although the ICJ has in recent years pronounced on the relationship between international humanitarian law and human rights law – affirming that human rights are applicable even during armed conflict, subject only to derogation, with international humanitarian law prevailing as *lex specialis* – the exact translation of this relationship into practice remains a conundrum.[43] An important aspect of the dilemma deals with the exact scope of a state's extraterritorial human rights obligations and the meaning of 'effective control'.

---

39 *Targeted Killings, supra* note 29, at para. 26.
40 *Targeted Killings, supra* note 29, at paras 34–7, 39. For critique, see, for example, Kristen E. Eichensehr, 'On Target? The Israeli Supreme Court and the Expansion of Targeted Killings', 116 *Yale Law Journal* (2007) 1873–1881; Amichai Cohen and Yuval Shany, 'A development of Modest proportions: The Application of the Principle of Proportionality in the *Targeted Killing* case', 5 *Journal of International Criminal Justice* (2007) 310–21.
41 Cf. my *Human Rights and Violence, supra* note 10, at 184–5.
42 See *supra* the text accompanying note 36; see also Aharon Barak, *The Judge in a Democracy* (Princeton University Press, 2008).
43 Cf. *Legality or Threat of Use of Nuclear Weapons (Advisory Opinion)*, ICJ Reports (1996) 226, at para. 25; *Legal Consequences of the Construction of a Wall in the Occupied Palestinian Territory (Advisory Opinion)*, ICJ Reports (2004) 136, at para. 106; *Armed Activities on the Territory of the Congo, supra* note 34, at paras 216–20. For commentary, see e.g., Françoise Hampson, 'The Relationship between International Humanitarian Law and Human Rights Law from the Perspective of a Human Rights Treaty Body', 90 *International Review of the Red Cross* (2008) 549–72.

It was to the appreciation of the requirements for 'effective control' that the House of Lords had to turn in 2007, when deciding in *Al-Skeini*, whether the Human Rights Act of 1998 (and thereby the European Convention on Human Rights) was applicable to the British forces in Iraq.[44] The case involved claims by the relatives of six Iraqi civilians who had been killed in Basrah in 2003, during the time when the UK was responsible for maintaining security as an occupying power. Five of the six civilians had been killed by the British armed forces in the course of patrols or during a raid or crossfire; the sixth death had been the result of maltreatment by British soldiers, occurring while the victim had been in custody in a British detention facility. The Law Lords had to consider whether the deaths took place within the jurisdiction of the UK so as to fall within the scope of Article 1 of the European Convention, and, if so, whether there was a violation of the requirements under Articles 2 and 3 of the Convention.[45]

As far as the death of the sixth applicant's son in UK military custody was concerned, the majority of the Law Lords found jurisdiction to attach by virtue of an analogy 'with the extraterritorial exception made for embassies'.[46] With regard to the five killings during patrol operations, however, they could find no jurisdictional link and accordingly held that the Convention was not applicable.[47] In interpreting the extraterritorial scope of the Convention, the House of Lords followed the lead of the ECtHR. In doing so, the House faced the problem that on the question of jurisdiction over foreign territory, 'the judgments and decisions of the European Court do not speak with one voice'.[48] It therefore had to decide to which of the European decisions it should be 'giving pre-eminence'.[49] It opted for the *Banković* decision of 2001.[50] This concerned the applicability of the European Convention to several NATO member states on the basis of an

---

44   *Al-Skeini and Others v. Secretary of State for Defence* [2007] UKHL 26, [2008] 1 AC 153.
45   See Convention for the Protection of Human Rights and Fundamental Freedoms, Rome, 4 November 1950, in force 3 September 1953, 213 UNTS 221, ETS No. 5, as amended by Protocol No. 11 (restructuring the control machinery established thereby, Strasbourg, 11 May 1994, in force 1 November 1998, ETS No. 155), Article 1 (jurisdictional requirement), Article 2 (right to life, the protection of which includes the requirement to effectively investigate deaths at the hands of security forces), and Article 3 (prohibition of torture).
46   *Al-Skeini*, supra note 44, at para. 132 (*per* Lord Brown). Consequently, under the European Convention the British government was obliged to conduct an independent, thorough and impartial investigation into the circumstances of his death, cf. the Rt Hon Sir William Gage (Chairman), *The Report of the Baha Mousa Inquiry: Presented to Parliament pursuant to Section 26 of the Inquiries Act 2005 Ordered by the House of Commons to be printed on 8 September 2011* (3 vols, HC 1452–I, The Stationery Office, 2011).
47   *Al-Skeini*, supra note 44, at paras 83 (*per* Lord Rodger), 97 (*per* Lord Carswell), 132 (*per* Lord Brown).
48   *Al-Skeini*, supra note 44, at para. 67 (*per* Lord Rodger).
49   *Al-Skeini*, supra note 44, at para. 68 (*per* Lord Rodger).
50   See *Banković and Others v. Belgium and 16 Other Contracting States*, Application no. 52207/99, ECtHR Grand Chamber, Decision of 12 December 2001.

aerial bombardment of a radio and TV station in Belgrade during the bombing campaign of Serbia in 1999. Rejecting applicability, the European Court had held that aerial bombardments did not constitute the exercise of territorial control so as to meet the test for 'jurisdiction' within the meaning of the Convention.

Ascribing primacy to the *Banković* judgement would have significant consequences for their Lordships findings in *Al-Skeini*.[51] As such, *Banković* could be seen to supersede all the previous, substantially different judgements in which the ECtHR had found that a state could indeed have jurisdiction under the Convention, if it exercised 'effective control' over an area outside its territory, and if without this control 'a regrettable vacuum in the system of human-rights protection' would be created 'by removing from individuals there the benefit of the Convention's safeguards'.[52] In contradistinction to such findings, the Court had in *Banković* emphasised that not only does the Convention operate in the regionally circumscribed legal space of the contracting states but that, moreover, it 'was not designed to be applied throughout the world, even in respect of the conduct of Contracting States', and therefore:

> the desirability of avoiding a gap or vacuum in human rights' protection has so far been relied on by the Court in favour of establishing jurisdiction only when the territory in question was one that, but for the specific circumstances, would normally be covered by the Convention.[53]

As this pronouncement in *Banković* could be seen to weaken the significance of any subsequent judgement that might appear to affirm a different view of the meaning of jurisdiction,[54] the Law Lords could read the 2004 decision in *Issa and Others v. Turkey* as being inconsistent with *Banković*. In *Issa* the Court

---

51   See Ralph Wilde, 'Case Note: *R (on the application of Al-Skeini) v. Secretary of State for Defence (Redress Trust Intervening)*', 102 *American Journal of International Law* (2008) 628–34 at 630–1.
52   See *Cyprus v. Turkey*, Application no. 25781/94, ECtHR Grand Chamber, Judgment of 10 May 2001; see also *Loizidou v. Turkey (Preliminary Objections)*, Application no. 15318/89, Decision of 23 March 1995.
53   *Banković*, *supra* note 50, at para. 80.
54   Cf., e.g., *Djavit An v. Turkey*, Application no. 20652/92, ECtHR Chamber, Judgment of 20 February 2003; *Ilaşcu and Others v. Moldova and Russia*, Application no. 48787/99, ECtHR Grand Chamber, Judgment of 8 July 2004. Cf. also *Isaak and Others v. Turkey*, Application no. 44587/98, ECtHR Third Section, Decision of 28 September 2006; *Pad and Others v. Turkey*, Application no. 60167/00, ECtHR Third Section, Decision of 28 June 2007; *Andreou v. Turkey*, Application 45653/99, ECtHR Fourth Section, Decision of 3 June 2008; *Solomou and Others v. Turkey*, Application no. 36832/97, ECtHR Fourth Section, Decision of 24 June 2008; *Al-Saadoon and Mufdhi v. United Kingdom*, Application no. 61498/08, ECtHR Fourth Section, Decision of 3 July 2009; and *Medvedyev and Others v. France*, Application no. 3394/03, ECtHR Grand Chamber, Judgment of 29 March 2010.

had, with regard to the applicability of the Convention to Turkish troops in northern Iraq, reiterated its earlier findings that jurisdiction could derive from effective control, adding that:

> a State may also be held accountable for violation of the Convention rights and freedoms of persons who are in the territory of another State but who are found to be under the former State's authority and control through its agents operating – whether lawfully or unlawfully – in the latter State ... Accountability in such situations stems from the fact that Article 1 of the Convention cannot be interpreted so as to allow a State party to perpetrate violations of the Convention on the territory of another State, which it could not perpetrate on its own territory.[55]

In choosing *Banković* over *Issa*, the House of Lords took great pains to distinguish the two judgements, emphasising that *Banković* had been a decision by the Grand Chamber while *Issa* had been decided by a mere chamber; the *Issa* application had not succeeded; the Court's observations on *Issa* had been *obiter dicta* because the Court had found on the facts that Turkey did not have 'effective control'; the parties in *Banković* had been 'represented by distinguished counsel'; and the chamber in *Issa* had made no express statement to the effect that it was departing from the finding in *Banković*.[56]

Echoing the Court's findings in *Banković*, then, the House of Lords adopted a decisively strict view to the concept of jurisdiction and held that as obligations arising under the European Convention could not be 'divided and tailored in accordance with the particular circumstances', the whole package of rights had to be secured where a contracting state has jurisdiction. From this, the House drew the conclusion that a state could be considered to have extraterritorial jurisdiction only where it 'has such effective control of the territory of another state that it could secure to *everyone* in the territory *all* the rights and freedoms'.[57] To boost the finding that such effective control was lacking, the Law Lords referred to the material facts and the evidence of senior British officers, according to which, on the ground, 'the available British troops faced formidable difficulties due to terrorist activity, the volatile situation and the lack of any effective Iraqi security forces' and thus even 'leaving the other rights and freedoms on one side, with all its troops doing their best', the UK could not be said to have

---

55 *Issa v. Turkey*, Application no. 31821/96, ECtHR Second Section, Decision of 16 November 2004.
56 *Al-Skeini, supra* note 44, at paras 68, 124, 127, and 132 (*per* Lord Rodger), 91 (*per* Baroness Hale), 169 (*per* Lord Brown).
57 *Al-Skeini, supra* note 44, at para. 79 (*per* Lord Rodger) [emphasis mine], also para. 128 (*per* Lord Brown).

held such control over the area that it would have been able to discharge the obligations of a contracting state under Article 2 alone.[58]

Moreover, the Law Lords concluded that it would be 'manifestly absurd' to hold that the UK was obliged to secure in Iraq the human rights established under the European Convention, since the Convention was 'a body of law which may reflect the values of the contracting states, but which most certainly does not reflect those in ... the utterly different society of southern Iraq'. To hold that the Convention applied in Iraq would therefore 'run the risk ... of being accused of human rights imperialism'.[59] Indeed, it was the interpretation of the House of Lords that the precedent set in *Banković* meant that the Convention could only apply as a result of the effective control by one contracting state over the territory of another contracting state.[60]

So, in *Al-Skeini*, the House of Lords held that the British troops in Iraq did not have obligations under human rights law, as opposed to those accruing under international humanitarian law, towards the five victims who had been killed during patrol operations, as the UK authorities had lacked effective control over the area where the killings occurred.[61] The war on terror was thus essentially determined to be an internal conflict in the area of Iraq controlled by the British troops, except in the very limited circumstances of British-run military prisons.

It is arguable that by choosing to apply such a strict test to the status of the UK forces in Iraq, the Law Lords did not really so much go against the universalist assumptions of the Convention as they sought to rule out the extraterritorial application of the Convention outside the territories of the Council of Europe. The UK is an active participant in the theatres of operation in the war on terror. The Law Lords were certainly wary of opening the floodgates of litigation to claims of human rights violations arising from the involvement of British troops in military operations outside Europe and around the world. A finding that every individual against whom the British forces might use force was, *a priori*, under the protection of the Convention, would have imposed unrealistic burdens on British courts.

---

58   *Al-Skeini, supra* note 44, at para. 83 (*per* Lord Rodger). For the purposes of international humanitarian law, though, the British troops can most probably be considered to have held effective enough control for the said territory to qualify as occupied.

59   *Al-Skeini, supra* note 44, at paras 78–9 (*per* Lord Rodger), also 90 (*per* Baroness Hale) and 97 (*per* Lord Carswell). For critique, see Tobias Thienel, 'The ECHR in Iraq: the Judgment of the House of Lords in *R (Al-Skeini) v. Secretary of State for Defence*', 6 *Journal of International Criminal Justice* (2008) 115–28 at 122–7.

60   *Al-Skeini, supra* note 44, at paras 71, 76–7 (*per* Lord Rodger), 109, 127 (*per* Lord Brown), also paras 91 (*per* Baroness Hale) and 97 (*per* Lord Carswell).

61   *Al-Skeini, supra* note 44, at paras 83 (*per* Lord Rodger), 97 (*per* Lord Carswell), 132 (*per* Lord Brown). Contrast this with the finding of the ICJ in *Armed Activities on the Territory of the Congo, supra* note 34, at paras 173 and 178 (holding that during a situation of occupation, a state's human rights obligations automatically apply).

Interestingly, when the case then came before the ECtHR in 2011, the Court decided to extend the protection of the Convention to Iraq.[62]

The ECtHR pinned its *Al-Skeini* decision on the enigmatic notion of 'public powers' – finding that the UK had exercised all or some of the public powers normally to be exercised by the government of the territory in question – and carefully avoided explaining its understanding of this notion.[63] Instead, the Court emphasised the exceptionality of the circumstances that underpinned its findings in *Al-Skeini*, reiterating that each case must be decided on its particular facts.[64] By thus, prudently, refusing to construe the concept of extraterritorial jurisdiction in clear and consistent terms, the Court left itself room to tailor the concept to suit the specific facts and circumstances of any given case. So, while the Court did not, after all, close the door on the possibility of applying the Convention outside the territories of the Council of Europe member states, it did not throw that door wide open.[65] The extraterritorial application of the Convention remains exceptional and needs to be justified by reference to general international law.

As is evident from the above, when faced with the question of what rights, if any, terrorist suspects have in the field of armed anti-terrorist operations, one cannot answer this question by applying the relevant rules. Rather, it is only after one has decided whether terrorist suspects have rights, that the relevant rules can be applied.

2   Making the right choice

To counter the excesses of the war on terror, we use the language and the institutions of law to set limits to discretionary and pre-emptive power. To be sure, formal rules are absolutely essential to upholding a sense of political accountability of those who are in positions of power and decide on such matters as the use of armed force against suspected terrorists.[66] By force of the pure form of legal statements the decision-maker will have to follow a certain procedure and base her decisions on general principles. Instead of taking her own preferences and values as a given, she must argue and justify those preferences in formal processes through generally accepted standards. Crucially, formally, these rules are available to everyone – even to the objects of her decisions, the terrorist suspects.

---

62   *Al-Skeini v. United Kingdom*, Application no. 55721/07, ECtHR Grand Chamber, Judgment of 7 July 2011, paras 149–150.
63   *Al-Skeini*/GC, *supra* note 62, at paras 133–136; cf. *Banković*, *supra* note 50, at para. 71. For critique, see Marko Milanovic, '*Al-Skeini* and *Al-Jedda* in Strasbourg', 23 *European Journal of International Law* (2012) 121–39 at 127–33.
64   *Al-Skeini*/GC, *supra* note 62, at paras 132 and 149.
65   See Anna Cowan, 'A New Watershed? Re-evaluating *Bankovi* in Light of *Al-Skeini*', 1 *Cambridge Journal of International & Comparative Law* (2012) 213–27 at 226.
66   See my *Human Rights and Violence*, *supra* note 10, at 345–7.

Rules are impossible as clear-cut behavioural directives, however. Rules are, and must be, diluted from black-and-white directives into broad informal standards that allow, and even necessitate, discretion because no text of a rule emerges from a single, uncomplicated purpose. And so the open-endedness of rules emerges already at the legislative level as rules are formulated as legislative compromises to reflect the different priorities. Any application of a rule, then, will inevitably imply a choice among the various priorities. This, as I have sought to illustrate in the preceding pages, makes policy and discretion determinative of outcomes – even within the fields of international humanitarian law and human rights law.

This does not mean, however, that rules could be applied in any which way. In all institutional contexts there is, and there should be, a constellation of forces that relies on some shared understanding of what the relevant values and rules are, and how they should be applied. The abrupt societal change that occurred on 11 September 2001 brought about a radical shift in the direction of political winds, as became evident immediately on September the twelfth. The resulting regimes of rules in the legal orders of most, if not all, pluralist democracies would from thereon generate a wholly different kind of legal culture from that which had prevailed on September the tenth. This would involve a wholly different set of shared understandings and stabilising conventions, leading to exactly opposite preferences and, accordingly, exactly opposite decisions.

Indeterminate as they are, rules do not in themselves offer any clear guidance as to how to choose among the various competing priorities that went into justifying them. And so the decision-maker may effectively choose the justification that best fits her idea of a just world. Her choice will of course be informed by the deeply embedded preferences of the institutional setting within which it is made. However, as disagreement will remain about, say, what counts as the appropriate institutional tradition and what counts as a coherent decision, human agency and individual choice will linger. Among a constellation of forces that make up the institutional setting, the decision-maker is thus wielding true power. Here, the possibility of abuse arises, the more so the more powerful the decision-maker is. After all, rules are indeterminate precisely because no substantive agreement can be reached on what constitutes a just world.

A legal technique that reaches directly to (one of) the purpose(s) of the rule, either evokes moral naturalism or licenses the decision-maker to realise her own purpose – or it may try to do both, as has been the case in the war on terror. On the one hand, the moral and theological rhetoric through which the ongoing anti-terrorism campaign was originally pushed from the paradigm of crime control to that of just war injected the 'war' with moral assurances. On the other hand, the insistence that governments have wider, more exclusive discretion in formulating and implementing limitations on rights and freedoms so as to be able to better assess and manage the risks posed by transnational terrorism, gradually started to detach rules from their formality.

The focus on the purpose of rules instead of rules themselves frees the decision-maker to act as if omnipotent. In a situation where there is no distance between the decision-maker and her preferences, formal rules and institutions offer a way out to a more just understanding of how to – and to whom to – apply the rules. They set limits to the use of power and hold the decision-maker responsible for her actions. Accordingly, formal rules have been a strategy of resistance in the war on terror.

While formal rules are absolutely indispensable to upholding a sense of political accountability of those who are in positions of power, they are not enough. Because of the discretion – the choice – that persists in applying the rules, also an active political community will be needed. As the 'right' choice will be sought on the basis of previous practice, on the basis of what the decision-maker feels and considers to be right, and on the basis of the audience to whom the decision will be addressed, any choice will turn into a dialogue between the decision-maker and the tradition of principles, the institutional history shaping and constraining the decision. What is crucial about the political activism within the community is the cacophony of voices it will inevitably produce.

Indeed, the ambivalent nature of rules is, of course, but a reflection of the ambivalence prevailing in human societies – or indeed in the human person: conflicting aims and purposes that cannot be brought to a logical conclusion will simultaneously continue to accompany the same experience. Acknowledging the irredeemability of such irresolution is one of the controlling ideas behind liberal democracy that accordingly accepts pluralism as a form of organising human co-existence. In such a plurality of equal voices there can be no markers of certainty. Of this, the authorities that perform the balancing act between the individual's right to freedom and the society's right to collective security will need to be reminded.

It was this sort of reminder that the courts offered to the executive in the examples above. The decisions I have recounted have been much criticised for not having been the dramatic and unambiguous rebukes to the executive branch that many hoped they would be, but having merely 'chipped away at the edges' of overreaches of power.[67] Rather than offering the final say on the questions under debate, the decisions on anti-terrorist measures have tended to focus on institutional levels. Rather than making a determination on the very substance of the particular action in question, the courts have sought to clarify issues and considerations that the executive must take into consideration in exercising its discretion, or have invited the legislature to reconsider a hasty or vague authorisation. I do not consider such holdings an embarrassment. Instead, I appreciate the prudent fashion in which these courts have engaged their political branches, signalling their intention to constrain measures they consider excessive.[68] The decisions I have cited can

---

67 Ip, *'Inter arma silent leges?'*, *supra* note 5, at 60.
68 Cf. also Benvenisti, 'Reclaiming Democracy', *supra* note 6, at 256–7.

be seen as a reminder to both the terrorists and the anti-terrorists alike: that while it may be the destiny of a pluralist democracy that not all the means and the methods that are available to its enemies are available to it, a pluralist democracy will always have the upper hand in that it has a choice.[69] It is this choice that is effected as the law is made in the application.

---

69 Cf. Judge Barak in *Targeted Killings, supra* note 29, at para. 64; and Lord Hope of Craighead, 'The Judges' Dilemma', 58 *International & Comparative Law Quarterly* (2009) 753–65, at 758.

Index

absolutism 22, 23, 34
Abu Ghraib 184
accountability 49, 57, 196, 287, 324; and transparency 42, 66; of informal law-making 77–8, 82–3, 92, 99–102; legal 160, 166; political 326, 328; versus responsibility 70–1
Afghanistan 313, 317
African Union (AU) 309–12
agency 53–5, 83–4, 99, 124–5, 149, 228
agreement 7, 13, 14, 34, 209, 270; informal 76–7, 80–1, 83, 101, 124–5, 132; international 136, 213–14, 282, 308; jurisdictional 302; liberal 158; mixed 216–19, 224; multilateral environmental *see* multilateral environmental agreement; pre-existing, of EU member states 220–2; presumptive legality of 60–1, 85–6
Akande, Dapo 310–11
Al-Qaida 225; sanctions regime 226, 237, 243; *see also* UNSC Al-Qaida Sanctions Committee
Alembert, Jean le Rond d' 26–7
Alvarez, Jose 75–6
Andean Committee for the Defense of Competition 93
Annan, Kofi 283, 287, 291, 297
Antarctica 104, 111, 116–18
anti-terrorism *see* counter-terrorism
Aquinas, Thomas 19–20
armed conflict 116, 268, 315, 317; internal 321–6; international 316, 318–21; non-international 317–18; *see also* international humanitarian law
Asia Pacific Economic Cooperation (APEC) 93
Aspremont, Jean d' 76, 85

Aust, Anthony 79
aut dedere aut iudicare/punier 300, 302
authority 57, 61, 101, 105; as limits 97; as validity 137–8, 141; conflicts of 137, 140–4; executive 90, 318; international public 75, 82–4, 87–9, 92–6, 167, 292; law-making 4–5, 31, 60; presumptive 73; religious 21, 108; sovereign 6–9, 11, 22, 295–6; of states 12, 182, 277–9, 298, 324; UNSC as the source of 289
autonomous institutional arrangement (AIA) 190–1, 195, 207

Ban Ki-moon 290–1
Barak, Aharon (Judge) 321, 329
Barth, Kate 243
Basel Committee on Banking Supervision 81
Bazaramba, Francoise 305–6
Belgium 11, 241–2, 309, 311
best practices 45–7
Bettati, Mario 285–7
Bianchi, Andrea 179
bilateral investment treaties (BITs) 162, 221–2
bin Laden, Usama 225, 245
binding: commitment (contractual) 61, 76, 79–81, 98–9, 230, 302; decisions 55, 86–9, 123, 194–7, 202–8, 255; law 20, 27, 84, 121, 130–4
bio-politics 40, 42, 49
black-box model 136–9, 143, 147
Bodin, Jean 21
Bogdandy, Armin von 75, 87–8
Brammertz, Serge 186
Brazil 100, 274
British Petroleum (BP) 271–3, 275, 277, 281–2

Brown Weiss, Edith 209–10
Brunnée, Jutta 202–3, 209, 293, 296
Butler, William 155–6

Camenzuli, Louise Kathleen 192–3, 196–7, 203–5
Canada 99, 100, 165, 306
Cançado Trindade, Antônio Augusto 179
Central American Group of Competition 93
Chayes, Abram 208, 210
Chayes, Antonia Handler 208, 210
checks and balances 46, 99, 135
Churchill, Winston 17–8, 38
Churchill, Robin 195, 257, 279
civil society 19, 35–6, 95, 97, 286, 296; global 39, 49, 53, 55; transnational networks of 290, 297
coastal state: authority of 277–9; jurisdiction of 11, 272, 276, 278–81
Codex Alimentarius Commission 59, 93
commerce 20, 24–5, 29–30, 36, 108–9
common heritage of mankind 111–12, 115–16
community interest 57, 59
comparative international law 155–6
complementarity 172, 178–9, 188, 294
compliance 4, 54, 102, 199, 205, 208–10, 246; mechanisms/procedures 190, 193, 196–8, 206, 210; regime 208, 210; *see also* non-compliance
Comte, Auguste 36
conference of the parties (to a treaty) (COP) 130, 191–2
constitution: domestic 83, 122, 138, 142, 163; European Union 136, 211; global 40, 53, 121; security-based 238, 240
constitutional law, domestic 53, 147, 154, 163, 315
constitutionalisation 58, 67, 101, 102, 126, 238
constitutionalism 40, 58, 159, 238
cooperation: duty of 212–17, 224; fishing 282; international 73, 78–87, 97–100, 116, 124, 209; judicial 311
Council of Europe 140–1, 325–6
counter-terrorism 226, 313, 316, 327; measures 238–40, 313; operations 315, 321, 326; *see also* war on terror
Court of Justice of the European Union (CJEU): European Court of Justice (ECJ) 13, 16, 138, 226–9; Advocate General 228, 230, 232–3, 244; and national courts 141; and the UN Charter system 126, 132, 133, 136; in Kadi I 226; in Kadi II 226, 230–3; in Kadi III 226, 234–7; in Kadi IV 226, 246–7; *see also* European Union courts
Court of Justice of the European Union: General Court 226, 229, 237; in Kadi I 226, 230, 232; in Kadi III 226, 229, 234–7; *see also* European Union courts
Craig, Paul 90
Crawford, James 186–7
crimes against humanity 291, 298, 308, 310
custom *see* customary international law
customary international law 4, 79, 113–14, 122, 240, 320; establishing/making 75–6, 299, 304–9; nature of 76, 268; obligations 11, 86; principles 53, 267, 302, 312; regional/special 303; *see also* opinio juris; *see also* state practice
customary law *see* customary international law

d'Alembert, Jean le Rond *see* Alembert, Jean le Rond d'
Darfur Commission *see* UN Darfur Commission
Davis, James 43
Davis, Peter 199–201
de-formalisation/deformalisation 85, 125
de-nationalisation 40, 121, 128–9, 132, 134, 145
de-territorialisation 123, 128
dédoublement fonctionnel 127–8, 163
deepwater and ultra-deepwater oil and gas: drilling and production 271–2, 274–5, 277–8, 280–2; exploitation 111, 274, 276, 278–9, 281–2; resources 111, 114, 271, 273–5, 278–81
deepwater ecosystem 272–3, 276, 280–2
deepwater oil rig *see* mobile oil drilling unit
delegation: of jurisdiction 303, 304; of power 52, 99, 159, 255, 303
democracy 17, 48, 52, 55, 97, 135, 239; deficit 70, 157; international norm of 157; liberal/pluralist 37, 198,

328–9; *see also* e-democracy; *see also* right to democracy
democratic 5, 79, 150, 166, 320–1; deficit/failure 4, 7; legitimacy 81, 92, 97–8, 100: process/participation 7, 87, 92, 135, 157, 232
development 47; economic 6, 40, 47, 157–8, 166, 291; of law-making 70, 121; legal 143–5, 152–5, 171–5, 190–3, 222, 287; of public law 22; of soft law 40, 97; technological 111, 214, 275; *see also* right to development
Diderot, Denis 26, 28
discretion 231–2, 245, 314; of the addressee 89, 92–3; administrative 66; legal 45, 54, 321–9; sovereign 15–6
Domat, Jean 22–3
domestic law 84, 94, 151–3, 271, 308; relation to international law 122–9, 132–4, 153–6, 163–8
Drumbl, Mark 187
dualism 122–3; *see also* monism
Dunant, Henry 48
Dupont de Nemours, Pierre Samuel 31–2
Dupuy, Pierre-Marie 179–80
Dworkin, Ronald 40, 52, 146

e-democracy 55
economy 25, 39, 44, 139; political 19, 30–1, 37, 153
effective control 321–5
Eichmann, Adolf 305
epistemic community 45, 47
erga omnes 8, 266–7
Europe 19–25, 34, 158, 211, 245, 325
European Commission 186, 236, 246; *see also* European Union
European Community 211; *see also* European Union
European Court of Human Rights (ECtHR) 133, 240, 247, 322–3, 326; Grand Chamber 241, 324; *see also* Council of Europe
European Union 3, 10, 16, 212, 220, 257, 247; competence 123, 126, 213–20, 227–30, 241; Counter-Terrorism Strategy 239; external relations 65, 211, 223; law/legislation 14, 136–9, 144, 147, 214–16, 220–2; legal order 54, 99, 136–45, 225–9; member states 18, 212–22, 242, 309
European Union courts 226–9, 233–4, 237–8, 242–3, 247; *see also* Court of Justice of the European Union
exclusive economic zone (EEZ) 46, 116, 276–9, 282
expertise 40, 91, 165, 243, 285; of stakeholders/NGOs/board members 49, 53, 87, 90, 95–6

Falk, Richard 154–7
field constitution 227–30, 233–4, 239, 241
Financial Action Task Force 81, 93
Financial Stability Board 93
Finland 221, 305, 306, 311
Fischer-Lescano, Andreas 139
formalism 126, 132, 134
Foucault, Michel 37, 40, 42, 49
fragmentation: of international law 148, 165–6; of international legal order 43, 229; of law 145; transnational legal 139, 144
France 19, 21–2, 29–30, 35–6, 83–4, 285–7
Franck, Thomas M. 157, 180–1, 210
Fuller, Lon 86, 94, 102

G7 61
G8 61
G20 81, 93, 124
garbage can model of decision-making 46
Gattini, Andrea 14, 16
general comments (by treaty bodies) 249–52, 257
genocide 180–2, 265–6, 269, 284, 291, 298, 306–10; in Bosnia 180, 185–8; in Rwanda 182, 305, 311
Genser, Jared 240, 243
Germany 80, 214, 303
global administrative law 42, 53–6, 57–67, 75–81, 159
global civil society *see* civil society, global
Global Food Safety Institute 93
Global Harmonization Task Force (GHTF) 93
Global Partnership for Good Agricultural Practice 93
globalisation/globalization 37, 39–43, 121, 128, 145, 211, 244
Gournay, Vincent 29–30
governance 18, 37, 190, 211;

democratic 157, 167 (*see also* right, to democracy); economic 30, 38; global 6, 39–46, 76, 81, 87–8, 150, 159; global, problems of 49–56; good 211, 239, 291; international/transnational/supranational 18, 37, 57, 96–100; legislative/regulatory 57–9, 64–6; legitimacy of 67–8, 89–92; multilevel 72, 83; private 49, 53, 67, 149–50
Greece 18, 214–15
Grewe, Wilhelm 105
Gros Espiell, Héctor 180
Grotius, Hugo 10, 26, 68, 103–4, 107–9, 112–18
Grundnorm 59, 137–8, 140–3
Gulf of Mexico 271–4, 281

Habermas, Jürgen 68–9, 74, 100, 115
Hardin, Garret 50
Hart, H. L. A. 60, 62, 136, 142–3; Hartian 60, 62, 146
Hartmann, Florence 188
Higgins, Rosalyn 63, 113–14, 302
high seas 107–8, 110, 116, 276, 279, 281–2, 298
Hirschman(n), Albert O. 30, 37, 47, 55
Hobbes, Thomas 26, 68; Hobbesian 24, 31
Holbach, baron d' 27–8
hostis/hostes humanis generis 116–17
Huber, Max 9–10
human rights 63, 81, 88, 226, 315–17, 321; adjudication of 41–3, 51, 73, 126, 159, 321–6; as trumps 40–1, 314; conflict of claims of 41, 48, 51, 132–3, 238–44, 284; emergence/proliferation of 43, 51–2, 144, 156, 158; fragmentation of 165–7; interpretation of 256–7, 314–15, 327; promotion/respect of 7, 8, 58, 134, 240, 255, 287; sovereigns as trustees of 8–9; treaties/institutions 153, 201, 210, 229, 240, 249–51, 254; violations of 116, 182, 187; *see also* field constitution; *see also* indeterminacy; *see also* natural rights; *see also* right of property; see also right to
Human Rights Watch 244, 299
humanitarian intervention 284–9
humanitarian law *see* international humanitarian law

immunities of high state officials 311–12
immunity from jurisdiction 230, 233, 234, 246
indeterminacy, of rules 135, 183, 314–15, 327
individual complaints, to a treaty body 249, 252–4, 255, 257
individual criminal responsibility 171, 188–9; and state responsibility 178–88; approach of the ILC 172–5; in the Rome Statute 175–8
informal law 78, 80–1, 92, 94, 96–7, 100
informal law-making 49, 80–3, 86, 92–4, 102
institutional legal theory (ILT) 88–9
intellectual property 44, 98
intergovernmental organisation (IGO) *see* international organisation
interim measures 214, 252, 254–5
interlegality 140, 144
International Commission on Intervention and State Sovereignty (ICISS) 283, 285–6, 288–9, 292–3, 295–6
International Conference on Harmonization of Technical Requirement for Registration of Pharmaceuticals for Human Use (ICH) 82, 92, 96
International Cooperation on Harmonization of Technical Requirements for Registration of Veterinary Medicinal Products 93
International Court of Justice (ICJ) 144, 158, 321; on corporate rights 52; on criminal jurisdiction 301; on domestic law 151–2; on global welfare 11–12, 113; on humanitarian necessity 288; on the immunity of state officials from jurisdiction 311–12; on implied powers 252; on international responsibility 180, 185–8; on the jurisprudence of the Human Rights Committee 253–4; on jus cogens 261, 264–70; Statute of 76, 149
International Criminal Court (ICC) 172–3, 182, 184, 187, 304; Statute of 175–8, 184, 284, 294, 308
International Criminal Tribunal for Rwanda (ICTR) 182, 187, 269; Statute of 176
International Criminal Tribunal for the

former Yugoslavia (ICTY) 113, 182, 186–8; Statute of 176
International Forum of Sovereign Wealth Funds 93
international humanitarian law 268, 306–7, 315–21, 325, 327
International Law Commission (ILC) 171–5, 177–8, 184, 186, 188–9, 266, 268
international organisation (IO/IGO) 5, 40, 67, 153, 246; in contrast to informal process 81–3, 207; influence of domestic law on 123–4, 126–9, 149–50; political decision-making of 212, 215, 216–20; proliferation of 43–4; responsibility of 171–3, 181, 183
International Organisation of Securities Commissions 93
International Organization for Standardization (ISO) 53, 61, 93, 149
international relations 85, 153, 208, 264, 296, 299, 309; discipline of 75, 96, 208
International Seabed Authority 111, 279, 280, 281
International Swaps and Derivatives Association 93
Internet Corporation for Assigned Names and Numbers (ICANN) 59, 93, 95, 125, 128
Internet Engineering Task Force 81, 93
Internet Governance Forum 93
Internet Society 93
interpretation: as law-making power 193, 199–204, 249–50, 253–6, 291–4; domination through 55–6; international responsibility as 183; judicial 146; judicial, by the ECtHR 133, 241, 322–5; judicial, by the EU courts 229–32, 247; judicial, by the ICJ 11–12, 152; judicial, by the UK House of Lords 322–5; judicial, by the US Supreme Court 318; legal order (global) as 62, 69–73, 141–4, 314–15; methods of 256–7; patterns in 314; of treaties *see* treaties, interpretation of
intervention *see* obligation to intervene, *see* right to intervene, *see* humanitarian intervention
Iran 235, 267
Iraq 181–2, 288, 322, 324–6
Ireland 217–18

Israel 305, 306, 309, 319–20; Supreme Court 319–21
ius naturae *see* natural law

Jacobson, Harold Karan 209–10
Jenks, Wilfred 152–5, 159–60
Jonas, Hans 71
judicial review 40, 54, 99, 229–37, 242, 248, 282
jurisdiction 105, 214, 231; of coastal states *see* coastal state, jurisdiction; conflict/contest over 137–8, 144, 212; exclusive 108, 113, 278; immunity from *see* immunity from jurisdiction; judicial 148, 176, 180, 234, 284; representative 303–4; sovereign 5, 8–9, 14, 111; universal *see* universal jurisdiction
jus cogens 81, 231, 261–70
justice 7, 22, 61, 109, 179, 227–9, 244; absolute 32–3, 48; as virtue 92, 135; inter-/transnational 62–3, 74, 158, 160–1, 186; judicial, domestic 164; judicial, international criminal 185–6; 187–8, 298, 303, 310; military 318; miscarriage of 245; procedural 227, 232; theory of 52

Kadi justice 227
Kadi, Yassin Abdullah (Yasin Abdullah Ezzedine Qadi) 225–7, 229, 232–6, 238, 240–8
Kant, Immanuel 46, 49, 51, 63; Kantian 63, 74, 138
Karadzic, Radovan 186
Kelsen, Hans 62, 138, 140–3; Kelsenian 58, 137, 139–43, 146
Kennedy, David 62, 115, 183, 243
Khaliq, Urfan 257
Kimberly Process 93
Kingsbury, Benedict 59, 64, 75
Klabbers, Jan 40, 60–1, 77–9, 84–7, 89, 92, 94–5, 100–2, 103, 121, 126, 130–2, 136, 189, 212, 221, 227–8
knowledge 17, 46–7, 79, 251, 281; legal 140, 162, 165, 226; organised/perfect/scientific 18–19, 21, 24, 33, 95; practical/professional 142, 246; special 91, 95
Koskenniemi, Martti 7, 20, 64, 68, 109, 138–9, 144, 147–8, 165, 227, 241
Kouchner, Bernard 285–7

Larrère, Catherine 29

Laski, Harold J. 91
law of the sea 44, 59, 63, 66; concept of mankind 103–4, 111–12; law-making 271, 282; legal uncertainties 271–2, 275–81
law-making interaction 150, 164–8
Le Bret, Cardin 22
Le Mercier de la Rivière, Paul-Pierre 32–5
legal culture 141–7, 314, 327
legal despotism 33–6
legal hybrid 59, 160
legal personality, of an informal law-making network 82
legal speech act 88–9, 137–40, 145–7
legal strategism 137–8
legal systems 53, 41, 143, 153, 180, 305; de-nationalized/de-territorialized 121, 123, 128–9, 143; domestic 122–9, 155–8, 163, 177–9, 303, 308; international 122–9, 150–2, 158–68, 178, 270, 286; interrelationships among 123, 126–7, 132–3, 144–5, 148; interrelationships among, horizontal 124, 129–30, 133, 150–5, 158–61, 184; interrelationships among, vertical 124, 129–30, 133, 150, 155–61, 209; new black-box model of 137
legal vacuum 315, 321
legislation 53, 71
legislation: as a formal expression of the society 23, 25–34; as the expression of truths 36–7; by sovereigns as trustees of humanity/community 5–13, 19–22; de facto 193, 204, 249, 299, 306, 312; domestic 94, 123, 132, 299, 306–9, 312; global/international 18, 57–9, 62–70, 72–4, 90, 306–12; for humanity 3–5, 16
legitimacy 67, 74, 81, 100, 179, 210; as opposed to legality 288; enhancing 53–4, 113, 292; expertise-based 90–2, 96; of different approaches 156–7, 161–2; of law/rules 89–90; problems of 4, 49–55, 68–9, 84, 97–8, 196, 206–9, 254
lex specialis 321
liberty 25–6, 29–33, 36, 41, 88, 108, 304
Libya 290, 293, 294
linguistic philosophy 88
Lipson, Charles 79

Luhmann, Niklas 139, 145; Luhmannian 146

Madison, James 9
Maduro, Miguel Poiares (as CJEU Advocate General) 228, 230, 232–3, 244–5
managerialism 64, 118
marine environment, harm to 272–3, 281
maritime industry codes 272–3, 275–9, 281–2
Marshall Islands 272, 277–8
materialism 27–8
Mechlem, Kerstin 257
Melon, Jean-Francois 29
memorandum of understanding (MOU) 80, 100
mercantilism 28–30
Mercosur 93
Meroni doctrine 99
military commission 315, 317–18
Mill, J. S. 7
mobile oil drilling unit (MODU) 275–9, 282
monism 122–3, 138; *see also* dualism
Montaigne, Michel de 21
Montesquieu 24–5, 28
Mueller, Gerhard 187
multilateral environmental agreement (MEA) 190–9, 205, 208, 210, 219

natural law 19–22, 25–31, 37, 103–6, 109–18, 261–2, 270
natural rights 27, 31–7, 108–9
Naturalism 19, 22–3, 28, 36, 327
nemo dat quod non habet 302
Netherlands, The 11, 99
network 29, 39, 42, 47, 290, 297; interjudicial/-legal 140, 160; transgovernmental regulatory *see* transgovernmental regulatory networks
New International Economic Order (NIEO) 47, 157
Nicaragua 11, 267–8
Nollkaemper, André 159–60, 179, 181, 186
non-compliance 196, 197, 202, 205, 208–9, 256; mechanism/procedure/regime 196, 198, 205, 206; *see also* compliance
non-governmental organisations (NGOs) 39, 49, 192, 284–5, 290, 292

non-governmental/non-state actor *see* private actor
North Atlantic Treaty Organisation (NATO) 287–8, 294, 309, 322

obligation to intervene (devoir d'ingérence) 285–6, 288
offshore installation 276–8
O'Keefe, Roger 301
Operation Allied Force 287
Operation Infinite Justice 313
opinio juris 264, 269, 304, 311; *see also* customary international law
Orford, Anne 292, 295, 296
Organisation for Economic Co-operation and Development (OECD) 81, 93
Othman, Omar Mohammed 226

pacta tertiis nec nocent nec prosunt 103, 302
Palestinian Authority 320
Palestinian Territories 320
paternalism 18, 65, 68
peacekeeping 47–8
People's Mojahedin Organisation 235
peremptory rules/law-making *see* jus cogens
perspectivism 136–7, 140, 142–8
Peters, Anne 58, 126, 295–6
physiocrats 30, 32, 34–6
Plato 46
positive law 27, 30–3, 104, 109, 263–4
post-national rule-making 150, 159, 161–3
presumptive law 77, 84–7, 89, 102
private actor 3, 35, 94, 112, 209
private law-making 53, 75, 125, 128, 132; emergence of 39, 62, 72, 131; informality of 78, 79, 81, 83–4; source of authority of 87–92; transparency of 97
progress 24, 43, 62, 116, 179–80, 250
Providentialism 37
public goods 4, 13, 16, 49–50, 107, 110, 116
publicity 53, 55

Quesnay, Francois 30–2, 34

Rawls, John 50–1
Raz, Joseph 7–8; Razian 60
referential legal order 142–3, 145
regime, jurisdictional 298, 303–4, 308, 312
regime, old (ancien regime) 19, 23, 25
regimes 33, 138, 227, 282; analysis of 44, 47; for the commons of mankind 104, 112; conflicting 139; environmental 195–6, 198–9, 207–10; interaction 164–8; legal 159, 314; of responsibility 171–2, 184, 188–9; static 161–2; trade 44, 69; of UN sanctions 229, 237, 239, 243, 246, 248
regulation *see* transgovernmental regulatory networks
Reisman, W. Michael 179
responsibility to protect (R2P, RtoP) 42, 283, 285, 286, 289–97
responsibility, fragmentation of 49, 82–4, 172–8, 181–8
right of property 32–6, 44, 50, 110, 229, 233
right to: communicate (ius communicationis) 105–9, 110; democracy 4, 2, 51–2, 157; development 40; equality 162–4; intervene (droit d'ingérence) 285–9; self-determination 6–8, 11, 105, 268; *see also* human rights
rights: as trumps *see* human rights; conflict *see* human rights
Rousseau, Jean-Jacques 25–6, 70
Rumsfeld, Donald 309
Russia 155, 202, 204, 256

Saint-Pierre, Abbé de 23–4
Salamanca school 20
sanctions 3, 85, 209, 232; economic/financial 221, 225, 242–3; list of targeted persons 226–7, 229, 233, 236; targeted 42, 132
Saudi Arabia 225, 240
Scelle, Georges 36, 127, 163
Schmitt, Carl 52
Scholasticism 21
seabed 111, 115–18, 272–6, 278–81
Searle, John 88
self-determination of peoples *see* right to self-determination
Serbia 180, 186–8, 288, 323
Shaw, Malcolm 114
Simpson, Gerry 180, 184
Slaughter, Anne-Marie 75, 81–2, 160, 296
Smith, Adam 32, 49
sociability 28–31, 35–7

social contract 26–7
soft law: as de facto law making 53, 206–7, 250–2; discomfort with 49, 79, 130–1; proliferation of 121–5, 132–4
sources of legal authority 59–63, 113; as an expression of legal culture 141–2; for informal norms 78, 87–92; redefinition of 102, 126, 149; stakeholder consensus as 95–8; *see also* customary international law; *see also* stakeholder
Sousa Santos, Boaventura de 140
sovereignty *see* authority, sovereign; *see* jurisdiction, sovereign; *see* legislation, by sovereigns as trustees of humanity/community
speech act *see* legal speech act
stakeholder 4–6, 79; consensus as a source of authority 95–8; foreign 4, 7, 12–13; problem of legitimacy of 49, 53, 56, 82, 87, 90
standard of review 15, 232
state practice 152, 171–2, 185–6, 252, 304, 306–7, 311–12; *see also* customary international law
state reports 249, 250–1, 257
state responsibility 178–88; and the Rome Statute 175–8; codification by the ILC 172–5; as for acts of genocide 180; *see also* individual criminal responsibility; *see also* responsibility, fragmentation of 117–18, 171, 179
Stewart, Richard 82–3
sub-national law-making 124
Sudan 182
Sunstein, Cass 55
Sweetser, Catherine 114
systems theory 139, 146

technocracy 18, 75, 90
technology 6, 116, 149, 198, 271, 274–6
territorial sea 276–9
terrorism *see* counter-terrorism
Teubner, Gunther 139
Tomuschat, Christian 9, 255
Toope, Stephen 209, 293, 293, 296
transgovernmental regulatory networks 49, 53, 75, 81–3, 92–4, 99, 149–50
transnational 54, 72
transnational civil society networks 290, 297
transnational governance 57, 87, 96, 166

transnational institutions 55
transnational law 62, 97, 125, 139, 141, 144–5, 147
transnational legal culture/legal order 136, 143–4
transnational offences 300, 327
transnational polity 136, 159, 162
transnational regulation 53, 75, 94
treaties 79, 103, 112, 136, 209; amendments to 193–5, 198, 203; conferences of the parties to *see* conference of the parties; domestic approval of 79, 80, 98; interpretation of 113, 163, 199–207, 210, 221, 224, 250–2, 292, 301; interpretation of, effective (effet utile) 222, 255; law of 173, 194, 201–7, 263–4, 302
treaty bodies 249–52, 254–7
Tuori, Kaarlo 238
Turgot, Anne-Robert-Jacques 35–6
Turkey 323–4

Ulfstein, Geir 126, 195
ultra vires 207, 229, 294
United Kingdom (UK): applying universal jurisdiction 309; domestic oversight of informal commitments 80; before the ECtHR 240–1, 326; before the EU courts 214–15, 217, 236; House of Lords 322, 324–5; before the ICJ 265; in Iraq 322, 325
United Nations (UN): Charter amendment 284; Charter system 47, 126, 133; on human rights 133–4, 240–1; peacekeeping 47–8; procedural deficiencies 242–4, 257; on responsibility to protect 285, 288, 294, 296–7; sanctions regime 229–30, 234, 236–9, 248; on state responsibility 187
United Nations General Assembly (UNGA): on genocide 266; Global Counter-Terrorism Strategy 238–9; on humanitarian assistance 287; law-making 61; on responsibility to protect 289–91, 294; on universal jurisdiction 175, 299
United Nations Human Rights Committee (HRC) 241, 242, 250–7
United Nations Secretary-General (UNSG) 283, 287, 290, 291; Darfur Commission (The International Commission of Inquiry on Darfur to the United Nations

Secretary-General) 182–3; International Strategy for Disaster Reduction (UNISDR) 93; UN Secretariat 81
United Nations Security Council (UNSC): collective security 132–3, 228, 231–2, 241, 285; 'good goals' of 66; on international responsibility 181–3; law-making 59, 61, 69; and responsibility to protect 283, 287–90, 292–7; sanctions lists 226, 234; UNSC Al-Qaida Sanctions Committee 225, 233–6, 239–44, 246–8; UNSC Monitoring Team 240; UNSC Office of the Ombudsperson 234, 278, 240
United Nations System Chief Executive Board for Coordination 83
United States (US) 44, 47, 100, 271–3, 278, 302; international law in the domestic courts/law of 80, 83, 154–5; torture by 184; transnational firms based in 54, 125; unilateral measures by 3, 10; on universal jurisdiction 306, 309; US Coast Guard 277–8; US Supreme Court 154, 164, 307, 317–18
universal code of legality 144
universal jurisdiction 116, 298–9, 312; customary 304–12; treaty-based 300–4
unlawful enemy combatant 315–18
utilitarianism 24, 27, 32

Vattel, Emerich de 9, 10, 103–4, 109–13, 116–18
Verdross, Alfred 261–2
virtue 20, 24–5, 33, 35, 71, 121; critique of 132–5
virtue ethics 92
Vitoria, Francisco de 20, 103–4, 105–7, 108, 112–13, 116–18
voluntas 17–8
Vorverständnis 138, 141, 143–5, 148

Walker, Neil 146
war crimes 291, 298, 310
war on terror 314–15, 317–18, 321, 325–8; *see also* counter-terrorism
Weber, Max 38, 42, 49, 67, 74; Weberian 37, 68
Weil, Prosper 114
Wiener, Antje 54
Wilt, Harmen van der 179
Wolff, Christian 10, 109
World Health Organization (WHO) 93
World Trade Organization (WTO) 81: Appellate Body 13, 151; as a regulator 59, 69–70, 72, 157–8; as a self-contained regime 144; conflicting with environmental law regime 137–8, 144; established interests ensconced in 44, 56–7; 'good goals' of 66; intellectual property rights 44

Taylor & Francis
eBooks
FOR LIBRARIES

ORDER YOUR FREE 30 DAY INSTITUTIONAL TRIAL TODAY!

Over 23,000 eBook titles in the Humanities, Social Sciences, STM and Law from some of the world's leading imprints.

Choose from a range of subject packages or create your own!

- Free MARC records
- COUNTER-compliant usage statistics
- Flexible purchase and pricing options

- Off-site, anytime access via Athens or referring URL
- Print or copy pages or chapters
- Full content search
- Bookmark, highlight and annotate text
- Access to thousands of pages of quality research at the click of a button

For more information, pricing enquiries or to order a free trial, contact your local online sales team.

UK and Rest of World: **online.sales@tandf.co.uk**
US, Canada and Latin America:
e-reference@taylorandfrancis.com

www.ebooksubscriptions.com

A flexible and dynamic resource for teaching, learning and research.